POSTERITY LOST

POSTERITY LOST

Progress, Ideology, and the Decline of the American Family

RICHARD T. GILL

Foreword by James Q. Wilson

ROWMAN & LITTLEFIELD PUBLISHERS, INC.
Lanham • *New York* • *Boulder* • *Oxford*

ROWMAN & LITTLEFIELD PUBLISHERS, INC.

Published in the United States of America
by Rowman & Littlefield Publishers, Inc.
4720 Boston Way, Lanham, Maryland 20706

12 Hid's Copse Road
Cummor Hill, Oxford OX2 9JJ, England

British Library Cataloguing in Publication Information Available

Library of Congress Cataloging-in-Publication Data
Gill, Richard T.
    Posterity lost : progress, ideology, and the decline of the
American family / Richard T. Gill.
        p.   cm.
    ISBN 0-8476-8379-6 (cloth : alk. paper)
    1. Family—United States.   2. Social values—United States.
3. United States—Civilization—20th century.   4. United States—
Social conditions—1945–   5. Family policy—United States.
6. Progress.
HQ536.G545   1997
306.85′0973—dc21   96-49901
                                                                      CIP

ISBN 0-8476-8379-6 (cloth : alk. paper)

Printed in the United States of America

∞ ™ The paper used in this publication meets the minimum requirements of
American National Standard for Information Sciences—Permanence of Paper
for Printed Library Materials, ANSI Z39.48-1984.

To my wife and our posterity—
Tom, Peter, Geoff, and their families.

CONTENTS

FIGURES AND TABLES

Figures

Tables

FOREWORD

James Q. Wilson

The American people believe that this nation is on the wrong track, not because it is constitutionally ill-founded or economically backward, but because its family life is deteriorating. By every available measure, this view has been in place for many years, and no public policy initiative seems to reverse it. When the president or Congress urges "welfare reform," Americans are pleased but not optimistic. They have heard such promises before, and note, correctly, that little seems to change after any "reform." At the same time, when Americans are asked by pollsters whether the government should help people in need, Americans say yes.

To some observers, this is a contradiction. How can Americans support cutting back on welfare and still claim that they want to help people in need? Of course it is no contradiction at all once one realizes how Americans distinguish between "welfare" (a collection of unmarried young girls getting pregnant in order to receive tax-supported benefits) and "people in need" (a collection of honest people disabled by disease, afflicted by hunger, or harmed by unemployment). Welfare reform means getting rid of the first group; helping the needy means responding to the second.

The real problem that Americans have is not any mistake about the gravity of the problem or any imaginary contradiction in their preferences as to it, but a narrow view of the scope of the problem. Their view, I think, is this: America has made a huge mistake in public policy. We created the Aid to Families with Dependent Children (AFDC) in

1935, originally to help the widows of dead miners and soldiers, and have found that as a result of the relentless operation of the Law of Unintended Consequences it was soon taken over by unmarried girls who used AFDC to acquire a home without a husband and an income without a job. The way to correct this problem is to get rid of AFDC, or slash its benefits, or tighten its rules, or convert it into a required work program.

This view has received next to no support from scholars who have looked at the program. Until recently there was virtually no social scientist who did not proclaim that the level of benefits did not explain the growth in welfare rolls. Some of them went further: There is nothing wrong with fatherless households. The demand for two-parent families is a mischievous legacy of a male-led, all-white, Victorian culture. Children can grow up perfectly well in "alternative" families led by an unmarried mother or whatever. Even asking for two-parent families reveals the extent to which America is a narrow, bourgeois mess.

The more extreme form of social denunciation did not last. It could not, because it was—literally—contrary to nature. There is no evidence that children prosper in one-parent families. In time, serious scholars got hold of the right data and established this beyond much doubt. Deborah Dawson, Sara McLanahan, Gary Sandefur, and others made very clear the harm that single-parent households inflict on most children.

But the first complaint—that however bad single-parent homes may be, they were not caused by AFDC payments—still lingered. That issue is still somewhat in doubt, but even here the evidence is shifting to support the view that welfare payments, taken as a whole, do make a difference. Charles Murray has published data showing this, as has Mark Rosenzweig of the University of Pennsylvania. My reading of the evidence leads me to accept this new view, but to assign it a still undetermined weight in explaining the magnitude of family decay.

The reason for being uncertain, not about the effect of welfare but of the size of that effect, is well told in this book by Richard T. Gill. He takes the largest view of the family problem of anyone I have read and urges us to accept the very real possibility that we are witnessing a great cultural transformation that has, out of what seem like admirable motives, dramatically weakened the social constraints that once guaranteed that the great majority of children would grow up in two-parent families.

In support of this view he draws our attention to data, not well known to the average American, showing how family disintegration has proceeded apace in most European nations as well as in the United States, and has been doing so since long before the enactment of modern welfare programs. To grasp at a glance what this book is about, look at the table on page 61 in chapter 3: For thirty years, the rates of divorce, illegitimate births, and single-parent families have been growing rapidly in Canada, Denmark, France, Germany, Sweden, Great Britain, and the Netherlands, as well as here.

Now, all of these nations have welfare programs that provide support to the parent of a child. But they also have rather different programs. The programs, in my view, have contributed to the growth of the problem, but they are far from the whole story. Richard Gill tells the rest of the story, and it is an important one.

His argument is best left to his own words, but involves the rapid spread of what he, and some other scholars, have called shortened time horizons. We think more about today, or at most tomorrow, and much less than once was the case about next year, or the next generation. That this should have occurred at all is quite odd, because the industrial West has become more prosperous, more scientific, more rational. We invent and build elaborate technological systems, we invest for a decade in finding a way to travel to the moon, and we spend vastly more than ever before on educating the young. Surely, one might suppose, these commitments suggest that we have acquired a longer, not a shorter, time horizon.

Gill's contribution in this book is to explain why, in his view, this natural assumption is wrong. His argument rests on the value we assign to a belief in the idea of progress. Once, we believed that tomorrow would be better than today; now, we are not so certain. Even though we invest in technology, education, and business creation, we are no longer so convinced that these investments will really make our children better off than ourselves. And our children, quickly taking up on this cue, act on the assumption that enjoying each moment today is much more important than deferring their happiness until tomorrow.

To use a phrase Gill does not employ and might not agree with, I think we have produced in a technologically forward-looking society a kind of adolescent culture that leads us, in our personal decisions, to look only at the moment. It is evident in television, clothing, popular music, and male-female encounters. Television is about now and is sent to us in thirty-minute bites; books are about yesterday and tomorrow, and take a long time to read. A child's clothes were once very different from an adult's; today everybody regardless of age wears identical blue jeans. Music once emphasized commitment and romance; today it emphasizes action and passion. Men and women once met through arranged marriages; later, as parents lost control, they began to go out on dates; today even dating is displaced in favor of spontaneous encounters. Adolescence was once a brief phase through which a child passed on the way to adulthood; indeed, the term did not even exist before this century. Now it is a state of mind and attitude that governs the daily lives of many of us without regard to age.

Gill argues that our short time horizons help us explain the decline of the family. For so vast a subject, one expects a bold, wide-ranging book, and this is such. But it is lively, vivid, and clear, and so no one need bring to its reading any specialized knowledge. It is one of the few volumes that places our common concern—the family—into a sufficiently broad context so that we can see how fundamental, and perhaps unalterable, are the forces shaping it.

PREFACE

The title of this book, *Posterity Lost*, was chosen for two rather specific and, to me at least, compelling reasons. The first was that it is, in fact, the concept of "posterity" that links together the two main subjects indicated by the book's subtitle and that are at the heart of our analysis: the decline of the American family and the fading of the Idea of Progress. In dictionary terms, the word "posterity" refers both to (1) our descendants and all succeeding generations, and (2) the future generally. The core function of the historical institution of the family, and very clearly of the traditional American family in particular, has always been to secure this succession of descendants and generations. In the past, whether rightly or wrongly, we stayed together "for the sake of the children." We also took enormous satisfaction in the thought that those children would be able to enjoy advantages and have happier and better lives than we ourselves had had.

Similarly, the Idea of Progress was always and inevitably focused on the future, the world that those children and descendants of ours would someday occupy. It was in fact this Idea, with its promise of an ever more abundant life stretching out into the indefinite future, that guaranteed that our children and grandchildren would prosper in the years, decades, and even centuries after we had passed from the scene. This guarantee gave meaning, depth, and an essentially optimistic tone to the core family project. Thus, the concept of posterity linked family and the ideology of progress in the days in which both were in the ascendant and also, as this book will attempt to demonstrate, in the present era in which both institution and ideology are in serious decline.

The second major reason for choosing this title, and one obviously requiring an apology to the memory of the poet John Milton, was precisely because of the relation of the notion of "posterity lost" to that of "paradise lost." For an intrinsic feature of the modern age (in contrast to our current postmodern age) was exactly the idea that paradise need not be sought in heaven or in any kind of other-worldly setting but might actually be found right here on this earth. Not immediately, of course. It would take a long time for scientific, economic, medical, political, and social progress to accomplish their terrestial work. Still, the potentiality was clearly there. This, in fact, was what the Idea of Progress promised us.

In his book, *Reaching for Heaven on Earth*, Robert H. Nelson has shown how even among apparently hardheaded, scientifically minded economists there has lingered an underlying spiritual impulse. "For many faithful of modern economic theologies," he writes, "economic progress has represented the route of salvation to a new heaven on earth, the means of banishing evil from the affairs of mankind."[1] The dream of Progress has always involved far more than simple economics. Ultimately, it spoke to humanity's longing for more freedom, equality, justice, brotherhood, and all the institutions and virtues that could one day produce a paradise not just in heaven but on this planet. The posterity guaranteed by the Idea of Progress was thus, in significant measure, a modern substitute for an other-worldly paradise that had come to seem, for many, an increasingly doubtful proposition.

The message of this book is precisely that this promise of a future earthly paradise has now itself become an increasingly doubtful proposition. We are rapidly losing our faith in the future. As we do so, we are also risking our posterity in both senses of the word—as a future in which our present labors, efforts, and dreams find imaginative fulfillment, and as the *raison d'etre* for the care, attention, and sacrifices we make on behalf of our children and heirs through the institution of the family. It is no accident that as we come more and more to abandon any conviction that earthly salvation lies ahead, we also seem willing to accept a society in which increasing numbers of our children are brought up in broken, fatherless, emotionally deprived, poverty-stricken homes. We are rapidly losing our posterity in both these senses, and this, I believe, is the most serious social tragedy of our time.

A book of this scope has many authors; in fact there are very few writers I have read over the past many years and even decades who have not influenced my thinking on this subject at least indirectly. But there are also specific persons who have been of signal help. I owe an important debt to James Q. Wilson, who not only has written the foreword to the book, but has also made many specific suggestions for additions and revisions that have greatly improved the overall manuscript. Brigitte Berger, whose significant work on the institution of the family has always been a source of stimulation for me, read the entire unfinished manuscript and was both helpful and encouraging. D. N. McCloskey suggested, at an earlier stage in the writing, that this book be separated off from a larger book on the myopic society on which he had already made detailed comments. Going back even further in time, Senator Daniel Patrick Moynihan encouraged me by commenting favorably on a draft article I wrote, "Progress and the Family," in which the basic themes of the present book were first articulated. Meanwhile, Nathan Glazer at Harvard is owed a permanent debt for constantly supporting my efforts to expand my horizons from purely economic issues to those affecting society at large.

I also thank my publisher, Rowman & Littlefield, and especially Stephen Wrinn, Julie Kirsch, Glenn Popson and Kermit Hummel, for putting up with my frequent questions and requests. David Popenoe introduced me to Stephen Wrinn at a conference on marriage chaired by David Blankenhorn. Both David Popenoe and David Blankenhorn have, of course, written extensively and with great effect on family issues.

Ultimately, I suppose, my main inspiration for what follows comes from my own family experience with three sons, their wives, and now several grandchildren. One son, Professor T. Grandon Gill, has in fact been deeply involved in this project and will soon, I hope, bring forth that complementary study of the myopic society of which this book was once a part. The rich family life I have been fortunate enough to share goes back to my own childhood and, above all, reflects my great good luck in convincing Betty Bjornson Gill to marry me many years ago. With such a wife, how could I not believe in the importance of marriage and the family and the need to do whatever one can to help preserve these ancient and honorable institutions?

INTRODUCTION

Two revolutionary changes characterize late twentieth-century
America. One change is institutional, one ideological. Together,
they can be regarded as the defining symptoms of what social observers
are now, almost universally, calling the "postmodern" era.

The first revolution involves a massive breakdown in what is without question the most durable and fundamental human institution: the
family. Hints of this breakdown can be found well back in our national
history, although there were also strongly countervailing forces that, at
times—for example, during the curious but highly fascinating episode of
the postwar Baby Boom—dominated and disguised the growing underlying weaknesses. Since the 1960s, however, the domination and disguise have been largely ripped away. Divorce, spouse and child abuse,
illegitimacy, shattered homes, fatherless children, the feminization of
poverty, latchkey kids, hopelessly inadequate day-care facilities, falling
test scores, juvenile crime, drugs, violence, and suicide —the pathology
of the American family, once thought to be the special province of the
Black family,[1] has now become epidemic across the nation.

This institutional revolution has reached the point where even the
most unperceptive observer cannot fail to wonder exactly what will happen to America's future when a generation brought up in a state of
personal and social disorganization often approaching actual chaos takes
over the reins of authority at the national level. What anger will then
emerge? What resentments will be played out? Is this the generation that
we are counting on to sustain our Social Security, Medicare, and other
retirement benefits thirty or forty years down the road?

The ideological revolution, though similarly profound in its effects,
does not extend so deeply into the history of the human race. That is to

1

say, whereas the breakdown of the family involves an institution that reaches back to the dawn of history, the ideological breakdown involves a reversal of concepts that have been dominant for only a century or two, certainly no further back than the beginning of the modern era. The concepts referred to are those embodied in what intellectual historians widely speak of as the "Idea of Progress." Much can, and will, be said about the lineaments of this Idea in the pages to follow. What is to be noted here is that it was an Idea born of the Scientific, Commercial, and later Industrial Revolutions, which have totally transformed the basic physical conditions of human life in our age. It carried with it the promise that, aside from occasional ups and downs, temporary defeats, and short-term set-backs, the long-run future facing the human race on this planet was on an ever-ascending trajectory. Things were definitely getting better. We lived better than our mothers and fathers had and they lived better than our grandmothers and grandfathers. Similarly, our children would live better than we had, as their children would, in turn, live better than they.

This Idea, and the faith that accompanied it, today seems almost quaint. Who could possibly foresee the future over such long stretches of time? How could anybody feel so much confidence in these rosy predictions? How could it have been during late nineteenth-century America that, as Henry George noted, "with the majority of thinking men, as with the great masses, the belief in progress is yet deep and strong—a fundamental belief which admits not the shadow of a doubt."[2]

How, for that matter, could it have been that there was a sharp (though temporary) resurrection of this Idea in the early post-World War II years? Had the greatest depression and the greatest war in history taught us nothing about the hazards of modernity? Yet, in fact, for a short time, and partially if never quite wholly, the faith did return. It was expressed in an unexpected renewal of confidence in our own continuing prosperity, but, perhaps above all, in our confidence in the blessings—especially economic development, but also ultimately freedom, democratic institutions, and world government—that this very same modernity would confer on the then-designated "underdeveloped nations" that comprised the vast majority of the world's population.

How naïve all this now seems! It is not that we have all suddenly turned pessimistic about the future. Actually, speaking of those underdeveloped—now called "developing"—nations, we can easily find justifications for our early postwar faith. In most cases, living standards have been rising in these countries; further, the forces of democracy, long held at bay by communism and/or right-wing dictatorships, seem increasingly vigorous; market economies are everywhere challenging the stranglehold of the "command economy" model; and so on. At the same time, however, one can also find justifications for pessimism—rapid population growth, tribal conflict, ethnic cleansing, the rise of religious fanaticism, to name a few concerns.

Reasons for pessimism then can be found, but reasons for optimism have by no means vanished. Both exist; neither wins out. For the truth (and a point that will have to be argued in some detail as we go along) is that pessimism fares no better in the postmodern world than optimism does. We can be confident of neither. What has really replaced the Idea of Progress in late twentieth-century America is Uncertainty.

To capsulate the ideological revolution of today in a few words, we can say that whereas the dominant modern ideology involved *faith* in the future, the dominant postmodern ideology involves *agnosticism* about the future. We simply can't tell what's going to happen over long periods of time. We don't know. Perhaps we never really did know, but now we also *feel* that we don't know. The world has become too complicated, too vast, too rapidly changing for us to comprehend in any simple way. Who can possibly tell where those "developing" nations will be heading one hundred, fifty, twenty, or even three years from now? Where, in fact, is the United States heading over similar time spans? Does anyone feel anything even approaching probability, let alone certainty, on this matter?

Another way to phrase the change in our ideology is with reference to religion. Speaking always at the level of the broadest generality, one could say that increasing faith in our terrestial future during the eighteenth and especially the nineteenth and very early twentieth centuries was accompanied by an increasing agnosticism about the existence (or, at least, the significant day-to-day earthly interventions) of God. Now we face an increasing agnosticism about that very terrestial future which was, for some at least, a kind of God-substitute in a secular world.

Could this mean that God may now make a strong comeback? Are the increasing signs of evangelical religion we see in our country harbingers of just such a change?

These questions take us beyond even the already extremely broad scope of our present inquiry. However, what is not beyond this inquiry, and indeed is central to it, is the connection that has to be drawn between the two revolutions we have been discussing—the institutional and the ideological, the breakdown of the family and the serious weakening of our faith in Progress and the future.

Actually, when one thinks about the matter, even quite superficially, this connection seems almost too obvious to require much of a defense. The Idea of Progress, however specifically defined, clearly places great emphasis on what happens in the future and on this earth, or if not literally on this earth, at least on future earths that the descendants of the human race may come to occupy. It has, that is to say, a this-worldly, rather than other-worldly, focus, and this focus is very much future-oriented in the sense that the great payoffs will come to us not directly but to our heirs. In his classic work, *The Idea of Progress*, J. B. Bury made this point emphatically:

> Consideration for posterity has throughout history operated as a motive of conduct, but feebly, occasionally, and in a very limited sense. With the doctrine of progress it assumes, logically, a preponderating importance; for the centre of interest is transferred to the life of future generations who are to enjoy conditions of happiness denied to us, but which our labours and sufferings are to help to bring about.[3]

Whatever other features may be associated with the Idea of Progress, the emotional weight of the doctrine depends crucially upon the importance we attach to the life enjoyed in this world by our successors after we ourselves have departed the scene.

And, of course, the institution that is, or at least always has been, associated with sheltering, nurturing, and preparing those younger generations who are to succeed us is the family. Whatever its other functions, the family has historically been the primary institution devoted to preserving the species over time and in which our interest in posterity has been most pointedly expressed. Varying from age to age and culture to culture, the family has nevertheless had a staying power over the centuries that exceeds that of all other human institutions, and its concern for the well-being of future generations, though again fluctuating from period to period, has never been totally absent. In the Middle

Ages, while celibacy and the monastic life may have been extolled and venerated, still the mass of humanity continued to produce its quota of children and grandchildren and it was largely through the family that these inhabitants of the future were nourished and sustained.

Since the Idea of Progress, as I shall refer to it, is basically a modern doctrine, the connection that I wish to draw between it and the institution of the family is also confined to the modern era, in this book predominantly, though not exclusively, to the United States in the nineteenth and twentieth centuries. I shall try to show specifically how the triumph of the Idea of Progress following the Industrial Revolution was accompanied by an enormous increase in the prestige of the family unit in the more economically advanced nations of the West, and the United States in particular. We had, on our own shores and in the same time frame, probably the greatest emphasis on, and belief in, Progress ever seen anywhere in the history of the world, and simultaneously the greatest celebration of home and family ever witnessed in any other country in any age. The triumphs of the Idea of Progress and of the Victorian family—the famous "cult of domesticity"— occurred together, a congruence that cannot have been purely coincidental.[4]

Nor would we expect these developments to be independent of each other since the analysis of this book will link them directly through their common attitude toward the future. A long time horizon, extending well beyond any individual's life expectancy and centered on the fate of descendants in this terrestial world as opposed to some other worldly afterlife—this is what joined together family and Progress, institution and Idea, in late-nineteenth-century America, and to some degree earlier and later as well.

By the same token, the breakdown of the American family and our declining faith in Progress in recent years are also joined together by a common attitude toward the future, in this case our growing agnosticism about what truly lies ahead of us. If, for whatever reason, we are increasingly unable to imagine even the general direction of future change, if, on that account, we have increasingly become unwilling to depend on the future or to invest it with our deeper emotions and hopes, then the Idea of Progress will have lost its motivational power over our lives, and the institution of the family, with its core function as rearing device for the species, will command our commitment to a much lesser degree.

PLAN OF THE BOOK

Is all this really happening? In the course of this book, I shall try to establish the reality of family decline and ideological change in America, and also the profound interconnection between these two revolutionary developments. Part 1, "The Problem," is largely devoted to establishing the nature of the questions we must address and especially to explaining my conviction that family breakdown in the United States can only be explained in a very broad socioeconomic and ideological context. A number of propositions will be developed, some rather obvious, others less so. The first such proposition, and I believe a fairly obvious one, is that the American family has, in actual fact, been breaking down, especially, but not exclusively, during the past three decades. Numerous statistics and other data will be adduced to demonstrate the exceptionally rapid decline in this most basic of institutions, and also the profound and potentially tragic consequences of this decline.

A second proposition, and again a fairly obvious one I would think, is that any acceptable analysis of family breakdown in America must locate its causes in the general socioeconomic processes characteristic of the economically advanced nations of the West. I am speaking here of those great modern trends involving scientific, technological, economic, political, and cultural changes that are sometimes grouped under the general heading of "development," sometimes "modernization," occasionally even the more limited term, "industrialization." Each of these terms seems to have more specific connotations than is appropriate and thus preference is here given to the broadest possible heading, which I designate "the process of progress." What clearly has to be avoided is confusing the empirical "process of progress" with the (capitalized) "Idea of Progress" with its ideological and actually moral implications.

However the empirical process of progress is labeled, the phenomenon itself is clearly implicated in the declining status of the American family. For such family breakdown is apparent in one degree or another throughout the industrialized world. Whether family decline has gone further in the United States, Sweden, France, Britain, or the Low Countries is an interesting question, but one we do not have to decide. The fact is that the same general trends observable in the United States are present in all these different contexts. A suitable explanation of those trends must be rooted in the common scientific-technological-socioeconomic background that these otherwise diverse nations share.

Already we can see a potential problem here. If the empirical process of progress is somehow related to, and, in fact, producing family breakdown in the United States and elsewhere, what has happened to the notion stressed above to the effect that strong families and faith in the Idea of Progress are intimately related? If the Idea strengthens the institution of the family, how can the process undermine it? Part 1 ends precisely on this paradoxical note, having established both that the process of progress tends to undercut family life, while the Idea of Progress, with its emphasis on posterity and the future, is its strongest ally.

Not surprisingly, part 2 is labeled "The Paradox" and focuses directly on the complex relationship between the empirical process of progress and what one would have assumed to be its spiritual counterpart, the Idea of Progress. The essence of the paradox is that while the process of progress initially launches and helps sustain the Idea of Progress, in the long run it tends to undermine that Idea. We shall spend considerable time dealing with what I shall call "predicaments of progress." Such "predicaments" are said to exist when the process of progress creates conditions which in one way or another impede further progress and, more especially, tend to undermine our faith in the Idea of Progress (capitalized).

An obvious example of a possible predicament of this nature is pollution. If the process of progress inevitably and in the very nature of the case generates intolerable amounts of pollution, then it may well (as certain so-called Doomsday writers suggested in the early 1970s) bring the process to a screeching halt and, at the same time, totally destroy our belief in the Idea of Progress—namely, that things in general get better and better over time. It is very doubtful that pollution (or other of the typical Doomsday factors) is the fundamental predicament of progress. However, such a fundamental predicament almost certainly does exist, and it crucially involves our growing agnosticism about the direction of future change.

Putting together the arguments developed in parts 1 and 2, and speaking in the most general terms, we emerge with this schematic structure:

- The empirical process of progress tends, in its direct effects, to be corrosive of all premodern institutions, including the institution of the family.

- One of the early indirect effects of the process of progress, however, is to suggest and sustain the Idea of Progress.

- The Idea of Progress, with its strong emphasis on posterity and a benign future, is a major factor elevating family life to what are, historically, almost unprecedented heights.

- Over time, the process of progress begins gradually to undermine the Idea of Progress through an increasing number of predicaments of progress, each suggesting grim if not disastrous future outcomes.

- While most of these specific predicaments prove resolvable, the process of progress by creating an ever more complex society, with constantly expanding ranges of individual choice and endless change, is also creating the *fundamental* predicament of progress: our inability to foresee, imagine, or in any way depend on, the long run direction of future change.

- This fundamental predicament undermines the Idea of Progress—which intrinsically depends on just such foresight and imagination—and, in so doing, leaves the institution of the family unprotected against the underlying, and always corrosive, direct effects of the process of progress. Result: both institution and ideology tend to break down simultaneously.

This is the generalized structure of the argument of parts 1 and 2, though the actual analysis is developed for the most part with specific reference to the historical situation of the United States. There is, moreover, a further and rather intriguing question that arises in the course of this discussion: How was it, during the earlier stages of the process of progress, that the notably long-run, future-oriented attitudes of the Idea of Progress could have become established? After all, the period during and immediately following the Industrial Revolution involved shattering changes of the then-existing pre-industrial society. How, in such a period of wrenching change, could the "long view" ever become so dominant?

The basic answer we give is that this period of actually revolutionary change was accompanied by, and in effect carefully channelled by, a very stiff and rigorous moral code. On this view, middle-class Victorian morality, however often dishonored in the actual observance, provided a kind of rudder for a society sailing through choppy and uncharted waters. It seriously restricted the available choices and options open to a modernizing society and thereby made possible the long-term outlook and interest in posterity inherent in the Idea of Progress.

By the same token, if this analysis is correct, the breakdown of this morality, and the consequent controversy over "family values" in our postmodern era must be seen as related to, and in fact part and parcel of, the fundamental predicament of progress. A detailed consideration of this controversy over values will be a primary topic for us in part 3, "The Battle." It will turn out that a somewhat self-restrictive general morality, an emphasis on family values, and the faith in the long-run future characteristic of the Idea of Progress, are all very much intertwined.

In part 3, also, we will discuss the possibility of reversing or at least ameliorating the current trend toward family breakdown. Interestingly, there is in the preceding analysis one general reason to be hopeful. Since the vast expansion of individual choice accruing from the process of progress is one of the major components of our problem, it could also in theory become a major vehicle for facilitating its solution. We *could* choose to promote a more orderly, satisfying, child-oriented family life in the United States if, individually and collectively, we so desire. There is nothing to prevent us from doing so. There are numerous institutional and attitudinal changes that would enable us to accomplish such a goal. Such changes would not, of course, be trivial. They would involve, if not a return to Victorian values (clearly impossible), a far more restrictive, self-restrained, even occasionally self-sacrificial, view of life than has recently become common.

There would, in short, be pain, but also potential reward. And one of those rewards might actually be an enhanced, if always somewhat imperfect, ability to envision and take comfort in the world we will be leaving to our children and heirs.

Part I

THE PROBLEM:
FAMILY BREAKDOWN AND ITS
RELATION TO PROGRESS

1

IN DISARRAY: THE AMERICAN
FAMILY APPROACHING YEAR 2000

I n 1980, a significant event occurred. President Carter, worried about the state of American family relationships, had called a White House conference to study the matter. The conference, like many such collective attempts to analyze complex social problems, produced little if any substantive knowledge or recommendations. It was nevertheless a signally important occasion: for what had begun as an indication of concern about *the* American family had a name change and became, officially, the White House Conference on *Families*.

And what that seemingly innocuous word change was saying is that there is no longer in America (or elsewhere for that matter) any institution that can claim the unique title "family." What we have instead is an enormous variety of institutions: some involving children some not; some involving two parents others one parent; some involving biological parents others step-parents; some involving marriages others not; some involving different sexes others the same sex; some involving permanence others involving year-to-year or even month-to-month changes; some involving a common place of residence others involving various forms of separation, drop-in lovers, children shuttling between different households (and, in fact, often receiving their "primary care" totally outside the home where they officially live). What an abundance of options and possibilities!

Are American famil*ies* on the decline? Hardly. There have never in our history been so many varieties to choose from. As long as Americans form any kind of attachment to other persons—social, sexual, emotional, spiritual—and for whatever lengths of time—weeks, months, years, decades—U.S. famil*ies* will be flourishing, and there will be no need for

13

a further White House Conference, or any other conference, on the subject.

All of which, of course, completely misses the real point. And this is that there is an historical institution, known as the family, with certain characteristic and defining features, and about whose breakdown in the Western world in the late twentieth century there is, or certainly ought to be, the deepest possible concern. Playing with plurals does not change this central point, nor avert the social tragedy that is likely to come from denying it.

THERE *IS* SUCH A THING AS "THE FAMILY"

When I speak of "the family," I am referring to a virtually universal institution by which human beings historically and even prehistorically have organized the succession of generations.[1] Although it is possible to have a "family" in this sense of the term without children—and numerous families throughout the ages have not borne offspring—nevertheless there is little question that an essential ingredient in the organization of the family unit is its role in propagating the human species, a role made necessary by the extraordinary dependence of the human child on others for care, nurture, and instruction during the early years of life. This dependence, moreover, has in many ways become increasingly prolonged over time as human society has grown more technologically complex. The family unit ultimately has this genetic purpose and is, as one writer has put it, "the rearing device for our species."[2]

However decisive this function of securing the succession of generations, the family has also historically fulfilled numerous other functions, and, in many periods and cultures, has become the basic unit around which human social life has been organized. In his survey of the changing American family, Carl N. Degler cites five characteristics that he believes are to be found in family life in virtually all known cultures.[3] They are, briefly:

1. "A family begins with a ritual between a woman and a man, a ceremony that we call marriage, and which implies long duration, if not permanence, for the relationship."

2. "The partners have duties and rights of parenthood that are also socially recognized and defined."

3. "Husband, wife, and children live in a common place."

4. "There are reciprocal economic obligations between husband and wife—that is, they both work for the family, even though the amount and kind of labor or production may be far from equal."

5. "The family also serves as a means of sexual satisfaction for the partners, though not necessarily as an exclusive one."

Clearly, these characteristics of family life are not wholly universal. There are, for example, known cultures where husbands and wives do not live together in a "common place." Also, we have to be careful about the meaning of the term "partners." Under polygyny, for example, a man may be married to more than one woman, and under polyandry, a woman to more than one man.

In general, however, these characteristics do describe fairly well an institution that, in the past, was common and accepted in virtually all societies. Thus, even in the many cultures where multiple partners were allowed, monogamy was still a common marital arrangement. Also, the view of some nineteenth-century theorists, like Friedrich Engels, that group marriages were widespread among primitive peoples, has not been confirmed by subsequent research. Writes Kathleen Gough: "All known hunters and gatherers live in families, not in communal sexual arrangements. Most hunters even live in nuclear families rather than in large extended kin groups. Mating is individualized, although one man may occasionally have two wives, or (very rarely) a woman may have two husbands. Economic life is built primarily around the division of labor between individual men and women."[4]

Our first conclusion then, is that, historically speaking, there is such an institution as "the family" that has very deep roots in human experience and culture.

THE FAMILY IN AMERICA: COLONIAL AND "TRADITIONAL"

Within this general framework, American families have exhibited many historical, geographical, racial and other variations. Thinking of predominant forms prior, say, to the early-to-mid-twentieth century, we can mention two in particular: (1) the colonial family, and (2) the "traditional," or, one might even say, the "Victorian" family.

The Colonial family

The colonial family is distinguished from later characteristic American families by two main features. The first involves the role of the family in production. Although the husband was considered the head of the family and although there was a sexual division of labor in terms of kinds of work, there was no sharp division between a provider-husband and a homemaker-wife. The father's place of work, in a world where 90 percent of colonial men were engaged in farming, was characteristically at home or very nearby. Meanwhile, the wife was heavily engaged in what was effectively a major manufacturing enterprise. Even as late as 1810, Secretary of the Treasury Albert Gallatin could note that "two-thirds of the clothing, including hosiery and of the house and table linen worn and used by the inhabitants of the United States, who do not reside in cities, is the product of family manufactures." He estimated this at ten times the value of what was produced outside the home.[5] The children were also engaged in productive work, either at home or in nearby apprenticeships, from an early age, and were often more accurately thought of not as dependents but as "little workers."

Thus the colonial family was clearly a major productive unit, in which all members of the family took part, though in different activities.

The second characteristic of the colonial family that sets its somewhat apart from later institutional developments was the extraordinary range of functions other than economic production that it also fulfilled. In his study of the Plymouth Colony, John Demos notes that, among other things, the colonial family was a school, a vocational institute, a church, a house of correction, and a welfare institution. Included in the last is the role the colonial family played at various times as a hospital, orphanage, old people's home, and poor house. As far as a house of correction is concerned, criminals were sometimes sentenced to become servants in the houses of citizens who could help discipline and reform them.[6] Thus, within the general framework noted by Degler, the colonial family obviously performed a great many detailed and vital functions for the society as a whole.

The "traditional" American family

A second predominant form the American family has taken historically (again, within the general framework noted by Degler) is what we now think of as the "traditional"—one might even say, Norman Rockwell-style—family. Although widely celebrated in the 1950s, this family form was really a creation of the post-Industrial Revolution, Victorian era in the United States, and reached its zenith in the late nineteenth and very early twentieth centuries. The post-World War II resurrection of Victorian "family values" was, it turned out, only temporary and was followed by a massive repudiation of these very same values. Briefly, as compared to the colonial family, the traditional American family was characterized by the following three traits:

1. *A change in the locus of economic production from home to marketplace.* This was accompanied by a change in the division of labor between husband and wife, as the former took on more and more the "sole-provider" role, while the wife became more and more exclusively a "homemaker." The children also increasingly ceased to be "little workers"; by middle-class standards, child labor came to be considered immoral and child labor law reform was eagerly sought.

2. *A shedding of many ancillary family functions.* As specialized hospitals, orphanages, prisons, and schools were developed in the surrounding society, the family gradually relinquished its all purpose role and concentrated increasingly on its basic functions: providing a relatively secure locus for the uniting of wife and husband around common purposes and interests, including centrally the siring, bearing, nurturing, rearing, and providing moral and other instruction to children.

3. *An attachment of great sentiment to home, family, motherhood, and children.* In contrast to the colonial period, when fathers played a much larger role, the rearing and teaching of children in the Victorian family fell increasingly to the mother. Whatever view one takes of woman-as-homemaker today, there is little doubt that opinion in the nineteenth and early twentieth centuries—certainly publicly expressed opinion—was that the raising of children and the domestication of men by women was a noble, almost holy, calling. According to Emerson: "women are . . . the civilizers of mankind. What is civilization? I answer, the power of

good women."[7] According to Catharine Beecher: the American mother "rightly estimates the long train of influence which will pass down to thousands, whose destinies from generation to generation, will be modified by those decisions of her will which regulate the temper, principles, and habits of her family"[8] And, according to the U.S. Congress: "the service rendered the United States by the American mother is the greatest source of the country's strength and inspiration."[9]

The last quotation is from the Congressional citation establishing Mother's Day in 1914. Since women still did not have the vote at that time, one is justified in feeling a certain skepticism about this, and other similar, expressions of sentiment about the value attached to women's roles at this time. Still, such sentiment was almost routinely expressed during the late nineteenth and early twentieth centuries; it is quite consistent with the view that children were achieving a new pride of place in the national consciousness and that, to a degree at least, women, who now had much larger responsibilities in rearing children, also shared that new pride of place.

Thus, the "traditional American family." This is the family that achieved an almost mythic quality at the turn of the century. It is also the family that made a surprise return engagement just after World War II—the family, if you will, of *Ozzie and Harriet* or *Leave It to Beaver*. And it is the family that is now deteriorating with extraordinary rapidity before our very eyes.

A CEREMONY THAT WE CALL MARRIAGE

A "ceremony that we call marriage" is how Degler begins his list of the more or less universal characteristics of the institution of the family across cultures and centuries. What is happening to the institution of marriage as we prepare to enter the twenty-first century? Numerous indicators suggest that the institution of marriage has been declining since the early postwar period and especially since the 1960s. In a 1985 study, Professor Thomas Espenshade of Princeton offered in evidence on this point such recent tendencies as the postponement of marriage, a lower proportion of people getting married, a lesser proportion of life spent in wedlock, and a shorter duration of marriage.[10] In 1940, married-couple families comprised 76.0 percent of all U.S. household units, but by 1995 their percentage had fallen to 54.4 percent. During the same period, family units in general fell from 91.1 percent of households to 70.0 percent.

One reason for the decline in family and married-couple households is that young people are delaying marriage. At the height of the Baby Boom in the mid-1950s, the median age at first marriage for women was 20.1 and for men 22.5. By 1990, the median ages were, for women, 23.9, and for men 26.1. And just as age at first marriage has been rising, so have the proportions of men and women who have never married. Figure 1.1 shows the extraordinary change in the percentages of never married women and men at various ages from twenty to thirty-four between 1960 and 1990. In every age category except one, the percentages of never married persons have more than doubled over these thirty years. The one exception is the category of men, aged twenty to twenty-four, where doubling would be impossible, but where the numbers have gone up from 53.1 percent to 79.3 percent.

As one would expect, there has also been a very sizeable increase in the numbers of individuals living alone over this period. In 1960, roughly 13 percent of individuals were living alone in this country; by 1995, this had almost doubled to 25 percent. Even more rapid has been the growth of unmarried couples living together. In 1970, there were only 523,000 unmarried-couple households in the United States, or about one for every one hundred married couples. By 1990, the number had grown to 3.5 million unmarried couple households and the ratio to six per every one hundred married couples.

Still another indicator of the weakening state of marriage in this country is the decline in the percentage of women who, upon discovering they are pregnant, get married before the baby is born. In the period 1960–64, of women fifteen to thirty-four years of age with a premaritally conceived first child, 52.2 percent actually married before the birth of the child. By 1985–89, the percentage who married was 26.6, or scarcely more than half the earlier percentage. And then, there is the question of the duration of marriages that do take place. It is quite significant that in a period of rising life expectancies at older ages, the average duration of marriages has been declining. Between 1940–45 and 1975–80, for example, the average duration of marriage for White women fell from thirty-two to twenty-three years and that of Black women from twenty-three to fifteen years. Also, if a given marriage

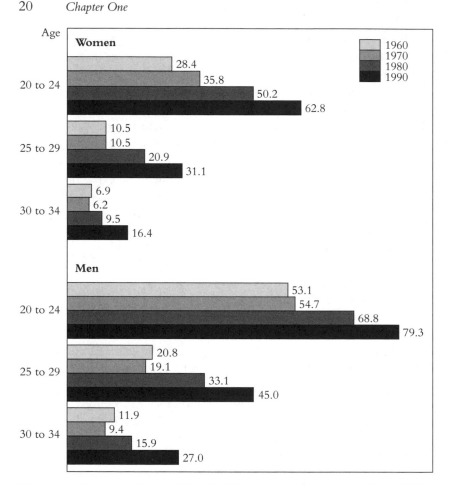

Fig. 1.1   Percent Never Married, by Age and Sex: 1960 to 1990

Source: U.S. Bureau of the Census, *Current Population Reports* (CPR), P23–181, 1992.

does break up, the remarriage rate is also falling—by 38 percent just between 1963 and 1986.

Later marriages, shorter marriages, fewer remarriages, more never-marrieds, more living alone, more cohabiting without the benefit of clergy, more pregnancies uncertified by marriage—can there be any serious question about what is happening to the institution of marriage as we complete the twentieth century? It is clearly fading fast as the basic institution in which "the family," in our sense of the term, is ultimately rooted.

THE DIVORCE REVOLUTION

A major reason for the changes we have noted, particularly the shorter duration of marriages, is a revolution in American attitudes towards divorce. Degler wrote of marriage as implying "long duration" if not "permanence" in the relationship between wife and husband. Divorce changes all that. For example, in 1988, the median duration of all marriages that end in divorce was 7.1 years. This duration varies, of course, according to the categories of age, sex, and marriage. We have spoken of couples today getting married at older ages. If we consider first marriages of women between the ages of thirty-five and thirty-nine, we find that, in 1988, the median duration of their marriages ending in divorce was a scant 4.7 years. For men in this age group, it was hardly better at 5.2 years.

Surprisingly perhaps, teen first marriages that end in divorce have a somewhat longer median duration, in 1988 roughly ten years for both men and women. However, the news for these very young marriages is not good at all since the chances of those marriages actually ending in divorce is much higher. In the period from 1970 to 1985, between a quarter and a third of all teenage first marriages broke up within five years. As demographers Teresa Castro Martin and Larry L. Bumpass put it, "The inverse relationship between age at marriage and the likelihood of marital disruption is among the strongest and most consistently documented in the literature."[11] Thus, these teenage marriages may last a bit longer on average before they end in divorce but the odds of having a divorce ending to the marriage is a lot higher.

One might add further that the odds of having a divorce ending are also higher for second as opposed to first marriages. You would think that experience would offer, if not total insurance against further family breakup, at least some protection against silly first-marriage mistakes. On the contrary, second and later marriages are even less stable than first marriages and their median durations even shorter.

What all this tells us is that, where divorce occurs, the notion of marriage as implying "long duration" if not "permanence" is simply inapplicable. The question then arises of how common such divorces are. Are these short-duration, impermanent marriages on the increase?

Everyone knows the basic answer to this question. With an occasional exception (see below, page 225), the number of divorces each year per one thousand married persons has been rising since the beginning of the twentieth century and has skyrocketed in recent decades. This rate rose from 35 divorces per 1,000 married persons in 1950 to 142 in 1990, or roughly fourfold. Figure 1.2 shows that this rapid rate of increase applies to both White and Black families, though the figure for the latter is more than twice as high. Interestingly, by 1980 the White divorce rate was higher than that of Blacks in 1970 and almost 50 percent higher than that of Blacks in 1960. By 1990, the White rate was twice that of Blacks in 1960. Thus, while divorce problems (and many other problems) are more serious for African Americans than for Whites, one must clearly reject the notion that they are in any way exclusively minority

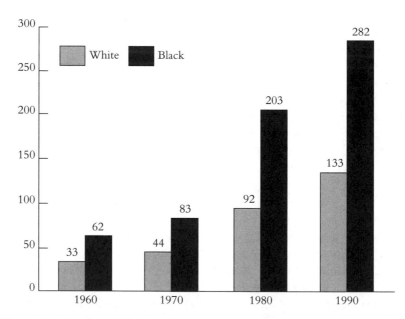

Fig. 1.2   Ratio of divorced persons per 1,000 married persons, by race and year

Source: U.S. Bureau of the Census, *Current Population Reports,* "Marital Status and Living Arrangements: March 1990," Series P-20, No. 450, 1991.

problems. Family breakup is now a massive phenomenon in the White as well as in the Black community.

But what of future trends? What is the likelihood that American marriages in the years ahead will end in divorce? In the same Castro-Martin and Bumpass article quoted above (and written in 1989), the authors reach this rather striking conclusion: "Taking into account well-known levels of underreporting, we find that recent rates imply that about two-thirds of all first marriages are likely to end in separation or divorce." However, this estimate has subsequently been revised downward somewhat and there is, in fact, some disagreement among the experts as to whether U.S. divorce rates are still going up, have plateaued, or are actually coming down.[12]

A very common estimate in 1995 is that half of first marriages are expected to end in divorce. This is a very high rate by any historical standard and, of course, has vast implications for the way in which American children are being raised. As a recent Census Bureau report put it: "About one-half of recent marriages may end in divorce and the children of these divorces will typically live in one-parent families. If their custodial parent remarries, these children will live with a stepparent. Hence, many of today's children will experience two or three different parental arrangements before they reach the age of 18."[13] Which is to say that high divorce rates deny "long duration"[14] or "permanence" not only to spouses but to children as well. And this is only part of the story where today's children are concerned.

SINGLE-PARENT FAMILIES

For one trend that has definitely not plateaued in recent decades is the having of children by the never-married. We have already mentioned that, in the case of premarital pregnancies, the percentage of women getting married before the birth of the child has fallen drastically in recent decades. Now we have to add the further fact that the number of women experiencing such premarital pregnancies has also been rising.

Figure 1.3 shows the course of birthrates for married and unmarried women since 1950. At the beginning, we were still in the midst of the post-World War II Baby Boom (1946–1964) and fertility among American women was quite high. It then began to fall sharply for married women. For unmarried women, however, there was no fall, and from the mid–1970s on, fertility among unmarried women has been rising

Fig. 1.3   Birthrates for women aged 15–44, by marital status: 1950–1991

Source: Sara McLanahan and Lynne Casper, "Growing Diversity and Inequality in the American Family," in *State of the Union: America in the 1990s,* Vol. 2, ed. Reynolds Farley (New York: Russell Sage Foundation, 1995), p. 11. Reprinted with permission. Data from National Center for Health Statistics, *Vital Statistics on the U.S., 1988,* Vol. 1; and National Center for Health Statistics, *Advance Report of Datality Statistics,* Vol. 41, no. 9, 1993.

strongly. By the end of the 1980s as compared to the early 1960s, the percentages of White women, ages fifteen to thirty-four, with a first birth occurring before first marriage, had more than doubled, from 8.5 to 21.6 percent. The figures for Hispanics and Blacks were even more startling, Hispanics going from 19.2 to 37.5 percent, and Blacks going from 42.4 percent to 70.3 percent over the same period.

The result of this development was that whereas even as late as 1970 only a very small percentage (6.8 percent) of children living in single-parent families were living with a never-married parent (the rest being with a divorced, spouse-absent, or widowed parent), by 1990 this percentage had zoomed up to 30.6 percent. In fact, it was almost equal to the number of divorced single parents (38.6 percent). Widowed single parents—the largest cause of single parenthood in olden days—had meanwhile become a positive rarity, falling from 20.1 to 7.1 percent over this same time period.

The upshot of all these changes has been a virtual explosion of single-parent families in the United States in recent years. Just in the years between 1970 and 1994, the percentage of single-parent families among all families with children increased nearly two-and-a-half times, from 13 percent to 31 percent.[14] The overwhelming majority of these families are headed by women, meaning that great numbers of fathers have not only been absent from home during working hours, but absent from the home, period. In many cases, these absent fathers see their children infrequently, occasionally not for months or even years on end.

In fact, the situation with respect to biological fathers is even more striking than these numbers suggest. Single-parent families do not include families where the wife (or ex-husband) has remarried. In 1990, about one of out of every six children living with two parents was living with a stepparent, nearly 90 percent of these with a stepfather. Thus, the percentage of children living apart from their *biological* fathers was even greater than the single-parent numbers might suggest. David Blankenhorn, in a 1995 book ominously titled *Fatherless America*, points out that official figures indicate that, in 1990, 36.3 percent of American children were living apart from their biological fathers. This was more than double the official figure for 1960 (17.5 percent). Blankenhorn notes further that "the trend shows no sign of slowing down. Indeed, it seems quite probable that, as of 1994, fully 40 percent of all children in the nation did not live with their fathers. Scholars estimate that, before they reach age eighteen, more than half of all children in the nation will live apart from their fathers for at least a significant portion of their childhoods." [15]

If this analysis is right, then by the time the nation reaches the twenty-first century we might even be facing a situation in which the percentage of children living with both biological parents is not only a minority but a fairly small minority. Blankenhorn subtitles his book *Confronting Our Most Urgent Social Problem*. Whether one agrees or disagrees with this evaluation, it is quite clear that this father-absence by decision—not by war, accident, or death—is a new phenomenon in American experience and that it conflicts sharply with Degler's account of the basics of the institution of "the family," that is, that "partners have duties and rights of parenthood," that "husband, wife, and children live in a common place," even, in the case of many of these absent fathers, that "there are reciprocal economic obligations between husband and wife" (the well-publicized "deadbeat dad" phenomenon).

If this behavior conflicts with the generalized responsibilities of family life, it conflicts even more sharply with what we have referred to as the "traditional American family." For in that once-treasured family unit, children, home and hearth, fatherhood and motherhood were considered priceless possessions. Certainly one would never ignore one's children. It would be unthinkable to abandon them. And, in fact, practically no one ever did.

Actually, one of the most telling statistics in this whole area has to do with the effect of having children on a couple's propensity to divorce. In the old days, the thought always was that, except *in extremis*, one should "stay together for the sake of the children." In consequence, the number of children in divorcing families was notably smaller than those in families staying married. No longer. The inhibiting effect of children on divorce behavior has ceased to exist. Divorcing couples have the same number of children as all married couples. The existence of children makes no statistical difference in parental decision-making with respect to divorce—perhaps, sadly, very little difference with respect to parental behavior in general.[16]

WHO'S MINDING THE KIDS?

Everything we have said so far has related to family structures. But the breakdown of the institution of the family can also take place within a superficially intact family structure. A fundamental—probably *the* fundamental—function of the family historically, and even prehistorically, was the raising and nurturing of children. And how, we now ask, are Americans doing on this score as we count down to the end of the twentieth century? One basic change, as compared to the traditional American family, is obvious to everyone. The husband is no longer the sole-provider for the family unit. As figure 1.4 indicates, labor force participation by married women has increased dramatically in recent decades—from less than a third (30 percent) in 1960 to almost double (58 percent) in 1990. If we were to carry these numbers further back in time to 1890 or 1900, the change would be even more dramatic, actually revolutionary. It was extremely uncommon then for married women to work in the paid labor force, and in the case of middle-class White women almost unheard of.

In itself, this new pattern of behavior, however much in conflict

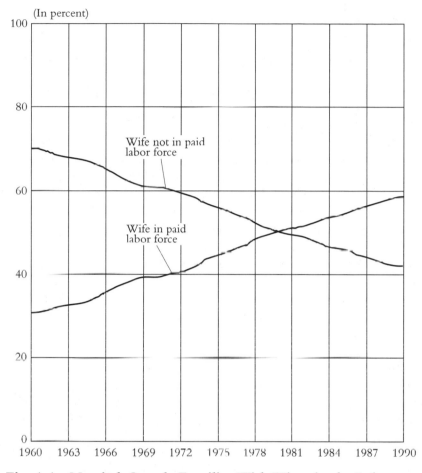

Fig. 1.4 Married-Couple Families With Wives in the Labor Force: 1960 to 1990

Source: U.S. Bureau of the Census; *Current Population Reports,* P23–181, 1992.
Note: Data for 1983 are not available.

with the traditional American family, would not mean a departure from a more general concept of family life. After all, we know that in the colonial family women were effectively active members of the labor force, just not officially in the paid labor force. In general, the family unit has always involved those "reciprocal economic obligations between husband and wife" to which we have frequently referred. What is more of a problem here is, specifically, the way in which today's families are taking care (or not taking care) of the basic needs of their children. For what is especially noteworthy here is not so much the increased labor force participation of wives as of mothers, and perhaps very especially, the mothers of infants and toddlers. Interestingly, wives who have no children under eighteen in the home have notably lower labor force participation rates than wives with children, even with children under the age of six. This is actually not so surprising as it might seem since "childless wives" in these statistics also include older, and even elderly, wives whose children have long since left home.

Still, the participation rates of mothers and especially mothers of very young children are dramatically different not only from American families a century ago, but even a few years ago. For example, in just fourteen years—from 1976 to 1990—the labor force participation of mothers of children under age one rose from 31 percent to 53 percent. This situation, where more than half of the mothers of American infants have employment in the paid labor force, is quite simply unprecedented in the nation's history.

What then happens to the role of the family in rearing and nurturing these children, and small children in particular, when both parents are employed, or, in the case of single-parent homes, where that single parent is employed? Has the American family, already shattered by divorce, separation, and illegitimacy, also forfeited this fundamental function?

Not completely, of course. There are still substantial numbers of families that are not only intact but in which one parent—almost always the mother—devotes herself largely to the rearing and nurturing of children within the physical confines of the family home while the other parent—almost always the father—is the sole provider, or a reasonable approximation thereof. What we have in these cases are what we might consider variations on the traditional American family theme. Sometimes the mother remains a homemaker only when the children are of preschool age and then enters the labor force. Sometimes the mother takes on part-time work, but still is the primary provider of care for the children, either while they are very young, or throughout their childhoods. Sometimes, in truth, the father becomes the primary provider of care for the children, either (in rare cases) becoming the homemaker himself, or (more commonly) adjusting his hours or working schedule so that he can take on major child-rearing responsibilities.

All this is to say that the situation with respect to child care in America at this time is a very mixed one, containing not only radically new elements, but also, in some cases, substantial roots in our historic past. Still, there is the massively important fact that three-quarters of wives with children age six and above are in the labor force and nearly two-thirds of those with children under age six are similarly employed. Who takes care of the children while this great majority of wives and mothers is working?

Fortunately, the Census Bureau provides regular and systematic information on this subject in a publication that comes out every few years entitled *Who's Minding the Kids?* or, most recently, *Who's Minding Our Preschoolers?*[17] This latest version, published in April 1996, is for primary child-care arrangements in the fall of 1993. The central results for children under age five are presented in table 1.1. And what they indicate is

Table 1.1   Primary Child Care Arrangements Used by Employed Mothers for Children Under 5, Fall 1993, by Percent

Type of arrangement	All children under 5	Children under 1	Children 1 & 2	Children 3 & 4
Care in child's home[a]	33.8	37.2	36.1	30.3
Care outside child's home[a]	66.2	62.8	63.9	69.7
Care by a relative[b]	47.5	52.5	51.1	42.0
Care by a non-relative[c]	52.5	47.5	48.9	58.0

[a] Includes small percentage of employed mothers giving primary care to children, arbitrarily divided half and half between at home and outside home care.
[b] Includes mother (at work), father, grandparent, and other.
[c] Includes care at home, in another home, organized child care facilities, or school-based activity.
Source: Adapted by the author from table 2, Lynne Casper, "Who's Minding Our Preschoolers?" U.S. Bureau of the Census, *Current Population Reports,* P70-53, April 1996.

that the primary care for these preschool age children of employed mothers was in the great majority of cases (66.2 percent) provided outside the physical premises of the child's own home, and that, in over half the cases (52.5 percent), primary care was provided by a nonrelative.

In a way, the most striking feature of these numbers has to do with infants, that is, children under the age of one. Recall that the majority of the mothers of these infants are in fact currently employed. And who provides the primary nurturing care for these totally helpless and dependent offspring? In nearly half of these cases (47.5 percent), primary care is not even provided by a relative of the child, and, in nearly two-thirds of the cases (62.8 percent), it is provided outside the infant's home. This represents a total break with the concept of the traditional American family, the colonial American family, and, in fact, any family structure represented on a substantial scale in the entire American experience. For this nation at least, what we are seeing in the farming out of infants to extra-family locations and persons is something new, untried, and, for many of us, very alarming.[18]

Nor does the problem stop with infants, or children under five generally. For, as already noted in passing, the effective dependency period of children has had a strong tendency to lengthen in the course of industrialization, or what, in this book, we shall be calling, the "process of progress." Children at ages seven or eight, or even fourteen or fifteen, are no longer "little workers" as they were in colonial times and even into the early nineteenth century. They still live at home; they still are economically dependent on their families (or, one has to add today, on the government welfare system); they still need attention, instruction, and guidance; even, one has to suspect, they still need nurturing, affection, and love.

Thus, we now ask, how are these older children, say, from ages five to fourteen, cared for in late twentieth-century America? The primary caregiver, in terms of waking hours, is, of course, the school system, either public or private. But how about after school hours? How many children return to a parentless, adultless, and, in fact, empty home when the school day is over?

What we are referring to here is, of course, the phenomenon of "latchkey kids," children who, in Census Bureau reports, are described as those "who are left alone or unsupervised during the day and return home to an empty house after school." In operational terms, the Census

Bureau considers latchkey kids to be "those children aged 5 to 14 whose parents reported 'child cares for self' as either the primary or secondary child care arrangement."[19] Actually this method of data collection—via the reports of the parents who may feel a bit guilty about announcing that their young child "cares for self"—is certain to produce underestimates of the phenomenon in question. In fact, wild underestimates. Thus, using this method, the Census Bureau reported in 1994 that 1.6 million children of employed women (7.6 percent of the total) were latchkey kids in the fall of 1991.

However, the report went on immediately to add that this number is almost certainly a "conservative" estimate and, using an alternative (and more objective) approach, came up with the figure of 4.6 million latchkey kids, or 21.7 percent of the group in question. Even this estimate is probably too low. As the report itself noted, some private estimates of the number of latchkey kids go as high as 15 million. Magazine surveys and polls suggest that as many as 40 percent of parents leave their kids on their own after school at least one day a week. Also, and very significantly, all these numbers in the Census reports are for the fall months. What about the summer? Here the primary care arrangement—the school—disappears, and other arrangements must be made by full-time or even part-time working mothers. The percentage of school-age children who go unsupervised more than doubles in summer as compared to the school year.[20]

Why are American children watching so much television these days? Why is it that the government has been instituting regulations to require television sets to have devices whereby parents, *in their absence*, can regulate the kind of programs their children watch?

The answers are pretty clear. In many of today's American "families" (I now purposefully use the plural), not only has the biological father completely fled the scene, but the mother, in her own way, is fleeing the scene as well. In all too many cases, the message is clear: "You're on your own, kids. Lots of luck!"

IS THE AMERICAN FAMILY ALREADY DOOMED?

So much has been happening to the American family in recent decades that one has to wonder whether the issue may by now have been

32   *Chapter One*

decided: Is "the family" already doomed? Are we already committed to those multiple, all-inclusive famil*ies,* which are certain to survive since they have no real content and say nothing whatever about the ultimate relationships of wives and husbands and, perhaps especially, about the substance of the parent-child nexus?

While this is clearly the trend of things, I will ultimately argue that there is nothing at all inexorable about what is happening and that, if we choose—and perhaps, above all, if we decide that we really ought morally to make this choice—we have it in our power to turn things around and restore something of the historic potency of family life to our national future.

But first things first. And the very first of these first things is what I have attempted to show in this chapter, namely, that family breakdown in America as we approach the year 2000 is no mirage. It is real, it is important, it is unprecedented in our nation's history. Where the most unequivocal change—and, in terms of the intrinsic functions of the institution of the family, the most fundamental change—has occurred is with respect to our children. Every statistic cited in the preceding pages bears on this point. Indeed, we can add one further statistic that, in many ways, sums up all the rest. It is estimated that between 1965 and the late 1980s, the amount of time the average American child spent interacting with a parent (either mother or father) *dropped by 43 percent*—from around thirty hours a week to around seventeen hours.[21] Project this kind of trend into the future and obviously "the family" in America would be doomed. It would be broken completely.

The second of our first things is to ask whether this trend, if we accept it as real and indeed overwhelming, is all that bad. Is there any clearcut, hard evidence to suggest that this trend has consequences that we really may not want to live with? This task we take up briefly in the next chapter.

And then it is on to the fundamental undertaking of this book: to try to explain why family breakdown in America has occurred and why we feel it is intrinsically connected with fundamental changes in our society's ideology, and very especially our society's view of the future as embodied in what we call the "Idea of Progress." Only when this large task is completed can we hope to come to any conclusions about the possibility of reversing current trends.

2

THE FUTURE AT RISK:
THE CONSEQUENCES OF
FAMILY BREAKDOWN

B ut does it really matter? Perhaps the replacement of the historical institution of the family with a multiplicity of families does no harm and conceivably may even be all to the good. One has to raise the question seriously because there is no reason to believe that Americans (or Swedes, or Britons, or French, or any other Western population) have been coerced, or in any other way intimidated, into accepting the new family regimes. It has been a natural evolution, a result of millions of individual choices, including choices of public policies, leading our societies down this more or less common road.

Further, as one reads the popular press or listens to the radio or watches television, one gets the sense that many American adults are, in fact, quite pleased with their own particular and individual current arrangements. Does this investment-counselor mother feel that she, and others like her, should be forced to leave her job and return to the kitchen sink and the diaper-changing table? Hardly. Or this battered wife? Does she feel that she should have stayed with her brute of a husband "for the sake of the children"? Or this young man of the streets? Does he feel he should be tied down for life to this young woman he doesn't care the least about just because he happened to get her pregnant? Or, for that matter, this gay or lesbian couple? Shouldn't they have the same rights and privileges of marital status that the state confers on the heterosexually married? Are they to be forced back into the closet, as in times past, because of some archaic and prejudicial concept of "the family"?

The point is that individuals in their special and particular situations have often benefited dramatically from recent changes in American family arrangements. It could hardly be otherwise since no *deus ex machina* has descended from the sky ordaining that all these choices be made in just these particular ways. Of course, not everyone, and very clearly not every adult, has benefited. Often they have not benefited from their own choices; that is, they have made bad mistakes, which looking back upon, they very much wish they had avoided. Also, they may have been very adversely affected by the choices of others, as, perhaps, was the young woman whose pregnancy is of no concern whatever to the father of her child-to-be. Still, in all, adults, at least beyond a certain age, have to take some personal responsibility for the situations in which they find themselves.

Which is to say that if we are looking to find the real victims of family breakdown in the United States in this last decade of the twentieth century, we had best look not at adults, young, middle-aged, or old, but at children. This is for three reasons. First, as already hinted, it is because, unlike adults, our children have not had any real choice in these matters. It was not their choice to be born, nor their choice of homes to live in (or not live in), nor of parents to raise (or not to raise) them, nor, in fact, of anything relevant to the family environment in which they are placed and in which they are expected to grow up.

Second, it is particularly appropriate to concentrate on the effect of family breakdown on children since, according to our general analysis, it is at a minimum one of the most fundamental functions of the family to shelter, nurture, and instruct the dependent young. The American family, whether colonial, traditional, or whatever other historical variation we might find, has always been charged with this function. If the institution is breaking down, how and by whom is this unavoidable charge being fulfilled?

Finally, and of particular relevance to our subsequent analysis, the effect of family breakdown on children can be considered a proxy for the effect of such breakdown on our society's future. I call this chapter "The Future at Risk." Ultimately, our analysis will tie together a diminished sense of the future, inadequate attention to our children, and the decline of the American family. It is finally our inability, and to some degree our unwillingness, to visualize and depend on the future that makes possible the kind of family breakdown and, in many cases, outright child neglect that would otherwise seem wholly incomprehensible in a civilized society.

CHILDREN IN TROUBLE

American children are not having an easy time growing up these days. Many are troubled; many are *in* trouble, often serious trouble. Violence among teenagers is exploding. The homicide rate for fourteen- to seventeen-year-olds tripled just in the decade between 1984 and 1993. The teenage suicide rate increased more than threefold between 1960 and 1990. Despite AIDS and other sexually transmitted diseases, sexual intercourse is occurring earlier and earlier among American young people, increasingly with multiple partners.[1] School performance is declining and U.S. children are now outranked by virtually every other industrialized nation on earth when it comes to competitive test-taking.

How bad is the condition of our young people? A recent (1995) statement by William Damon, director of the Center for Human Development of Brown University, sounds a clear alarm: "Practically all the indicators of youth health and behavior have declined year by year for well over a generation. None has improved. The litany of decline is so well known that it is losing its ability to shock. . . . Unfortunately, I am also aware that the data will be significantly worse by the time this statement reaches the press."[2]

The Fordham Institute for Innovation in Social Policy has published an Index of Social Health of the U.S. for the past twenty-five years. The 1996 edition traces this Index from 1970 to 1994 and finds a massive decline in the country's social health over this period. From a high of 77.5 in 1973, the index declined to 37.5 in 1994. The index includes some sixteen measures, of which six are specific to children and teenagers: infant mortality, child abuse, children in poverty, teen suicide, drug abuse, and high school dropouts. The declines in some of these measures over the past quarter century are stunning: teen suicide worsened by 83 percent, children in poverty by 48 percent, and child abuse by an extraordinary 346 percent. In the latest report, high school dropouts and drug abuse were also found to be on the increase.[3]

Clearly this is a deeply troubled generation. The harder question is, how much of this trouble can fairly be attributed to the kind of family breakdown we discussed in the last chapter? A quite general difficulty here is that the same cultural factors that produce changes in the behavior of older generations—including the parents of these children, and specifically their neglect of these children—may also directly affect the attitudes and behavior of the children themselves. The fading of the Idea of Progress, a subject to which I devote the whole of part 2 of this book, is likely to influence all generations, young and old, and this independently of the strength or weakness of the institution of the family.

Also, there is the problem that there are so many things going on simultaneously, so many changes interacting with each other, that it is difficult to separate out any one particular influence—say, divorce, or single-parenthood, or lack of parental attention during infancy, or any other specifically familial factor—as dominant. A very good example of the difficulty is given by a 1995 *New York Times* poll in which an attempt was made to find what Americans think is causing the current explosion of teenage sex and violence.[4] TV was apparently considered the prime suspect. "Americans have a starkly negative view of popular culture," the opening sentence reads, "and blame television more than any other single factor for teen-age sex and violence." Evidently, it is the media, not the family that is the real culprit.

But wait a second. Read on a bit. Presently one finds that the media in general is in a dead heat with family factors in the answers of poll respondents with respect to teenage violence. Each has 33 percent of the votes for the most responsible factor. It just happens that the family factor is divided into three categories: "lack of supervision," "parents, unspecified," and "breakdown of family." Even more significant, perhaps, are the detailed comments about television reported from people who had taken the poll. Many said that they felt "powerless" to prevent their children from watching inappropriate television shows. Why this sense of powerlessness? The response of David Hull, a forty-year-old father of two, is telling: " 'Parents are not around,' said Mr. Hull, who works days as a cook and whose wife works nights as a security guard. 'So kids are going to get a hold of what they want no matter what. I don't see how you can keep them away.' "

The *Times* then goes on to quote political pollster Mark Mellman, who suggests that concern about the media "has been rising precisely because many people feel that parents no longer spend enough time with their kids." The family is where good values should be taught, he suggests, but parents don't have time to do it, and hence TV does it, only "they're the wrong values." Which factor then is really to blame? The media or family breakdown? Even the most sophisticated polling techniques are unlikely to be able to unscramble this kind of omelet.

A further difficulty in singling out the effect of family breakdown on the condition of American children is that, although moving in the same downward direction, the decline of the family is obviously much further advanced in the case of minority, and especially Black, families as compared to non-Hispanic Whites. This leads to a tendency (comforting to some, alarming to others) to locate the problems of American children more or less exclusively in the minority community. American children in general are doing just fine, it is sometimes said. The only real problems are with the children of the largely Black "underclass."

Take, for example, the matter of declining academic performance and test scores. Test scores for American children have fallen substantially since the 1960s, the median verbal SAT, for example, falling from 477 in 1960 to 423 in 1992, the math SAT from 498 to 476 over the same period. These declines represent a reversal of a previous trend toward higher SAT scores over time. The seriousness of the decline is confirmed by very recent efforts to change the tests so as to raise the median scores. Also, as noted above, there is the extremely low ranking of U.S. children on all international achievement tests, coming in at or near the very bottom of the list of nations, even including some which are far less "developed" than the United States.[5]

Is this a general problem affecting American children, or can it safely be relegated to minorities and others at the bottom of the socioeconomic ladder? Sophisticated observers, like Robert Haveman and Barbara Wolfe of the University of Wisconsin, warn against attributing measures of declining child welfare to children in general when what they may really reflect is "drastic declines for children at the bottom of the distribution." In the case of test scores, which they acknowledge as "low," they note that "the increase in the proportion of high school students taking the test may account for all or most of the decline since 1970."[6] But is this really a correct way of looking at the matter? John Bishop of Cornell University has pointed out very clearly that the test score decline has been larger for Whites than for minorities, larger in the suburbs than in the central cities, evident in private as well as public schools, as large or possibly larger for more able students than for less able students, and particularly large for higher level skills in contrast to basic skills, including an especially large decline in the number of students achieving above 700 on the verbal SAT. Also, when tests like the Iowa Test of Educational Development, which largely rule out the changing composition of the test-taking population, are examined, the same pattern of declining scores is evident.[7]

None of which is meant to deny that minority children are having a particularly tough time of it in America these days—after all, family breakdown in Black and some Hispanic communities often approaches the level of total disaster. It does strongly suggest, however, that non-Hispanic White Americans proceed at their own peril if they feel that they can consider themselves somehow immune from the deep viruses affecting our youngest generation. To quote Brown University's William Damon again: "The youth crisis that we face in our society is a general one. It is not confined to a particular class, ethnic group, gender, or any other social grouping. . . . (T)he affliction that I have observed threatens children of the wealthy as well as children of the poor."[8] Not just a few, but increasingly a large number, perhaps even a majority, of our children are seriously at risk.

FAMILY STRUCTURE AND CHILD POVERTY

The foregoing comments are all impressionistic. They convey a general sense that our children are not doing at all well these days without pinning down exactly why. This is, I believe, a necessary starting point—after all, if there is no problem, there is no need to analyze it—but clearly we need to go further and, in particular, to suggest as concretely as we can how family breakdown may be a major contributor to the troubles our children are experiencing. We begin with one of the broadest factors affecting children's well-being, their economic condition, and, in particular their poverty status. It is indisputable that, relative to other groups in our society, and, indeed, relative to their own situation, children's economic condition has decidedly worsened in recent decades. For example, over the period 1967 to 1989, while working-age adults (age eighteen to sixty-four) were experiencing a roughly constant poverty rate of around 10 percent, and elderly Americans (sixty-five and over) were experiencing a drastic reduction in poverty, from 30 percent to just over 11 percent, children (up through age seventeen) saw their poverty rate increase from 17 percent to 20 percent. The most recent numbers (for 1995) show children with a poverty rate (20.8 percent) almost exactly double that for elderly Americans (10.5 percent).[9]

Furthermore, within the age group of children, it is the youngest children who tend to get hit hardest. For example, in 1988, a year of general prosperity, children aged 0 to 5 had a poverty rate of around 23 percent. In a recession year in the early 1980s, over a quarter of these youngest children were being brought up in poverty. Ironically, these increases in child poverty have been taking place long after the War on Poverty, which only began to have effect in the late 1960s, was launched.

What, you ask, does all this have to do with family breakdown in the United States? A very great deal. Take divorce, for example. A 1991 study found that after divorce, the percentage of children in poverty doubles from 19 percent to 38 percent and that, if the mother neither remarries nor reconciles with the father, the rate remains at a startling 35 percent sixteen months later.[10]

Actually, divorce isn't the worst of it. Children of never-married parents generally fare far worse than those of divorced parents. Thus, while 50 percent of all families receiving federal welfare under the Aid to Families with Dependent Children (AFDC) program are headed by an unmarried parent, just 12 percent are headed by a divorced parent. In 1991, the median family income for divorced mothers with children was almost double that of never-married mothers with children—$16,156 as compared to $8,758. It might be added that both income levels were far below that of two-parent families, $40,137![11]

Since most of America's divorced families and never-married families with children are headed by women, the extremely low standard of living of such families has led to what has been called the "feminization of poverty." Looking at it from the child's point of view, we might equally well term it the "impoverishment of children." The extent of this phenomenon is suggested by figure 2.1. Owing to the rapid growth of single-mother families, combined with the very high poverty rates in such families, single-mother families with children in 1990 accounted for 53.1 percent of all U.S. families below the poverty level. As the 1993 Report of the National Commission on America's Urban Families put

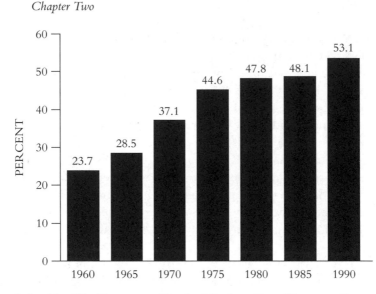

Fig. 2.1   Family Poverty: Single-Mother Families as a Percent of all Poor Families (1960–1990)

Source: Families First: Report of the National Commission on America's Urban Families (Washington, D.C.: U.S. Government Printing Office, 1993). Data from U.S. Bureau of the Census.

it: "Poverty historically has derived primarily from unemployment and low wages. Today it derives increasingly from family structure. In the 1980s, the U.S. experienced an important turning point: for the first time in recent history, a majority of all poor familes were one-parent families. Today, single-parent families are six times more likely to be poor than married-couple families with children."[12] Although there is a heavy concentration of Black and other minority families among these poor single-parent families, nevertheless the Commission noted that child poverty "is prevalent in all communities." "Surprisingly," they added, "the number of children in poverty has been rising more rapidly in the suburbs than in the central cities."

In short, family breakdown, if not the sole cause of child poverty in the United States, is certainly a major contributor to this unhappy outcome. Had our family structure remained what it was thirty or forty years ago, child poverty would unquestionably be much lower than it is today.

THE MULTIPLE ILL EFFECTS OF FAMILY BREAKDOWN

Poverty affects children's attitudes, behaviors, and general well-being in a variety of ways, but it is by no means the only cause of harm to children in a society in which the family is breaking down. Broken homes themselves can be a direct cause of harm in many different dimensions of life.

Take juvenile crime, for example. We have mentioned the explosion of crime and violence among children and teenagers in recent years, a phenomenon that is occurring even while adult crime, as in the mid–1990s, may actually be declining.[13] As we know, many factors are involved in this behavioral change, including television and/or parental failure to supervise television watching. Juvenile poverty itself is undoubtedly a factor. Also frequently mentioned is the easy availability of handguns and other lethal weapons. Yet the fact is that the most important factor is almost certainly the prevalence of single-parent families and especially the absence of a father in the household. Fully 70 percent of all prison and reform school inmates come from fatherless homes. This is a dramatic finding that underlines the critical importance of a caring and competent father to serve both as a role model and disciplinarian during the often wild teenage years, particularly for young males.

This effect of broken homes is so major that it very probably dominates all other factors contributing to the explosion of juvenile crime and violence. Thus one study concludes the following about the "relationship between crime and one-parent families": The relationship is "so strong that controlling for family configuration erases the relationship between race and crime and between low income and crime."[14] But what about things like handguns and automatic weapons? Compared to family factors, the gun problem, in and of itself, seems rather minor. As Richard Neely, Chief Justice of West Virginia, notes: "In West Virginia, where I live, the average household has several guns, yet West Virginia has the lowest crime rate in the U.S." He himself attributes this low rate to the somewhat better family conditions in West Virginia compared to the rest of the nation.[15]

Juvenile crime is probably the most dramatic single effect of family breakdown on our children's lives but hardly the only one. Figure 2.2 presents evidence on a variety of indicators of children's well-being taken from the National Longitudinal Survey of Youth. These bars are

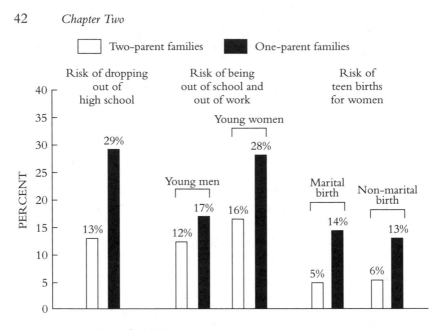

Fig. 2.2   Risks of children in one-parent versus two-parent families

Source: All percentages are taken from the National Longitudinal Survey of Youth as presented in Sara McLanahan and Gary Sandefur, *Growing Up with a Single Parent* copyright © 1994 by the President and Fellows of Harvard College. Adapted by the author from figures 1, 3 and 4 with permission of Harvard University Press.

presented in some different form, along with a variety of other study results, in a 1994 book by Sara McLanahan and Gary Sandefur, *Growing Up with a Single Parent.*[16] The other studies generally tend to confirm the results shown here.

The results are striking. In three of the categories—the risks of dropping out of high school, of having a baby as a married teenager, and of having a baby as an unmarried teenager—the chances are more than twice as great for the children of one-parent families. In this compilation, it should be noted, "one-parent families" also include "stepfamilies." In the other two categories—the risks of schoolless young men and young women being out of work—the adverse results are not quite so strong but still quite serious.

Very forceful evidence of the harmful effects of family breakdown also emerged from the 1988 National Health Interview Survey of Child Health covering 17,100 American children. In a study based on this survey, Nicholas Zill and Charlotte A. Schoenbron found the incidence of developmental, emotional, and behavioral problems among today's children "alarmingly high." They argued further that the survey results are likely "underestimates of the true prevalence of the conditions." And they found that family structure was far and away the most important factor producing these "alarmingly high" (and probably underestimated) results.[17]

Another study, by Deborah Dawson, based on the same extensive National Health Interview Survey, divided families into biological mother-father families, formerly married mother-no father families, and mother-stepfather families. Excluded from this comparison then was the family type probably most injurious to the young—namely, that of the never-married mother family. Even so the results were striking. The apparent advantages of the intact biological-parent family for children's welfare stand out boldly. For example, the percentage of children between the ages of three and seventeen who were treated for emotional or behavioral problems over a twelve-month period was 2.7 percent in families with both biological parents, 6.6 percent for mother and stepfather families, and 8.8 percent for formerly married mother-no father families. Children in these disrupted families were also much more likely to have to repeat a grade in school, to be expelled or suspended from school, and to suffer more from accidents, injuries, and poisonings than those in the intact family units. In general, the results for stepfather families were closer to those of no-father families than to those where the biological father was still present—that is, where no divorce had taken place.[18]

A later (1993) study suggests further that the effects, and particularly the psychological effects, of divorce on children are quite long lasting. Children were followed up from ages seven to eleven to ages twelve to sixteen, and then again to ages eighteen to twenty-two. Among the last group, those from disrupted families had poor relationships with their fathers in two-thirds of the cases and with their mothers in almost a third of the cases. Many of these children of divorce had exhibited, and were currently exhibiting, serious behavioral problems, and 40 percent had required some psychological help.[19]

Can we then, as a society and at long last, agree unequivocally that divorce, separation, single-parent families, illegitimacy, and other aspects of family breakdown—whatever their other merits or demerits—are clearly and distinctly harmful to our children and do, in fact, place the future of our nation at risk? My own personal belief is that the evidence is now overwhelming on this score. Indeed, this would seem, at first glance, to be the opinion of McLanahan and Sandefur in the study referred to above. They "reject the claim that children raised by only one parent do just as well as children raised by both parents." They add, in italics, the results of their ten years of study:

> *Children who grow up in a household with only one biological parent are worse off, on average, than children who grow up in a household with both of their biological parents, regardless of the parents' race or educational background, regardless of whether the parents are married when the child is born, and regardless of whether the resident parent remarries.*[20]

They then go on to refer to the kinds of material we have displayed in figure 2.2. Interestingly, in both this statement and in the graphs shown in figure 2.2, single-parent families and stepfamilies are treated as having rather similar (and negative) effects on children. The stepfather, it turns out, is, at least for most children, a very poor substitute for the biological father, as many other studies have pointed out.[21]

The McLanahan and Sandefur statement—on the very first page of the book and in italics—seems as direct and unguarded as one would wish. It expresses my own conclusions on this matter exactly. And yet almost immediately, and really quite curiously, the authors back away from their own declaration. For on page 2, they go on to ask, "Are single motherhood and father absence therefore the root cause of child poverty, school failure, and juvenile delinquency?" And proceed to answer: "Our findings lead us to say no."

How's that again? What is going on here? The puzzle only deepens when they explain themselves further. Thus, with respect to the problem of high school failure, they note that "during the 1980s, the dropout rate was about 19 percent overall and about 13 percent for children who lived with both their parents. So even if there were no family disruption, the high school dropout rate would still be at least 13 percent. Clearly, most school failure is being caused by something other than single motherhood."

Now quite apart from the question as to whether at least a certain fraction of that 13 percent dropout rate for two-parent children was more or less inevitable and perhaps even desirable, the comparison of 13 percent and an overall 19 percent (which includes that 13 percent) misses the whole point. Their own data show that the dropout rate for single- (and step-) parent children was 29 percent, or well over twice the rate for intact family children. The problem becomes massively more serious because of family breakdown.

If this family breakdown were limited to a relatively small group in the society then the "overall" rates of school dropout, unemployment, poverty, teenage pregnancy, illegitimacy, juvenile crime and violence might be our central concern. But this isn't the case. A third of our children are now born to unmarried mothers. Divorce will break up half or more of our families. The majority of American children born today will spend some or all of their childhood years apart from one of their biological parents, most commonly their fathers. This is why attention is needed to the *big* numbers—29 percent versus 13 percent high school dropouts, 70 percent of reform-school and prison inmates, 53 percent of families in poverty, twice the risk of psychological problems, childhood poisonings, illegitimate teenage births. These surely are the numbers, and problems, to have firmly in mind, and not the fact that the other parts of American society are, after all, not quite perfect.

The "pathology" that Daniel Patrick Moynihan noted in the Black family thirty years ago—and for which analysis he took a terrible beating—is now permeating the majority population in American society. When this harsh fact is not faced squarely, it is little wonder that Moynihan's more recent piece, "Defining Deviancy Down," is precisely concerned to show how, when things really deteriorate, we lower our standards so that nothing seems that bad at all.[22] Unfortunately, lowered standards, even when lowered out of good will, do not change realities!

WORKING PARENTS AND CHILD CARE

The tendency to qualify, or even gloss over, the increasingly massive evidence of the harm family breakdown is doing to our children is not only widespread but is actually itself part of the underlying problem causing family breakdown. We shall consider this matter further in part

3, and particularly in our final chapter. However, even in our present discussion we cannot avoid the issue completely, particularly as we come to a further aspect of family breakdown: the care and nurturing of young children and particularly infants. Here, of course, we are dealing not with a structural breakdown of the family unit but rather with the way in which parent-child relationships are handled *within* families, regardless of their structures.

Actually, this problem applies quite as directly to two-biological-parent, intact families as it does to step- or single-parent families. What are the consequences for the nation's future of the fact that the mothers of children, whether single, divorced, married or remarried, are now overwhelmingly engaged in the labor force? Especially, one might ask, what are the consequences, both short-run and long-run, of the facts that nearly two-thirds of mothers of children under six are employed, and that primary care for these young children is increasingly provided by nonrelatives, and outside the child's home?

The most honest answer one can give at this point in the life of our nation is that no one really knows. By the time, twenty or thirty years into the future, when we truly understand what kind of generations we are raising by our current methods, it will, of course, be too late to change; the die will have been cast. Still, something can be said on the subject—three main things in fact.

1. *There is a very curious tendency in the face of our basic lack of knowledge in this area to believe that better day care, as opposed to more parental care, is the appropriate solution to the problem.*

Although so-called conservatives are often considered advocates of family values and parental child care, this is not really a "liberal" versus "conservative" issue. One of the major planks of conservative policy-makers at the moment is to promote workfare as opposed to welfare for single mothers. This "solution" to the welfare problem would, of course, greatly aggravate the present tendency toward less and less parental care for children. Indeed, everyone who proposes the workfare approach clearly recognizes that it could function only if much more adequate day care were to be provided these single, now-to-be-employed mothers.

On quite different grounds—thinking perhaps of the desirability of liberating women from house and home in order *to* work, that is, to have interesting jobs, careers, and professions—liberal commentators end up with essentially the same conclusion. What we really need, they say, is not more parental care but much better, or to use the common term, "higher quality," day care.

Now the interesting thing about this, if you will, "shared" conclusion is that there is very little evidence to suggest that such care will provide an excellent, satisfactory, or even adequate arrangement for the children involved, particularly for children under five, and even more especially for infants and toddlers. Extremely telling in this regard was the extensive 1990 report on child care in the United States from the prestigious National Research Council (NRC).[23] This report urged a series of legislative and other actions, all of which effectively promote maternal employment and the subsidization and increased availability and accessibility of day care for preschool children from birth on up. If the recommendations of this report had been enacted, the bizarre result would be that a two-parent family where one parent stayed home to take care of a baby would not only be forgoing a second income, but would be paying taxes some of which would go to subsidize another two-parent family where both parents were working, and which consequently was enjoying two incomes plus publicly supported day care. All the economic incentives, in other words, would go to promoting day care as opposed to parental care.

Why? Was it because new research had established that such out-of-home care is equivalent to parental care and that our children will probably benefit, and certainly not suffer, under these alternative arrangements? Hardly. The main assertion in the report about nonparental versus parental care for young children is that we do not yet have enough information to make a judgment. With regard to social competence, the evidence is "extremely limited." With regard to worrisome findings about bonding and the attachment relationship, studies haven't followed up day-care children sufficiently "to assess directly the stability of the pattern or its developmental implications." In general, there is "insufficient evidence to predict the magnitude of the effects of alternative policy and program proposals on children's development." And yet the NRC did come up with definite "policy and program proposals," apparently without the least hesitation.

2. *There are at least some general reasons for believing that day care, particularly full-time day care for infants and one- and two-year olds, may be an inadequate substitute for parental care.*

Not everyone would accept this contention, although probably most observers would agree that, on average, parental care is likely to be superior to poor quality day care. The reasons we are referring to here, however, are more or less independent of the quality of the day care and reflect basic structural deficits in any kind of outside-the-home, nonrelative day care arrangement. For example, there is the fact that the day care provider cannot, any more than a public school second- or third-grade teacher, maintain a truly lasting relationship with the children in question. If any kind of bonding does take place, it will involve bonds that, of necessity, are quickly and usually permanently broken. A short-term relationship with a child, or characteristically several children, often involving a number of care-givers, is intrinsically, and no matter what the quality of the providers, a different matter from the lifelong one-on-one relationship of mother and child.

In effect, the NRC report concedes this in a paragraph that is far more revealing than convincing. As a defense of day care, they offer the following: "Children can benefit from 'multiple mothering' *if* [emphasis in the original] it provides affection, warmth, responsiveness, and stimulation in the context of enduring relationships with a reasonably small number of caretakers . . . who have come to know the child's individual needs and style." The giveaway word here is "enduring." One doesn't have an "enduring relationship" with a day care worker. That is what one has, or should have, with a parent. What is being said here effectively is that if day care closely mimics parental care it can be quite sucessful. But it doesn't. It can't.

There is, by now, a fairly substantial general literature suggesting that the forming of deep attachments of infants with a single care-giver—in most cases, historically, the mother—is of great significance to a child's ultimate personal and psychological development. Names associated in one way or another with these attachment studies include John Bowlby, Rene Spitz, Mary D. Salter Ainsworth, Selma Fraiberg, Marshall Klaus and Phyllis Klaus, John H. Kennell, and T. Berry Brazelton.[24] The degree of this early attachment relationship is sometimes measured by what is called the "Strange Situation Procedure" (or the

"Ainsworth Strange Situation Procedure," after its originator, Mary Ainsworth). The test involves watching the child's reactions as he or she is subjected to a variety of stresses, including the mother's departure, the presence of strangers, reunion with the mother, and the like. The question is whether day care children show excessive insecurity as indicated by this and other tests and observations.

As it turns out, this is a very complicated matter. Consider, for example, the work of Professor Jay Belsky of Pennsylvania State University. In studies beginning in 1985, Professor Belsky found that infants under such care did show signs of insecurity, particularly those exposed to such care for more than twenty hours a week. Since he had long believed that "a primary social task for the infant is to establish a close emotional relationship with another human being," he worried that replacing parental care, even by quality day care, during the first year of a child's life might be harmful to later development.[25]

Subsequently, he and his colleagues began to wonder about the advisability of extensive day care even during the second and third years of the child's life. He and collaborator David Eggebeen published an article in a 1991 issue of the *Journal of Marriage and the Family* dealing with the effects of maternal employment during the first three years of children's lives.[26] They concluded that children who spent these years in day care tended to be more "noncompliant"—i.e., they don't turn off the TV when told, protest going to bed, won't eat meals at the proper time, and so on. Since noncompliance can be a "harbinger of more serious problems to come" (drinking, delinquency, and the like), there was, they felt, some cause for concern about extensive day care during the first three years of life.

Belsky and his colleagues' work produced a flood of protests and rebuttals—a phenomenon I will touch on later in this book—and was followed by a number of further studies, including a major effort from the National Institute of Child Health and Human Development (NICHD) Early Child Care Research Network, in which Belsky (among many other researchers) was a participant. The announcement of the results of this study in April 1996 produced a flurry of newspaper articles, all suggesting in one way or another that day care for infants, even extensive day care, had little effect on "mom–child relations" or on the child's basic sense of security. In the words of the report itself: "The results of this study clearly indicate that nonmaternal child care by itself does not constitute a threat to the security of the infant-mother attachment relationship."[27]

Does this mean that, contrary to Belsky's (and others') earlier findings, and despite its obvious general disadvantage (lack of permanent attachments) as compared to parental care, day care, even extensive day care, poses no real problems for our youngest children? Such a conclusion, certainly at this point in time, is clearly unwarranted. Indeed, the more one studies the matter, the more complex it becomes. Here are a few of the problems:

1. Belsky's studies were concerned not only with effects in the first year or so of the children's lives but also with later effects during the preschool and early elementary school years. Since the NICHD results pertain solely to the first fifteen months of the children's lives, only continuing study will be able to sort out these later effects.

2. Although the NICHD study found that day care did not in and of itself directly affect the infant-mother attachment relationship, it also found that this relationship *was* affected adversely by day care (its quality, extent, and variability) in the case of children who were receiving poorer quality maternal care. In other words, the more vulnerable the children were to begin with, the greater the likelihood that they would be placed at additional risk. In the words of the report, "There was consistent evidence that poor quality, unstable, or more than minimal amounts of child care added to the risks already inherent in maternal insensitivity. In other words, the combined effects of these child care variables and maternal insensitivity were worse than those of maternal insensitivity alone."[28]

3. Also, there was some evidence in the NICHD study that, while girls seemed to profit from day care, boys were adversely affected by more than thirty hours a week of such care.

4. The NICHD considered only the attachment relationship and did not deal with other aspects of child development at fifteen months, for example, cognitive, language, and health development. Clearly, any judgments, pro or con, on day care will ultimately have to take these other factors into account.

As one of the researchers connected with the NICHD study, Belsky finds no fault with the procedures employed, although he does caution against drawing any unqualified conclusions from their results. Considering, for example, the four problems noted above, he points out that any real conclusions concerning the effects of early day care obviously must wait upon the promised follow-up studies into later childhood. Also, he stresses that the findings that day care intensifies the effects of other factors (as, for example, those due to insensitive maternal care) might possibly mean that the adverse effects of day care manifest themselves *first* in the case of the most vulnerable children, and only later will show up in the case of less vulnerable children as they continue with extensive, and/or poor quality, day care. He writes: "Such a scenario, should it turn out to be true, will very much resemble how animals respond to drought or other challenging ecological conditions, with the weakest succumbing first and the stronger taking longer to succumb but succumbing nevertheless (should adverse conditions continue and accumulate)."[29]

He also notes that his own earlier analysis was focused on "risk-factors" and that risk-factors characteristically exert their influence principally in *combination* with other sources of risk, in this case insensitive maternal care, and, possibly even more significantly, with boy children as opposed to girls.

What this means, as Belsky would agree, is that all our studies so far, including his own, are too incomplete to give any definitive answers about the long-run effects of day care on small (and, indeed, older) children. What it does not mean is that we should overlook the obvious general disadvantage of day care in terms of permanent, lifelong emotional relationships, nor, for that matter, the direct personal judgments of many highly experienced day care professionals. Take, for example, Dr. Burton L. White, former head of the Harvard Preschool Project, and an expert on the first three years of life. In the revised edition of his widely admired book, he has made it clear that he endorses "the view of the family as the first and most fundamental educational delivery system." He takes this stand: "Simply stated, I firmly believe that most children get a better start in life when, during the majority of their waking hours of their first three years, they are cared for by their parents or other nuclear family members, not by any form of substitute care."[30]

Other experts also express concern, for example about the aggressiveness of some day care children. Fredelle Maynard, author of *The Child Care Crisis*, notes that "a recent report found day care children performed *fifteen* [emphasis in the original] times as many aggressive acts as home-reared agemates."[31] Marion Blum, educational director of the Wellesley College Child Study Center, agrees: "It is another irony about day care that ignoring the issue of aggression in day care may eventually impact on future aggregate costs to society."[32]

This is not to imply that there is anything like general agreement on these issues. Day care, like parental care, for the very young has its strong advocates. At least, quality day care does. But what *is* the quality of the extra-family care currently being given our youngest generation? And this leads to our third point:

3. *There is almost universal agreement that actually existing out-of-home, nonparental day care in the United States at this point in time is of extremely poor quality.*

If quality day care may involve certain intrinsic structural problems, what are we to say about the extremely questionable arrangements in which we are actually placing our youngest children these days? On all sides, there is vast dissatisfaction with these arrangements. In most day care centers, the pay is low, the turnover rates of child care workers are extremely high, the staff-to-child ratios are totally unsatisfactory, and conditions are often unhealthy and unsanitary. Labor department estimates are that child care workers in the early 1990s were earning less than waitresses, kitchen workers, and hairdressers. Care by nearby relatives, neighbors, and various other unlicensed caregivers is so variable that it is hard to generalize about it, except perhaps to say that such settings are often far from hygienic and are frequently transitory. Nearby female relatives, for example, may themselves decide to enter the labor force and thus cease to be available while the mother is at work.

At the present time, the fastest growing arrangement for child care for working mothers in the United States is in the form of organized child care facilities. In 1993 they accounted for 30 percent of all such preschooler care. In the case of these child care centers, we are fortunate to have a comprehensive four-hundred page, 1995 study, *Cost, Quality and Child Outcomes in Child Care Centers*.[33] The findings of this report about the quality of current U.S. child care centers are especially telling since the authors of the report clearly support increased private and governmental subsidization of such centers. Indeed, their major recommendation, set in bold-faced capitals is:

THE NATION MUST COMMIT TO IMPROVING THE QUALITY OF CHILD CARE SERVICES AND TO ENSURING THAT ALL CHILDREN AND THEIR FAMILIES HAVE ACCESS TO GOOD PROGRAMS. THAT IS, GOOD-QUALITY CHILD CARE MUST BECOME A MERIT GOOD IN THE UNITED STATES.

A "merit good" is, for economists, a good that may deserve extensive public subsidy when private funding is inadequate.

This, then, is the general point of view of the report, and places in context their findings about the quality of *actual* child care centers in today's America. I quote at some length:

> *Child care at most centers in the United States is poor to mediocre, with almost half of the infants and toddlers in rooms at less than minimal quality.* The level of quality at most U.S. child care centers does not meet the children's needs for health, safety, warm relationships, and learning. . . . Only one in seven centers (14%) received a rating of developmentally appropriate . . . and one in eight (12%) were less than minimal. Child care for infants or toddlers is of particular concern. . . . In fact, of the 225 infant or toddler rooms observed, only 1 in 12 (8%) were in the developmentally appropriate range, while 2 in 5 (40%) rated in the poor range. Babies in poor-quality rooms are vulnerable to more illness because basic sanitary conditions are not met for diapering and feeding; are endangered because of safety problems that exist in the room; miss warm, supportive relationships with adults; and lose out on learning because they lack the books and toys required for physical and intellectual growth.[34]

They then add, rather ominously, that, comparing their (1995) study with an earlier (1990) study, "there is some evidence that the quality of infant/toddler care has declined in the interval between the studies."[35] This is ominous from the overall point of view of the report because it casts into considerable doubt the realism of their major recommendation. If day care quality for young children is already declining, what reason is there to hope, or expect, that the nation is suddenly going to turn completely around and start subsidizing such care on the massive scale required? Indeed, what hope, or expectation, of this sort could possibly exist at a time (the late 1990s) when the overall mood of the country is clearly to cut back on government in virtually all areas of life? From our immediate point of view, the issue is simply this: How is the transfer of much of the traditional family function of rearing and nurturing small children to outside caregivers actually affecting those children? Not what some observers feel *should* be done; what *is* being done.

And, in this respect, the answer seems all too clear. As in the cases of divorce, separation, and never-married mothers, the sharp reduction of parental care for infants, toddlers, and all preschool children, even within perfectly intact families, has almost certainly lowered the general well-being of the coming generation. Poor quality extra-family care is simply no substitute for parental care in the vast majority of cases. Again, this form of family breakdown is placing the future at risk.

AND THE REAL QUESTION IS: WHY?

We now begin to face a real dilemma. If, as I believe, the American family is rapidly breaking down, and if this breakdown is having a sharply deleterious effect on our children, why is it we are letting it happen? Is it because we no longer care about our children? Or care much less about them than we once did? Is it because we are somehow too economically poor to take care of them properly? But how can that be since, compared, say, to a century ago, our real (inflation-adjusted) incomes per capita are perhaps five times higher? Even over the past fifty years, our real incomes have more than doubled. And, as far as caring about our children is concerned, we certainly *say* that we still worry greatly about them. Indeed, the report I have just quoted is full of care and concern for children, strongly (if perhaps unrealistically) urging a major governmental crusade to promote quality child care.

But something very deep is missing here. The family is such a fundamental institution that only very profound changes in our socioeconomic condition and ideology could produce what we now see before our eyes. To understand the nature of our problems with the family, therefore, we must begin to outline the basic connections that exist between those problems and underlying developments: the "process of progress," as I call it, and its sometime companion, the "Idea of Progress." And in this long and necessarily somewhat complicated analysis, we shall discover that the focus of this chapter—a "future at risk"—is not an incidental but a central feature of our current social dilemmas. In a meaningful sense, we are in serious danger of forsaking our posterity.

3

WHY CONVENTIONAL
EXPLANATIONS ARE INCOMPLETE

I have tried to establish that the American family is breaking down, and that this breakdown has deeply harmful effects on our children and, in consequence, on the potential future of the nation. It is time now to begin asking the apparently simple question: Why are we allowing this to happen? Why, when Americans continue to say that they really do care about their children? Why, when most U.S. opinion polls in the 1990s suggest that "the family," in something like or fairly near its traditional form, is still a quite popular institution? Why, when, as already noted, this is essentially a matter of our choices? No external power or authority is forcing us to abandon traditional, or other, family values. In a word, why?

In this chapter and the next, I will try to set forth what I believe to be the essential characteristics that the answer to this question must possess. Once we have determined the form that our answer must take, we will be able to understand the relevance of what, in the Introduction, I called the central "paradox" of our analysis. I said then (with terms yet to be fully defined) that the paradox is that while the process of progress initially launches and helps sustain the Idea of Progress, in the long run it tends to undermine that Idea. All this seems a far cry from the issues of divorce, child poverty, day care, single-parent families, and the like that we have focused on so far. Thus, it will be an important task for these two chapters to show why an analysis of this paradox is not only helpful in understanding family breakdown in America, but absolutely essential to its explanation.

Also, I might add, the contemporary decline of the Idea of Progress is a major, and fascinating, phenomenon in its own right. It provides, in itself, one of the two central themes of this book.

CONVENTIONAL EXPLANATIONS: I

In clearing the decks for this general analysis, I must try to show why conventional explanations of family breakdown in America fail to account for certain major features of the problem. In some cases, this is really quite easy to do. I refer to a wide variety of explanations that find the causes of U.S. family breakdown essentially in post–World War II, or even post-1960s, events and developments. Three such explanations are widely, but much too casually, discussed at the present time. One locates family breakdown basically in the growth of the welfare state, particularly following the initiation of the Great Society and War on Poverty programs in the mid-1960s. A second attributes the problem largely to the economic difficulties facing young men in recent years, both unemployment and their declining earning power relative to that of women. A third explanation focuses on cultural factors and especially the so-called "sexual revolution" of the 1960s. Increasing sexual free-dom allowed people to have intimate relations (and babies) before, and/or without, marriage, and also justified them in abandoning marriages through divorce when marital relations, including sex relations, were deemed to be less than satisfactory.

While these explanations have something to them, they are all fa-tally flawed when it comes to locating the basic causes of declining fam-ily life in America. In some cases, they don't even fit the immediate facts very well. Thus, it has frequently been pointed out, with respect to the welfare state explanation, that the actual trend of welfare payments since the 1960s does not accurately track the increase in single motherhood. Also, nonwelfare, well-to-do mothers are increasingly becoming single parents. Particular flaws, like these, mar all three explanations.[1]

Their main flaws, however, go much deeper than this. One such central flaw reflects the fact that they take a far too *short-run* view of the problem. This is easy to understand in that changes in family structures and behavior have occurred so rapidly since the 1960s. But this appear-ance is quite deceiving. It arises in great part from the fact that the experience of the Baby Boom period (1946–1964) was, by most indicators, out of step with longer run trends. Thus, the reversal of family values following the Boom—when, for example, birthrates, which had been falling for a century and a half prior to the Boom, simply resumed their decline—can be interpreted primarily as a restoration of a much longer-run pattern which had been temporarily distorted just after World War II.

In general, most of the elements that we see as part of the overall picture of family decline today have roots that go back well before the 1960s and, indeed, long before World War II. While it is true that most married mothers did not participate in the labor force a hundred years ago, nevertheless the general trend toward greater labor force participation by single women reaches way back into the nineteenth century and was, of course, given a patriotic nudge by Rosie the Riveter during the Second World War. As far as divorce is concerned, Andrew Cherlin has tracked a rising trend in the U.S. divorce rate ever since 1860 or 1870. Actually, one of the sharpest upward departures from this trend took place in the 1920s.[2] In point of fact, the twenties themselves have usually been thought of as a period of greatly increased sexual freedom. Scandalously, women began to "bob" their hair, and the short skirts and kicking heels of the "flappers" suggest a mini-sexual revolution well in advance of the 1960s.

As far as the welfare state is concerned, we can hardly date its growth exclusively from Lyndon Johnson and the Great Society programs. Most critics of such programs trace their roots back at least as far as Franklin Roosevelt and the New Deal. In truth, what we saw in the 1960s was a continuation of a general expansion of government in the economy that had been going on at least since the turn of the century. In 1900, all governments (federal, state, and local) spent about $20 per capita, or around 8 percent of U.S. GNP. By 1927, this was already up to 12 percent of GNP, and, by 1960—before the Great Society programs were launched—to more than 25 percent.[3]

Essentially what we have with government programs, as in the cases of divorce, women in the labor force, the relative decline in men's wages, and general changes in cultural mores, are long-standing trends that themselves are reflective of the great technological, scientific and socioeconomic developments that have characterized the United States since its industrial revolution in the early nineteenth century.

THE INTERNATIONAL CONTEXT

And such trends are by no means limited to the United States alone. For a second major flaw in the explanations for family breakdown just discussed is that they are too specifically tailored to the political and socioeconomic conditions existing in this country. Indeed, one of the most important stages in understanding family breakdown in America comes with a recognition of the fact that such breakdown in one form or another is now characteristic of most of the industrialized world. It is present not just in this country, but in Scandinavia, the Low Countries, continental Europe, and the British Isles; there are even some signs of family problems beginning to emerge in Japan.

Needless to say, the political and socioeconomic conditions in all these countries vary quite widely. Take welfare systems, for example. In most cases, certainly in Europe, the industrialized nations have far more elaborate welfare arrangements than is common in the United States. This is a point that I will be referring to from time to time in later chapters, noting among other things, that these very elaborate systems are currently under considerable political and economic stress. Or consider unemployment: In the early postwar decades, European countries tended to have lower rates of unemployment than the United States. Recently, however, their unemployment rates have been running at around 11 or 12 percent, roughly twice the U.S. rate.

Consider further the very important differences in racial and ethnic compositions of European nations (and Japan) as compared to the United States. Although immigrants, including "guest workers," have become something of a problem in Europe, there is probably no industrialized country in the world that has the extraordinary mixture of racial, ethnic, and national groups we take for granted in our own society. This difference obviously has a considerable bearing on the issue of family breakdown, since, as is well known, such breakdown is much further advanced among U.S. inner-city minority populations, especially African Americans, than it is, say, among non-Hispanic White families living in our middle-class suburbs.

Given all these differences, one would not expect family decline to display exactly the same manifestations in all these different countries. Still, the striking thing is that the basic trends throughout the industrial world are so similar. Table 3.1 is interesting because it shows not only

Table 3.1 International Comparisons: Divorce Rates, Illegitimacy Ratios, Single Parents and Employed Women

	Divorce Rate[a]		Illegitimacy Ratio[b]		Single Parents[c]		Employed Women[d]	
	1960[e]	1990[f]	1960	1990	1960	1988	1970[g]	1988
United States	9	21	5	28	9	23	45	73
Canada	2	12	4	24	9	15	41	75
Denmark	6	13	8	46	17	20	NA	90
France	3	8	6	30	9	12	52	75
Germany[h]	4	8	6	11	8	14	48	62
Italy	1	2	2	6	NA	NA	44	61
Netherlands	2	8	1	11	9	15	24	55
Sweden	5	12	11	47	9	13	61	89
United Kingdom	2	12	5	28	6	13	43	66

Source: Sara McLanahan & Lynne Casper, "Growing Diversity and Inequality in the American Family," in *State of the Union: America in the 1990s*, Vol. II, ed. Reynolds Farley (New York: Russell Sage Foundation, 1995), table 1-3. Data from U.S. Bureau of the Census, Statistical Abstract of the United States, 1993; Constance Sorrentino "The Changing Family in International Perspective," *Monthly Labor Review* 113, no. 3 (1990): 41–58.

NA = Not Available.
[a]Divorce rate per 1,000 married women.
[b]Percentage of all births to unmarried women.
[c]Percentage of all family households that are single-parent. 1971 and 1986 for Canada. 1976 and 1988 for Denmark. 1968 and 1988 for France. 1972 and 1988 for Germany. 1961 and 1985 for Netherlands. 1960 and 1985 for Sweden. 1961 and 1987 for the United Kingdom. Age restrictions for children differ by country.
[d]Percentage of women aged 25–34 (25–39 in Italy) in the labor force.
[e]1970 for Italy.
[f]1989 for France; 1988 for United Kingdom.
[g]1977 for Italy.
[h]For former West Germany.

that, as we would expect, many differences do exist among industrialized countries, but also that there is a fundamental commonality of the direction of change in every case. Look at divorce, for example. The United States in 1990, with a rate of twenty-one divorces per one thousand married women, was clearly the world champion in this department. Note, however, that the divorce rate between 1960 and 1990 was increasing in the case of every single country on the list. And also note that the *rate of increase* in a number of these countries (Canada, the Netherlands, and the United Kingdom) was actually more rapid than that of the United States over these three decades.

In the case of Illegitimacy Ratios (percentage of all births to unmarried women), the United States, though high at 28 percent, was well behind Sweden at 47 percent. In this case, however, it is the United States that has the more rapid rate of increase over the 1960–1990 period. To complicate matters further, we find that although Sweden, and also Denmark, have higher Illegitimacy Ratios than the United States, they both have a smaller percentage of single-parent families. The reason for this is that whereas in the United States about 25 percent of nonmarital births in the 1970s and 1980s were to cohabiting couples, in Sweden and Denmark nearly all nonmarital births were to cohabiting couples.[4]

To add one more complication to the picture, it should be noted that not all children in these cohabiting families were being brought up by their biological mothers and fathers. Just as divorce in all industrialized countries means that many two-parent families are now step-families, so cohabiting couples, including biological parents at the outset, can also break up over time. In the late 1980s, for example, sociologist David Popenoe estimated that, in Sweden, cohabiting couples—so-called "consensual unions"—tended to break up at three times the rate of formally married couples.[5]

In short, what we have in the industrialized world are these universal tendencies toward family breakdown, each showing certain particular national features, but each manifesting the same underlying trends. What this means, first, is that it is very unlikely that the ultimate explanation for American family decline will be found in the special peculiarities of the U.S. welfare system, our unemployment rates, our national version of the sexual revolution of the 1960s, or even our particularly worrisome inner-city minority problems. Second, it strongly suggests that, in order to find that deeper explanation of the American situation, one will have to deal with the very most general features of scientific, technological, and socioeconomic change that apply in all these different contexts. In this book, I call this vast process of change that has seized the developed and industrializing world during recent centuries, the "process of progress." And what I am suggesting about family breakdown is that, occurring in such a variety of modern situations, it must ultimately be explained by certain general features of this same "process of progress."

To develop this theme further, we must now say a few words defining this phrase more precisely.

THE PROCESS OF PROGRESS: A PANORAMIC VIEW

The *process of progress*, as I shall use the term, refers to an objective, empirical, historical phenomenon and (unlike the capitalized *Idea of Progress*, which I define later) involves no particular moral or value judgments. Furthermore, we shall be limiting the term to changes that began to occur, largely in the Western world, during the past three or four centuries. It was during this period, following the Scientific, Commercial, and then Industrial Revolutions, that scientific, technological, and socioeconomic changes began to accelerate mightily and in such a way as to alter basic attitudes and motivations over the whole of society.

Indeed, a major characteristic of the process of progress, in our usage, is precisely the rapidity and scale of the changes that it has entailed, particularly since the British Industrial Revolution of the late eighteenth and early nineteenth centuries. Perhaps the single most striking example of these changes is the growth of total production, and especially total product per capita. The rapidity of this growth was quite simply unprecedented by any previous historical standard. For example, estimates of the annual growth of Gross Domestic Product (GDP) per capita in the United States since the early nineteenth century range from 1.5 to 1.8 percent, or around a fivefold increase per century.[6] In constant, inflation-adjusted, dollar terms, this suggests an increase in per capita output from, say, $4,000 (1987 dollars) in 1890 to around $20,000 in 1990. As Nobel economist Simon Kuznets used to say, if you wish to realize how extraordinarily rapid this rate of increase is, just project it backward, or forward, in time a century or two and see where you end up.

Along with this extraordinary increase in incomes, and in part a response to it, came an equally extraordinary increase in life expectancies. In the United States, by no means an unusual case, average life expectancies at birth have more than doubled since the late eighteenth century—from an estimated thirty-five years or so in 1789 to over seventy-five years in 1990. Actually, more years have been added to life expectancies in the developed countries of the world in the past century alone than in the entire previous history of the human race. Interestingly—and a fact that will be of some importance to us in our study of family breakdown—whereas earlier advances were largely in infant and child mortality, more recent decades have seen major extensions of life expectancies at older ages. Eighty-, ninety-, and one hundred–year-olds are now our most rapidly growing age categories. Where, one wonders, will children fit in in this increasingly aging society?

The rapidity of all these changes has completely altered the scale of the modern world. Consider population growth. Today, we tend to associate the population explosion with Third World nations (who have borrowed their medical and public health technologies from the West), but actually we need look no farther afield than the United States. With immigration, but mainly through natural increase, our population grew from just under 4 million in 1790 to around 250 million in 1990—over sixtyfold!

Scale, in turn, has been a factor revolutionizing the way our economy, and indeed our society in general, is put together. In one of the most famous sentences in *The Wealth of Nations*, Adam Smith wrote, "The greatest improvement in the productive powers of labour, and the greater part of the skill, dexterity, and judgment with which it is any where directed, or applied, seem to have been the effects of the division of labour."[7] Specialization, professionalization, interdependence of functions—all this has grown strikingly over the past two hundred years. A result, according to Smith, of the increased scale of the economy, or, in his own words, the "extent of the market."

Size has also meant important transformations in the nature and direction of work. In his classic study of the English Industrial Revolution, Paul Mantoux subtitled his book: *An Outline of the Beginnings of the Factory System in England.*[8] The growth of factories and large-scale enterprises in general was, in turn, associated with increasing urbanization, and the vast movement out of agriculture into manufacturing industry, and, in our own period, into the service industries. In the United States, three-quarters of our population now lives in urban areas as compared to less than 7 percent in 1800. At the beginning of the nineteenth century, the characteristic American worker was a farmer; now farmers comprise less than 3 percent of our labor force.

Dramatic changes continue. One of the most important is the increasing emphasis of today's society on knowledge and education. As social analyst Peter Drucker has recently put it: "The social center of gravity has shifted to the knowledge worker. All developed countries are becoming post-business knowledge societies. Access to good jobs and career opportunities increasingly require a university diploma."[9] In fact, and despite well-publicized flaws in our educational system, the past fifty years have seen an enormous increase in the percentage of Americans aged twenty-five years or older who have completed four or more years of high school (from 25 to over 75 percent), and four or more years of college (from under 5 to around 20 percent).[10]

I mention all these numbers concerning output per capita, population growth, education, and the like to bring home the point that whatever "progress" may have been in earlier times, the brute transformations of life during the past one or two hundred years in countries like the United States really dwarf all past human experience. The process of progress, as we are defining it, has produced such large quantitative changes in crucial aspects of economic and social life as to alter their essential quality.

FOUR IMPORTANT CHARACTERISTICS OF THE PROCESS

With so much going on in so many different compartments of life over the past century or two, it is, to say the least, difficult to single out particular characteristics of the process of progress as the essential, or pivotal, features we must attend to. The risk is that one will single out only those features that fit one's particular theoretical structure.

While keeping this caution in mind, I nevertheless believe that some areas of agreement are possible. The following four features of the process of progress have been widely noted. They seem not only to have been quite characteristic of our empirical experience with the process since the Industrial Revolution, but, if anything, to have exhibited a tendency to increase in intensity over time.

1. *The rapidity of modern change*

We have essentially discussed this characteristic of the process of progress above when we were noting the really huge changes (incomes, life expectancies, places of residence, occupations, etc.) that have been compressed into the last two or three centuries. Premodern societies were by no means stable and unchanging, and the adjective "traditional," sometimes applied to them, is in many ways a misnomer (see pages 110–12). Still, the persistent tidal waves of socioeconomic change characteristic of the process of progress really have no historical equivalents.

Whether the commonly used current phrase—"change is accelerating these days"—is appropriate is a more complicated question. One can find certain criteria—say, the number of scientific papers published per year, or the memory capacity of computers, or the speed of land, air, or space travel—where change really does appear to have accelerated measurably in the twentieth as compared to the eighteenth or nineteenth centuries. On the other hand, it is very doubtful (though not impossible) that per capita real incomes will increase during the next century at rates measurably faster than the fivefold increase of the present century, or that life expectancies at birth will more than double (say, to 150 or more years) during the next two hundred years. In its literal meaning, therefore, the phrase "change is accelerating these days" is hard to credit either way. The frequent use of this phrase is, however, very telling. For what it really seems to mean operationally is that the future is rushing toward us, that is, that the future about which we can make any kind of confident predictions is ever closer at hand. In a word, our effective time horizons are becoming shorter and shorter. And this, as it turns out, is a point that will prove to be of great significance for our overall analysis.

2. *An increasing power to affect the environment*

This is meant to be a value-free characteristic, since no claim is made that this effect is either generally "good" or generally "bad." Nor is it claimed that the process of progress in any way confers on humanity total control over the forces of nature. The sun may still cool one day, or an errant comet collide with and destroy all life on earth, and all this in ways quite impervious to even the most heroic efforts and intentions of the human species. Still, the ability to use the laws of nature to modify, amend, control, and even master the forces of nature has always been considered, and is, in fact, intrinsic to the process of progress in our meaning of the term. If this ability is not today increasing more rapidly than a hundred or two hundred years ago (again, the "acceleration" question), nevertheless the effects of its exercise tend at least to be cumulative. By this, I mean that the process of progress has involved an increasing transfer of powers from nature to humankind over time. We are more insulated now from natural disasters of various sorts than we were fifty, one hundred, three hundred years ago, and, by the same token, more vulnerable to the effects of human decisions.

3. *An increasing range of choices facing humanity, both individually and collectively*

In a certain sense, as just indicated, this third point is a corollary of the second. Insofar as we have greater control over nature, and are less passively recipients of the cards nature deals us (flood, drought, plague, infant mortality, etc.), we have numerous choices and options available to us that would have been precluded in a more restricted time. Years ago, trying to define what progress meant, historian Charles Beard spoke of a general evolution from "necessity to freedom."[11] A major specific "necessity" is, of course, food to live on—likewise clothing, shelter, and protection from the elements. Freed from these natural constraints to a greater or lesser degree by the process of progress, humanity can choose its path through life from a whole host of new alternatives and is in that sense increasingly "free." One has to be a bit careful, however, in using the concept of "freedom" too cavalierly in this context. For, in theory—and, as we have witnessed in many actual instances—human beings are quite capable of using their new powers to restrict, regulate, enslave, and even exterminate their fellow humans. Freedom under the Nazis or in Russia under Stalin was a very scarce commodity indeed. The very scientific and technological tools that give humans increasing control over nature can be, and obviously have been, used to exert much more effective control over other human beings.

Still, as an empirical, historical matter, the process of progress has, in fact, overwhelmingly tended to increase human choice and decision making over time. The major attempts to curb and control individual decision making in our time by political domination—by the aforementioned Nazis and Soviet Communists—have been notable failures. They were no more a central and determining element of the process of progress than, say, the Luddites were in relation to the process of technological advance. Thus, if not certifiably in principle, nevertheless in preponderant practice, freedom has been winning out in the course of the process of progress. And nowhere more obviously, one might add, than in today's United States with our almost infinite variety of different, increasingly acceptable, or at least tolerable, lifestyles and cultural affinities.

4. *Increasing scale, specialization, and interdependence*

Finally, one makes the fairly obvious point, already noted above, that the whole scale of life has become increasingly vast, and the particularized roles of individuals within that scale have become increasingly specialized and detailed. One consequence of the combination of increased scale and specialization is interdependence. Although, in the course of the process of progress, one experiences a vastly increased range of choices and options and thus is, in that sense, more "free" over time, still one's situation becomes increasingly dependent on the choices and decisions of others, and thus one's sense of "control" over one's destiny may actually diminish even with this greater freedom. Under any circumstances, specialization dominates developments in many ways. Jobs, institutions, whole regions of a nation may become increasingly specialized over time. As the "extent of the market" becomes literally the entire world, Adam Smith's "division of labour" can proceed to a degree that might have surprised even that canny Scot. In the knowledge industry—that increasingly important "factor of production" of our information age—specialization by experts has become so intense that communication even between fairly adjacent fields has become difficult and rare. The bonus is the production of new knowledge at an extraordinary rate, and thus the foundation for still further increases in the possibilities of choice, scale, specialization and change.

These then are certain of the historical (and current) characteristics of the process of progress that might command fairly general, if not universal, agreement. In the nineteenth century, long before Beard had characterized the process as a move from "necessity to freedom," the British philosopher and sociologist, Herbert Spencer, spoke of evolution as involving a movement from the simple to the complex, from the homogeneous to the heterogeneous.[12] Indeed, one way we might summarize this brief discussion is to say that while the process of progress has on the whole made life in the United States freer, and certainly more comfortable than in times past, it has also made it more complicated.

Complexity, like the psychological sense of accelerating change, is the daily companion of late-twentieth-century America.

CONVENTIONAL EXPLANATIONS: II

With this sketch of the process of progress in mind, it is quite easy to see how this process can be related to family breakdown in America, certainly of the colonial family, but of the "traditional" family as well. Indeed, we now turn to a set of conventional explanations of family breakdown that are far more convincing than those we mentioned (and discarded) earlier. They are more convincing because they do take the required long-term view of the problem. Also, they specifically relate family decline to various characteristics of the process of progress: the variability of all institutions in a rapidly changing world, the increasing specialization of those institutions, the emergence of an abundance of choices and options outside the family circle, the rising opportunity costs within that circle, and the growing independence of men and especially women as rising living standards permit increased freedom from "necessity."

Since the basic elements of this conventional analysis are well known and since I have no quarrel with its fundamental contention—namely, that it is the process of progress that ultimately undermines the institution of the family—I can summarize this literature quite briefly. What I will then insist on is not that this analysis is wrong but that it is seriously incomplete. It fails to explain, not just details, but major features of American family life as it developed in the late nineteenth and early twentieth centuries.

But first the summary:

PRODUCTION MOVES OUT OF THE HOME

One of the first major effects of the increasing specialization of functions characteristic of the process of progress is to remove many of the traditional productive functions of the domestic economy into the external market economy. In the colonial family, as we know, production was largely carried out in or near the home. This was true of the husband who was both farmer and craftsman, the wife who was not only the homemaker but also a manufacturer of clothing and other assorted goods, and even the children who, either at home or apprenticed to nearby homes and shops, became "little workers" from a very early age.

What happened then, with the Industrial Revolution, was "the sharpest ecological and physical cleavages ever experienced between workplace and domicile."[13] The husband and father now increasingly carried out his productive labors outside the home in a factory, shop, or office, often in an urban setting, making goods for a regional, national, and ultimately international market.

The wife and mother also saw many of her productive functions effectively taken over or at least substantially reduced by the market-place.[14] The clothing, linens, canned foods, and other goods she had produced in the home increasingly were purchased in the market. As time went on, moreover, many former household chores—cooking, housecleaning, and doing laundry—were substantially alleviated by appliances and other goods also purchased from the external marketplace.

Taking a long bird's eye view of the matter, one can even argue that, like the husband's, the wife's productive work also was largely transferred to more specialized markets outside the home. Like him, too, though later in time, she moved her major, lifetime labors to that same external market place. We have already noted the clear upward trend in the labor force participation of single women during the late nineteenth and early twentieth centuries. In more recent decades, as we know, single women were joined in great numbers by married women, and, by 1990, the majority of mothers of children under age six were in the labor force and around two-thirds of them were working full time.

Even the children were affected by the increasing specialization of the times. As the father's work departed the home and the mother's work in the home effectively diminished, children largely ceased to be "little workers," or, rather their work was transferred to the task of education, which the more complicated and specialized industrial society now required. In short, the explicitly productive functions of the household, by all members, were being reduced by the process of progress, depriving the family of what had once been a key role in society.

SPECIALIZATION OF OTHER FUNCTIONS

Other functions were soon to follow. The colonial family, we noted, had once been a school, hospital, old people's home, even occasionally prison. Increasingly, these functions were carried out by specialized institutions, often sponsored by the state. These institutions were not necessarily, and perhaps not even typically, in opposition to the interests of the family. Public education in the nineteenth century represented in many important ways an extension of family interests into the public sphere. (See pages 95–98). Still, the fact was that functions once performed largely, even solely, by the family, were in more and more matters taken over by extra-family institutions.

The relation of all this to specialization and the process of progress in general is quite close. Take, for example, the schooling function of traditional families. Where the son or daughter might expect to follow roughly the same occupational path as father or mother, schooling within the family, both general and vocational, may prove reasonably adequate. As we move into a progressing society, with the vast range of new and different career opportunities constantly opening up, home-training becomes in most cases patently insufficient. As Gary Becker has put it,

> In modern societies markets facilitate trade and production, and dynamic economic environments rapidly change technologies, income, and opportunities. The knowledge accumulated by older members is much less useful to younger members than in traditional societies because the young face a different economic milieu. Small family schools that prepare members for a traditional activity are not as efficient as large schools with students from many families that teach general knowledge adaptable to new environments.[15]

The same is true of other functions. Becker notes, for instance, that one of the key functions of the traditional family was to provide insurance for individual members against the numerous hazards and uncertainties of life. However, family insurance through gifts and loans to members in distress are less necessary in modern societies. Individuals can self-insure by borrowing in the capital market during bad times or saving during good times. Moreover, market insurance based on the experience of thousands of families provides more effective protection against fire, death, old age, ill health, and other hazards than any single family can. To which one adds further that still broader-based insurance can be, and increasingly is, provided by society collectively through the State. The vast increases in state-sponsored social and health insurance in all modern industrial societies, and the growth of the "welfare state" in general, reflect again the increasing scale and specialization character-istic of the process of progress.

INCREASED OPTIONS THROUGH PROGRESS

Through specialization, then, many of what would now be re-garded as ancillary functions of the family were displaced over the course of the nineteenth and early twentieth centuries, and the family was ren-dered, in Parsonian terminology, a "more specialized agency than be-fore" with only two remaining functions: "the primary socialization of children" and the "stabilization of the adult personalities of the popula-tion."[16]

Indeed, by the mid-twentieth century, some social theorists were extending the principle of specialization to include even these core func-tions of the family. Writing in 1958, for example, Harvard professor Barrington Moore, Jr. suggested the possibility of eliminating the role of motherhood almost entirely: "The trend towards a continually more efficient technology and greater specialization, may conceivably supply an answer. . . . Specialized agencies . . . might assume a much larger share of the burden of child rearing." And why not? This burden has been "greatly lightened by machinery for feeding and the removal of waste products," and, anyway, "a nurse can perform these tasks of af-fection and socialization just as well as parents, often better." Overall, noting that one after another of society's traditional institutions have fallen before the forces of progress, Moore argued that "the burden of proof falls on those who maintain that the family is a social institution whose fate will differ in its essentials from that which has befallen all the others."[17]

It was not just specialization and efficiency that undermined core family functions, however. There was also the growing economic abun-dance, the greater freedom, the increasing range of choices and options that the process of progress was making available. Mind you, growing abundance could, in theory, actually strengthen certain core functions, notably the time and attention given to children within the family circle. In principle, it could even prompt a desire for a greater number of chil-dren. This actually seemed to be happening after the Second World War during the Baby Boom period. Thus, W. W. Rostow, in his best-selling book, *The Stages of Economic Growth*, noted that Americans were behaving "as if they preferred the extra baby to the extra unit of consumption." He wondered, indeed, if other countries, when they had achieved levels of mass consumption comparable to that in the United States, might "follow the Americans and reimpose the strenuous life by raising the birth rate?"[18]

This conjecture, as it turned out, was quite wide of the mark. Still, it does bring home the point that an increased range of options would not necessarily mandate a diminished role for the family. With all the hours released from household drudgery—washing, ironing, cleaning, baking, sewing, mending, not to mention planting, milking, egg-collecting, and wood-chopping—one might have thought that parents would have a much greater opportunity for, and interest in, dedicating themselves to the always fascinating process of watching their children grow and develop over time. In other words, *one* of the added options made available by the process of progress could be to devote oneself more wholeheartedly than ever to one's children.

Against this line of argument, however, is an important psychological consideration: namely, that contrary to the thesis once advanced by John Kenneth Galbraith—that "scarcity" is essentially irrelevant in the "affluent society"—the process of progress may actually increase our inner sense of scarcity.[19] It is true, of course, that the process of progress generally makes people feel that they have many more options than in the past. Contrasted, say, with people living a century or two before, the move from "necessity" to "freedom" seems obvious and undeniable.

At the same time, however, the presence of additional options means that we have to select from a wider range of possibilities, thus forcing us to rule out more possibilities than in earlier times. "Scarcity" is best thought of as a relationship between the number of options we are able to achieve and the number of options potentially achievable. The process of progress increases *both* numbers and therefore the sense of scarcity—and hence the necessity of choosing among alternatives—may be as great or greater in a society that has progressed than in one that has remained at a basic subsistence level.

Among the alternatives we have to choose from in this option-rich society—the argument goes on—is how much of our time and energy to devote to ourselves and how much to others: our spouses, friends, and especially our children. It is notable that despite nearly two centuries of unprecedented economic progress, the reason most frequently given today for mothers of very young children having to work outside the home is economic necessity. And, in truth, psychologically speaking, necessity now includes many possibilities, including labor force possibilities that simply did not exist in an earlier era. When this happens, there really doesn't seem to be enough time both to take care of children and to exploit the vastly increased number of other opportunities that earning money and having careers outside the home now provide.

This explains, among other things, why a sense of pressure and necessity is felt equally, or even more deeply, by comfortably off, highly educated mothers as compared to mothers who are poor and have little education. Between 1960 and 1988, for example, the labor force participation of mothers of children under six increased by 274.8 percent for women married to husbands in the top income quartile as compared to 113.9 percent for women whose husbands were in the bottom quartile.[20] Raising children in conditions of relative isolation may simply not compare with the exciting options offered by the wider world outside the home.

OPPORTUNITY COSTS AND DEMOGRAPHICS

Furthermore, raising those children becomes increasingly expensive over time. As the knowledge base of the society has become larger and more specialized over the course of the process of progress, the time and resources necessary to prepare children for entry into society has increased substantially. Moreover, the educational enterprise, as it is carried out in home, school, college, graduate school, and the like, is essentially a labor-intensive process. That is to say, even in the age of computers, it has not proved to be greatly susceptible to automation or mass-production methods such as are characteristic in most industrial processes. Thus, education has become relatively more and more expensive, and, indeed, one of the reasons the wives of well-to-do husbands most often cite for being in the workforce is precisely the huge college expenses they anticipate when their children finish high school.

Another way in which children become more costly over time is by their effect on parental, and in the usual case, maternal earning power. The point here, as noted above, is that the options opening up for women in the marketplace are becoming more and more attractive over time. Women's wages are rising, and an increasing range of professional opportunities is opening up. If the woman gives up working to take care of her young child or infant, the cost in terms of forgone income and future advancement possibilities—what economists term "opportunity cost"—tends to rise over time. Even if the woman does continue to work after having children, she usually pays a price in terms of a lack of job flexibility, and an inability to focus single-mindedly on her work, because she will usually be bearing the major responsibility for such child care and homemaking as is undertaken within the family circle. Thus, children not only take more resources directly, but also indirectly increase parental, and especially maternal, opportunity costs.

And bring much less in return. Ceasing to be "little workers," modern children add little or nothing directly to the family exchequer. Moreover, the functions that they used to perform for their parents later in life—sustaining them economically, medically and otherwise in their old age—have now largely been taken over by specialized, government-financed systems and agencies. Mind you, Social Security, Medicare, veterans' benefits, and so on, all must ultimately be sustained through the productive efforts of those children as they form the working force on which the elderly of the society must heavily depend. Still, this support does not come from one's own children, or through the specific vehicle of the family unit, and consequently it has little bearing on the domestic calculations that parents and potential parents must make. Thus those calculations all tend to come to one conclusion: children are an increasingly bad bargain. Insofar as economics has played a decisive role in our thinking, we would do well to have fewer and fewer of them.

This, of course, is exactly what has happened over the past two centuries. We have had fewer and fewer children. Exceptional periods (like the postwar Baby Boom) aside, there has been a massive downward trend in the number of children borne by American women. From an average of seven or eight children per woman at the end of the eighteenth century to around two per woman today. This has been a universal tendency and, indeed, in many industrialized nations, the so-called "fertility rate" has fallen well below replacement levels.[21]

This "demographic transition," as it is usually termed, was, of course, affected by many specific factors that occurred during the process of progress, most notably the decline in infant and child mortality. As

Kuznets has written, the Western world's "long-term decline in fertility" was at least in part, "a free and rational response of would-be parents to higher survival rates of children."[22] Actually, the fall in fertility rates has far more than compensated for the increase in survivorship rates in the United States and elsewhere in the West. The number of family members per U.S. household declined throughout the nineteenth century. Thus, the percentage of households with six or more members fell from 49 percent in 1790 to 35 percent in 1890.[23] This trend continued sharply in the twentieth century with the comparable percentages reaching 5 percent in 1970 and 2.3 percent in 1990.[24] In other words, the number of babies declined not only because more babies survived, but also because the apparent costs and benefits of having children were being altered significantly by the process of progress.

HUSBAND AND WIFE: AN INCREASINGLY FRAGILE TIE

This brief summary of the conventional analysis of family breakdown can be concluded now by pointing out that all the factors already mentioned—fewer children, less attention to children, greatly increased opportunities for women outside the home, displacement of many traditional family functions—have also conspired to render far more tenuous the relations between husbands and wives. Indeed, as the welfare state has also taken over financially as a kind of surrogate spouse, the necessity for having any father present in the home at all has been sharply diminished.

Just as the *father* has become less necessary as a result of the increased role of the state, the increased earning power of mothers, and the historic reduction in the number of children per family, so also have these same factors made the *husband* less necessary. In its direct effects, the process of progress almost certainly tends to undermine permanent, or even long duration, relationships between men and women. As earning opportunities for women were increasingly opened up, and as the demands of housework and child-rearing were continually diminished, women entered the labor force in growing numbers and achieved a kind of independence of their husbands that was difficult, if not impossible to achieve, in a much poorer society. With the increased economic independence of women, the man's sense of responsibility to wife, cohabitor, or simply, lover, was diminished. Her freedom, after all, opened up options of new freedoms for him as well. When the smaller role of children in family life was added to the mix, the need to accept or prolong even a mildly unsatisfactory marital, or nonmarital, union became much less pressing.

In many cases, as we know, such unions were, in fact, no longer accepted or prolonged. Divorce rates soared. Out-of-wedlock child-bearing increased. The historic union of husband and wife, like the putatively deep biological union of parent, and especially father, and child was shattered. The result was that we face the serious, and in deep ways, unprecedented breakdown of family life occurring in today's America.

WHY THE CONVENTIONAL ANALYSIS IS INCOMPLETE

So goes, in simple outline, the conventional analysis of the decline of the institution of the family in the United States, and, indeed, throughout the developed world. All by itself, it would seem, the process of progress is sufficient to explain this decline as a more or less continuing phenomenon since the Industrial Revolution.

The only trouble with this account of the matter is that it doesn't fit the facts. Or at least not all the facts. For example, if the American family has basically been on the decline ever since the Industrial Revolution, how do we explain the astonishing upsurge of family feeling that occurred in the two decades after World War II? Not only were Americans having a sharply increased number of children, but the ethos of the period was saturated with what today we would call "family values."

Far more significant is the actual family experience of nineteenth-century America. Throughout that entire century, while the family was shedding its productive and other special functions, the basic trend was toward an elevation of the spiritual significance of family life and especially a significant increase in the care and attention given to children within the family unit. This is a major point that simply cannot be overlooked:

> *During the course of the nineteenth century, the status of the American family was not declining, but rising, reaching by the turn of the century almost mythic proportions. This was especially true of the treatment of children, who were*

now considered treasures of great value even while their actual net economic benefits to the family were diminishing.

Despite all the negative effects we ascribe to the process of progress, the overall trend in nineteenth-century America was toward a greater emphasis on the core functions of the family, and especially on its historic role as bearer and nurturer of the future generation. This trend was probably most obvious and clearcut in the United States, but it was actually common to the industrializing world in general.

The great Joseph Schumpeter, indeed, described "the family and the family home" as "the mainspring of the typically bourgeois kind of profit motive." The purpose of the early entrepreneurs and capitalists was "to work and save primarily for wife *and children*" [emphasis in the original]. The capitalist ethic, indeed, was precisely "working for the future irrespective of whether or not one is going to harvest the crop oneself."[25] What Schumpeter was saying, in our terminology, is that the process of progress, at least in its early stages, was accompanied by an ideology that strongly favored the family. This is a conception that we will be developing at great length in the analysis that follows.

But, first, we ask, is it really true? That is, was the family, and especially the care and attention given children, actually strengthening during these early stages of the process of progress? Here are a few recent comments by a range of scholars who have studied the history of the American family:

- By the end of the nineteenth century the child-oriented family became a reality for all classes in Western society.

- The attention, energy, and resources in the emerging modern family were increasingly centered upon the rearing of their offspring.

- The ideal bourgeois family . . . everywhere manifest(ed) similar characteristics (including) an enormous interest in the welfare of children and their proper education.

- In nineteenth-century America, the increasing differentiation between economic production and the home transformed the basis of family cohesion. As instrumental ties weakened, the emotional value of all family members—including children—gained new saliency.

- The Victorians believed deeply in the sanctity of children and the family.

- With the rise of the bourgeois family in the last century, the institution of the family became centrally focused on children and child-rearing.

- Sometime around a century ago the image of the child reached its highest point in Western civilization. The exaltation of "childhood" to such heights directed attention to the needs of children as never before in history.

- Prosperous and middling women in cities and villages, and some living on farms . . . devoted increasing time and attention to rearing their children. Their letters and diaries began to be full of careful and loving observations of their children's growth and activities, and anxious concern for their physical and spiritual welfare.[26]

These are not nineteenth-century but twentieth-century evaluations, all written by scholars during the 1980s or 1990s. And the general point is that, at a time when children were ceasing to play a significant role in the family's domestic economy, their place in the emotional and affectional lives of their parents, and especially their mothers, was increasing. Children in nineteenth- and early twentieth-century America achieved a kind of priority in the adult imagination greater than anything that had occurred before, and, with the possible exception of the immediate post-World War II decades, that has occurred since. The "cult of domesticity" dominated nineteenth-century America, and within that domestic circle children attained an unprecedented prominence. With reason, Carl Degler has referred to the nineteenth century as the "century of the child."[27]

VIEWS AND INTERPRETATIONS

Needless to say, on such a complex matter, there are bound to be different views. And this is quite apart from the question of whether all this emphasis on family and children was, or was not, a Good Thing. The theme of much feminist writing is certainly that it was not a Good Thing at all, that women were effectively imprisoned in these Victorian families, that all this attention to domestic life and children was purchased at the expense of the realization of women's potential growth and development.

The value issue aside (for the present), there is the simple factual question, particularly with respect to children: Was the modern interest in their well-being truly exceptional, as our own view suggests? Were children really treated all that well in the Victorian family?

Some scholars think not. Lawrence Stone, for example, suggests that, at least during certain periods, the treatment of children prior to the nineteenth century was fairly benevolent and that it was actually *during* the nineteenth century—with the "cruel" and even "terrifying" figure of the Victorian father—that there was a decline in the well-being of children, at least in Britain, and presumptively in the United States as well.[28] This view conflicts with that of the numerous testimonies quoted above and also with evidence that the "old ideals of patriarchal authority" were actually losing ground during the nineteenth century.[29] Given the enormously increased role of the mother (as opposed to the perhaps "cruel" but increasingly absent father) in the domestic sphere at this time, it is hard to credit the father with quite such a negative influence.

Furthermore, one should note that there is also a considerable body of scholarship these days suggesting that our analysis does not go far enough. The claim is made that it was *only* in the modern period that children were given anything like decent treatment by society, their families, or even their mothers. Edward Shorter, for example, asserts that "good mothering is an invention of modernization. In traditional society, mothers viewed the development and happiness of infants younger than two with indifference. In modern society, they place the welfare of children above all else."[30] Lloyd deMause goes still further and begins a study of the evolution of childhood with this dramatic sentence: "The history of childhood is a nightmare from which we have only recently begun to awaken."[31]

Although these views are quite compatible with my own general thesis, they seem extreme and, indeed, carry us far beyond the requirements of that thesis.[32] I would rather rest my case on the preponderant view, which is that children, though by no means wholly neglected in the past, generally received more familial attention and concern during the nineteenth century than they had in earlier times, and that this was very clearly true in the United States. The point is further supported, I believe, by the evidence of what was happening outside the family unit during this period, i.e., the great new emphasis on the education of children, the growing concern about child labor and the demand for child labor laws. The "century of the child" remains, in my view, an apt description.

The real puzzle, then, is not so much what was happening during the nineteenth century as why it was happening. There are, it should be noted, some general theories on this score. Gary Becker, whom we have quoted earlier, has developed a model in which there is a clear tradeoff between the number of children we have (quantity) and the time, attention, and investment we make in them (quality).[33] Under this model, the nineteenth century, which saw a clear decline in the numbers of children born to women, would be expected to see an increase in their care and concern for their well-being. Quantity was falling, quality was increasing, just as predicted.

Unfortunately, this tradeoff does not seem in any way generalizable over a longer time-span. For example, if we look at the half century following World War II, we can divide it into two quite different periods. In the first period, roughly to the mid–1960s, the fertility rate was high (quantity) and the attention and general priority given to children was also high (quality). One can hardly accuse America in the late 1940s and 1950s of not being sufficiently child-centered!

The second period—from the mid–1960s to the present—has, by contrast, seen a sharp reduction in fertility (the Baby Bust) and also a sharp reduction in the time, attention, resources, and general care and concern given children. Whereas in the earlier period, quantity and quality both went up, in this second period quantity and quality both went down. Clearly, the notion of a general tradeoff here is seriously incomplete. Quantity and quality were inversely related during the nineteenth and early twentieth centuries. During the second half of the twentieth century, they were directly related.

What this means is that, in order to explain the main and central characteristics of family developments during the nineteenth century, and especially the changing attitudes toward the core function of raising children, we need to go beyond the direct and obvious effects of the process of progress. In particular, we need to go beyond process to ideology. This ideology, it will come as no surprise, was embodied in what historians call the Idea of Progress. And it is ultimately in the changing fortunes of that great and once-dominant Idea that we will find the further key we need to unlock the secrets of the evolution of the American family and its current, widely lamented, decline.

4

THE CRUCIAL ROLE OF THE
IDEOLOGY OF PROGRESS

The direct and obvious effects of the process of progress explain much of the modern history of the American family, at least according to the conventional wisdom. Increased specialization resulted in many traditional family functions being taken over by nonfamily institutions. At the same time, expanding personal and economic options, especially for women, accelerated the departure from the home of the wife-homemaker, and ultimately even the children themselves.

Where the conventional wisdom notably fails is in explaining how it was that, while these same forces were operating in nineteenth-century America, the family unit—including the very high priority given children—became such a celebrated and almost holy institution. On a smaller and briefer scale, something similar happened in the 1940s and 1950s. It wasn't just that parents had more children then. It was the attitude toward home, family, and the raising of those more numerous children that was so striking. If anything, the "togetherness" of that period was a bit much to take, and, of course, it was a massive contrast to what was almost immediately to follow.

The key to this dilemma is, I believe, to be found in one of the more indirect effects of the process of progress—its ideology, or what historians most commonly refer to as the "Idea of Progress." For this Idea, which was of dominating importance to much of the post-Industrial Revolution Western world, and especially to nineteenth-century America, placed enormous emphasis on the future, on posterity, on life as it was to be lived by one's children and heirs. It was, in fact, perfectly suited to a worldview in which the institution of the family played a crucial and highly elevated role.

83

LIMITING THE RANGE OF DISCUSSION

The *Idea of Progress*, as I shall use the phrase, represents in the first instance a commentary on the modern process of progress discussed in the previous chapter. It should be noted immediately that such a characterization already substantially limits the term compared to a number of other uses common in the literature. We are focusing on the Idea of Progress more or less exclusively as it developed and gained strength during, and especially after, the Industrial Revolution of the late eighteenth century. We will be concerned with this ideology largely in the specific context of the United States, and, of course, will be relating it to the fate of the American family during this period.

These limitations to a particular country (for the most part) and to a defined period of time have many advantages, not the least of which being that we can avoid the voluminous discussions and controversies that have developed as to when, where, by whom, and to what degree the Idea of Progress was first espoused, developed, amended, criticized, rejected, or overlooked. For it turns out that there is virtually no thinker in the history of Western civilization who did not have at least some thoughts on the subject, and usually more than one set of thoughts as his or her ideas developed over time.[1]

The main advantage of these limitations, however, is that they enable us to focus on the place and period in history when the Idea of Progress, far from being an occasional notion developed by an occasional philosopher, or even being a dominant notion but only or largely among philosophers, became a general article of faith with the public at large. From the point of view of the intellectual historian, the development of the philosophic foundations of the Idea of Progress, particularly associated with the eighteenth-century Enlightenment, is a source of endless fascination. Our interest, however, is in the extension of this Idea as a widespread popular belief capable of influencing and motivating human actions and decisions in society at large.

There is very little doubt that such an extension did occur in the United States in the nineteenth and early twentieth centuries. Testimony on this point by American historians during that period is virtually unanimous. Thus, the Idea of Progress was variously described as the way in which God was "made visible in history," "the greatest single idea in the whole history of mankind," and "one of the most profound and germinal ideas at work in the modern age." Even a critic of Progress, or at least of the inevitability of Progress, confessed that, as far as the American people in general were concerned, the Idea was "a fundamental belief which admits not the shadow of a doubt."[2]

Historian Oscar Handlin once summed up the general mood of late nineteenth-century America in this way: "The past, by 1875, had acquired the attributes of continuity and regularity. It proceeded in a chain of natural causes and effects, not subject to interruption or caprice. Any given moment in time was inextricably linked to all its antecedents. . . . The plan was progress. Americans confidently believed that history was a record of man's improvement which would continue indefinitely into the future."[3]

In what was, during the nineteenth and early twentieth centuries, probably the most "modern" of modern nations—these very United States—the Idea of Progress became, not only a commonly held belief, but something close to a national religion.

MAIN CHARACTERISTICS OF THE IDEA

What, then, did this peculiarly "modern," notably American, "fundamental belief" consist of? In terms of our specific inquiry, what kind of commentary did it make about the process of progress as the latter evolved, and transformed life, in the nineteenth and early twentieth centuries?

In the crudest possible terms, the Idea of Progress stated that the process of progress is a "good thing," that this "good thing" will continue indefinitely into the future, and that the future in which this "good thing" is expected to continue matters—greatly. In short, progress is good, inevitable, and important.

This formulation, though basically correct, is a bit too short and crude for our purposes. These three adjectives need amplification and in some respects qualification. Taking them in order, we have the following:

1. *The process of progress is good*

This first claim, though obviously debatable on moral grounds, would appear at least to be fairly straightforward as to meaning. Actually, the claim is quite complicated. It involves a hidden issue that is easy to overlook but that is quite important. The problem may be framed as a question: Do we mean "good" with reference to the values of the present observer (i.e., believer), or "good" with reference to the values of a later observer who is on the scene when that subsequent stage in the process of progress actually occurs? Is the present observer willing to accept as Progress (a "good thing") a drift in the direction of a future world that violates his or her basic moral convictions? Would it in any way comfort that present observer to know that later generations might regard this drift as desirable (a "good thing")—in effect, rejecting previous moral standards as outmoded?

As in most of these matters, the question could in theory be answered either way. As present believers, we could insist on our own fixed moral standard, or we could acknowledge that the future observer would have advanced morally and would be able to see and understand things that we, in our present and relatively underdeveloped moral state, would be unable to appreciate. The latter position is certainly quite compatible with a progressive outlook, since included in that outlook is the possibility of a continuing improvement in human morality.

I am not, however, so much concerned with the theory of the matter as the practical and especially psychological impact of the Idea. In fact, there is a direct impact of this nature involved in the relations between generations. Would the typical believer consider it a good thing if his or her children, or grandchildren, act on beliefs that are distasteful, and possibly even abhorrent, to the believer but which the children or grandchildren are quite confident are preferable to those of their forebears? Or would such a believer tend to conclude that his or her faith in Progress had in fact been misplaced, and that, contrary to expectations, the world was going to hell in a handbasket? Economists might well think of this issue as a kind of Moral Index Number problem.[4] That it is in no way a purely abstract matter may be proved by consulting almost any American parent whose children were of college age in the 1960s.

Although some parents and grandparents might well take the benevolent, and in some ways truly "progressive" view, these will surely be more the exception than the rule. Indeed, in order to take any real psychological satisfaction from the benefits of the process of progress accruing to future generations, one must have at least some mental image of the kind of world they will be enjoying, and this mental image, or even range of images, must be conceived from some relatively fixed vantage point. This vantage point may well allow for changing social mores in the future; indeed, it almost certainly will. However, the direction of these changes will have to be foreseen. A believer in the early part of this century may, for example, feel that women, Blacks, and other minorities will be accorded increasingly equal rights over time—that is, that then-existing prejudices will gradually fade away and that this fading away is in fact part and parcel of the process of progress. In approving these anticipated changes, this believer is expressing a fixed set of values toward which the rest of society is seen as gradually moving. What is *not* compatible with this believer's credo is the possibility that future generations may prefer to restore Black slavery and/or start binding girls' feet as in the ancient Chinese custom.

The only way in which such future behavior could be accepted imaginatively by a present believer would be as a temporary aberration, a brief lapse in the upward and onward movement assured by the Idea of Progress. Bad things obviously can and do happen from time to time. What the believer will say is not that these bad things are, in fact, good things because later observers believe them so. On the contrary, the believer will say either that these bad things are only temporary— basically departures from trend—or, possibly, that these bad things, while bad in themselves, may well serve a higher purpose—that is, will prepare the way for even better things to follow.

A clear case in point here from our own period, is the Holocaust in Nazi Germany. The leaders of the German nation—and, one suspects, more of the German people than will now acknowledge the fact believed it acceptable to commit genocide on Jews, gypsies, and other "undesirable" races and individuals. Our question is this: Could a believer in the Idea of Progress at, say, the turn of the century conceivably have accepted this possibility as a continuation of the good things promised by Progress on the grounds that it was so regarded by the later generation that perpetrated these acts? The answer seems almost self-evident. Armed with such foresight, the early believer would have either lost his faith, or found some way of interpreting such future incidents as aberrations or instruments of some still later higher good.

Our conclusion, therefore, is that the belief that the process of progress is a good thing requires a reasonably fixed, though of course not totally rigid, set of values from which vantage point the future, and especially the direction of future change, is to be visualized and judged. Without such a standard, it seems doubtful that the assertion that the process of progress is a good thing has any real psychological content at all. Or, if it does, it would have content only with respect to the past (whose Progress would, of course, be judged by a present-day standard of value), and not to the future.

As far as nineteenth- and early-twentieth-century America is concerned, it seems abundantly clear that it was not just the past, but particularly, and especially, the future whose unfolding was regarded as a good thing. Also—and a point I will return to often—it seems equally clear that there was, in fact, a basically fixed standard of values that could be applied to this unfolding process. Although profession and actual practice often differed, one is not likely to accuse Victorian America of excessive moral laxity.

2. *The process of progress is inevitable*

This brings us to the second characterization of the Idea of Progress: the view that the continuation of the process of progress into the future is inevitable. Here, both an amplification and qualification are necessary. The amplification has to do with the distinction between the certainty of future progress as (a) independent of conscious human motives and intentions; or (b) a result, at least in part, of those conscious motives and intentions. Thus, studies that classify Progress thinkers often divide them into two categories, those who believe in "necessary" Progress and those who believe in "contingent" Progress only. Although there are many possible contingencies that might affect the issue here, the main consideration is the degree of human freedom involved.[5] Is Progress more or less guaranteed no matter what human beings choose or decide, or is it largely guaranteed because humans will make wise decisions, or, perhaps more appropriately, will make increasingly wis*er* decisions over the course of the centuries?

Philosophically, the problem is the ancient one of predestination versus free will. If the continuation of the process of progress is truly "inevitable," then in what possible sense can conscious human choices have any real bearing on the matter? Many ideologies have quite similar problems. In Calvinist terms, if the Elect are already decided, isn't human choice and behavior a complete irrelevance? In Marxist terms, if the ultimate triumph of communism is scientifically ordained, why bother agitating for it, even giving up one's life for it? Similarly, if the process of progress is inevitable, why concern oneself with promoting "progressive" policies? And so on.

Again, and as always, our primary interest is psychological, not philosophical. And, as is well known, it is quite possible to be psychologically stimulated and sharply goaded into action by the very sense of inevitability of the outcome (and thus the seeming irrelevance of one's actions). Calvinists can prove to themselves, and possibly to others, that they are among the Elect only by living the kind of life and enjoying the kind of success that would inevitably come to them if they were, in fact, among the Elect. Marxist revolutionaries have the psychological satisfaction of knowing that history is on their side and that, although the outcome may be foreordained, they may very possibly affect its timing. Similarly, the believer in Progress may feel that humans can affect the pace of change in a given desirable direction, and may also take a deep psychological satisfaction in being part of a general process much larger and more meaningful than the life of any single individual.

Such psychological responses are not only possible but undoubtedly of signal importance in actual historical reality. Indeed, it is almost certainly true that faith in a process that somehow occurs independent of conscious human volition is likely to be a stronger faith than one in which that volition plays a serious, or in any way crucial, role. This is the important qualification that we referred to above, namely, that "inevitability" is, or at least seems psychologically to be, on a surer footing when it can be associated directly with some force external to conscious human volition, either God's Will, or the process of evolution as working through natural selection, or, very possibly, natural selection as an exemplification of God's Will. At a minimum, introducing conscious human volition as a factor on which the future process of progress depends makes that process contingent on an additional variable and one whose actual past "variability" is likely to be widely recognized.

This point is significant because, just as the process of progress has been seen to go through a certain evolution over time—with a growing emphasis on human choice and decision making—so the Idea of Progress is likely to go through a similar evolution. Increasingly, or so I will argue, predictions of the continuation of the process come to involve predictions about human choices and behaviors. For some believers, this may pose no problem. They may have all along associated the Idea of Progress with the increasing perfectibility of human nature. For others, a slow drift may begin to occur along a kind of predictability axis from inevitable to probable to merely possible. When combined with a shifting morality that may seem, to some at least, increasingly questionable, this slow drift may easily go from merely possible to effective abandonment of the whole Idea.

3. *The process of progress is important*

We come now to the third basic characteristic of the Idea of Progress, namely, that what happens in this more or less indefinitely prolonged future is important, that is, that the future matters, that it "counts." The proof that it "counts" is that we are willing to make sacrifices today for results that are likely to accrue mainly in the future, and, indeed, often after we are long dead. We have already quoted Schumpeter and historian J. B. Bury to this effect. The former spoke of working for the future whether or not "one is going to harvest the crop oneself." The latter noted that it was "the life of future generations" that justified our current "labours and sufferings."

Nineteenth-century morality is full of future-directed injunctions. One must be industrious. One must be frugal and saving. "Abstinence" looms large among the economic virtues (and in Victorian America, among the more intimate virtues as well).[6] One must work hard today, save, invest, accumulate wealth, partly for one's own private purposes, partly to impress one's neighbors, friends, and society in general, but also partly, and significantly, to leave an inheritance behind.[7] Whether it be a small family business or a substantial fortune, it matters greatly that it be carried forward after one is gone, ideally expanded further, then handed on to still later generations. The "American dream," to this day, is usually interpreted precisely to include this notion that one's children and heirs will have a better head start and be able to lead happier lives than were their parents and grandparents.

The future referred to here—the future that "counts"—has to do with events taking place in this world and not in some kind of other-worldly afterlife. Such a view of the future is not inconsistent with a belief in an afterlife and, indeed, it is almost certain that most nineteenth-century believers in the Idea of Progress in the United States also retained a vestigial, and in some cases quite vivid and active, belief in Heaven and Hell. Which is to say that there is no theoretical reason that a person cannot attribute importance both to happiness on this earth and to happiness in the Hereafter, and this both for oneself and for one's children, grandchildren, and later descendants.

Still, from a psychological point of view, there is little doubt that the Idea of Progress has its greatest motivational impact when secular events assume increasing importance in human thought. If one seriously balances the few short years of one's earthly existence and those of one's descendants against eternity, there is really no contest. It is only when the terrestrial years take on special priority in one's thoughts that the Idea of Progress becomes a truly dominating force in shaping those terrestrial years. If the religious connection is to be maintained in this increasingly secularized context, it is likely to be less in the form of acute visions of the afterlife than in the belief that Progress on this earth is, in fact, guaranteed, commissioned, or in some other way assured by a divine power.

Indeed, the easy companionship between religious faith and the full enjoyment of industrial and commercial success in nineteenth-century America has often been noted. As Tocqueville put it succinctly: "Americans not only follow their religion from interest, but they often place in this world the interest which makes them follow it. . . . The American preachers are constantly referring to this earth, and it is only with great difficulty that they can divert their attention from it."[8]

The special importance of the future in the Idea of the Progress thus implies a substantial secularization of thought, certainly as compared to premodern Europe and to colonial America as well. But this is not the only implication of the assignment of a strong priority to the future and especially to the distant future. What is also at stake here is a different conception of time, as compared to previous ages. At a minimum, the Idea of Progress requires that there *be* a distant future, and specifically a distant terrestial future. This is true in part because the process of progress can hardly bring on the millennium all at once; its essential characteristic is to move incrementally ahead, always tending to improve things, but always with a great distance to go before anything approaching an ideal world emerges.

It is also true, moreover, that few believers in the Idea of Progress would imagine that there are never any periods in which things temporarily regress. Setbacks will occur from time to time. Setbacks may even be necessary to enable subsequent large advances to take place. The point is that for the Idea of Progress to have a serious psychological impact on people's attitudes and actions, they must: (1) feel some assurance that there is extensive future time available in our earthly setting, and (2) believe that the basic direction of the course of events over that considerable span of time can be envisioned and counted on with at least some degree of confidence. As it turns out, the process of progress, through various scientific discoveries, was very good at providing assurance on the first of these two points. The relationship of that process to the second point is a far more complicated matter. We will have much to say on both points as we continue on with our study.

IDEOLOGY AND THE FAMILY

First, however, we must consider the obvious question: What, after all, does all this talk about the Idea of Progress have to do with what was happening to the American family during the nineteenth and early twentieth centuries? What is its bearing on attitudes to family life in general?

Three points are relevant here. Two suggest a strong connection between the ideology of Progress and the institution of the family. The third raises a problem that we will have to spend a moment discussing at somewhat greater length.

The first point is quite simply the *historical simultaneity* of two events in the late nineteenth and early twentieth centuries: the triumph of the Idea of Progress, and an emphasis on home, family and children that was exceptional by past historical standards. However much one may dislike, or even reject, Victorian attitudes, most historians have, as we know, argued that there was a new stress on the importance of home and family during this period and that, as far as children went, there was a greater manifestation of concern for their well-being. This concern, as indicated earlier, extended well beyond the family unit as, for example, in the matter of child labor laws, and the like. In any case, the rearing of the next generation was considered a deep personal and social responsibility and the agency overwhelmingly charged with this important task was unquestionably the Victorian, or what we would now call the "traditional," American family. Historical simultaneity in no way proves causation, but it does give us a starting point, and is, at a minimum, highly suggestive.

The second point is that there is in fact a very clear *logical connection* that one can draw between these two simultaneous developments. To put it in the simplest and most unequivocal terms: The Idea of Progress involves a celebration of posterity, and the family is the institution responsible for nurturing and sustaining the generations that will constitute that posterity. The Idea of Progress occupies imaginatively the same future space that successor generations will occupy in fact. Emotionally, as already indicated, the tie is suggested by the satisfaction each present generation gets from imagining the better, happier, more fulfilling lives that will be enjoyed by its children and heirs. Although this satisfaction was not the only force motivating the success-oriented, future-directed attitudes so prevalent in nineteenth-century America, it almost certainly added depth, resonance, and point to many otherwise prosaic day-to-day activities. All one's hard work and careful husbanding of resources was given a purpose that was at once personal (one's family) and universal (the future in general). In striving for the betterment of one's own, one was thus also part of a larger scheme of things, a scheme which, in America perhaps more than anywhere else, really seemed to reflect our special national destiny. For over a century, this marriage of the particular and the general proved to be an extremely fruitful union.

Because of this logical, and really emotional, connection, one can see good reason why the celebration of Progress and the celebration of the family should go together. The historical conjunction of these two phenomena at the end of the nineteenth century need not, for this reason, cause us any particular surprise. And yet there is a problem here.

Which leads us to the third point, or rather question: Did the spirit of Progress actually infuse the family sphere in the nineteenth century as suggested by the above two points, or, on the contrary, did the Victorian family in crucial respects involve a *rejection* of the whole enterprise represented by the process of progress? Was that family unit less a participant in the process than an explicit retreat from it?

The notion of the American middle-class family as a retreat from the nineteenth-century world of commerce and industry has been advanced by a number of writers. In his book, *A Haven in a Heartless World*, Christopher Lasch wrote: "The withdrawal into the 'emotional fortress' of the family took place not because family life became warmer and more attractive in the nineteenth century, as some historians have argued, but because the outside world came to be seen as more forbidding."[9] Similarly, John Demos, when offering a capsule contrast between the nineteenth-century family and that of colonial times, speaks of the change from a "building block" to a "refuge."[10] Roughly the same point of view is presented by Kirk Jeffrey in his often-cited essay, "The Family as Utopian Retreat from the City: The Nineteenth Century Contribution." In it, he notes the "sharp disjunction between the private world of the family and the larger society."[11]

None of these writers presents quite as simplified an analysis as these brief quotations suggest.[12] Still, the general picture that emerges is that of an institution that is in essence protective, disapproving, and at best corrective of the surrounding society. Domestic values, it would appear, stand in sharp contrast to those observed in the crude and scarcely moral world of production, industry, and commerce.

But if this is so, how could the Idea of Progress, so clearly based at this time on the underlying process of progress, have come to affect those domestic values in a positive way? Why would the family have become so optimistic and future-looking when the only warrant for such an attitude was a process from which the family was apparently in retreat? This, then, is the problem that has to be addressed.

IMPORTANCE OF THE "SUCCESS" THEME

There is much that could be said on this matter, since it ultimately involves the question of how morality, centered in family and also increasingly in the schools of nineteenth- century America, related to the large technological and socioeconomic forces that were remaking the nation, and that we are calling the "process of progress." In our very next chapter, we will be arguing that this morality was a complement to that process and, far from being a rejection of, was in fact a necessary component of, the Idea of Progress.

For the moment, however, all we really have to do is to reject the basic premise of the descriptions we have just presented. The late-nineteenth-century American family as retreat, haven, refuge, critic of the world outside its doors? As a basic characterization? It makes no sense at all! In fact, if my overall thesis has any real difficulty, it would very likely be the exact opposite, namely, that the family, like the society in general, was becoming so wrapped up in dreams of quick-and-easy material "success" that even thoughts of the future might occasionally take a back seat. However, the central point is that the family could never have been so isolated as to escape the feverish spirit of the times. These were the decades that have been labeled "the age of optimism."[13] The generation that grew up in the seventies, eighties, and nineties of the last century has been called "the most titanically successful generation in our history." Could the world outside the putative "family fortress" seem so alarming when, according to the words of Emerson, "there is in America a general conviction in the minds of all mature men that every young man of good faculty and good habits can by perseverance attain to an adequate estate; if he have a turn for business . . . he can come to wealth?"

Wasn't the real problem for the late-nineteenth-century family, not that the outside world seemed too "forbidding," but that it seemed too alluring and attractive? This was, after all, the period when success as exemplified by the Horatio Alger stories was becoming an intrinsic part of our national mythology. In 1906, William James could write to H. G. Wells: "The exclusive worship of the bitch-goddess SUCCESS . . . is our national disease."[14] This hardly sounds like a society in which middle-class families were huddled protectively in their domestic shelters for fear that the rude winds of commerce might shatter their lives.

EDUCATION: INTERCONNECTED "SPHERES"

In a way, what really has to be rejected, or seriously qualified here, is the notion that the two "spheres" of late-nineteenth- and early twentieth-century life—the private, domestic sphere occupied largely by women and children (the family), and the public, business and commercial sphere occupied almost solely by men (the process of progress)—were totally disconnected, or, if connected, were joined together by a basic antagonism of attitudes and purposes.

How far such a picture is from the real truth of the situation may be indicated by considering the role of education during the nineteenth century. It was, of course, during that century, that the battle for universal, tax-supported public education in the United States was fought and won. In the late 1830s, industrial states began adopting laws that required poor children working in factories to attend school three months a year. In 1852, Massachusetts adopted the nation's first universal compulsory education law. New York followed in 1853 and other states soon joined in (although the last state, Mississippi, did not follow until 1918). Most public education throughout the century was primary school education, although high school education also began to expand rapidly. On the eve of the Civil War, there were three hundred or so public high schools in the nation; by 1900, there were around six thousand.

While this growth of public education might seem, on the surface, to be simply part of the increasing specialization and professionalization of functions that was ultimately to weaken the family, it is more accurate during this period to consider it largely an extension of the family sphere into the public sphere. Indeed, if we think of the "separate spheres" doctrine in terms of a male/female dichotomy, then it can be argued that the task of children's education in both home and school became increasingly the sole possession of women. Thus we have two simultaneous developments: (1) The father, who had previously been considered the primary educator of children, increasingly works outside the home. This task is taken over by the mother. In fact, the work of rearing and educating children in the home is now more or less universally accepted as occurring within "woman's sphere." (2) When public education, occurring outside the family, expands over the decades, so also does the employment of women as teachers. By the middle of the nineteenth century, 60 percent of U.S. school teachers were women, and, by 1900, 74 percent. In the more urbanized Northeast, the number by the end of the century was 85 percent.[15] Thus teaching in the "public" sphere had become clearly associated with "woman's sphere."

To complicate the family-society relationship even further, we could also add (3) that children's education at this time continued much longer within the family sphere itself. The period of childhood dependency and the age at which children left home continually increased during the century. Thus, while formal school influences were becoming more important in the preparation of children for participation in the world outside the home, family influences were becoming no less and in some respects even more significant than in the past.

What we have then is a total commingling of spheres in the matter of children's education during the nineteenth century. What is more, this whole educational project was clearly and directly connected with both the process of progress and the Idea of Progress. A commercialized, industrialized, urbanized society clearly needed greater literacy and numeracy in its workforce. This demand of the process of progress continues, and, in fact, has become greatly intensified in our own day. No one would doubt that education in the nineteenth century was needed to, and did in fact, increasingly perform this crucial function.

But it was not just a matter of teaching the three "R's" (resulting, one might note in passing, in a dramatic increase in women's literacy during the century), it was also a question of teaching attitudes appropriate to a progressing society. Discipline, hard work, saving for the future were among the important virtues taught. "A penny saved is two pence clear," "Save and have," "Industry, Perseverance & Frugality, make Future yield," "Lost Time is never found again," and other adages from *Poor Richard's Almanack* were a staple of the educational process. It comes as no surprise that Benjamin Franklin was one of the most quoted of all American authors in the schoolbooks of the period.[16]

Even more to the point of our present analysis is the fact that the entire nineteenth-century educational enterprise was strongly motivated, and quite specifically, by the Idea of Progress. A leading scholar of the history of American education, Lawrence A. Cremin, describes the purposes of Horace Mann (1796–1859) thus:

> The commanding figure of the early public-school movement, he had poured into his vision of education a boundless faith in the perfectibility of human life and institutions. Once the public schools were established, no evil could resist their salutary influence. Universal education could be the "great equalizer" of human conditions, the "balance wheel of the social machinery," and the "creator of wealth undreamed of." Poverty would most assuredly disappear, and with it the rancorous discord between the "haves" and "have-nots" that had marked all of human history. Crime would diminish; sickness would abate; and life for the common man would be longer, better, and happier.

Mann was by no means alone in this attitude for, as Cremin writes, "if anything had been established in the public mind by a half-century of public-school propaganda, it was the sense of an inextricable relationship between education and national progress. The great pre-Civil War architects of universal schooling—Horace Mann in Massachusetts, Henry Barnard in Connecticut, John Pierce in Michigan, and Samuel Lens in Ohio—had hammered relentlessly at this theme in their quest for political support."[17] That "national progress" could be usefully employed as a rallying-cry for public support suggests both the connection between education and the Idea of Progress in the public mind, and also the hold that that Idea already had in the public imagination even by mid-century.

In chapter 5, we will indicate an even further, and more subtle, connection between nineteenth-century education in both home and school and the Idea of Progress—the crucial role of the teaching of morality as a guide to personal lifestyles and behavior—but enough has already been said to indicate that home, family, school, and society were at this time engaged in a huge common mission. And that mission was to promote both the process of progress and the ideology that went with it. Ruth Miller Elson concludes her study of more than a thousand popular textbooks used in American schools in the nineteenth century with these words: "All of these books accept as an axiom that the law of history is one of steady and inevitable progress toward greater material wealth and comfort as well as toward greater virtue and freedom. These two aims of evolution are inextricably linked and the progress of the United States sufficiently substantiates their importance as keys to man's development."[18]

To deny that families (and women) were deeply involved in this grand educational project, or to claim that that project was somehow disconnected from the process of progress and its commanding Idea, would simply be to overlook overwhelming historical evidence. Just as the increasingly materialistic, success-oriented attitudes emerging at this time inexorably embroiled the nineteenth-century family in the process of progress, so also the rapidly expanding educational enterprise brought the purposes of family, home, school, and nation into shared territory. The Victorian family was not a retreat from the Idea of Progress. It was a vehicle for its vital expression.

THE PARADOX EMERGES

Our analysis has now reached a point where a crucial link in the argument of this book—its central paradox, as I have called it—begins to emerge quite clearly. In the previous chapter, we discussed the many ways in which the process of progress during the nineteenth century—and, indeed, to this very day—tends to displace family functions and thus to undermine the family as society's basic institution. The problem with that analysis was that it was incomplete. It failed to explain why, despite the loss of so many functions, the American family during the nineteenth and early twentieth centuries reached such a revered and almost mythical status. (It also fails to explain the great wave of family feeling that seized the American psyche in the Baby Boom era, another matter we must discuss in due course.)

In the present chapter, we have tried to amend the earlier analysis by adding another component of change in the nineteenth century, namely, the triumph of the Idea of Progress. Denying the view that the family during this time was in essence a retreat from, or a fortress walled up against, the surrounding society, I have maintained that it was very much a party to the great changes that were transforming that society and, indeed, was deeply influenced by the Idea of Progress. Among other things, the whole educational process in both home and school was drenched with the notion that the national future, and the children who would create and share in that future, was to be ever better and brighter because of the process of progress. On this view, the greatly increased attention to children, noted in the previous chapter, has an easy and obvious explanation.

What is not at all easy and obvious, however, is the paradox we are left with. The process of progress undermines the family. The Idea of Progress strengthens the family. But surely these two phenomena, process and Idea, are not unrelated. Without the process, the Idea in the sense we are using the concept could never have arisen in the first place. By what warrant can we treat process and Idea as though they were somehow not united at all, but separable?

Such a warrant almost certainly does exist but it is not something that can be spelled out in a few words. The whole of part 2 will, in fact, be devoted to an analysis of the relationship—and especially the changing relationship—between the process of progress and the Idea of Progress. Our major, and final, claim in part 2 will be that while the process of progress initially suggests, supports, and sustains the Idea of Progress, in the long run, it undermines that Idea. And when the Idea begins to weaken and fail, so the ideology that was protective of the institution of the family is also seen to be weakening and failing.

Without too much exaggeration, it can be said that the rise and fall of the American family and the rise and fall of the Idea of Progress are directly—and, from the point of view of present-day America, perhaps tragically—related.

Part II

THE PARADOX: RISE AND FALL OF THE IDEA OF PROGRESS

5

HOW THE PROCESS GAVE RISE
TO THE IDEA

Enough has already been said to suggest not only that the process of progress and the Idea of Progress are different phenomena but also that they have borne a changing relationship to each other over time. In particular, it has been mentioned—and is crucial to the argument of this book—that, whereas the process of progress initially suggests and appears to confirm the Idea of Progress, in the long run it tends to undermine and ultimately to destroy it. I speak always of the Idea of Progress in the sense of a doctrine that influences and motivates not just a few intellectuals but the whole of, or at least very substantial segments of, society at large. This particular doctrine did, in fact, exert exactly that kind of influence in America during the late nineteenth and early twentieth centuries.

Part 2 will be devoted to charting the course of this changing relationship between the empirical process of progress and the Idea of Progress, explaining in broad terms the rise and fall of what can well be considered the defining ideology of the post-Industrial Revolution era, if not of the entire modern era. In the present chapter, what would appear to be the "natural" relationship—a basic harmony between process and Idea—is explained, thereby showing why, in the nineteenth and early twentieth century, the Idea of Progress was widely triumphant, certainly in its American setting. Subsequent chapters in part 2 will suggest how this happy relationship became unhinged, not so much because of specific difficulties often cited, as because of the less-noticed but nevertheless intrinsic character of the underlying industrialization process.

INITIAL HARMONY

There is little doubt that, at the outset, the Idea of Progress was born from and nurtured by the process of progress. Indeed, to some degree, this is a consequence of the definitions we are using. The Idea of Progress, in our specific sense, involves a commentary on the modern process of progress. Before that process took place—essentially, before the Industrial Revolution—there may have been many ideas or visions of "progress," but clearly not in terms of the conception we are employing, and certainly not as a general article of faith throughout society. Apart from definitions, however, it is difficult to see how such a general faith could have become established until the fruits of rationality, science, invention, and innovation began actually to affect the conditions of ordinary life.

Indeed, the most likely pattern of events in the early stages of the process of progress is that the process fostered the Idea and the Idea in turn buttressed the process. As Carl Becker once put it: "Of all the inventions yet made by the ingenious Europeans, the doctrine of progress is the most effective. . . . If then the idea of progress emerges from progress itself, progress is in turn reinforced by the idea of progress that is in men's minds."[1] A philosophy predictive of continuing and rapid change could hardly occur in the relatively static long-run conditions of an agrarian, preindustrial society. And the relationship also works in reverse—that is to say, rapid and continuing change in social and economic institutions and structures could hardly take place without an accompanying philosophy that was at the very least permissive of change.

This harmonious interaction seems both natural and really quite obvious, and is the starting point for any serious analysis of the relationship of process and Idea. Still, this early relationship was far more detailed and intricate than this. Specific scientific discoveries cleared the way for a philosophy that was predicated on long stretches of evolutionary time. Technological advances permitted an unprecedented rise in the general standard of living with the obvious possibility of endless further advances over future time. Humankind was clearly achieving mastery over the ancient adversaries of nature—drought, famine, disease—and, suitably instructed, might well also achieve mastery over human nature itself.

Later on, these same forces of science, technology, economics, and social control might prove actually threatening to the Idea of Progress. In the beginning, however, they conspired in very specific ways to underline the conception of a beneficently and indefinitely unfolding future.

SCIENCE, GEOLOGIC TIME, AND EVOLUTION

The first specific requirement that enabled the Idea of Progress to secure a foothold as a general social philosophy was the provision of time, enough time, very long stretches of time extending back into the earth's past and, by analogy, forward into the world's future. Without extensive historic time, who could possibly determine whether things had, in fact, been getting better and better over the course of the human past? Without extensive future time, who would even care?

The simple ability to measure time is a necessary prerequisite here. Lewis Mumford, more than any other scholar, has pointed up the importance of the widespread use of clocks as the quintessential innovation ushering in the modern age.[2] More generally, the gradual development of objective measures of time, through both clocks and calendars, as opposed to subjective measures as determined by various different activities in response to the seasons, weather conditions, patterns of light and darkness, and so on, was necessary to enable individuals to conceive of changes over lengthy periods of time.

The measurability of time was clearly a necessary prerequisite for the Idea of Progress, but hardly sufficient. What was needed was that there be a very extensive quantity of time, both past and future. Extensive past time was required to establish the historic progressiveness of the world, and extensive future time was required to enable the process of progress to bring forth its promised benefits. And here, modern science, a key feature of the process of progress, played a decisive role.

It must be remembered that an extended timescale, permitting imaginative reconstructions of distant past events and foreshadowings of distant future events, is a surprisingly recent conception. Not only in the medieval period but well into the modern age, the entire time span of the earth was believed to be no more than a few thousand years. As late as 1650, Archbishop James Ussher could set the date of creation at 4004 B.C. In doing so, he was very much in line with Joseph Scaliger, a sixteenth century French philologist, who combined two astronomical cycles with one sociopolitical cycle to calculate our beginnings at 4713 B.C. Such views were similarly held in other cultures, the Mayan calendar placing the beginning of the world at 3113 B.C., and the Indian at 2850 B.C.[3]

And if the beginning of the earth was long believed to be rather recent—measured in a few millennia rather than billions of years—the ending of the earth was believed to be even closer. The doctrine that the end of the world was coming shortly was by no means limited to medieval Catholicism. If anything, early Protestants were even more convinced of the imminence of the Last Judgment. Luther wrote: "The world will perish shortly. The last day is at the door, and I believe the world will not endure a hundred years." Even so scientifically minded an observer as Francis Bacon wrote in the seventeenth century of contemporary life as the "Old Age of the Earth."[4]

Most astonishing perhaps, geologists were apparently divided (or at least politically very cautious) about this whole subject of the earth's age and future prospects even into the nineteenth century. As Stephen Toulmin and June Goodfield note, "When the Geological Society of London was established in 1807, it was resolved as a deliberate policy to take no sides about the Theory of the Earth, and to accept meritorious contributions from geologists of any theoretical persuasion or none."[5]

Still, among scientists, at least, the debate was not to last very long. A key event was the appearance in 1830 of Charles Lyell's book, *Principles of Geology*. He summed up previous thinking on the matter thus: "It had been the consistent belief of the Christian world . . . that the origin of this planet was not more remote than a few thousand years; and that since the creation the deluge was the only great catastrophe by which considerable change had been wrought on the earth's surface. On the other hand, the opinion was scarcely less general, that the final dissolution of our system was an event to be looked for at no distant period."[6]

Neither opinion nor belief could Lyell accept. For the geological record left little doubt in his mind that successive strata "could only have been formed by slow and insensible degrees in a great lapse of ages," and that the age of earth, accordingly, was to be calculated not in thousands but in millions or billions of years.

This discovery made it possible for the Idea of Progress to spread its wings historically and created the conceptual possibility of virtually endless future time. It should be said that, while this discovery was, in point of historic fact, a product of the empirical process of progress, it was not really an intrinsic feature of that process. Is there any necessary reason that the facts *had* to come out this way? Was the biblical story of creation not only empirically wrong, but in some sense logically or philosophically impossible? Hardly, unless we write off many of the best Western thinkers prior to the modern era as guilty of sophomoric error.

A similar point can be made with respect to another, and in many respects the decisive, scientific advance that made the Idea of Progress widely acceptable during the nineteenth century: the development of the theory of evolution. Was it in any way logically necessary or otherwise mandatory that the world should turn out to have an evolutionary, or developmental, structure? In the Great Chain of Being—a concept of no small importance in the premodern *weltanschauung*—every life-niche is filled by one creature or another but development is distinctly not part of the picture.[7] Nor was it part of the biblical picture, nor, one might add, of the artistic imagination of Michelangelo. In the Sistine Chapel, God offers life to a fully formed modern man—a man without ancestors and, indeed, without any past at all.

Thus, it was only factually and empirically—not logically or necessarily true—that the fossil record and observational knowledge of the world developed within the process of progress should reveal a world subject to constant evolutionary change. Still, this is what that process did in fact reveal. The crucial event was the publication of Darwin's *Origin of Species* in 1859. Even before then, however, evolutionary thinking was very much in evidence. Herbert Spencer, for example, clearly anticipated Darwin in terms of an evolutionary worldview, though not with respect to the specific mechanism of natural selection. Indeed, it has been argued that by mid-century the ground was so well prepared that, even if Darwin had never written, the theory of evolution would have had to have been invented out of thin air.[8]

However that may be, the facts are that Darwin did publish his monumental work, that despite numerous attacks on religious grounds (as, of course, still happens even in our own day), it was quite widely and quickly accepted in Britain and the United States, and finally, that the theory easily lent itself to the view that there was an underlying, elemental force in the universe leading the human race to higher and higher levels of ability and well-being. Darwin himself occasionally succumbed to this roseate view. In the famous penultimate paragraph of the *Origin*, he wrote: "As all living forms of life are lineal descendants of those which lived long before the Cambrian epoch, we may feel certain that the ordinary succession by generation has never once been broken, and that no cataclysm has desolated the whole world. Hence we may look with some confidence to a future of great length. And as natural selection works solely by and for the good of each being, all corporeal and mental endowments will tend to progress to perfection."[9]

Thus evolutionary science joined geological science to provide a conception of an ancient world with an indefinite future in which evolutionary advance toward a more and more elevated destiny seemed built into its inner mechanism. In this fashion, the process of progress before and during the nineteenth century cleared the decks for the triumph of the Idea of Progress.

TECHNOLOGY, INVENTION, AND MATERIAL ADVANCES

Cleared the decks, but hardly assured that triumph. In fact, on logical grounds, it would not take any exceptionally gifted mind to recognize that the "perfection" achieved through natural selection might have very little to do with human well-being. Witness the perfection of the cockroach, or worse, some especially hardy and virulent strain of bacteria. Further, evolution at best was excruciatingly slow. To become a general article of faith, the Idea of Progress required much more rapid change, and change more specifically directed toward human welfare.

Science again provided the ultimate groundwork for such a faith since it soon became clear that scientific advance proceeded at a far more rapid rate—indeed, by previous standards, a dizzying rate—than evolutionary, biological change. Further, the essential characteristics of science suggested that things in general would tend to get better and better over time. Science was clearly cumulative in nature, leading to the widespread view among eighteenth- and nineteenth-century intellectuals that since the future can build on the past, the later is almost always better than the earlier.[10]

From the point of view of the general acceptance of the Idea of Progress by the common man, however, much more significant was the embodiment of this cumulative knowledge in inventions—the steam engine, textile production, agricultural improvements, coal, iron, steel, railroads, ultimately electricity, the internal combustion engine, and on and on and on. All these led in due course to enormous general advances in living standards. "This evident material progress which continued incessantly," Bury noted in the early twentieth century, "has been a mainstay of the general belief in Progress which is prevalent today."[11] Indeed, insofar as any faith in Progress remains in our own period at the end of the twentieth century, most believers are likely to point to the succession of life-enhancing economic and technological advances that continue to revolutionize our material standards of living. Similarly, loss of faith in Progress today is often substantiated (though never more than partially) by the claim that median family incomes are no longer rising, the middle class is losing ground, the poor are multiplying, and only the rich continue to prosper.

However, before considering those often-heard laments of today's critics—a subject for later discussion—we must note in advance that there is almost certainly a basic difference in societal attitudes toward material improvements at the beginning of the process of progress as compared to later on in conditions of greater affluence. This is not necessarily a difference in the intensity of the desire for material advance. There is strong historical evidence that the desire for "more" tends to increase *pari passu* with the provision of "more." Whether demand ("wants") grows more or less rapidly than supply (quantities of goods and services) over time is a matter of debate, not easily determined from the factual record.

What does seem fairly certain, however, is that the character of "wants" changes over time; in particular that they tend to go from the more simple to the more complex. On the very first page of *The Affluent Society*, John Kenneth Galbraith notes a crucial difference between the aspirations of the rich and those of the poor: "The poor man has always a precise view of his problem and its remedy: he hasn't enough and he needs more. The rich man can assume or imagine a much greater variety of ills and he will be correspondingly less certain of their remedy."[12] When "wants" involve very basic "needs"—food, clothing, shelter, elementary protections against disease and death—there is, at a minimum, a much greater simplicity of one's desire for "more." Since the process of progress promises to meet these basic needs, and through large-scale, mass-production methods that can reach a very large proportion of the whole population, it is easy in the early stages of the process to believe that the direction of future change is unambiguously toward the "better." Indeed, it is very probably for this reason that in today's poor societies making the move from underdevelopment to development, interest in and faith in Progress often remains far more vigorous than it does in the economically advanced nations of the West.

In short, in its early stages, the process of progress provides strong evidence of improvements in standards of living in directions that few (if any) members of society regard as anything but highly beneficial. During this period, the Idea of Progress seems almost self-evidently valid. Later on, it will turn out that even the definition of "beneficial" change is subject to dispute and uncertainty.

INCREASING MASTERY OF NATURE

Another feature of the scientific and technological advance embodied in the process of progress that is likely to have an especially great impact on ideology in the early stages of development is the implicit promise of greater and greater human control over the forces of nature. Intrinsic to the entire modern scientific enterprise has always been the view that there are laws of nature that humans can comprehend and use to their advantage. Thus, instead of being a pawn in nature's hands, subject to her perpetual and changing whims, mankind is able to study nature's methods and operations and, through this study, learn to master or at the very least defend against her frequent onslaughts.

The reason that this aspect of the process of progress was so important at the early stages of the process is that preindustrial society was so obviously and in many cases devastatingly rocked by those natural onslaughts. I have spoken, correctly I believe, about the relatively static long-run conditions in the preindustrial world. Certainly as measured by rates of population growth, rises in output per capita, speed of transportation, rates of urbanization, and the like, this generalization holds.

Comparatively static long-run conditions are, however, consistent with very considerable short-term instability. In point of fact, premodern European life was assaulted by all sorts of particular events and changes which could not be accounted for by traditional methods and institutions nor by syllogistic reasoning from universal principles. Miracle, mystery, providence, fate, fortune, and other agencies incomprehensible to the secular mind had to be called on to account for the unpredictable flow of actual day-to-day and year-to-year events.[13] And this flow was highly erratic.

Lawrence Stone's characterization is telling:

> It is now generally admitted that the life of premodern man was the very opposite of the life of security and stability depicted by nostalgic romantics. Both groups and individuals were under constant threat, at the mercy of the hazards of weather, fire, and disease, a prey to famines, pandemics, wars and other wholly unpredictable calamities. This insecurity produced a condition of acute anxiety, bordering at times on hysteria, and a desperate yearning for relief and reassurance.[14]

Stone goes on to point out that there are three ways in which man has attempted to remedy this problem: "He has tried to relieve the symptoms of his anxiety by recourse to magic, or by placing his confidence in the providence of God as revealed by religion; and he has tried to remove the causes of his anxiety by expanding his control over the environment through scientific and technological invention." This third method, clearly, was that introduced in a serious and pervasive way by the process of progress.

In a word, premodern man was under assault by both nature (pestilence, drought, earthquake, famine, infant mortality) and by man himself (wars, injustice, various forms of servitude). The process of progress, with its constant stream of new innovations and methods of production, brought at least a degree of order into this picture by diminishing the violence due to one of these assaults—those of nature. Disease and early death had been a devastating human companion through the ages. In the fourteenth century, the bubonic plague wiped out a third of the population of Europe. Infant mortality was always high and life expectancy at birth for the average European prior to the Industrial Revolution was probably no more than a half or a third of what it is today.[15] The prospect that, by more fully understanding the laws of nature, these dreadful onslaughts could be modified, and ultimately removed, could hardly fail to appeal to the human imagination. Was there any limit to the control over the future that this understanding and application of the laws of nature to human purposes could sustain?

Moreover, in the specific American context, this general appeal was further underlined by the very fact that, from the beginning, and well into the eighteenth and nineteenth centuries, man was in effect pitted against the wilderness. In the harsh New England landscape with its rock-strewn, overgrown soils and its brutal winters, how would nature appear other than as a significant adversary? Conditions for the early pioneer families as they moved westward were hardly an improvement. In short, nature in those days posed huge challenges and difficulties. For that reason, subduing, controlling, and using nature for human advancement was a necessary precondition for the Idea of Progress to flourish. And this precondition the underlying process of progress appeared amply, and increasingly, to provide.

THE PROBLEM OF MORALITY

The obvious joker in the picture was mankind. For premodern society was clearly in danger not just from nature but from assaults from humans themselves. Stone mentions "wars" among his premodern calamities. Huizinga's well-known description of the pessimism of fourteenth-century Europe involved, beside the cruelty and unpredictability of nature ("scarcity, misery, and pestilence"), the barbarous misbehavior of man ("bad government, exactions, the cupidity of the great, wars and brigandage").[16] Furthermore, when the process of progress did begin to emerge on the scene in eighteenth-century Britain, the human assaults on various groups in the society were, or seemed to many to be, far more cruel and devastating than had been known in, or at least been characteristic of, the past. The middle classes may have been flourishing but what of the poor? For that matter, what of the increasingly displaced landed aristocracy?

Finally, and very important for our purposes, one has to recognize that increased human mastery over the forces of nature implies, in and of itself, a transfer of increasing powers to human beings. In a certain sense, what nature loses in terms of disruptive impact, mankind potentially gains. The future course of the society will more and more hinge on what human beings do with their newfound powers. Human behavior—in effect, human morality—always important, now becomes decisive.

Central to the argument of this book, this point needs substantial elaboration even at this stage of the proceedings. The basic claim is the following:

> In the nineteenth and early twentieth centuries, both Britain and the United States witnessed a massive effort by society to shape individual morality and social institutions in such a way that the changes unleashed by the newfound powers of human beings could be channeled into a restricted, predictable, and desirable direction. Capital "P" Progress meant not just any future development but development specifically along certain morally approved lines. The Idea of Progress is ultimately a moral concept, given real meaning only when the morality that defines "Progress" is understood. When thus channeled, and only then, does the process of progress give clear support and confirmation for the Idea of Progress.

The following points, some of which will be discussed in more detail later, are relevant here:

1. There was, from the very beginning of the Industrial Revolution, an awareness of the basically disruptive features of the process of progress. The benign view embedded in the Idea of Progress was by no means universal. The Luddite riots of 1811 and 1812 which "spread terror throughout the industrial Midlands" were only extreme examples of the anxiety felt by workingmen who, threatened by the new industrial system, wreaked their vengeance on the new machinery that was costing them their jobs. All through the late eighteenth and early nineteenth centuries, the British Parliament was "flooded with petitions" to prevent the use of the new textile machinery—Cartwright's combing machine, mechanical shearing, the gig mill, and other innovations in both the cotton and woollen industries.[17] Whether the workers hated the machinery most, or the factory system in which the machinery was increasingly installed, it is clear that the advent of the process of progress brought new possibilities of unemployment and also an increased sense of powerlessness to many groups in society. Not only were fellow men the source of a new coercion, but even nature was, in some respects, more formidable than before. Urbanization was frequently characterized by highly unsanitary living conditions, the rampant communication of disease, and, in many cases, actual declines in life expectancies.

2. Although the rising middle classes escaped much of this disruption and uncertainty and could much more easily approve of what was going on, they were also on the whole keenly aware of the dangers, and in fact positive evils, of industrialization. The rearing of children in nineteenth-century America actually reveals a curious love-hate relationship with the process of progress. In chapter 4, we discussed how the entire public school movement was infused with the Idea of Progress. Also, the lessons that were taught—the three R's obviously, but also the need for disciplined hard work, the importance of saving one's pennies, building for the future, and the like—were clearly and positively related to fostering the process of progress. American children were unequivocally taught that the United States was to be admired as the most advanced, technologically accomplished nation in the world.[18]

However, they were also taught that the only really good life was to be found in simple, rural circumstances. One would have thought that to achieve any kind of real independence and peace of mind, one would have to be a farmer, surrounded by fresh air, open fields, chickens, pigs, and cattle. The pastoral, natural, unspoiled life was to be preferred above all. By contrast, the world of cities, factories, money, commerce and even striving *too* hard for success—the world that the process of progress was rapidly creating on all sides—was clearly suspect, and very probably perilous to the soul. In a word, the process of progress was both praised and warned against in the same breath! Beware of temptation, children were effectively taught! Don't be seduced by the lures and easy promises of urban living! Keep things simple, restrained, and on an even keel!

3. This acknowledgment of the problems and potential evils of the process of progress really reflected a growing awareness that the process involved increasing power in the hands of mankind and that, in order to secure the better and more ample future that the new technology also promised, it was essential that human beings be brought under control. One way to do this was through instilling in every child who could be reached either through home or school a very strict code of moral behavior. In America in the nineteenth century, the teachers of this code were the women, and the main objects of their teaching the men and boys. In effect, there were really two codes to be imparted: one was the behavior to be expected of those who were exercising the new powers

that the process of progress had afforded—they were expected to behave in a self-restrained, honorable, gentlemanly way even in their crudest commercial dealings; the other was the behavior to be expected of those who bore the brunt of the disruptions of the new order—they were to avoid envy, resentment, and, above all, crime, liquor, and licentious women.

4. As the nineteenth century wore on, this effort to instill a rather rigid personal morality—Victorian morality, as we now think of it—in all young men and boys (it was assumed that women, being far more moral than men by nature, needed much less guidance in such matters) was increasingly combined with efforts to plot a sure and certain moral course for society as a whole. The end of the nineteenth and beginning of the twentieth century in America was widely known as the "progressive era." By this time, the power of man to affect his environment was so evident and potentially threatening that society—and especially again, the women of society—couldn't take the chance that moral education in home and school would be sufficient to keep men on the straight and narrow path. Society itself must be reformed through expanded educational opportunities, abolition of child labor, temperance laws, and, of course, the extension of direct political power to the natural moral leaders of the nation through woman's suffrage.

5. The use of the term "progressive" in connection with these reforms is not coincidental but essential. For the Idea of Progress—which historians agree was virtually *the* dominating idea in turn of the century America—included this specific Victorian personal morality and increasingly this reformist social morality as part of its very definition, that is, as constituting an essential element of the "good thing" that the process of progress had been bestowing on a fortunate and grateful country and that it could be expected to bestow in even greater measure over a promising future. *The Idea of Progress was, in fact, a specific way of narrowing and limiting the choices and options increasingly opening up for mankind as a consequence of the process of progress.*

Victorian morality and reforms, on this interpretation, were responses to the threat that a free-wheeling, uncontrolled process of progress posed. They said, in effect, all this will work only if we take one clear-cut, definite, certifiable, morally appropriate path into the future. This is the path of capital "P" Progress. We must do this, for otherwise the new onrushing forces of change produce not a better future, but chaos.

6. At the turn of the century, America had in fact a remarkably consistent and self-contained view of life centered upon the Idea of Progress. A fixed morality strictly limited the acceptable range of the process of progress, reduced complex decision making to the application of a set of predetermined, well-defined rules of behavior, and effectively permitted the long-term time horizons so essential to that Idea. Even in a period of wrenching social and economic change, a vision of the distant future could be assured by placing strict limitations on acceptable attitudes, plans and behavior, constraining the process of progress within specific personal and social guidelines and, in effect, denying society and individuals within the society the new freedoms which the process of progress intrinsically makes available. The moral code was the key. It made very clear what the "good thing" that was Progress was, and also provided marching orders into the future, thus promising that this "good thing" would get better and better over the long and foreseeable years ahead.

7. Remarkably, for the better part of a century, this approach worked quite well. Despite the massive changes that were taking place in American society during and immediately after the Industrial Revolution took hold, personal behavior, all things considered, remained remarkably orderly and controlled. Here is what James Q. Wilson has written about the effects of Victorian morality in Britain and the United States at this historical juncture:

> During the nineteenth century . . . informal methods of control reached their greatest strength; we in the United States and Great Britain refer to these teachings as "Victorian morality." As applied to male behavior, that morality was, in essence, the code of the gentleman. . . . The requirements of gentlemanly behavior included everything from table manners and the obligation to play games fairly to one's responsibilities toward ladies and one's duty to country. So successful were these moral exhortations and codes of gentility that, so far as we can tell, both alcohol abuse and crime rates declined in England and America during a period—the second half of the nineteenth century—characterized by rapid urbanization, massive immigration, and the beginnings of industrialization.[19]

In the case of alcohol abuse, these informal methods of control, increasingly supported by legal restrictions, appear to have been extraordinarily effective. In 1855, long before national prohibition was enacted, numerous states already had adopted laws that in one way or another limited drinking. As James Collier notes, "Where 18th century Americans were drinking . . . six gallons of absolute alcohol annually . . . the figure for the second half of the 19th century was less than half that, despite the influx of millions of Irish and Germans with fairly heavy drinking patterns."[20]

Some of this reduced drinking has been attributed specifically to the process of progress, in that businessmen in the new industrial establishments required workers who would not show up on Monday mornings with hangovers, or indeed fail to show up altogether. But there was additionally a clear moral imperative being asserted here. The concept of a "straight and narrow path"—so suggestive of the entire Victorian approach to life—indicates not only what sobriety was to provide, but also what was required to keep the process of progress within fixed, determinable limits.

SUMMARY

In its early stages, the process of progress provided the raw materials from which the Idea of Progress could potentially be fashioned. Science showed humanity an ancient world, with a possibly limitless future, subject, moreover, to evolutionary changes that could easily, though not necessarily logically, be interpreted as grounds for optimism. More significant perhaps was the fruit of science in invention, innovation and technological change, which permitted the mass production of the necessities of life with the promise of ever-increasing abundance ahead. Further, growing mastery of the laws of nature put into human hands powers which previously had had mankind largely at their mercy. No longer merely a passive recipient of change, humanity could now, and increasingly as time went on, decisively affect the pattern of future change.

Ultimately, as we shall see in due course, this increased ability to decide, choose, opt for this alternative, then that, then both, then neither, this enormous human variability, when freed from external constraints, would pose very deep problems for the Idea of Progress. However, in nineteenth-century Britain and perhaps especially in America, the increasing range of choices implicit in the process of progress was gravely and and with quite remarkable effectiveness constrained by an imposing moral code. Control over the newly empowered human beings was quite as important as, and indeed was really required by, mankind's increasing control over the natural environment. Historian David Landes describes the Industrial Revolution generally as involving "what we may call a Faustian sense of mastery over man and nature."[21] Both components were needful. Not only physical nature, but human nature, had to be mastered if the Idea of Progress were ever to carry any real emotional weight.

This was the "Victorian solution," if you will. It worked quite well for a time, but not indefinitely. In our own age, it has broken down almost completely, a development that we must now start to trace with some care.

6

THE FIRST GREAT PREDICAMENT
OF PROGRESS

D uring the nineteenth and early twentieth centuries, there was, in America at least, a basic harmony between the process of progress and the Idea of Progress. We are not speaking of a logical connection here so much as an emotional, visceral, almost religious, connection. Most Americans of that era felt in their hearts that the present was better than the past and that the future would be better than the present. Furthermore, the future counted. That is, it mattered that one's children and heirs would have better, happier, more fulfilling lives than one had enjoyed. Building toward that better future was, in fact, an exciting life-project in the here and now, and, for some at least, provided something like the consolation once offered by thoughts of an otherworldly afterlife.

This happy connection of process and Idea was not, as I say, a necessary or logical one, and, as was shown in chapter 5, really depended upon a whole series of specific scientific discoveries and very particular mental and moral attitudes and practices. This means, also, that at all times, from the beginning of the process until today, the Idea was vulnerable and subject to qualification or outright rejection.

THE PREDICAMENTS OF PROGRESS

For one thing, it is quite clear that nature, however subject to human mastery and control in certain respects, is never fully so. Every hurricane, earthquake, volcanic eruption, or flood gives ample proof that when Mother Nature is sufficiently aroused her powers easily dwarf those of boastful human beings. Scientific research on such matters as the K-T extinctions also tends to confirm an underlying uneasiness about the ultimate duration of mankind's residence on earth, or elsewhere for that matter. In our day, science fiction depicting human migration to other planets and galaxies conveys both this sense of unease and also the slimness of the reed to which future solutions are attached.

Still, as indicated earlier, the real problem, both logically and viscerally, is less nature than man. The obvious question is: How can we be sure that man, as he masters nature, will also be able to master himself? Even in the Victorian period, as many subsequent critics have been happy to point out, hypocrisy often reigned supreme and actual observance of the lofty moral code frequently failed miserably.

More generally, history demonstrates time and again that human character is, to say the least, less than ideal from almost any conceivable moral vantage point. Every time that anyone decides that human beings are either basically good, or at least getting better over time, brute facts—indeed, brutal facts—intervene to cast a huge shadow over this sunny perception. There is little question that a major factor contributing to the beginning of serious doubts about the Idea of Progress in the early years of our own century was the pointless and horrible slaughter of men, women, and children in World War I. This event, as we shall indicate later, served as a kind of wake-up call in the Western world, rousing many from the dream of Progress that had so dominated the nineteenth century. Other horrors were, of course, to follow—World War II, the Holocaust, Korea, Vietnam, Biafra, Somalia, Rwanda, and "ethnic cleansing" in Bosnia.

However, when we are talking about matters of faith—and it is as a matter of general and widespread faith that the Idea of Progress is of interest to us—we have to be careful not to assume that bad news is, in itself, sufficient to undermine the beliefs of the faithful. For one thing, there is usually good news too, and the naturally optimistic, when sufficiently determined, can usually find a way to suggest that the balance tips at least slightly to the positive side of the scale. If man occasionally performs horrible deeds today, think of the unbelievably barbaric deeds he often performed in the past—slavery, serfdom, the suppression and sometimes mutilation of women, the denial of rights to minorities and, indeed, to the vast majority of common people, and so on. Would one really like to go back to those "good old days"?

'There is also the further fact that no believer in the Idea of Progress ever truly claimed that the upward trend was absolutely monotonic, with never the least deviation. Like the business cycle around the secular upward trend of GNP, so the actual course of human events in general may spiral up and down around that basically favorable long-run trend. Indeed, departures from that trend—even such horrors as World Wars I and II—can be looked upon as necessary learning periods, preparing the way for still higher levels of well-being to come, in this case a possible world in which world wars (if not "little" wars) have been effectively ruled out. For the determined believer, periods of suffering can thus always be viewed as stages paving the way toward some greater good.

All this may simply be taken to signify that when people want seriously to believe in something, they can almost always find rationalizations that will permit that belief to survive. In terms of our own analysis, however, it also signifies something further, namely, that loss of faith in an ideology like the Idea of Progress is likely to be caused by something more systematic than the occasional untoward event, however horrific. In particular, if it can be shown that the process of progress, by its own natural and intrinsic character, is inexorably weakening, undermining, or even totally destroying the foundations on which the Idea of Progress was built, then our explanation of the failure of that Idea will be far more convincing than one based on particular disasters.

This brings us, then, to the concept of the "predicaments of progress." As defined earlier (see page 7), such "predicaments" are said to exist when the process of progress creates conditions that in one way or another impede further progress and, more especially, tend to undermine one's faith in the Idea of Progress. The original example we considered was pollution. In the present chapter, I have suggested that world wars, made increasingly devastating by scientific advances, may have played an important role in undermining our faith in Progress. In this and future chapters in part 2, various other possible predicaments will be analyzed.

Before starting this analysis, however, one point should be mentioned and kept in the back of our minds throughout. It is that although the process of progress will prove very good at creating new and seemingly overwhelming problems, it is also very good at solving the problems it has itself created. This is why I have used the word "predicaments" as opposed to a harsher and more definitive-sounding word, like, say, "contradictions." In common usage, a predicament is a difficult problem but one from which it is at least theoretically possible to disentangle oneself. In the case of the process of progress, the very nature of that process, involving the application of reason, rationality, scientific method, and the like to whatever difficulties emerge, tends to be especially adept at finding ways to disentangle society from the messes it has itself created.

Thus, in most of the predicaments we will consider, we will find, I believe, that there are potential, though never airtight, ways around them. The process of progress may very well resolve them, but then again it may not. It is an uncertain future, rather than a doomed future, that is likely to be the biggest problem of all.

But this is taking us well ahead of the present stage of the analysis. Let us therefore return to where the last chapter had brought us, namely, to the early stages of the process of progress.

THE MALTHUSIAN PRINCIPLE

It was suggested in chapter 5 that the harmony between the process of progress and the Idea of Progress was never complete even in the relatively early stages of the process. The Industrial Revolution brought great social and economic dislocations whenever and wherever it was launched, Luddite and other protests against the introduction of machines and factories being but one example of what would prove to be vain efforts to turn back the clock.

But disbelief in the inevitability of Progress was by no means limited to the dispossessed or disaffected. Indeed, it is little exaggeration to say that such disbelief was characteristic of mainstream thought, at least of mainstream thought in the vital area of political economy, during much of the late eighteenth and early nineteenth centuries. The "first great predicament of progress," as I shall call it, was announced and codified by the British classical economists at the height of the Industrial Revolution. Indeed, this particular predicament, in a somewhat revised form, continues to attract heated attention to this very day. I refer here to the Malthusian population doctrine as presented in the first edition of his *Essay on the Principle of Population*, published in 1798.[1] In analyzing this doctrine and its subsequent variations, we can begin to see both how predicaments of progress can be generated and also how, in some cases, the threat they pose either to the process of progress or its Idea can be exaggerated.

Although we begin with the Malthusian statement of the problem, we shall be more directly concerned with the way in which the principle of population was embedded in classical economic theory through the works of David Ricardo in the early nineteenth century. The reason for this is that Malthus's doctrine was modified in later editions of the *Essay*. On this basis, Robert Nisbet, for example, includes Malthus as a "progress" author.[2] Even more important perhaps is the fact that, as Keynes remarked in a different context, Ricardo's theories conquered England "as completely as the Holy Inquisition conquered Spain."[3] Being a quite systematic writer, Ricardo presents the population principle within a more comprehensive, overall theory.

Malthus clearly should be cited first, however, if only because it was his *Essay* that so dramatically brought the population problem to the world's attention. Also, population problems even today are still often referred to as "Malthusian" problems. Further, and more to the point of this analysis, it is possible to draw two important lessons directly from Malthus's work.

The first lesson is that the population problem was, from the beginning, conceived explicitly as an attack on the Idea of Progress, specifically in Malthus's case on the notion of the perfectibility of man. As is well known, the *Essay* was written as a response to Malthus's father in a controversy over the doctrines of William Godwin and other proponents of a progressive view, such as Condorcet. Godwin had written that man was perfectible in the sense not that he "could be brought to perfection" (implying an end to the process), but in the sense of "being continually made better and receiving perpetual improvement." Thus, "every perfection of excellence that human beings are competent to conceive, human beings, unless in cases that are palpably and unequivocally excluded by the structure of their frames, are competent to obtain."[4] Unassisted, human beings clearly cannot jump fifty feet into the air; apart from such feats, however, very little else is ultimately denied them. Malthus rejects this sense of the "unlimited improvement" of man as "not applicable to man under the present laws of his nature." In fact, it is the limit imposed by human nature that ultimately prevents the process of progress from working any beneficial effect on "the most important part of the human race."[5]

The second lesson that becomes clear from the early Malthusian version of the population principle is that it is the process of progress that creates the problem that ultimately defeats the process—that is, that the problem is a predicament of progress in the sense we are using the term. The difficulty arises because of the discrepancy between two famous ratios. Food supply, through increased labor and agricultural improvements, can be expected to grow at a maximum at an "arithmetic" rate: 1, 2, 3, 4, 5, . . . During the same period, however, population growth can easily expand at a "geometric" rate: 1, 2, 4, 8, 16, . . . Since it is the increase in food production that makes possible the growth in population, we can regard the latter as a human response to the process of progress. It is human nature, when the means are available, to have as many children as possible; more food makes possible the increased survival of children and also encourages earlier marriages and higher fertility. The predicament arises because the ensuing population growth quickly swallows up all gains and reduces the mass of population to the subsistence level again.

"Progress," with its clear implication of improving living standards, can occur for a time. But ultimately—and, if we take the geometric ratios seriously, very quickly—the advance is defeated. Nothing has been gained.

THE RICARDIAN CODIFICATION

David Ricardo treats the population response to the process of progress within his general economic theory as presented in his *On the Principles of Political Economy and Taxation,* the third edition of which appeared in 1821.[6] We can summarize this part of his theory as follows:

A country's population is treated, like any other "commodity," through a supply and demand analysis. This population, apart from relatively small numbers of capitalists and landlords, is composed of laborers and their families. The "natural" wage of labor—what we might today call its "equilibrium" wage and what the classical authors often called a "subsistence"" wage—is that at which the supply and demand for labor are equated. At this wage, the country's population will be stationary.

Introduce now the process of progress through, let us say, technological improvements in agriculture, which increase labor productivity in the production of food and other necessaries. At a given wage rate, there is a larger gap in real terms between output and wage, increasing the profit margin for the capitalists who employ the labor. Their profits increased, the capitalists strive to hire more laborers—thus, the demand for labor goes up. This demand is, in the first instance, frustrated, because the population (and the number of laborers available) is unchanged. Hence this increased demand simply goes into raising the wage-rate. In particular, it raises it above the "natural" or "subsistence" level.

The Malthusian principle now comes into play. Better wages mean higher living standards, earlier marriages, an increased desire for children, better survival rates for children, better survival rates for mothers during their childbearing years—in short, rapid population growth. This population growth has the effect of increasing labor supply, and bidding the wages of labor back down again.

We cannot return to the status quo ante, however, because of a crucial economic principle: the law of diminishing returns. The larger population forces us to use increasingly inferior lands or to use existing land more intensively. In either case, we have a factor that in effect counteracts the improved productivity due to the agricultural improvements. Essentially because of the given human response to higher living standards, wages tend almost irresistibly to return to the subsistence level, and capitalists, forced to use increasingly inferior land, find their profits squeezed as well. The only group in society that really benefits from the exercise are the landowners whose land, because of the increased pressure from a larger population, tends to rise in value over time.

Ricardo summarizes his conclusions as follows:

> The natural tendency of profits then is to fall; for, in the progress of society and wealth, the additional quantity of food required is obtained by the sacrifice of more and more labour. This tendency, this gravitation as it were of profits, is happily checked at repeated intervals by the improvements in machinery, connected with the production of necessaries, as well as by discoveries in the science of agriculture which enable us to relinquish a portion of labour before required, and therefore to lower the price of the prime necessity of labour.

Unfortunately, however, these effects are "limited," and in the long run, "the very low rate of profits will have arrested all accumulation, and almost the whole produce of the country, after paying the labourers, will be the property of the owners of land and the receivers of tithes and taxes."[7]

Since these landowning receivers of tithes and taxes contribute little or nothing to the process of progress in the Ricardian world, the "natural" end of this entire development is a stationary state. The country's population will have reached "its highest point," and the process of progress will effectively be over.

HOW THE FIRST GREAT PREDICAMENT WAS RESOLVED

In fairness to both Malthus and Ricardo, one must recognize that, in each case, the analysis just presented was modified in one way or another. In the case of Malthus, as already indicated, later editions of the *Essay* gave increased emphasis to the possibility that human nature might not be quite as inflexible an obstacle to advance as previously advertised. Thus, in the second edition (1803), he gives special emphasis to the preventive check of "moral restraint." In contrast to the positive checks (famine, starvation, general misery), man also has a "distinctive superiority in his reasoning faculties, which enables him to calculate distant consequences." Thus, instead of his earlier view that the "passion between the sexes" is likely to remain unchanged, he now allows that, anticipating these distant consequences, many persons will refrain "from pursuing the dictate of nature in an early attachment to one woman."[8]

Ricardo is also more flexible in his outlook than the bare-bones representation of his theory would suggest. Thus, while he can state in one part of his discussion that "no point is better established, than that the supply of labourers will always ultimately be in proportion to the means of supporting them," he can at other points suggest that the natural wage is wholly a matter of habit and custom and, furthermore, that it can vary from country to country and even over time in the same country. If the natural wage really is conventionally determined and can vary over time, then the ground is ultimately laid for a genuine theory of capital "P" Progress, not too unlike that of the much maligned William Godwin. For when people can calculate "distant consequences," and change their attitudes and behaviors accordingly, then any predicament of progress relying on the basic constancy of those attitudes and behaviors tends to evaporate into thin air.

And, of course, this is what happened in the specific case of the population problem as witnessed in the context in which both Malthus and Ricardo conceived it—that is, in what we today call the developed countries. Actually, two things happened. First, the actual rate of invention, innovation, and technological advance clearly exceeded the Malthus-Ricardo vision by a huge margin. It would have been inconceivable to them that the developed countries of the world today could produce mountainous quantities of food with, in many cases, no more than a very small percentage of the population engaged in farming at all, and this after unprecedentedly rapid population growth during the nearly two centuries since they wrote. Diminishing returns, their nemesis, were simply and unequivocally routed by the process of progress.

The second point is even more interesting: namely, that human attitudes and behavior did change notably in the course of this process, and nowhere more strikingly than in the very area of reproduction that so concerned them. For a variety of reasons, many of which we have already discussed (see above, pages 75–76), families in the progressing societies of the Western world, including the United States, determined purposefully and self-consciously to have fewer and fewer children over time. The drop in fertility in the United States from seven or eight children per woman two centuries ago to two or less today represents as profound an alteration in human behavior as one could wish for. Not only did fertility rates fall below any biological or near-biological maximum, as suggested by an unchanging "passion between the sexes," but they frequently—and in Europe characteristically—have dipped below replacement levels. To take an extreme case, Italy in 1993 showed a fertility rate 30 or 40 percent below replacement level and an actually declining total population.

This second point is particularly interesting for two reasons. One is that the change in attitudes and behavior involved in this massive fertility decline is not to be thought of as fortuitous or incidental to the process of progress but rather as an integral part of it. Thus, when historian David Landes wishes to cite an example of the characteristic features of modernization ("rationality, and . . . a Faustian sense of mastery over man and nature"), his main example is precisely European success in population control: "This is evidence presumably of self-restraint—an effort to restrict commitments to means—and as such is an excellent example of rationality in a particularly crucial and sensitive area of life.''[9] The same scientific, rational, innovative, manipulative frame of mind that permits man to master and use the laws of nature to human advantage also permits him to calculate the consequences of his own behavior and that of others around him. As always, of course, such calculations necessarily involve the future. In this case, the Idea of Progress—with its elevation of the claims of the future—clearly acts to facilitate the process of progress. As suggested earlier, the interaction between process and Idea often goes in both directions.

The other way in which this resolution of the Malthus-Ricardo dilemma is interesting is through its suggestion that the process of progress may in the long run survive its predicaments only through human intervention. That is to say, the search for any analysis of the process such that its continuation is independent of human choices and decisions seems very likely to be vain. The basic reason that the Western world was able to escape the Malthusian problem was that individuals chose to behave in certain ways and not in other ways. His telling phrase is "moral restraint," thus hinting at our own suggestion that the Idea of Progress does intrinsically involve some kind of self-limiting morality.

In one respect, this emphasis on human choice and decision making is comforting. It strongly suggests that when the always available prophets of doom (such as some we will discuss in the next two chapters) conclude that there is no way out of forthcoming disasters—no way out except by abandoning the process of progress—they will often have failed properly to account for the human ability to adjust to new circumstances, to invent new possibilities, and thus to stave off the supposedly "inevitable" outcome.

In another respect, this emphasis on choice is far less comforting, at least to believers in the Idea of Progress. For it places an ever-growing weight on the quality of human decisions, decisions that, over time, become increasingly numerous and complex. Indeed, as we shall see, the very attributes of the process of progress that enable it to resolve particular predicaments—as it did in fact resolve the Malthusian predicament in the Western world—may be the source of its underlying, general, and very probably most difficult, predicament.

IS THE POPULATION PREDICAMENT REALLY RESOLVED?

Before continuing with the overall development of our argument, however, we should focus our attention at least briefly on the present state of the population problem. It is obvious that many observers, considering especially what is going on in the Third World, believe that unchecked population growth constitutes the main, and very possibly decisive, obstacle to the initiation of the process of progress in the developing countries, and, for that matter, to its future continuation in the developed countries. Whether this should be considered a belated tribute to Malthus, who envisaged a very different situation, is problematic. As Nobel laureate George Stigler once observed: "It is an odd theory that may not some day and somewhere find a role; for every answer one can find a correct question."[10]

Still, there is a clear family resemblance between the Malthusian positive checks of famine and misery and the predictions of certain twentieth-century observers. Here is the assessment given by Dr. Paul R. Ehrlich in his book, *The Population Bomb*, which sold two million copies in the decade following its first publication in 1968:

> The battle to feed all humanity is over. In the 1970s and 1980s hundreds of millions of people will starve to death in spite of any crash programs embarked upon now. At this late date nothing can prevent a substantial increase in the world death rate, although many lives could be saved through dramatic programs to "stretch" the carrying capacity of the earth by increasing food production and providing for more equitable distribution of whatever food is available. . . . So far most of the evidence seems to be on the side of the pessimists.[11]

Has the population problem, like a virus we thought we had eliminated, mutated into some new, especially virulent and progress-resistant form, such that this time mankind is truly at its mercy? Is it, in fact, the fundamental predicament that is already undermining the Idea of Progress and will soon undo the process as well?

No one, of course, can be sure of the answer. The question is, however, important and deserves (as do the other predicaments we will be discussing) at least a clear statement of my own position. The following five points are relevant:

1. *Formally, the modern population problem can be regarded as a predicament of progress.*

Since the modern population explosion in the developing countries resulted from contact with Western technology, especially in the fields of medicine and public health, it can be regarded as created by the process of progress in at least an indirect sense. The main initiating factors were sharply falling death rates due to Western health technology combined with traditionally high birthrates. In the absence of the process of progress in the West, it is evident that no such explosive population growth would have taken place in the Third World, certainly not within the present time frame.

2. *Although similar in some respects to the Malthus-Ricardo predicament, present-day population problems differ substantially in other ways.*

As Ehrlich suggests in *The Population Bomb,* some contemporary commentators still worry about population pressures in terms of starvation, limited land resources, and the ultimate inability of the planet to feed such vast numbers of people. This is in line of descent from the Malthus-Ricardo approach. In point of fact, as I will suggest in chapter 8, concerns about population growth today are more commonly focused elsewhere, especially on the external effects of GNP growth, to which population growth is only one and by no means the main contributor. Pollution and resource depletion are the characteristic concerns here, concerns that, if anything, apply even more to the developed world (where population growth is now minimal) than to the developing world. Even if we restrict ourselves for the moment to the problem of population pressures on food supplies—that is, to a Malthus-Ricardo-style population problem—we have to recognize a very significant difference in this modern predicament. Homegrown development as it occurred in the West was accompanied not only by medical-public health progress but also by a vast range of other changes, including rising living standards and those attitudes of rationality, interest in controlling and changing the environment, and so on, that we have frequently referred to. Many have in fact argued that the conscious decision to control population growth through lowered birthrates was in fact part and parcel of this more general process. When the process of progress is imported from abroad—and especially when only some *parts* of the process are so imported—it is by no means clear on theoretical grounds that the Western resolution of the earlier population problem will be applicable to the version of the problem facing poor countries today. It can be argued in principle that the present form of the predicament is far more intractable than its prior form.

3. *In point of fact, Third World countries, on average, have shown more rapid economic advance during the period of their population explosions than in any earlier period.*

This conclusion applies both to food production per capita and to output per capita in general. Clearly, there are important exceptions—sub-Saharan Africa is a case in point, in many instances a tragic case in point. Furthermore, no one claims—or at least only a few claim—that there is any causal relationship between rapid population growth and consequent increases in output per capita. Still, the predicted arrival of mass starvation in the huge population centers of the Third World has not materialized. What *has* happened in the post-World War II era (the era of the population explosion) has been "unprecedented growth in national output and the value of output available per person in poor countries" and, from an economic point of view, "the best period in history for people in the poor countries of the world."[12] If it is true that the Malthusian version of the population problem has "the dubious honor of receiving from history one of the most emphatic refutations any prominent economic theory has ever received,"[13] the recent predictions of imminent mass starvation among the billions of people in Third World nations would seem to be serious competitors for this same honor. Unanalyzed facts in themselves prove nothing. Still, facts *are* facts, and not unimportant in these matters.

4. *Fertility rates are beginning to fall in many developing countries, in some cases far more rapidly than they did at comparable stages of Western development.*

This is another important fact. As is fairly obvious, in the long run the only solution to population problems in the developing countries is lowered birth rates and ultimate cessation of population growth. Compound interest is so powerful that even rather small annual percentage increases (1 or 2 percent per year) lead to astronomical-size populations over sufficiently long periods of time.[14] Fortunately, there is by now considerable evidence that such reductions in fertility are beginning to occur, and on a significant scale. In a study of thirty-seven poor countries (not including China), Lloyd Reynolds found that birthrates declined in thirty-five over the period 1960 to 1980 (the two exceptions being in Africa).[15] China—the largest of the developing countries with well over a billion people—has practiced what many in the West fear are overly stringent policies to reduce the birthrate. Estimates are that her annual rate of population growth fell from 2.6 percent in 1962–73 to 1.1 percent in 1985. Some analysts predict that because the problem is such an obvious one, and since governments now frequently and explicitly promote family planning, birthrates will keep falling rapidly and that the population explosion will, indeed, prove to be a "transient phenomenon."[16]

> 5. *The world population explosion can be seen as an important argument for promoting, rather than limiting, the process of progress.*

This fifth point is quite important in relation to the general argument of this book. What it claims is that today's population explosion, though in its indirect and complex way a result of the process of progress, is not likely to be further intensified by that process. Indeed, if anything, it is only through the continuation of that process that a resolution of the problem is likely to take place. In his study, Reynolds found that the developing countries that were making the most rapid economic progress were also the countries experiencing the most rapid (and in some cases very rapid) declines in birth rates. Richard Easterlin and Eileen Crimmins concluded, again with respect to the developing world, "that the process of socioeconomic modernization that lies behind the increased growth rates both of population and per capita income is also operating to bring about fertility reduction." The process of progress, which creates the problem also, it would appear, holds the key to its solution.

Needless to say, no one can ever know in a specific case whether particular solutions will or will not work. However, in terms of attitudes toward the process of progress—and, specifically, with respect to the Idea of Progress—it is very important to know whether reasonable resolutions of any given problem require limitations on, cessations of, or even significant reversals of the process of progress, or whether, on the contrary, the better bet is to continue on the modern path and even to attempt to promote it more vigorously. These questions are not limited to the population problem, and they are definitely not new. When the first worker in the modern era was replaced by a labor-saving machine, the issue became immediately explicit: do you fight the machine to save the job or do you argue that, in the long run—in that always significant path to the future lying ahead of us—there will be both more jobs and more output if such machines are introduced? In one case, you limit, in the other you try to accelerate, the process of progress.

In making such a decision—a decision that ultimately rests on faith since one can never actually know what the future holds—one is also very likely deciding for or against the Idea of Progress. Thus, whether any given predicament of progress seems likely to be aggravated, or potentially relieved or even solved, by further progress is a key to the future of the Idea of Progress. In the case of the first great predicament of progress, the believers in Progress were justified and the doubters clearly rebutted by historical experience. Although different in many respects, the present version of the population problem seems likely to share the same fate.

At a minimum, we can conclude from this discussion that population problems, past or present, provide no really convincing evidence that the process of progress is fatally flawed and that, on that account, the Idea of Progress must be abandoned. For the source of any waning of our faith in that Idea, therefore, we must pursue our search elsewhere.

7

A "HORRIBLE CAPACITY FOR MASS ANNIHILATION"

An ancient and unchanging "passion between the sexes" was the central roadblock on the path of progress in the original Malthusian version of the population predicament. Human nature was at fault.[1]

Human nature is also at fault—or deemed to be at fault—in the group of predicaments of progress I will consider in this and the following chapter. Collectively, this group of predicaments might be labeled "Doomsday" predicaments, and we shall discuss them roughly in the order in which they have attracted public attention in the Western world during the course of this century. They are, in brief: war, resource depletion, and pollution. In this chapter, I will focus on the problems posed by the development of instruments of mass destruction; in Chapter 8, we will turn to resource and pollution problems.

While these "Doomsday predicaments" share some common features with the original population predicament, they also differ from it in important ways. In the case of the Malthus-Ricardo problem, if the process of progress—especially in the specific form of improvements in agricultural technology—is rapid enough, then the tendency of wages to rise and the standard of living to improve can be sustained over very long periods of time, perhaps indefinitely, even in the absence of basic attitudinal changes. In the case of war, resource depletion, and pollution, however, the process of progress, through the development of massively more powerful technologies over time, would appear to magnify rather than offset what were originally far more limited problems. The same technological advance that enables us to feed ourselves with vanishing percentages of our labor force—thus helping to solve the first great predicament of progress—also gives us the power to destroy the human race, to plunder the earth of its fossil fuels, and to create havoc in the planet's ecosphere. The very tools of progress which help meliorate one problem are the creators, or at least significant amplifiers, of others.

Thus, the changes in human attitudes and behaviors required to resolve the predicaments considered in this and the next chapter may be even greater than those required in the case of population problems. Our discussion in the following analysis will be largely confined to the effect of these "Doomsday predicaments" on the fortunes of the Idea of Progress. This discussion, in turn, involves two main questions: (1) Is the process of progress, in the future, likely to meliorate these problems or simply to intensify them even further? Is our best bet to place our faith in future progress, or is our only recourse to halt the process, or at least to try to slow it down significantly before it is too late? (2) Can a waning faith in the Idea of Progress, such as appears to be so common today, properly be attributed to any or all of the Doomsday predicaments?. This is not basically a logical question, but an empirical, psychological question. Are we losing faith because of the bomb? The energy crisis? The greenhouse effect? All three together? Or is a deeper and more complex psychological mechanism involved? That further possibility we consider in chapters 9 and 10.

THE SHOCK OF GLOBAL WARS

There seems little doubt that the first truly major challenge to the Idea of Progress in the twentieth century was the outbreak of World War I. The challenge was particularly severe because it took place in a context where there was an increasing faith that humanity and society could be so shaped and molded as to bring greater happiness, freedom, dignity, and equality to all. By the end of the nineteenth century in the United States, and throughout the then-developed world, there was widespread recognition of the fact that, as man's control over nature had increased, the importance of controlling man himself had also increased.

At that very time, as already mentioned, America was embarking on a series of major experiments to achieve the required changes in human attitudes through widespread public education, agitation for temperance legislation, crusades for women's rights, regulation of business through the Sherman Act and other laws, attempts to limit and ultimately eliminate child labor, and so on. During the Progressive Era, faith in the adaptability, malleability, and above all improvement of human nature was at its height and formed, for many, a clear psychological basis for the Idea of Progress.

And then came the Great War with its horrendous destruction, not only of the flower of European manhood, but of millions of innocents, a war begun not so much by inevitable historical forces as by nearly accidental circumstances magnified by monumental miscalculations, but a war that nevertheless revealed so-called civilized man to be very much the same bloodthirsty, aggressive, barbaric destroyer as the hordes of Genghis Khan or the pillagers of ancient Rome. The only difference, of course, was that modern societies now had guns, artillery, tanks, aeroplanes, and bombs at their disposal. And with much more devastating weaponry predictably on the way!

Although it was possible for a time to believe that the war itself might be simply one more—if rather painful—agent for reform, this faith was quickly challenged by the obvious weaknesses of the Versailles Treaty and the League of Nations, and, within a very short time, by the apparent readiness of Europe to prepare for and launch a still greater war and to commit even more barbaric atrocities on the human race than those of just a quarter of a century earlier.[2] Technological "progress" could now be used by the leaders of the most theoretically advanced countries to control people's minds (propaganda through the radio and other forms of mass media), to transport and scientifically exterminate people by the millions (the Holocaust, Stalin's purges), to incinerate cities and vast civilian populations (from London and Coventry to Dresden and Tokyo), and, finally, to create weapons and delivery systems capable of directly destroying most of the world's population or indirectly rendering the planet unfit for human habitation (Hiroshima, the hydrogen bomb, ICBMs, the whole present and projected array of space-based technologies, and the like).

Ironically, the near-term ending of the world predicted by the medievalists and the early Protestant reformers could now logically make a respectable comeback. The vast extension of future time required as a basis for the Idea of Progress was arguably to be cut short by the process of progress itself. The Doomsday Clock began to approach "midnight." Serious scientists could predict the coming of Armageddon, not only as a possibility, but as a "statistical certainty."[3]

What particularly fueled this depressing view was the fact that, no sooner had World War II ended, than an even deeper national, now "superpower," rivalry emerged. Hitler could be regarded as an anachronism, a throwback, a genetic mutant. But the post-World War II rivalry was between two vast and well-articulated ideologies, each proclaiming itself the wave of the future, each intent on destroying the other, each, in fact, specifically regarding the other as "evil." Was it any wonder that people on both sides of the Iron Curtain began building bomb shelters—fruitless gestures in a world soon to be consumed by its own technological virtuosity.

THE COMPLICATED RELATIONSHIP BETWEEN PROGRESS AND WAR

But it didn't happen. World War III didn't happen. The new instruments of mass destruction have not been used. Furthermore, if they are used in the future, it will be in a far different context from the one in which apprehensions about their employment were originally entertained. The specifically ideological conflict between the two rival superpowers is now over. The Soviet Union no longer exists. Russia and the United States are, for the moment, cooperating in relative harmony and (admittedly tentative) friendship. Logically, there were far more preconditions for World War III (accidents, miscalculations, provocations, specific acts of aggression, inherently incompatible philosophies, and actual combat) than there had been for World War I or even, arguably, for World War II, but, in fact, the conflict didn't come and the circumstances making that conflict seem virtually unavoidable have largely evaporated.[4]

All this suggests that the relationship between the continuation of the process of progress and the greater or lesser likelihood of massively destructive future wars is far more complicated than a simple statement of this particular predicament would suggest. Let us turn now to the first question mentioned above: Is the process of progress likely to meliorate or intensify our future problems in this area? The following four points, not all of which tend in the same direction, seem relevant:

1. *Historically speaking, it is possible, or at least it has sometimes been argued, that war was a stimulus to the process of progress under certain conditions.*

Some years ago, W. W. Rostow remarked that wars occasionally "accelerated the development of new technology relevant to the peacetime economy and shifted the political and social framework in ways conducive to peacetime growth."[5] Rostow also suggested that a "reactive nationalism" has been a usual precondition for economic development. Thus past wars or threats of foreign domination were seen as helping to precipitate the "take-offs," as he called them, in Germany, Russia, Japan, and even to some degree in modern China.

Stretching matters a bit, one could even argue that in the case of the United States, World War II, by enabling the country to emerge from the Great Depression, paved the way for the extraordinary growth spree that occurred after the war. This is apart from the possible technological advances of a military nature, like the atom bomb itself, which had at least some favorable peacetime side effects.

More generally, the claim has been made that the process of progress, like the underlying process of biological evolution, of which it is sometimes regarded as the cultural equivalent, is basically a matter of competition among different groups with the natural outcome being the "survival of the fittest." It is understandable that the author of that particular phrase (nineteenth-century philosopher and sociologist, Herbert Spencer), should have regarded war as a central instrument by which societies in the past had progressed.[6] In his *Principles of Sociology*, Spencer wrote: "We must recognize the truth that struggles for existence between societies have been instrumental for their evolution. Neither the consolidation and re-consolidation of small groups into large ones; nor the organization of such compound and doubly-compound groups; nor the concomitant development of those aids to a higher life which civilization has brought; would have been possible without inter-tribal and inter-national conflicts."[7]

Actually, Spencer believed that in the future, human nature would improve to the degree that industrial progress would lead not to war but to peace. "Evil and immorality" would "disappear," and the "ultimate development of the ideal man (was) logically certain."[8]

In point of fact, many historians reject the idea that the process of progress was in any serious way facilitated by war even in the past. In his classic study, *War and Human Progress*, John U. Nef found very little evidence that war was ever a positive factor promoting human progress, and a good deal of evidence to suggest that its negative impacts were often massive. At the same time, moreover, he very much questioned the assumption that progress had any clear tendency to lead to peace. "One of the principal errors which led to world wars," he wrote in 1950, "was the assumption that material progress is necessarily favorable to peace." Looking back over the nineteenth and early twentieth centuries, indeed, he found that "the role of war in promoting industrial progress had been small compared with the role of industrial progress in bringing on war." An important element in this unfortunate development was that increasing wealth not only "helped to provide men with weapons" but also gave them "resources that add to the time they can devote to the luxury of fighting."[9]

Whatever weight we give to these various arguments, it would seem that their general impact is quite clear: namely, they suggest that this particular predicament of progress is very likely to get worse over time. If war is in any way a stimulant to the process of progress, then the cessation of wars would tend to undermine that process to some degree. On the other hand, the continuation of wars would lead through increased technological advance to ever greater destructiveness, thereby ending the process through global devastation. If, moreover, the process of progress, by freeing mankind from the pressures of necessity, makes the "luxury of fighting" ever more available, then this, too, could lead to greater future destructiveness. Thus, we begin in effect with an intensified predicament and have to ask whether there might be some offsets to these lines of argument in a positive direction.

2. *Since the development of more potent offensive weapons tends to stimulate the production of compensating defensive weapons, the process of progress over time may have some tendency to neutralize the threats posed by even the most devastating weapons of mass destruction.*

There is no doubt that, in a world of serious nationalistic rivalries of one sort or another, the invention of any new offensive weapon of major significance will produce intense efforts both to duplicate the weapon in question and to find some kind of defensive response to it. For a long time in the nuclear era, the Soviet Union followed both offensive and defensive strategies, while the United States effectively abandoned the search for defensive responses and relied on what is widely referred to as a MAD strategy (MAD standing for Mutually Assured Destruction).

Then, quite dramatically, in a speech to the American people on 23 March, 1983, President Ronald Reagan announced a wholly new approach: "I call upon the scientific community in our country, those who gave us nuclear weapons, to turn their great talents now to the cause of mankind and world peace, to give us the means of rendering these nuclear weapons impotent and obsolete." Thus was born the Strategic Defense Initiative (SDI), and a major national debate which, in some respects, is not over yet. In terms of our discussion, this was a clear case of trying to counteract new technology by the development of still newer technology—that is, to use the process of progress to solve one of its outstanding predicaments.

Since the potential and actual grounds for criticizing the SDI approach are so obvious, it may be worthwhile to indicate my beliefs: (1) that the Reagan proposal did, in point of actual fact, have enormously favorable repercussions on the prospects for world peace; and (2) that, just as the nation is preparing to curtail or even abandon the SDI approach, we are entering a period when it would likely have its most significant and effective use. Belief (1) stems from the fact that, if American critics often scoffed at the program, Soviet scientists clearly did not. While obviously not the sole element involved, SDI was undoubtedly *an* element in convincing the Soviet leadership that they were in a no-win military competition with the United States, and that their creaking economy simply could not bear the additional strains of a major new research effort and defensive buildup.

Belief (2) stems from the very strong possibility that future nuclear threats will come not in the form of all-out attacks by a nation seeking our total destruction, but rather singular, and relatively isolated, attacks, or even threats of attack, on targets such as New York City, Washington, D.C., Los Angeles, or other particular metropolitan areas. While as a total defensive umbrella, SDI has always provoked justifiable skepticism, as a thin line of defense against small numbers of isolated missiles, it has a much greater—and to my mind much more pertinent—chance of success.[10] In short, SDI proved itself useful in assuring the ultimate downfall of communism and could easily prove of great practical use in situations in which the United States, or other industrial nations, might otherwise be held hostage by local tyrants.

All the above is an aside, since on the main issue here there is overwhelming evidence that, on the whole and over time, there is no chance whatever that defensive technologies could be counted on regularly to offset their increasingly destructive offensive counterparts. With regard to SDI in particular, it could be pointed out that it wasn't an abandonment of MAD at all, but rather simply a more effective way of protecting our means of retaliation; that it would very probably be cheaper to develop weapons to shoot down our SDI defenses than to put them up in the first place; that SDI could very easily have been a destabilizing factor in the arms race since the Russians could conclude that the United States was preparing to strike first (SDI might actually give us protection against a weakened retaliatory strike, thus giving us an incentive to strike first), thereby giving *them* an incentive to strike first; and that the argument that SDI is technologically feasible since past history shows that almost nothing is "impossible" where science is concerned also leads to the conclusion that it will not be "impossible" to develop technologies that completely overcome any given SDI strategy; and so on.[11]

Actually, the last point probably presents the major difficulty not only for any all-encompassing protective SDI shield, but indeed for any general effort to count on future technological advance to offset the powers (in this case destructive powers) conferred by advances already on the books. Because very few things are scientifically "impossible," one simply cannot predict that new technologies will regularly and comfortably take exactly the shape and form required by present circumstances. They may do so, there even may be some tendency for them to do so, but this surely is only a tendency, and no one can be sure how, when, where, or even if it will eventuate. In the meantime—as at present—the world may go through long periods of time in which it is totally unprotected in a technological sense from its ability to destroy itself.

3. *The process of progress makes the prospects of global war increasingly horrifying and thereby causes changes in human attitudes making such wars increasingly unlikely.*

If the evolution of technology cannot be counted on to save us, can we place our hopes on the natural evolution of human attitudes to war? That such an attitudinal evolution had not manifested itself by the mid-twentieth century is not necessarily a decisive argument against this view. It could be that what is necessary is to reach a certain critical point of destructiveness, the point relied on by the MAD strategy: that is, one can launch a major assault on the enemy only if one is willing to accept guaranteed self-destruction as a consequence.

The view that the real solution to the problem of destructive weaponry is even more destructive weaponry goes back at least to Alfred Nobel whose words near the end of the nineteenth century provided the title for this chapter: "I should like to be able to turn out a substance or a machine of such horrible capacity for mass annihilation that thereby wars would become altogether impossible."[12] As both the inventor of dynamite and the founder of the world's most famous peace prize, it may be said that the Swedish industrialist did his own personal best to promote this particular solution.

And it is clearly a solution that has explained to many observers why despite the Berlin Wall, the subjugation of Eastern Europe, the Korean War, the Cuban missile crisis, the Vietnam War, the crisis in Angola, the invasion of Afghanistan, constant troubles in the Middle East and elsewhere over a period of nearly a half century, we did not in fact have World War III. Virtually every leader in both East and West during these decades proclaimed more or less constantly that nuclear weapons had made war unthinkable. Richard Nixon became convinced that World War III would never come, and precisely because of the atomic bomb. Margaret Thatcher held a similar view. Had there been no bomb (and no indestructible means of delivery) and had the world, with its merely "conventional" weapons, behaved as it had during the first half of the twentieth century, the toll in additional lives lost would almost certainly have exceeded one hundred million. The bomb, some would say, far from being the seed of our ultimate destruction, has already saved millions of souls and prevented incalculable material devastation.

While granting the power of this argument—and it is hard to deny that far greater caution in the matter of all-out war has been evidenced in the second as opposed to the first half of the twentieth century—one has every reason to treat it with a certain skepticism, at least in the absence of further supporting developments. The MAD concept has always seemed to some observers to be fatally flawed, in that it is a strategy that fails the moment it is in fact called into use. This may be a merely logical conundrum, but the fact is that students of warfare and foreign policy have easily been able to describe scenarios in which a MAD strategy confronts one or both opponents with alternatives neither of which is acceptable.[13] Also, there are suicidal leaders in the world, deranged and unbalanced individuals who, like Hitler in his bunker, would not hesitate to bring down the rest of humanity as they plunge to their own fiery destinations. Extend one's time horizon sufficiently far so that weapons of mass destruction become ever more sophisticated, dispersed, easier to hide and transport, and with unequal advantages developing first in this corner of the globe, then in that—view the matter in this broad perspective and the comfort provided by point 3, while real, is less than wholly convincing. In this regard, however, the following point is at least somewhat helpful.

4. *It is the case, or at least can be argued, that the process of progress tends in the long run to promote the global strength and influence of peace-loving, democratic societies.*

The West won the Cold War—peacefully. Military encounters, whether victories or, as in Vietnam, defeats, had very little to do with the matter in a positive sense. The fact is that, over the long pull, both freedom and peace are allies of the process of progress, and the process of progress is, over that same long pull, the ally of national strength and influence. The good guys came in first. The superpower that gobbled up half of Europe at war's end and suppressed its critics and dissidents now lies in shambles. The superpower—for a few years after World War II the only superpower—that took no territory for itself, helped rebuild its allies and enemies, and subjects itself daily to a barrage of self-criticism amounting at times almost to a kind of self-hatred, stands if not proud at least triumphant in victory.

No one can prove that this had to be the outcome, but what one can almost prove is that the nondemocratic, centrally-planned, command economy—contrary to Khrushchev's famous boast about "burying" us—is an ultimately unsustainable vehicle for coping with the modern process of progress. There are actually two sets of questions to be addressed here. The first is whether democracy and freedom, broadly defined, tend to promote growth and economic progress generally. The second is whether growth and economic progress tend, again broadly speaking, to promote democracy and freedom.

Each of these questions, in turn, can be subdivided into a number of others. In the case of the first question, in particular, one might wish to separate the early from the later stages of economic development. A common view used to be that while central planning might be highly useful for late-starting developing countries—a view, indeed, that was often encouraged by Western advisors and aid-givers—such planning was doomed to failure as a country became more developed and complex. Today, the question is more likely to be whether central planning, command mechanisms, and generally authoritarian political systems are *ever* conducive to rapid growth, even in the very earliest stages of the process.

Actually, there is disagreement on this point among the experts. There are a number of recent studies suggesting that developing countries would probably have done much better had they been freer, more democratic, individualistic, and market-oriented from the beginning. Thus, for example, a chart in the *American Economic Review* showed that, comparing industrial democracies with communist centralized economies, nations that took the central planning route tended to have lower rates of economic growth at all levels of per capita income than did the freer, more democratically organized countries.[14]

A general survey of statistical studies in this area found a considerable change in the conclusions professionals have reached since the late 1980s. This 1993 survey reported that "among the 11 results published before 1988, eight found that authoritarian regimes grew faster, while none of the nine results published after 1987 supported this finding."[15] Among eight of the most recent studies, averaging seventy-four countries per study, mainly less developed countries, five showed democracies growing faster economically, and the remaining three had statistically insignificant results.

On the other hand, Robert J. Barro of Harvard argues that democracy has, at best, a mixed performance record with respect to promoting economic development and rising living standards among very poor countries. He does not doubt that economic freedom, per se, is favorable to development. Indeed, recent studies by the Heritage Foundation suggest that an index of "economic freedom" is highly correlated with a country's living standards for all nations, rich and poor. However, democracy, Barro points out, does not always promote economic freedom, and, in a number of cases (he cites Chile, Peru, and several East Asian countries), authoritarian, even dictatorial, regimes have effectively advanced the cause of economic freedom. Thus, while economic freedom may be almost universally associated with the process of progress, democracy has a somewhat more ambiguous role in advancing that process.[16]

Still, when it comes to our second question—whether the process of progress tends to promote increased democracy and political and economic freedom—Barro appears to agree with a conclusion that virtually everyone now accepts, namely: Yes, the process of progress in the long run does promote politically democratic and usually much freer economic systems. This second conclusion is very hopeful. In general, democracies tend not to wage war on democracies. If, in the long run, democracy and the process of progress tend to go together, then the "zones of peace" in the world may, as Henry Rowen of Stanford argues, tend to increase "as the world becomes richer and more democratic. Terrible things will still happen, but wealth-creating forces will probably dominate poverty-sustaining ones for more of the world's peoples and should have widely beneficial political consequences."[17]

In other words, thinking in terms of the over-all question—the effects of further progress on the dangers of mass annihilation—most students of the international scene suspect that the greatest hope for peace on earth resides not in the stemming or suppression of the strong drive to achieve development in all corners of the globe but in encouraging that process to take hold as widely and productively as it can. Thus, despite some disagreement as to what happens in the very early stages of the development process, there seems to be unanimity about the more general conclusion. And this is quite simply that, in the long run, the process of progress will, other things equal, tend to promote peaceful, democratic attitudes, and to reward peaceful, democratic attitudes with increased national strength. The basic tendencies are self-supporting and benign.

THE BOMB AND THE IDEA OF PROGRESS

All the above points relate to the first of our fundamental issues—the effects of further progress on the dangers of mass destruction. But what of the second fundamental question, about the psychological impact of concerns in this area on the Idea of Progress? Have two World Wars, the Cold War, several minor wars, and above all, "the bomb" been major factors in undermining our faith in Progress as Idea and, indeed, Ideal? If the first question has been difficult to answer and our comments filled with reservations and notes about contrary tendencies, this second question is—surprisingly—very easy to answer. And the answer is quite simply, No. No, despite all the talk about Day One in the history of the world (6 August, 1945), Doomsday Clocks, and the anxiety produced by knowing that our children would never be able to sleep soundly in their beds again. Despite all this apparent evidence, there is overwhelming counterevidence to show that concerns over the bomb, nuclear weapons generally, World War III, mass destruction of the planet, and even that popular concept, "nuclear winter," were always quite superficial. Or to put it more accurately, they were quite superficial relative to the issue of greatest importance to our study, namely, the fate of the Idea of Progress as a general article of faith throughout the society at large.

The reason one can make such a strong and unequivocal statement has basically to do with timing. Taking the post-World War II period as a whole, we find (1) great anxiety over the bomb and the possibility of nuclear war in the earlier part of the period followed by increasingly less, and indeed currently almost vanishing, concern in this arena; and (2) a surprisingly strong recrudescence of faith in Progress at the beginning of the period followed by a gradual decline in faith until, at present, the Idea of Progress has really ceased to be a dominant article of American beliefs.

I will come back to a number of aspects of these two points in later chapters. For the moment, I simply note that there are three main periods involved. The *first* period extends roughly from the end of the war until the mid–1960s. During this period, we had a sense both of maximum danger in terms of superpower confrontations and of intense interest in growth and development both nationally and internationally.

Dangers seemed to crop up on every side—Greece and Turkey, Soviet development of the A-bomb and H-bomb, Korea with its sudden introduction of massive Chinese forces, Sputnik, and, above all perhaps, the Cuban missile crisis. President Kennedy is believed to have calculated the risk of all-out global war during this crisis as one in three.[18] At the same time, in a variety of ways that we shall discuss as we go along, there was a striking revival of the Idea of Progress during this period. Economic growth became virtually the be-all and end-all of governmental policy. The same Kennedy who operated on the brink during the missile crisis had been elected on a platform filled with what one might call "progress talk": the New Frontier; "Let's get this country moving again;" passing the torch to a "new generation;" and so on. Worldwide, it was simply taken for granted that the achievement of the process of progress in the then-designated "underdeveloped countries" was the central goal to which all these countries would naturally be dedicated.

The *second* period lasted roughly from the second half of the 1960s to the late 1980s. This period began with very serious international concerns—especially the Vietnam War—though it is doubtful that the fear of nuclear war was as great even then as it had been a few years earlier. In any event, the period as a whole showed a sharp refocusing of national interest on domestic as opposed to international issues. We launched the War on Poverty and the Great Society programs, withdrew from Vietnam, and saw the beginning of major drives in the areas of civil rights, women's rights, and other issues involving equality in one form or another. I shall argue in some detail (see chapter 13) that this increasing focus on equality represented a serious downplaying of the process of progress. In any event, at least among intellectuals, this second period was marked by serious and well-publicized critiques of the process of progress, many predicting its ultimate collapse in the very near future. These critiques—the various "limits-to-growth" models—will be considered in the next chapter. Thus we had during this second period increasingly less concern about the bomb and increasingly serious doubts about the process of progress.

Finally, the real clincher for this line of argument comes in the *third* period—the last few years. Actually, even before the Berlin Wall fell and the collapse of communism was assured, Americans already regarded Japanese economic competition as a greater threat to the nation's future than Soviet nuclear arms by a three-to-one margin.[19] And what is so striking about the subsequent developments is that the virtual disappearance of fears about all-out nuclear war within the foreseeable future has brought almost no sense of joy, relief, or even notice to most Americans. Huge disarmament agreements hardly make the third pages of our newspapers. And this despite the fact that recent disarmament agreements, unlike some earlier ones, have actually, and in fact, reduced nuclear capabilities. For example, Russia, following treaties signed in 1987, 1991, and 1993, had, by 1994, reduced her stockpile of nuclear weapons by about a quarter. This contrasted with a steady and massive buildup of this stockpile for the preceding quarter of a century.[20]

Amazingly, the ending of the Cold War, at least in its critical superpower confrontation phase, seems to have made no Americans happy in any measurable sense. When one talks about defense in the United States today, the main concerns appear to have to do with the implications of base closings on jobs, and other short-run, and decidedly nonmilitary, considerations. This focus on the short run, so evident in other areas of our national life as well, is actually one of the clearer indications that the Idea of Progress, with its very long-term emphasis, is losing its commanding position among our national priorities.

Thus, in this third and most recent period, we have at once the greatest freedom from fear of nuclear war since the late 1940s and, at least in practical terms, the lowest interest in the long-run future since World War II, arguably since the founding of the republic.[21]

SUMMARY

While it is difficult to determine unequivocally what effect the continuation of the process of progress may have on the threat posed by weapons of mass destruction (though my own conclusion is that, on balance, further progress is likely to meliorate this predicament), it seems indisputable that our declining faith in the Idea of Progress in recent decades has little or nothing to do with the bomb, missiles, fear of World War III, or fear of wars in general. We feel far safer with respect to the likelihood of nuclear attack than we did thirty or forty years ago, yet we seem to be more confused and apprehensive about the future than ever before.

8

LIMITS-TO-GROWTH
PREDICAMENTS

Although World War I undoubtedly played an important role in
pricking the balloon of the Idea of Progress in the first half of
the twentieth century, the last chapter suggested that the fear of mass
destruction—even when greatly aggravated by the development of nuclear technology—had become an increasingly modest concern by the
last decade of the century. If our children do not sleep soundly these
days, it is very unlikely to be because of their nightmares about incoming
nuclear-tipped missiles.

Indeed, the Doomsday models that appeared in great numbers in
the 1960s and especially the early 1970s—the so-called "limits-to-
growth" models—did not particularly play up the dangers of nuclear
war. They did not deny the possibility that such wars might occur (no
opportunity for increased pessimism was ever completely overlooked
during this period), but their prophecies of gloom did not require this
particular *deus ex machina*. They could achieve all they needed by stressing resource depletion, pollution, and population growth; and what they
claimed to have achieved in this negative direction was quite considerable. Here is the opening paragraph of "A Blueprint for Survival," a
widely-read British document published in 1972:

> The principal defect of the industrial way of life with its ethos of
> expansion is that it is not sustainable. Its termination within the life-
> time of someone born today is inevitable—unless it continues to be
> sustained for a while longer by an entrenched minority at the cost of
> imposing great suffering on the rest of mankind. We can be certain,
> however, that sooner or later it will end (only the precise time and

circumstances are in doubt), and that it will do so in one of two ways: either against our will, in a succession of famines, epidemics, social crises and wars; or because we want it to—because we wish to create a society which will not impose hardship and cruelty upon our children—in a succession of thoughtful, humane and measured changes.[1]

Similar conclusions were reached in MIT professor Jay Forrester's *World Dynamics* (1971) and the Club of Rome's *Limits to Growth* (1972). Thus, Forrester argued that "a society with a high level of industrialization may be nonsustainable," and that "we may now be living in a 'golden age' when . . . the quality of life is, on the average, higher than ever before in history and higher now than the future offers."[2]

FOSSIL FUELS AND THE "ENERGY CRISIS"

What is particularly striking about these various documents is how rapidly the Day of Judgment was expected to descend upon the earth (suggesting, indeed, that millennial considerations may have remained more deeply lodged in the human psyche than all the subsequent processes of modernization have led us to believe). The Blueprint speaks of the end of the process of progress arriving "within the lifetime of someone born today [1972]." Actually, since someone born in 1972 could live nearly to the end of the next century, they indicate subsequently that it is really inconceivable that the process could go on for as long as sixty or seventy years more, and, indeed, that resource depletion could easily occur much sooner than that. The illustrative example they offer with respect to world oil reserves and consumption is worth reproducing here (fig. 8.1). It purports to show that while "as late as 1975 there will appear to be reserves fully ample to last for considerably longer," the world will in fact totally run out of oil by the year 1990 (i.e., when the annual production curve intersects the reserves curve). According to this illustration, the world would have only 15 years before all our oil reserves were consumed!

This diagram was, as I say, meant as illustrative only. What it actually illustrates, however, is something its authors certainly never intended, namely, an enormously exaggerated view of the speed with which the world was exhausting its petroleum reserves and, by implication, its main

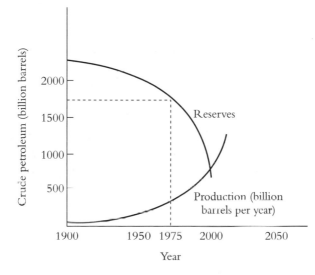

Fig. 8.1   World reserves of crude petroleum at exponential rate of consumption

Source: "A Blueprint for Survival," Copyright © 1972 by *The Ecologist*, published by Tom Stacey Ltd. and Penguin Books. Reprinted by permission of Deborah Rogers Ltd., London, and Houghton Mifflin Company.
Note that in 1975, with no more than fifteen years left before demand exceeds supply, the total global reserve has been depleted by only 12½ percent.

energy sources and, indeed, its reserves of nonrenewable natural resources generally. In the light of subsequent experience, the degree of exaggeration would seem to approach the edge of hysteria. The 1990s— the very decade when it was imagined that the world might conceivably have zero oil reserves left—have so far been marked mainly by attempts of oil-producing countries to limit production so as to avert serious gluts on world markets.

At the time, however, such images were accepted as by no means unreasonable and, indeed, seemed almost immediately to be verified by actual facts. It was an enormous boon to the Doomsday writers, certainly as far as their American audience was concerned, that hardly had their dire predictions rolled off the presses than the first of the great "energy crises" burst upon a dismayed and astonished nation. The collapse of the

West apparently might occur even sooner than expected—we might not even reach the 1990s!

If concern over the increasing destructiveness of war was the twentieth century's first major predicament of progress, alarm about nonrenewable natural resources, and especially fossil fuels, was clearly the second. From OPEC I in 1973–74 through OPEC II in 1979–80, the United States suffered major "supply shocks" involving not only sudden sharp rises in the price of oil, but also temporary physical shortages and actual "gas lines" at the pumps. Most significant perhaps, was the dawning awareness that, during the postwar period, we had been transformed from an exporter to a major importer of oil, and that our domestic oil reserves, absent these major imports, would last only a few years more at best.

The generalization of these specific problems to a basic predicament of progress was easy to make—in fact, had already been made by the Doomsday theorists, and evidently "proved" by computer demonstrations. The process of progress in the West, it was claimed, had basically rested on an unsustainably rapid exploitation of nonrenewable resources, and especially energy resources. The continuation of this process in the industrial nations—not even to mention its extension to the billions of people in the less developed world—was possible at best for a few decades more.

Indeed, it could be argued that the entire process of progress from the Industrial Revolution on had really been a one-shot affair, resting crucially on the depletion of unreplaceable fossil fuels, first coal, and then oil and natural gas, and would end as soon as this depletion was completed. What we really had been doing over the past two centuries was not advancing economically but simply using the world's stored up capital for our own present purposes. Instead of living for the future, as we may have imagined, we were actually passing along to the future a sadly drained and depleted shell of a planet. The problem of global pollution (which I turn to in a moment) obviously only intensified the problem, suggesting that the planet we were passing along would not only be woefully short on resources but positively unpleasant to live on and quite possibly unfit for human habitation.

FAILED MODELS AND DISAPPEARING CRISES

There is no question that it is theoretically possible to exploit our natural resource base at a rate that, from the vantage point of a given standard of value, may be judged to be "too rapid." This standard of value will be significantly affected by the priority we give to the interests and needs of future generations. It can be argued that if the present generation neglects the interests of its descendants (or even "myopically" neglects its own interests a few decades down the road), it may well deplete a nation's natural resource base at a rate that other observers—say, members of those future generations when they arrive upon the scene—may decide to have been excessive and damaging. Interestingly, the Idea of Progress, with its tendency to give a high priority to future generations, would actually constitute a major safeguard against this abusive use of our natural resource heritage. This is an important point we shall return to in the next section when we discuss pollution, and also in future chapters.

For the moment, however, we need not linger long on the energy crisis as a central threat to the process of progress for the simple reason that this concern has, twenty years after OPEC I, virtually vanished from view. The predicament itself remains as logical (or illogical) as it ever was; what has disappeared is any serious effect of its consideration on American attitudes and behaviors.

Our two questions, as in the case of the armaments predicament, are: (1) Will further progress tend in general to intensify or ameliorate the resource depletion predicament? (2) Has the existence of this problem seriously contributed to the waning of our faith in the Idea of Progress? Relevant to these two questions, only the following brief comments are necessary:

First, almost everyone now agrees that the computer models that produced the collapse of the process of progress within the next century (or usually much sooner) were extremely naïve and in fact very bad science indeed. In the case of resource depletion, they produced their cataclysmic results only by ignoring virtually all the mechanisms by which individuals, societies, and especially markets and price systems adjust to shortages of specific resources as they develop over time. Taken seriously, these models would actually prove that the British Industrial Revolution could never have occurred in the first place since increased production at that time required wood as a major fuel and the supply of forests in Britain was being very rapidly decimated. Of course, what happened in fact was that wood was essentially replaced by coal; not only did production not suffer but productivity increased by leaps and bounds.

It is important to recognize that the mechanism just described—substituting new and plentiful resources for resources in increasingly short supply—is not an incidental but a central feature of the process of progress. Actually coal itself was replaced in turn by oil and natural gas. In the United States, for example, as late as 1920, coal accounted for 78 percent of total energy use; by OPEC I in 1973, it had fallen to 18 percent. The development of new technologies and shifts in the use of resources, plus conservation and the increased discovery of scarce resources, all in response to higher prices—these several counteracting tendencies are built into the process of progress and are, for the most part, completely left out of the Doomsday calculations. In a short article published in 1973 in response to the Doomsday models, Nobel prize winner-to-be Robert M. Solow pointed out that their most "glaring defect" is "the absence of any sort of functioning price system." Remove the critical adjustment process, and, of course, things collapse. Who would ever have imagined otherwise?[3]

In other words, in response to the question as to whether or not further progress is likely to intensify or meliorate the predicament posed by any specific energy or other natural resource shortages, the answer is almost certainly more positive than negative. Getting around such shortages as they develop is exactly what the process of progress is *good at.* This is its strong suit. Possibly—nothing in the future can be claimed to be absolutely "impossible"—some day the process will fail us with respect to one particular requirement, or class of requirements. Even if it did, however—and historical experience gives us no reason whatever to believe that it will fail us in any vital area of economic life—there are so many adjustment possibilities available to a scientifically minded, technologically oriented, change-accustomed society that it seems unnecessarily perverse to believe that we have at last found a crucial roadblock that no one will be able to figure out a way to get around. The process of progress, in short, remains basically unchallenged in this area of concern.

But how about the effect of possible resource depletion on the Idea of Progress? This takes us to my second question. Is the fear of running out of something (oil, coal, natural gas, aluminum, iron ore, or whatever) a major component of our ebbing faith in a basically improving and bountiful long-range future? In the 1970s and even possibly in the very early 1980s such a case might have been made. By the early 1990s, however, such fears would appear to rank even lower in the popular consciousness than the already very much dissipated fear of all-out nuclear war. For all practical purposes, they have vanished from public consideration.

A clear case in point here has to do with President Clinton's proposal of a BTU tax in 1992, its withdrawal in favor of a gasoline tax, and the subsequent reduction of that proposed tax to a few pennies (4.3 cents) per gallon. Two conclusions immediately emerge from this exercise. In the first place, the debate over this proposed tax and its size had almost nothing whatever to do with the need to spur conservation of a natural resource that was being rapidly depleted at the expense of future generations. Insofar as the future was brought into the original debate, the concern was over pollution by carbon-based fuels (a problem potentially lessened by the long-run depletion of coal, oil, etc.), and much more significantly and explicitly by concern over the national debt. The gasoline tax seemed mainly to be thought of as a revenue-raising measure, like a tax on beer or tobacco (hardly commodities in short supply), and not as in any essential way a conservation measure.

In the second place, even if conservation of a scarce resource did figure in some marginal way in the original decision to raise gasoline taxes, the very smallness of the increase is indicative of how low this priority ranked in the national consciousness. In real (inflation-adjusted) terms, Americans pay far less for a gallon of gasoline today than they did in the 1970s when the Doomsday theorists were predicting imminent and massive gasoline shortages. Yet any attempt even to match that earlier price by increased taxation would have been rejected out of hand and, indeed, would not even have been—as it was not—brought to the table for consideration. Actually, in the present period of quite low gasoline prices, the whole concept of conservation, which achieved a certain prominence in the OPEC era, has virtually disappeared from public discussion.

In short, when the immediate energy crises ended, so also did major attention to the problem of depletable natural resources. In 1992, when an Energy Department study suggested that the United States has significantly more recoverable oil reserves than previously believed and that recoverable reserves were estimated to be equivalent to thirty-five to seventy-five years of continued U.S. production at current rates—when this seemingly great news burst on the national scene, it was buried in the back pages of a few newspapers and was hardly even noticed by the public at large. Similarly, a 1995 study by the U.S. Geological Survey (USGS) made virtually no national impact whatever. This study corrected an earlier (1989) USGS study that had calculated that the U.S. had roughly 78 billion barrels of oil and 504 trillion cubic feet of natural gas recoverable by current technology. The 1995 study raised these numbers to 110 billion barrels of oil and 715 trillion cubic feet of gas. Indeed, when a new category of gas-containing reservoirs was included, the new estimates came out to 1,070 trillion cubic feet of natural gas, or more than twice the projection just six years earlier.[4]

Again, the public sighs of relief were not just muted; they never occurred at all. Only a few specialists even noticed this apparently very desirable development. The simple fact of the matter is that the resource depletion problem, having had its brief, dramatic run, has essentially vanished from our national consciousness. The problem could return. It could even conceivably return in a serious way. What cannot be said, however, is that it is a problem that has to date offered any really major psychological challenge to the Idea of Progress.

THE ENVIRONMENTAL PREDICAMENT

An interesting implication of the foregoing discussion of resource depletion is that if it is, or ever does become, a serious threat to the process of progress it is likely to be only because, in one way or another, we are undervaluing the just claims of the future. What this suggests is that rather than resource depletion creating a major problem for the Idea of Progress, it is, or could be, the weakening of the Idea of Progress that effectively creates the resource problem. If we cease to care seriously about the future, if the future after we have personally departed the scene no longer much matters to us, then we could conceivably do major damage to our resource base. But notice here that the basic causation goes in the opposite direction from that with which we started—from failing Idea to predicament, rather than from predicament to failing Idea.

In fact, this very point has considerable relevance to the predicament of progress we turn to now—problems connected in one way or another with pollution and environmental damage generally. For it can be argued that such problems can be solved, but that to do so will require particular concern and attention to the future and, in many cases, even to the quite distant future. Failure of the Idea of Progress, at least insofar as it derives from or is associated with a shrinking of time horizons, could in fact create or at least greatly intensify the possibility of future environmental disasters.

Although, as just suggested, there are some family resemblances between the problems of resource depletion and pollution, it is customary to treat them as two different questions— or, in the present terminology, two different predicaments of progress. One important reason for this is that while the price system, as already indicated, tends on the whole to be quite effective when resource shortages develop, it is notably *ineffective* when economic processes involve pollution or other forms of environmental damage. Such damage occurs when the production or consumption of economic "goods" (potatoes, houses, cars, etc.) is accompanied by the production of economic "bads" (agricultural runoffs, destruction of wildlife habitat, air pollution, etc.)

Technically, what are involved are "external diseconomies"— economic, personal, health, or other costs that are "external" to the price system. The market does not in any direct or automatic way charge the polluter for the costs he or she is imposing on society. Hence it provides no incentive for individuals or business firms to reduce or in any way limit these costs. Environmental externalities are thus commonly cited as clear cases of "market failure." While, as Solow pointed out, the omission of a functioning price system is in many respects the major weakness of the Doomsday models of the early 1970s, the inclusion of such a system would, in itself, do little to remedy the problems of future environmental damage, which these models foresee.

This is not to say, however, that the market mechanism is irrelevant to such problems. On the contrary, as I will point out in a moment, probably the most effective way of resolving environmental problems is by using market incentives to change the behavior of individuals and firms—so to speak, by "internalizing" these "externalities." Not surprisingly, we shall also find out that our willingness to apply such a resolution will depend very much on our time horizons—that is, the weight we give to the well-being of future generations.

A second reason for treating environmental problems separately from resource-depletion problems is that, while the latter—as exemplified in the "energy crises" of the 1970s—have almost disappeared as a matter of public concern, environmental problems—as exemplified by such concerns as animal habitat, acid rain, ozone depletion, and, probably most publicized of all, the "greenhouse effect"—are extremely widely discussed and debated and, for many in the 1990s, are obvious sources of considerable anxiety. Although something of a simplification, the progression of public concerns in the United States during the past half century has been from war and the bomb, to energy crises, to fears of possibly looming environmental catastrophes. As indicated in chapter 6, the population explosion in the Third World is widely viewed as a contributor to the forthcoming environmental dangers, as for example through the destruction of rain forests and a general encroachment by growing numbers of people on wildlife habitat. If any predicament of progress appears to be threatening the Idea of Progress at the present time—certainly in terms of public displays of concern and demands for action—it would clearly be that involving pollution and environmental problems generally.

EFFECTS OF THE PROCESS OF PROGRESS ON POLLUTION

Again, I limit my comments to a few points about the two general questions relevant to our overall argument. The first question, as before, is will the process of progress generally tend to intensify or to meliorate this particular predicament over time?

One's comments here are necessarily somewhat ambiguous and for two main reasons. First, it is extremely difficult to judge the scale of environmental damage that the process of progress may or may not cause in the future because we do not even know the extent of the damage it is causing at present or has caused in the past. There are tremendous uncertainties here. Second, it is very easy to point out ways in which the process of progress may both create and help solve environmental problems. Judging the balance of effects here is extremely difficult. We comment briefly on each of these points:

1. *The great uncertainty concerning the environmental effects of the process of progress*

There is probably no global environmental effect that has caused more concern and been more intensively studied than the so-called greenhouse effect (often referred to as "global warming"). According to many studies of this phenomenon, the earth's mean temperature during the next century will rise due to the increasing concentration of greenhouse gases—especially carbon dioxide, but also methane, nitrous oxide, and chorofluorocarbons—resulting in large part from human activities and particularly the burning of oil, coal, and wood in industrial and other processes. This increased warming, occurring because these gases trap infrared radiation emitted by the earth's surface, will according to some scientists have possibly major effects on weather patterns, loss of precipitation, melting of polar ice caps, coastal flooding, and other potential disasters. In annnouncing President Clinton's plan to reduce these greenhouse gases in October 1993, Vice President Al Gore declared that "climate change is the highest-risk environmental problem the world faces today."

Does this mean that there is general scientific agreement about the seriousness of future global warming? Hardly. Indeed, as there has been no environmental problem more publicized and studied than the greenhouse effect, there has also probably been none on which such basic disagreements have developed. Have we in fact any persuasive evidence that the greenhouse effect has been operating during the massive industrialization of the Western world over the past century and especially the last fifty years? In 1988, James Hansen, a climate expert at the NASA Goddard Institute of Space Studies in New York City, told a U.S. Senate committee that he was 99 percent certain that the greenhouse effect was already here.[5] On the other hand, three years later, a well-known critic reported that "a just completed survey of climate experts . . . shows no such consensus [on the greenhouse effect] and demolishes the notion that energy use must be drastically constrained to avert a hypothetical climate disaster."[6]

Such disagreement about the basic fact of global warming during the past century (let alone its probable path in the decades ahead) is so common that almost every few days some new and contradictory report on the subject seems to emerge. Thus, while Hansen found that in 1988 the average global temperature had risen 0.4° C relative to mean temperatures for the period 1950 to 1980, a 1993 study led by Jonathan Kahl of the University of Wisconsin-Milwaukee found no evidence of warming over the Arctic Ocean during the last four decades (and, in fact, some evidence that surface temperatures had cooled in winter and autumn). This finding was particularly significant because many computer models predict greater than average warming in the Arctic region.[7]

The *New York Times* coverage of the subject is quite typical. On 27 August 1995, for example, the *Times* reported the apparently good news that plants absorb far more carbon dioxide from burning fossil fuels than had previously been imagined. This could counteract much of the greenhouse effect. Before one could properly enjoy this new development, however, on 10 September 1995, the *Times* reported that a new study marked "a watershed in the views of climatologists," that the "smoking gun" had now been found, and that a clear "pattern of climatic response to human activities is identifiable in the climatological record." James Hansen was apparently right after all. Reading on further, however, one discovered that the debate is hardly ended. Thus, Dr. Richard S. Lindzen of MIT is quoted as saying that there is "no basis" yet for saying that a human influence on the climate has been detected.[8]

Actually, the uncertainty in this latest round of research is underlined by the fact that the authors of this new study (the Intergovernmental Panel on Climate Change), while concluding that humankind is responsible for altering the earth's climate, also concluded that their previous (1990) projections for increased warming were too high by one third. Thus, we can apparently expect an increase in global temperature by the year 2100 not of 3^0 C, but of 2^0 C, with a consequent reduction in the projected rise in sea levels.[9]

One of the problems in all this is the matter of timing. If there has been some actual global warming over the past century, it should have been greatest during the massive industrialization occurring over the past half century, but in fact, at least according to such experts as Sallie Baliunas, chair of the Harvard-Smithsonian Center for Astrophysics, most of the (minor) warming that occurred over the past century occurred before 1940, prior to the significant buildup of man-generated greenhouse gases. At a December 1994 conference on environmental issues, she stated flatly that "no evidence can be found in the temperature measurements to support the theory of catastrophic global warming caused by human activities."[10]

What comes through most clearly in any survey of studies in this area is the enormous complexity of the problem. To achieve any kind of definitive answer to the question one would have to model such complicated phenomena as cloud formation; ocean currents; sulfur pollution caused by the combustion of fossil fuels (exerting a cooling effect); smoke aerosols produced by burning tropical forests and grasslands (also cooling); variable solar activity (it has been argued that sun changes are actually forcing climate changes); the complicated effect of decreases in snow coverage (increasing the heat-absorptive capacity of the earth but also possibly promoting cloud cover to block out incoming solar radiation); and even such basic questions as the lifetime of carbon dioxide in the atmosphere, the effect of carbon dioxide consumption by plants and oceans, the heat properties of sea ice, and, in general, the degree to which such greenhouse effects that exist are due to natural versus manmade causes. Thus, while some scientists believe that man-made global warming has already arrived, there are others who regard it as not only uncertain but as an "outright invention" of environmental extremists. As indicated in the next chapter, such high degrees of complexity and uncertainty are critical elements in virtually all predicaments of progress and, indeed, form part of what I consider to be the "fundamental" predicament.

2. *The process of progress may both cause and help solve our environmental problems*

The second reason for the difficulty of determining the effect of future progress on environmental problems is that the process has such definite effects on the problems, but in such opposite directions. Assuming that the concerns expressed by many scientists that human-generated pollution is producing global warming are basically correct, then it is clear that the process of progress as it continues in the developed countries, and perhaps even more significantly as it spreads to the burgeoning populations of the developing world, will tend to exacerbate the problem further. No one claims that this effect of industrialization is anything but generally negative in direction.

As against this, however, one has at least three major reasons for believing that the process of progress can help resolve the greenhouse effect or any other negative environmental effects. There is, first, the ability of science and technology to come up with pollution-reducing or even pollution-eliminating methods of industrial production and consumption. Totally nonpolluting hydrogen-powered cars and home heating units may never come to fruition, but something else may. Interestingly, at the time of the 1992 Earth Summit in Rio de Janeiro, over two hundred prominent scientists, including twenty-seven U.S. Nobel Prize winners published a so-called Heidelberg Appeal, in which they expressed concern over "the emergence of an irrational ideology which is opposed to scientific and industrial progress and which impedes economic and social development," and called for an increased emphasis on "Science, Technology and Industry whose instruments, when properly managed, are indispensable tools of a future shaped by Humanity, by itself and for itself."[11]

In the second place, pollution control is costly, and the process of progress by generating higher levels of Gross Domestic Product (GDP) here and abroad provides resources with which pollution-control measures—from smokestack scrubbers on coal-fired plants, to the development of new fuels for cars, to the replacement of chlorofluorocarbons (CFCs) in refrigerators, air-conditioning units, plastics, and the like—can be financed. To subtract the costs of pollution abatement from a constant or declining GDP would not only be painful, but also very possibly politically and practically unacceptable.

When these two points are combined, one might well conclude that, as in the case of economic growth lowering fertility and ultimately solving the population problem, the process of progress may in the long run actually be the best way to reduce pollution. An interesting 1994 study by Princeton economists Gene Grossman and Alan Krueger found that although economic growth may initially lead to a deteriorating environment, after a certain level is reached—a national income of $8,000 per capita—growth leads to an improvement in environmental quality.[12] Some support for this view is given by the facts that in the United States, smog has declined 40 percent over the past quarter century; toxic emissions have declined 43 percent in just the last seven years; we have more forested land now than in 1920; and so on.

Third, and finally, although this point takes us to the borderline of our second main question—the effect of environmental concerns on the Idea of Progress—there is little doubt that the ideology motivating the process of progress is characteristically future-oriented. Such an orientation is extremely important since the characteristic feature of most environmental problems is that the costs that they impose (however great or small) are generally borne in the future while the costs of preventing or eliminating these problems must usually be borne in the present.

We might summarize the underlying issue this way: Although the price system may be relatively ineffective in solving environmental and other "external diseconomy" problems, this fact is well known and, in principle, one can, through various tax and subsidy policies, rearrange marketplace incentives so that these problems are internalized. Basically, it is a "polluter pays" principle. One is not allowed to foist on society costs engendered by one's own production or consumption activities; one is forced to take these into account and thereby is given strong incentives to reduce or eliminate these social costs.

The point is that all this is well known and what is needed to eliminate the predicament in question is primarily (1) to understand what the specific problems are, and (2) to approach them with a willingness to accept short-term sacrifices for long-term gains. The process of progress should, one would think, be a help both in promoting the scientific understanding of the problems and in sustaining the required future-oriented ideology. But will it in fact sustain such an ideology? Here we come directly to our second main question: What effect has the environmental predicament had on the waning faith in the Idea of Progress?

THE ENVIRONMENTAL PREDICAMENT AND THE IDEA OF PROGRESS

Compared to concerns about the bomb or the energy crisis, there is little doubt that anxieties about potential or actual environmental damage are far more prevalent and intense today, both worldwide and in the United States in particular. Mind you, these anxieties are by no means universal. How could they be when the popular mind is constantly assaulted by laymen's books and articles taking radically different positions on the central issues involved? In 1995, for example, journalist Ron Bailey edited a book, *The True State of the Planet*, in which the authors of the various included articles more or less totally debunked modern environmental concerns. In that same year, a few months later, the *New York Times Magazine* published an article by Bill McKibben, "Not so Fast," totally debunking the debunkers, and calling for Americans massively "to change their lives." Meanwhile, not long before this article, another journalist, Greg Easterbrook, had published *his* book, *A*

Moment on the Earth: The Coming Age of Environmental Optimism, in which he took the positions (1) that environmentalists had vastly over-stated their case, but (2) that enviromental regulations had nevertheless done a lot of good. How could the general public possibly decide where the real truth lay?[13]

Still, it remains true that, compared to the other predicaments we have considered, the environmental issue is currently much more in the forefront at the present time. Furthermore, for many of those expressing the greatest concern, there is also little doubt that they find the answer to the problem in the large-scale abandonment of the process of progress as we have known it since the Industrial Revolution. As compared to the basic tenets of the Idea of Progress, which viewed the process as basically good and as sustainable into the more or less indefinite future, many environmentalists clearly wish to call the whole process to a halt and to promote a vastly different lifestyle from that which has become characteristic in the developed nations over the past two hundred years.

This is certainly true of the McKibben article, just cited, where he lambastes our habit of always "doubling or tripling our economies." It was also true of the various Doomsday reports that came out in the 1960s and 1970s. They frequently focused on the necessity, and also desirability, of moving toward some form of stable, as opposed to grow-ing or progressive society. In "A Blueprint for Survival," for example, the authors urged a massive decentralization of society into "neighbor-hoods of 500, represented in communities of 5,000, in regions of 500,000, represented nationally, which in turn as today should be repre-sented globally." These small communities would be largely self-suffi-cient; they would contain a balance of agriculture and industry; many modern appliances would have to be given up, but handicraft skills would make a comeback, and the arts, generally, would flourish. "It is probable," the report says, "that only in the small community can a man or woman be an individual. In today's large agglomerations he is merely an isolate." Thus, the stable economy emerges not merely as the only hope of mankind to avoid collapse, but actually a preferred environment in which, by reducing its impact on nature, humanity achieves a new personal and social harmony that is lost in a growth-oriented society.[14]

In effect, that very central element of the process of progress on which the Idea of Progress so heavily depended at the outset—man's ability to master and control the forces of nature—is now not only rejected, but reversed. Human beings are to adjust themselves to nature, live close to nature, befriend nature, commune with nature. Nature—read "ecosphere"—is in control and within its ample structure humanity is to find its small but agreeable niche. So too, of course, is the spotted owl and the snail darter. Whether certain prominent late twentieth-century viruses are to be included in this all-inclusive chain of being is another question. Presumably, as both arts and sciences flourish in these benign communities, a few species eradications would be permitted.

Is it such thinking as this that, in point of major and significant fact, has undermined the Idea of Progress in our time? Certainly, many environmentalists do share a preference for a stationary state. Still, before we conclude that the environmental predicament, unlike the weapons or energy or original population predicaments, is at the core of our waning faith in Progress, we must note three points at least:

1. *Although there are some believers in the imminence of societal collapse under a progress-growth-style regime, there remain many others who find the logic and conclusions of the environmentalists rather extreme.*

The weakening of contemporary society's general faith in Progress is not, I believe, by any means confined to those who expect—or feel that they have somehow proved by computer-generated simulations—future environmental catastrophe. As we go along, indeed, I think we will find that a main characteristic of those worried about where we are heading is a state of generalized anxiety and uncertainty. The clearcut, vividly painted threats of the environmentalists are not, in my estimation, really typical. Whereas the environmentalists are quite definite about what lies ahead, most people are rather unsure about what lies ahead. If Progress is God, environmentalists are convinced atheists; the rest of us tend toward rather uncomfortable agnosticism.

2. *The very fact that the focus of our worries about future progress has shifted so dramatically over time suggests that each specific predicament is more an occasion or outlet for an underlying malaise of one sort of another rather than a direct cause.*

It is, in fact, very interesting to note that in some cases the dominant worries in one period can actually reverse themselves in the next. Who could possibly have thought when Ehrlich was writing his alarming treatise *The Population Bomb* that twenty years later a best-seller in the United States would be titled, *The Birth Dearth?*[15] Who would have thought when the rivalry between communism and capitalism was ended and massive disarmament agreements and destruction of weapons systems were being undertaken, that many people could conclude that the world—beset by fractured nations, tribes, religions, sects, and assorted terrorists—was now *really* headed for trouble? For that matter, who could possibly have anticipated in the 1970s that in the early 1990s, even with Kuwait damaged and Iraq virtually, if temporarily, out of business, the complaint of oil producers around the world would be a tendency to glut rather than to shortage?

In truth, this kind of exact reversal of concerns even applies occasionally in the specific area of global warming. In the hot summer of 1995, it was very easy to believe in this phenomenon, but what about the cold winter of 1994? In its 31 January 1994 issue, *Time* magazine ran a major article entitled, "The Ice Age Cometh?" It featured the freezing of Niagara Falls, the shutting down of New Jersey's interstate highways, and temperatures of twenty-two degrees below zero in Kentucky. Most strikingly of all was its basic theme: "The next Ice Age could start tens of thousands of years from now. Or tens of years. Or it may have already started."[15]

Considering all these zigs and zags, we are strongly reminded of the amusing quote from George Stigler cited in chapter 6 re the Reverend Malthus: "For every answer, one can find a correct question." Which we might well rewrite for the present context: "For every anxiety, one can find a looming disaster."

3. *There is really no fundamental reason that the environmental crises described in the Doomsday tomes should make us abandon the Idea of Progress.*

There is intrinsically no reason why the process of progress, which has been so efficient in the production of economic "goods," should not be equally proficient in the elimination of economic "bads." For there were numerous "bads" in the world before the Industrial Revolution was ever dreamt of: poverty, disease, early death, back-breaking physical labor, drought, flood, plague, infestation, malnutrition—the list goes on endlessly. Why should the "bads" of global warming, acid rain, or ozone-depletion prove more resistant to the forces of progress than these more ancient maladies? Furthermore, as has been mentioned a number of times now, the Idea of Progress, with its strong future orientation should be considered an ally, not an enemy, of the environmentalists, or so one would have thought.

Indeed, the suspicion grows—justifiably, I believe—that it is not the bomb, population explosions, gas lines, or greenhouse effects that lie at the heart of society's current difficulties. The real problem lies in our seeming inability to maintain that very future orientation on which so much else depends. To this more fundamental predicament, let us now turn our attention.

9

THE FUNDAMENTAL PREDICAMENT
OF PROGRESS

The generalized anxiety of contemporary America, and, indeed, of the Western world as a whole, has usually been able to find an apparently "objective" warrant at any given moment of time. But the warrants keep changing. The analysis in the last three chapters strongly suggests that the distinction between "good reasons" and "real reasons" is appropriate here. The reasons Americans offer to explain their malaise are never fully convincing. The malaise itself, however, seems very real.

In this chapter, I will try to explain this underlying malaise in terms of what I will call the "fundamental predicament of progress." In doing so, I will be analyzing the paradox that I have repeatedly noted as central to this study, namely, how the process of progress ultimately undermines the very same Idea of Progress to which it originally gave birth.

TRYING OUT (BUT THEN REJECTING) A "SUCCESS" EXPLANATION

As we have considered the different predicaments of progress in the preceding pages, we have usually found that the process of progress, while the cause of these particular difficulties, often seems to offer if not definitive keys to their solution, at least possible keys, and many times what seems the most plausible of the available approaches. The process not only poses problems, but disposes of problems. Historically, it has, in fact, and on the whole, been very good at disposing of problems.

This brings to mind a curious thought: Is it possible that the dethronement of the Idea of Progress in recent decades is due not so much to the failures of the process of progress as to its successes? If true, this would involve a paradox to explain a paradox—and a very fascinating and challenging mental exercise for both author and reader.

Actually, I do not believe this approach is valid, but it is worth discussing, if only briefly, since it seems implicit in many discussions of contemporary American attitudes. Also, it is a form of analysis with a rich intellectual pedigree. I refer here specifically to Joseph Schumpeter's highly provocative analysis of a predicted breakdown of capitalism. Part 2 of his *Capitalism, Socialism, and Democracy* is entitled, "Can Capitalism Survive?", to which he gave the immediate answer: "No, I do not think it can." And this was followed by his argument that capitalism would break down "not under the weight of economic failure," but because of its "very success."[1]

His topic, though clearly different, is not totally unrelated to the subject of this book. Also, his approach is in many ways similar. While I have questioned the validity of some of the earlier predicaments of progress, he tried to dispose of many of the problems that seemed to others to be confronting capitalism. Thus, for example, he showed that the "vanishing of investment opportunity"—a great concern of the so-called "stagnationists" at the time he wrote—was completely unreal, and that it was a highly successful capitalism that ultimately undermined its own protective institutions and ideology.[2]

A similar approach applied to our problem would involve the notion that the enormous success of the process of progress in providing unprecedented material abundance has somehow undermined the institutions and ideology that were historically associated with that process. Not long ago, for example, Christopher Lasch suggested that "the concept of progress can be defended against intelligent criticism only by postulating an indefinite expansion of desires, a steady rise in the general standard of comfort, and the incorporation of the masses into the culture of abundance."[3] The corollary might well be that, were this "indefinite expansion of desires" to falter, then the "concept of progress" would be *un*defended against intelligent criticism. After a point, desire might fail us. We might lose interest in further accumulation. We might simply wish to sit back and conserve what we have—that is, choose a stationary future above a progressive future as a matter of preference.

Something rather like this idea was proposed over sixty years ago by John Maynard Keynes in a famous essay, "Economic Possibilities for our Grandchildren." He envisaged a future process in which economic growth would so raise incomes and well-being that interest in further growth, and, indeed, in the future in general would disappear. He derisively characterized the "purposive man" of the past who was:

> always trying to secure a spurious and delusive immortality for his acts by pushing his interest in them forward into time. He does not love his cat, but his cat's kittens; nor, in truth, the kittens, but only the kittens' kittens, and so on forward for ever to the end of cat-dom. For him jam is not jam unless it is a case of jam tomorrow and never jam today. Thus by pushing his jam always forward into the future, he strives to secure for his act of boiling it an immortality.

We can see in this statement a critique not only of the "purposive man"—the saver, investor, and accumulator of the process of progress—but also of the Idea of Progress with its central emphasis on the importance of the future above the present. Fortunately, Keynes thought, in a hundred years or so the process of progress would have completed its (rather disagreeable) work, we would have a world of almost limitless abundance, and much more salutary principles would apply. In particular, we would adopt the view that "those walk most truly in the paths of virtue and sane wisdom who take least thought for the morrow. We shall once more value ends above means and prefer the good to the useful. We shall honor those who can teach us how to pluck the hour and the day virtuously and well, the delightful people who are capable of taking direct enjoyment in things, the lilies of the field who toil not, neither do they spin."[4] Thus, with our material desires largely satiated, we would abandon the race, purge the future from our thoughts, and start practicing the simple and direct art of living.

Such a development is, of course, possible, and a number of individuals, perhaps especially in the late 1960s and early 1970s, did choose to pull out of the race, to move from city to countryside, to engage there in the more humane pleasures of communal sex, farming, candlemaking, basket-weaving, and other handicraft occupations. Happiness did not always follow, including for those left behind. One woman reported that her husband had abandoned her because he had fallen in love with his loom. Nor did those who left always find the simple life—for example, farming the rather obdurate soils of rural New England—as satisfying in detail as in principle.

The main problem with this point of view, however, is not the success or failure of those who decided to limit, rather than to fulfill, material desires, but the fact that this philosophy never captured a majority of Americans, even young Americans, during the unrest of the late 1960s, and certainly is far from characteristic of the outlook of the 1990s. What one hears constantly today is how difficult it is for young people to achieve and maintain a "middle-class standard of life."

Indeed, it can be argued that, if anything, desire has had a tendency to outrun achievement, even historically unprecedented and really quite massive achievement. As we have noted before, American median per capita income has risen perhaps as much as fivefold during the past century. If the expansion of desire has had any notable difficulty in keeping up with this tremendous growth of economic abundance, we have yet to hear major public testimonials to that effect. On the contrary, as I say, the usual complaint in the early 1990s is that young people find it so hard to keep up. They can't afford mortgages and proper houses, they can't afford college educations for their children, in fact they can't afford many children or to forgo second incomes to take care of those few children they do have.

Actually, the "success" argument can easily be given exactly the opposite form from the above, namely to emphasize not desire satiation but desire insatiability. This is a commonly heard theme these days. The material abundance brought about by progress has, it is said, engendered an overwhelming desire to enjoy every possible good thing in life. It has created a hedonistic mood so intense that one cannot think of anything but present satisfactions.

Needless to say, it is a bit disconcerting when both a proposition and its negation can be used to explain the same phenomenon. Also, whereas the desire-satiation theme does at least offer an explanation for our lack of interest in building for the future—that is, we have no need for more material wealth—the desire-insatiability theme gives no particular reason for a strong preference for the present above the future. Our children and heirs presumably also have this great need for "more." Why then are we neglecting their future desires in favor of our present desires? Why is the thought of their future well-being not an integral and vital part of our present well-being?

Above all, both theories, insofar as they rest on a foundation of the huge success of the progress enterprise, fail to catch the real mood of contemporary America. Consider all the predicaments of progress that we have just been discussing. Do they suggest any great sense of satisfaction or accomplishment as a consequence of two centuries of progress? On the contrary, most of them involve a vague disparagement of prior achievements, a sense that they are not truly real, that they may come to an end—the globe will become hopelessly overpopulated, we will run out of resources or choke ourselves to death on pollutants, or, possibly, anticipate all these problems via a nuclear Armageddon. Monday's problem du jour may, of course, disappear by Tuesday. But then there is Wednesday's problem du jour to consider.

What we have today is some small sense of satisfaction about the past along with a comparable anxiety about the future. We are both vaguely satisfied and vaguely apprehensive. And we have not quite yet decided what we are apprehensive about.

A CENTRAL CHARACTERISTIC OF THE FUNDAMENTAL PREDICAMENT

The Idea of Progress, one of the great, dominating ideas of modern Western, and certainly American, history expressed, perhaps above all else, faith in the future. It was a faith that the future would almost certainly be better, probably much better than the present, and that, in consequence, one could emotionally count on that future to provide purpose and justification for today's not always appealing (as Keynes would have it) attitudes and activities. It is, indeed, the importance attributed to the future that precisely links the Idea of Progress with the fate of the American family.

The great, though not necessarily more appealing, postmodern idea is agnosticism about the future. At least, this is our large claim. We no longer know, or, more accurately, we no longer *feel* that we know, the general shape of the future of humanity on this earth. We are not totally pessimistic. We are certainly not buoyantly optimistic. We are unsure—agnostic. We basically feel that we can't see that far ahead in time. And not being able to imagine the far future, even in broad outline, let alone detail, we no longer can count on it emotionally in terms of our purposes, plans and behaviors. And this new, postmodern idea is also linked to the fate of the American family, and especially to the role of children in our lives—and not happily.

If all this is true, one will be able to claim—as I in fact will in chapter 10—that the Idea of Progress, once so dominant in this country, is now dying a not-so-slow death before our very eyes. Our immediate task, however, is to try to link this putative failure of the Idea of Progress to the underlying process of progress, that is, to construe this development as a bona fide predicament of progress. But if we have already shown that neither the failures of the process of progress nor its successes seem to be undermining the Idea of Progress, at least in any obvious way, then what could possibly be the problem?

My answer, if not quite as paradoxical as Schumpeter's analysis of capitalism, is, I believe, sufficiently provocative in its own terms. It is essentially that the process of progress is, by its intrinsic nature, in conflict with the Idea of Progress. The process is really at war with the Idea from the very beginning. The conflict is always there but it emerges and becomes dominating only over the course of time. It is this underlying and ever-growing conflict that I call the "fundamental predicament of progress."

When I suggest that the process of progress, by its "intrinsic nature," involves a real, or certainly potential, conflict with the Idea of Progress, I do not mean to claim more than can be fairly readily justified. As always when I speak of the process of progress, I am speaking of an empirical phenomenon about which certain generalizations can be made. The "intrinsic nature" referred to here has no particularly mystical properties but refers only to the basic empirical characteristics we considered in chapter 3 (see pp. 65–69). To repeat that description here, I suggested that the process of progress historically has been characterized by at least four major features, some of which at least have tended to increase in depth and intensity over time: (1) the rapidity of change; (2) mankind's increasing power to affect the environment; (3) an increasing range of choices and decisions facing humanity, both individually and collectively; and (4) increasing scale, specialization, and interdependence. Taken altogether, these various characteristics, we noted, often lead to popular descriptions of today's world as increasingly "complex" and involving constantly "accelerating change."[5]

The Idea of Progress, in its turn, also has certain characteristic features as were described in chapter 4 (see pp. 85–92). In the sense in which the Idea became a widespread article of faith in the nineteenth and early twentieth centuries and actually motivated people and affected their actions and decisions in daily life (speaking always primarily of the United States, Britain, and a few other "early developers"), the Idea involved three major claims: (1) that the process of progress was a "good thing;" (2) that it would continue over at least a very extended future; and (3) that the extended future over which the process was expected to continue was important psychologically, that is, that what was to happen *then* (in a terrestrial setting, of course) mattered *now*. Again, summed up briefly, the Idea of Progress states that the process is good, inevitable, and important.

To say then that the fundamental predicament of progress reflects a conflict between process and Idea is to state simply that there is a basic dissonance between the characteristics embedded in the process as empirically observed, and the view of the world implied in the central features of the Idea. To put it a bit more accurately, since, in the case of the process of progress, we are talking about characteristics, some of which increase in depth and intensity over time: there is a tendency toward conflict and dissonance, which tendency can be expected to grow more serious with the passage of time.

SOURCES OF CONFLICT BETWEEN PROCESS AND IDEA

But are there convincing reasons to suggest that a conflict between process and Idea, or even a tendency toward such a conflict, actually might exist? The analysis here, when organized around the three basic characteristics of the Idea of Progress, is in fact fairly straightforward.

1. *The process of progress is inevitable*

Let us begin with the second basic characteristic, namely, the notion of inevitability, or, more accurately, the degree of inevitability, involved in the Idea of Progress. Clearly, if anyone is to depend in any serious psychological way on the future for present satisfaction and/or the direction of present behavior, he or she must be able to entertain at least a strong presumption that the process of progress will continue substantially in its present form over the distant future. By the use of such terms as "degree," "presumption," and "substantially" I indicate that we are dealing only with general tendencies—tendencies, moreover, in a psychological, not logical, sense.

In such terms, it seems fairly obvious that each of the four main features of the process of progress as it has evolved historically tend to undercut any real sense of the inevitability of future outcomes, whether involving a continuation of the process of progress or not.

Consider first the rapidity of change under a regime of progress. Whether or not change in the later stages of the process "accelerates" in any objective sense, the fact is that many people have a subjective sense of such acceleration. Certainly there is no reason, objective or subjective, to believe that change is in any way "decelerating" as the twentieth century comes to a close. Indeed, as one contemplates the continuing developments that have revolutionized one after another of the basic features of our daily lives over the last two centuries, the question almost automatically arises: How did the Idea of Progress ever take hold in the first place? Whatever else it does, the process of progress is certainly involved in creating the new, the novel, the unexpected. By contrast, the Idea of Progress requires a relatively dependable, certifiable future. How could these two approaches—the one free-floating, the other apparently constraining—ever have come to lie down together?

Chapter 5 presented a number of specific factors of a scientific, economic, and moral nature that enabled the process to give credence to the Idea in those early stages. As we now contemplate the rapidity of change under a regime of progress, it is hard to avoid the conclusion that the main burden of explanation may concern that initial harmony of process and Idea, not their later dissonance. How could anyone ever have imagined that any particular future configuration was "inevitable" given the massive changes that science and technology continually bring forth?

The psychological problem is further deepened by the other characteristics of the process of progress. Consider the increasing power of human beings to affect their environment. In the case of this second characteristic, we have a tendency that clearly does grow in force and effect over time. While never reaching complete mastery over nature, the process of progress continually gives humanity more and more tools by which the natural course of affairs can be shifted, altered, diverted, and in an ideal world converted to human betterment.

There is a certain irony in putting the matter this way in the sense that the predicament of progress causing most global concern these days involves exactly man's increased capability of doing harm to the environment. Of all the specific predicaments we have had to deal with, this may well prove the most difficult to find practically acceptable solutions for. What is involved here (as in all the other predicaments to a greater or lesser degree) is our uncertainty over what humans will, in fact, do with their new powers. Which is to say that, as power over the environment is gradually transferred from nature to man, the future becomes more and more dependent on a factor of known, or at least highly suspected, variability. In the beginning, as already suggested in chapter 5, nature tends to be the main adversary. It is thus possible, and even probable, that man's increasing power over nature initially gives him a greater sense of the reliability of the future—a future which is now less subject to the unexpected and heretofore completely uncontrolled forces of nature.

But in lessening the variability due to one agent, the process of progress greatly enhances the power of the other suspect agent, man himself. It is no accident, but of the essence, that in all the predicaments we have been discussing, the real question always comes down to what people will actually decide to do—whether it be having too many babies or polluting the planet or deciding to blow up the world in a nuclear holocaust. At a minimum, this second feature of the process of progress makes all future scenarios increasingly dependent on how predictable human beings themselves are likely to be in the decades and centuries ahead.

And this predictability of human behavior is likely not to increase but to diminish considerably as the process of progress continues over time. Partly, this involves the question of morality, which we come to in a moment. But it is also a direct result of a third characteristic of the process of progress, namely, an increasing range of choices and decisions facing humanity both individually and collectively. The number of paths into the future that we may choose to take—those that are not ruled out by harsh and immediate consequences like sudden death, starvation, excruciating pain, or whatever—increases enormously. This effectively is what we mean by economic abundance, the enormous growth of GNP per capita, and like measures. But also, as earlier noted, it is empirically (though not logically or necessarily) true that the process of progress has conferred enormous political and social freedom on most countries, at least over a sufficiently long run. This further increases the range of choice available to us. We can decide to go this way or that. Very little is predetermined. In terms of our present question, very little is in any sense "inevitable."

Being aware of the multiplicity of paths available to us—whether it be choice of career, political party, television channel, make of automobile, or general lifestyle—we are simultaneously aware of the multiplicity of paths being followed by others. Who can possibly figure out where one will oneself end up? I am not going to run a corner grocery store the way my parents did, nor will I (according to the ad) be buying "my father's Oldsmobile"! What *will* I be doing down the road? What will *others* be doing? Who can possibly put the whole thing together?

All of which becomes even more complicated when one takes into account the fourth and final characteristic of the process of progress: the overall increase in scale, specialization, and interdependence. It is perhaps here more than in any other aspect of the matter that the feeling of the enormous complexity of modern life is engendered. The process of progress creates at once a world that is very big and a world that is very small. It is very big in the sense that Americans, say, are clearly affected by events taking place in Europe, Japan, Africa, and God knows where else, in a very powerful, day-to-day way. It is very small in the sense that, because of the highly specialized nature of work in the progressing society, one's own vantage point tends to be very limited and particularized. This is why, despite the obvious increase in options and choices available to us, we often feel that, in many major matters, we have very little control over our own destiny.

Certainly most of us are aware of a gravely impaired ability to predict the direction of change in that larger world of which we are such a miniscule part. It is just too complicated to figure out. How often are we forced to say, "That's actually outside my field," or "To tell the truth, I deal mainly with the financial not the technical side of things," and so on. And, to tell the real truth, when it comes to the future, most of us don't have a clue as to how things are going to turn out five, ten, twenty years down the road, let alone the long vistas of posterity once envisaged by the Progress dreamers of the nineteenth century.

In a word, even in the loosest sense, the vision of any inevitable, or even highly probable, future course of events over a prolonged period of time has largely departed the scene. In itself, this is really enough to doom the Idea of Progress in any powerful, society-dominating sense. And there is more.

2. *The process of progress is a "good thing"*

I turn now to what we earlier listed as the first characteristic of the Idea of Progress, namely, the view that the process of progress has been and will be, assuming it continues, a "good thing." As indicated in chapter 4, this feature is more complicated than may appear on the surface for the simple reason that it has real content only when a particular standard of value is specified. For a believer today to imagine that the future world will shape up in a way that he or she considers appalling, but which is considered perfectly acceptable, or even delightful, by those who inhabit that future world, will hardly do much to support that believer's faith. Indeed, he or she may very well conclude that those future generations have deteriorated beyond any hope of redemption.

This point is really quite important for it suggests that underlying the Idea of Progress is the belief that human morality, or certainly the direction of change of human morality, is invariant over time. Capital "P" Progress essentially inhabits the world of absolute values. The believer needs some faith that the process of progress will in the future as in the past be guided by an appropriate moral code.

Now what the process of progress does over time is to (a) intensify this moral requirement, and (b) make it increasingly difficult to fulfill. The tension created between (a) and (b) is such as eventually to become unsustainable. The result is a total fragmentation of social morality. Terms like "multiculturalism," "diversity," and, perhaps above all, "moral relativism" suggest the factual reality of this fragmentation in today's American culture. More of this later. For the moment, let us examine only the direct effects of (a) and (b) on the standing of the Idea of Progress.

First, why do I say that the process of progress intensifies the need for a rather strict and firm moral viewpoint if the Idea of Progress is to persist over time? The essential reason is that only with such a built-in and even rigid morality can the increasing power of man to impact the world around him and his ever-expanding range of options and choices be constrained to follow a morally acceptable future path, or even general range of paths. This problem is, as I have already noted, with us from the very beginning of the process. When it was asked, how was it that the process of progress, which involves such wrenching changes in all aspects of life, could have produced the concept of a dependable, certifiable future, I gave a number of reasons, but large among them was the strength of society's moral code, in the historical case of Britain and America, the code of Victorian morality. If society knows what its goals and purposes are, then it is much less difficult to visualize the future that will emerge as a result of the wrenching changes that are in fact taking place. There is a prescribed path, and consequently the educational enterprise, both at home and at school, and society's reform movements, whether dealing with the elimination of drink or the liberation of women, are designed to ensure that society does in fact follow that morally appropriate path. In this fashion, one might say, morality not only specifies the good thing that is Progress but makes it possible to visualize a future world in which this good thing continues to occur.

Now as the power over the future is, by the process of progress, increasingly transferred from nature to mankind, the need for human behavior to conform to such a moral code only grows stronger. This is what is meant by (a) above to the effect that over time the morality requirement tends, if anything, to become more stringent.

But then we go on to (b), which claims that this requirement becomes increasingly difficult to fulfill in the course of the process of progress. Society begins the process with, as it were, a gift of morality from the past. This morality is drenched with religious phraseology and concept. There is, of course, a vast literature discussing the relationship of religion, and especially Protestantism, to the rise of capitalism and the modernization process generally.[6] I take no particular side on the issue of causation here, but only stress the obvious point that the process of progress from, say, the Industrial Revolution on did not take place *ab ovo* in a morally or religiously neutral world. The industrializing nations clearly began with an inherited, if you will "old-fashioned," set of values, which reflect an earlier stage of society in which the religious impulse was strong, and often dominating.

In the early days of the process, and, in the United States really through much of the nineteenth century, there is a very strong effort to retain these "old-fashioned" values. An important piece of evidence on this point is the way nineteenth-century schoolbooks for children were written. As indicated in chapter 4, these books combine an enormous pride in the rapidity of the nation's progress in material wealth with the apparent view that the rural life, close to God's beneficent natural world, is the life in which real virtue and contentment lie. Indeed, in the earlier part of the century, such hymns to agriculture and its way of life seem to reflect a view of America's essential and unique character.[7]

I interpret this emphasis on an apparently premodern view of life not as a rejection of the process of progress but as an attempt to maintain a set future course in a morally salutary direction. This attempt, however, becomes increasingly difficult to sustain over time. Indeed, already by the end of the nineteenth century, the paeans to agriculture and rural life in America's schoolbooks have begun to change tone. The mood is increasingly one of nostalgia, a celebration of what was once a simpler, nobler life, and is now rapidly passing, much as in our own age we mourn the passing of the small town, the village, the sense of community that once putatively characterized our daily lives.

Nostalgia, of course, carries with it the recognition that what once was is no more, and probably will never be again. And this is essentially what tends to happen to "old-fashioned" morality under a persistent regime of progress. In the first place, however much the forms persist, the religious warrant certifying this morality tends inevitably to be weakened as the process continues over time. The process of progress is a secular, this-worldly phenomenon. The Idea of Progress is also in substance a secular concept. Early religious leaders themselves were aware of the potential conflict between specific religious injunctions and their real-world consequences. Thus, if we morally exhort people to work hard and to save, how can we avoid the fact that they will become rich and that, when rich, they are likely to turn away from religion?[8] More generally, the process of progress, focusing on mankind's ability to master nature in a very clearly this-worldly setting, tends, at a minimum, to place religious justifications somewhere off on a back burner.

The theory of evolution provided a further challenge to the "old-fashioned," and specifically religious morality, though at the same time it provided a possible basis for a "progressive" morality of its own, and also could, without too much strain, be itself interpreted religiously. Thus, one could say, as many eventually did, that evolution was simply the mechanism God chose for humanity to work out its higher destiny on earth.

It was not, however, at all clear that the morality of the evolution-ist—natural selection, "survival of the fittest," Social Darwinism, and the like—described a future world that would be all that attractive, at least by previous conventional standards. Most important of all, how-ever, was the fact that insofar as the evolutionary process provided any warrant whatever for standards of social and personal morality, that war-rant was continually being weakened by the process of progress. For an essential feature of man's increasing mastery of nature was man's increas-ing ability to change and shape the course of evolution itself. Far from providing a standard by which human morality could be judged, evolu-tion became simply another natural process that human beings could modify, alter, or divert according to their own standards.

But where then would those standards come from? If "old-fash-ioned" values tend to fade, if religion is increasingly undercut by secular-ism, and if evolution becomes not a parameter but a dependent variable, then how exactly are those standards to be formed? Particularly, one adds, when all sorts of different lifestyles become sustainable in a world of increasing material abundance. Since an ever-widening range of choices and options is intrinsic to the process of progress, how, in the absence of prior warrants, can anyone justify restraint, limits, confine-ment?

All of which raises the strong probability that the future under a prolonged regime of progress becomes not only empirically indetermi-nate—it is increasingly difficult to know exactly what will be happening next—but morally indeterminate as well. What path will the process of progress take in the future? Who knows? Can we at least be certain that the path will ultimately lead to a better world? Who knows? In fact, who knows what a "better world" is? Your "better world" is a lot a different from hers which is different from his which is, sad to say, very different from mine.

In short, our agnosticism about the future extends not only to facts but to values. It is an all-pervasive phenomenon.

3. *The future is important, it "counts"*

Given this increasing difficulty in limning the shape of the future in terms either of factual or moral content, it would be no surprise to find that, over the course of time, Americans give a lower and lower priority to future as opposed to present events. A bird in the hand has perhaps always been worth two in the bush. But how many is it worth when one has great difficulty in determining what the future status of both birds and bushes will be? When uncertainty rules, the tendency is to apply a very high discount rate to future possibilities. The present reigns supreme.

I am speaking, as always, from a psychological rather than logical point of view. Uncertainty about the shape of the future could conceivably lead to a greater interest in, even an obsession with, the future. For example, there are without question today many environmentalists who are so worried about the future shape of planet earth that imaginings of things to come, often very dire things, fill their waking hours, and very possibly, their dreaming hours as well. It would be quite inaccurate to say in these cases that the future was losing priority, that it no longer really "counted."

Still, in the form in which the future mattered, and mattered greatly, under the aegis of the Idea of Progress, there is no doubt that any kind of agnosticism about what is likely to happen in the years and centuries ahead would very much tend to undercut one's emotional commitment to the future. If one could be sure that one's efforts were creating an ever-better world for one's children, heirs, and posterity in general, then a rough secular equivalent of religious purpose could be given to one's life. If, by contrast, that future is pretty much up for grabs, the question is bound to arise: Will all those efforts of mine pay off? Why should I work so hard? Save so much? Sacrifice to erect some kind of edifice that may be swept away by circumstance, or mere fashion, after I am gone? Why, in short, continue to be that future directed, "purposive man," who, in the extreme Keynesian description, actually prefers postponing jam consumption until a distant tomorrow to its consumption today?

Two major points can perhaps be established here: The *first* point is that increasing evidence that American society is, by its actual acts and behavior, showing little interest in the distant future would be sufficient evidence to prove that the Idea of Progress is in fact rapidly losing ground in our minds and hearts. The Idea of Progress is intrinsically focused on the long run. Shrinking time horizons are incompatible with that Idea as a significant ideological force.

Time horizons are, certainly in theoretical terms, a rather complex subject. Also, as political scientist Edward C. Banfield pointed out many years ago, they are very difficult to measure with any precision. Banfield was particularly interested in the differences in the degree of present-mindedness among socioeconomic classes at any given moment of time.[9] By contrast, our interest is in the increasing degree of present-mindedness—the shortening of time horizons—over the course of time, especially in America over the course of recent decades.

Although difficult to define and measure theoretically, shortened time horizons are not that hard to find in many real-life situations. Any behavior in which future consequences seem clearly and obviously to be overlooked or very highly discounted would qualify. I shall speak of a number of gross examples of such behaviors in chapter 10—everything from the increase in teenage sexual activity to the mounting burdens of the national debt to declining personal savings to the wildfire growth of the gambling industry. A general condition of temporal "myopia" is, I believe, now rampant in our nation.

As will become clear as the discussion continues, however, even this first point must be interpreted with some care. Although it is not perhaps an intrinsic characteristic, it has nevertheless been a persistent characteristic, of the process of progress that it results in longer life expectancies and, most recently, longer life expectancies at older ages. This explains why I have spoken above of little interest being shown in the "distant future." For with respect to the near-term future, there are reasons to expect a possible increase of interest, at least of personal interest due to the simple fact that one has a definite and clearcut stake in those years in which one can still expect to be around. This combination of an increasing agnosticism about the distant future with an increasing preoccupation with the near future—in the case of today's elderly Americans, with such things as Social Security, Medicare, pension plans, and the like—is likely to lead to a particularly strong focus on one's own life relative to the lives of one's children and heirs. I should note here that Joseph Schumpeter exactly anticipated this particular point a half century ago. On somewhat different grounds from those presented here, he nevertheless came to the same conclusion I have, namely, that as modern society evolves, people's interest in the far future will contract and will more and more be confined to their own life expectancies.[10] As Schumpeter also noted, and as I will try to show presently (see pages 243–44), this particular configuration of change has very serious implications for the institution of the family in a postmodern society.

The *second* point to be made here is that while this shrinking of time horizons seems clearly to follow from the agnosticism about the future bred by the process of progress, the connection is (as always) psychological, and not logically necessary. Indeed, to say that we are somehow "inexorably" or "inevitably" required to abandon our interest in the possible course of future events after we ourselves have departed the scene would actually be to contradict fundamental characteristics of the process of progress. In particular, it would contradict the tendency of that process to increase, not eliminate, our choices, options, and possible paths into the future. The original problem, after all, is in great part that nothing about the future any longer seems "inevitable." This is a major reason for our agnosticism. It is a question of not one, or too few, but too many potential avenues lying ahead of us. Of too much choice, not too little.

A PREDICAMENT FUNDAMENTAL BUT NOT INEXORABLE

Another way of putting this last point is to say while I believe the predicament of progress we have been discussing to be fundamental, I do not consider it to be inexorable. It is fundamental in the sense that the process of progress tends to undermine the Idea of Progress not because of highly specific features—running out of oil, depleting the ozone layer, lobbing nuclear-tipped missiles, and the like—but because of very general characteristics. The rapidity of change, the increasing dependence on the choices and actions of human beings as we succeed more and more in mastering the laws and forces of nature, the growing variability of people's choices as "necessity" loosens its grip on the human condition and as justifications for particular cultures or moralities increasingly weaken—all these intrinsic features of the process tend to lead to the same psychological outcome: a feeling that the distant future, and specifically the future that we will not live to see, is really beyond our comprehension. Feeling thus, many of us are unwilling to place any great hopes and dreams on the possibility of an ever better and happier world that lies ahead. The proof that we have taken this stance would be that our behavior shows an increasing disdain for the future consequences of present actions. And this same proof would indicate clearly that the Idea of Progress was beginning to wither and die as the guiding principle of postmodern society. Rooted in the present, we would no longer find any compelling satisfaction in building for a better world in the decades and centuries ahead.[11]

Fundamental, but not inexorable. Not irrevocable. At least such is the argument that can be made. For the increasing range of choice that makes the future so difficult to predict also implies the existence of one particular kind of choice: self-restraint, self-limitation, confining oneself, if not to the "straight and narrow" path, nevertheless to a relatively small sample of acceptable paths into the future. To many, such limitations, even if relatively loose and specifically self-imposed, are anathema. To others, as I shall try to show in due course, they offer a way out of what now seems a highly unsatisfactory cultural dilemma. They offer hope.

10

DECLINE AND FALL OF THE IDEA OF PROGRESS

So far I have been talking as though it were more or less generally agreed that the Idea of Progress, if not actually dead, is at least withering on the vine in late-twentieth-century America. However, I have not yet assembled any kind of systematic evidence to show that this is in fact the case. What I have done, or tried to do, is something rather different, namely to show that there is a basic dissonance between the psychological vision of the world embodied in that Idea and certain intrinsic characteristics of the process of progress. In short, having examined those factors that could be expected to bring about a decline in the Idea of Progress, we must now ask whether such a decline has actually taken place in present-day America.

This chapter will attempt to show that this very Idea that was so buoyantly dominant during the late nineteenth and early twentieth centuries has, as we enter the twenty-first century, virtually fled the domestic scene. This point is shown in two ways: (1) by evidence of changing intellectual and popular attitudes, and (2), more significantly, I feel, by indicating how our actual actions, in the most diverse departments of life, show an extraordinary present orientation, a dramatic shortening of time horizons, and, in general, a remarkable neglect of even quite obvious future consequences and ramifications. If the distant future still seems to "count" with us in many of our public utterances, our day-to-day actions appear to tell a very different story.

POPULAR ATTITUDES ABOUT PROGRESS

I take up the question of general attitudes first, asking whether there has, in fact, been a loss of faith in, and growing agnosticism about, the

189

distant future among Americans since, say, the early decades of this century. Is there any really convincing evidence to this effect?

I believe there is such evidence but, as usual in such complex matters, we have to begin with a caveat. The difficulty is that while almost everyone agrees that American faith in the Idea of Progress has waned seriously over the past seventy-five years or so, this development has by no means been uniform or uninterrupted. As mentioned in passing before, there was a substantial rebirth of the Idea of Progress in the United States in the first two decades after World War II. Like the Baby Boom which accompanied it (and which, in fact, I believe to be significantly connected to it), this renaissance of faith was short-lived. Also, like the subsequent collapse of the Baby Boom, the abandonment of the faith, when it occurred, was shockingly rapid. During the late sixties, the United States (and to some degree the entire industrial world) went through a kind of cultural revolution, a major victim of which was the view that the process of progress—industrialization, urbanization, affluence, and the like—was inevitable, good, or even satisfactory as a future way of life.

A similar, but smaller scale and less universal, recrudescence of the Idea of Progress took place in America in the 1980s during the Reagan Administration. In the late 1970s, during the Carter years, there was much talk about a national "malaise," while the Reagan presidency was, at least on the surface, highly vocal in promoting pride in America's past and also in America's future. However, this rebirth of faith, such as it was, reached far less deeply into our national consciousness than had the expansive optimism after World War II, and before the 1980s were over it had vanished almost without a trace.

Granting these occasional departures from trend, nevertheless virtually all historians and other social commentators on the American social scene have noted that the overwhelming general tendency since World War I has been in the direction of a declining general faith in Progress. "For two centuries the Western world has been sustained by a profound belief in the doctrine of progress," wrote Carl Becker in *Progress and Power*. However, "since 1918 this hope has perceptibly faded. Standing within the deep shadow of the Great War, it is difficult to recover the nineteenth century faith either in the fact or the doctrine of progress."[1]

This sentiment has been echoed in one form or another by numerous authors over the course of the last fifty or sixty years. Ralph Gabriel, writing in 1935, observed the "intellectual confusion of a generation that has lost its moorings and has failed to find a guiding principle in a cosmos where all appears to be flux."[2] Charles Beard, whose early paeans to progress we have mentioned, gradually moved over the course of the century from a sense of the inevitability to a much weaker sense of the possibility of future progress.[3] Literary historian Harry Levin wrote in 1961 that "the idea of progress no longer commands our undivided confidence," and, indeed, suggested that it took a "leap of historical imagination" to "project ourselves back to the point of time when it began to prevail."[4]

In the late 1960s and early 1970s, the Doomsday writers, whose theories we discussed in chapter 8, clearly rejected both the fact of progress and its Idea. Indeed, the whole period of rebellion in the late 1960s—the repercussions of which we still feel today—can be construed as involving a basic rejection of the values of Western civilization, including centrally the Idea of Progress.

The attack continues. In 1980, Robert Nisbet, in an elaborate study of the history of the Idea of Progress, found that the "crucial premises" of the Idea were being widely challenged. After referring to the "triumph of the Idea of Progress," which reached its zenith in the period 1750–1900, he titles the section dealing with contemporary trends, "Progress at Bay," and raises the possibility of a religious revival in the future.[5] Christopher Lasch in his 1991 discussion of "progress and its critics," seems to suggest that we now have to substitute for nineteenth-century "optimism" late twentieth-century "hope," the latter apparently admitting the possibility of serious defeats along the way.[6]

In that same year, 1991, a conference was held at MIT to study the current status of the Idea of Progress. Invitations to paper writers for the conference were to take into account the fact that, in some quarters, the Idea of Progress was considered to be "an idea whose time is past because it is no longer intellectually defensible," and "an idea in crisis." In his own essay, published later in book form, one of the organizers of the conference, MIT history professor Bruce Mazlish, wrote: "Whatever else, it must be clear that a major crisis in our time is the breakdown of our belief in the idea of progress."[7]

Still more recently, Robert Heilbroner, in *Visions of the Future* (1995), forms a contrast between what he calls the "Distant Past" (essentially all world history prior to 1750 A.D.), "Yesterday" (basically Western history from 1750 to very recent times), and "Today" (recent decades or what we would call the postmodern period). The Distant Past is characterized by a vision of the future as essentially changeless, or, worse, as a continuation of a general decline from some previous golden age. By contrast, Yesterday is characterized by a notion of the future as a "great beckoning prospect," or, in our terms, prospects for an almost indefinite continuation of capital "P" Progress.

And what of Today? "Today's mood," according to Heilbroner, "is somber rather than black; uncertain rather than despairing." Generalizing with respect to all three periods, he writes: "Resignation sums up the Distant Past's vision of the future; hopefulness was that of Yesterday; and apprehension is the dominant mood of Today." In short, like our other commentators, he sees the Idea of Progress as in substantial retreat in the present postmodern age.[8]

These are, of course, intellectuals speaking and not the general public. In most cases, however, they are intellectuals speaking about the general public and what they conceive its mood to be. In any event, there is strong evidence that a general weakening of the faith has percolated through all levels and layers of American society. Sometimes this weakening is expressed in the increasingly common view that America is losing ground to the rest of the world (read especially Japan, but also potentially Korea, Taiwan, China, and other Asian nations). The American century is apparently over. As many would have it, we are already, like ancient Greece, Rome, and the British Empire, fully launched on a downward spiral.

At other times, our loss of faith is shown in a tendency to denigrate Western civilization in general and American history in particular. The emphasis shifts from our past accomplishments to our multiple sins and failings. Columbus is no longer a hero but a villain. Racism not only existed under slavery but continues to dominate our society today. World War II was fatally flawed not only by our use of nuclear weapons but also by our cruel and unjustified internment of Japanese Americans during the war. While nineteenth-century textbooks uniformly saw a record of continuing advances, both material and moral, in American history, an increasing emphasis today is on our historic iniquities, suggesting, in effect, that capital "P" Progress in the American past was largely an illusion—it never really happened!

Perhaps most commonly of all, our waning faith in the Idea of

Progress is reflected in the plethora of newspaper and magazine articles wondering whether the "American dream" is "still alive." This concern has been taken over not only by the media but by politicians of every perusasion, so much so that it produced an outburst of exasperation from Irving Kristol: "I am tired of hearing our politicians, liberal and conservative, pontificate on 'the American Dream'—and how we are falling short of it, frustrating it, neglecting it, and in general allowing ourselves to be cheated of it. Is that the way adults are supposed to talk?" He then went on to specify what all this "talk" is about: "What, precisely, is this American Dream meant to signify under current conditions? The most common frustration of this dream that is now alluded to is that we Americans no longer are confident that our children will be better off than we are, thereby foreclosing the American future. Now, it is true that such confidence has eroded, but that is a perfectly natural phenomenon, not any kind of crisis."[9]

Kristol's contention is that this "natural phenomenon" essentially results from the maturing of the American nation and is nothing in particular to be worried about. From our point of view, however, what is interesting about his comments is that they show how widespread the concern about the "American dream" has become, and how the focus of that concern is specifically on the shape of our national future.

Popular polls show the same tendencies. A 1996 *Wall Street Journal/NBC News* poll found that 60 percent of voters said that they no longer expect that their children's generation will live better than their own has. Even the children themselves seem to have caught the contemporary mood. A 1993 poll of school children by Northwestern National Life found that, when asked whether today's children will grow up to be as healthy as today's adults are now, 63 percent of the children responded in the negative. Indeed, an extraordinary pessimism pervaded the answers of these young people in general. Responding not about themselves but about other children, 87 percent of these school children said that they felt that "most other kids" were sometimes "depressed," 71 percent felt that these other kids had "a lot of stress," and 63 percent thought that most other kids had considered suicide at one time or another.[10]

Equally apprehensive about the future are today's young adult Americans, those born between 1964 and 1975. This is the generation that immediately followed the Baby Boom generation, and their attitudes have become strikingly more pessimistic about the future. For example, according to a 1993 Roper Organization poll, only 21 percent of this group think that they have a "very good" chance of achieving a "good life." This is the lowest percentage Roper has ever recorded, and is down from 41 percent in 1978 when Baby Boomers were being polled. Roper views this twenty-percentage-point drop as "a huge shift in 15 years." Roper comments further that the contrast between the Baby Boomers and the current eighteen- to twenty-nine-year-olds "stems from growing up with confidence vs. uncertainty." Even among the most affluent of the current group, "uncertainty is profound."[11]

This sense of uncertainty, apprehension, and fear of the future is so widespread in the 1990s as really to be beyond questioning. It often involves an incredibly pessimistic reading of the actual facts of contemporary American life. An excellent example of this was given by the Presidential campaign of 1992. Without much doubt, the central issue in the campaign was the economy and especially employment. Now no one would claim that the U.S. economy in 1991–1992 was perfect, yet the facts are that our unemployment picture was far superior to that of most other industrial economies at the time, that our civilian employment-to-population ratio at over 61 percent was higher than in any previous year in our history prior to 1987, that the dozen years after 1980 had seen the creation of over eighteen million new jobs in the United States and that—contrary to constantly repeated myths—the greatest demand for new workers was for skilled, educated workers and not for mindless hamburger flippers.[12]

And yet, despite all this, the nation apparently bought into the idea that we were suffering from a monumental crisis, that the crisis was centrally economic, and that the central fact in this economic crisis was unemployment. This seems overwhelmingly to be a case of a prior anxiety in search of a justifying disaster. The "malaise" of the Carter years, has only become more pervasive and impenetrable in the 1990s. Who today has any real confidence that the future will be substantially improved over the present a century from now? A decade from now? Next year? Whether the process of progress will or will not persist over time, the Idea of Progress is, for the moment at least and to put it rather gently, in limbo.

CHANGES IN BEHAVIOR

All that we have said above has to do with general attitudes. But general attitudes, and the polls that try to measure them, often vary and are sometimes almost impossible to interpret. Thus, for example, a 1996 *Time*/CNN poll found that 63 percent of respondents agreed with the statement that "the American Dream has become almost impossible for most people to achieve," yet an equal number believed that their children would have a higher standard of living than they do.[13] What on earth, one wonders, did these respondents understand by the concept of the "American Dream"?

Given these often mystifying poll responses, observed behavior is likely to be a better guide to what is going on with respect to the actual impact (or waning of impact) of the Idea of Progress in today's America. We can ask, in particular, is there any evidence that Americans are taking actions and making decisions that reflect any abandonment of the Idea of Progress? What practical indicators are available to support this view?

As it turns out, such indicators are available all around us. Indeed, critics of the process of progress would claim that virtually every specific predicament we discussed earlier in our analysis is evidence of a basic neglect of, or even contempt for, the future. Pollution, resource depletion, the arms race, insupportable population growth—all have been cited at one time or another as evidence of a criminal lack of concern about future generations. American business behavior has also been cited, though from a totally different point of view. Here the charge is that, unlike our competitors (especially the Japanese), American businessmen take a much too short run view of investment opportunities and product development. By myopically concentrating on bottom lines and quarterly profits, we are, it is alleged, handing the future over to our foreign competitors. Whether we are in fact losing out to foreign competitors is a complicated question. What is not so complicated is the claim that American businesses almost have to adopt an increasingly short-term outlook in order to satisfy their stockholders. It is notable that the average holding period for stocks has declined from over seven years in 1960 to two years in the early 1990s. This, according to a well-known analyst from the Harvard Business School, Michael Porter, "is perhaps the most telling evidence of shortening investor horizons."[14]

From the wealth of available material, I choose four examples: (1)

the rapid growth of the national debt; (2) the saving habits of the Baby Boom generation; (3) promiscuous sex, and the generally self-destructive behavior of many teenagers; and (4) the recent, and spectacular, growth of the U.S. gambling industry. In one way or another, each of these examples shows a sharp focus on what is present and near at hand, even when the behavior involved is almost certain to affect the future adversely. Since the Idea of Progress, as we are using the term, includes a deep interest in, and concern for, the distant future, any such indications of short-sighted, future-disregarding behavior would be prima facie evidence of our diminished allegiance to that Idea.

"UNTHINKABLE DEFICITS"

If securing advantages for present generations at the expense of imposing burdens on future generations could be considered almost the exact antithesis of the morality dictated by the Idea of Progress, then most Americans would probably place the federal government at the top of the list of offenders.[15] The reference here, of course, is to the increased size of federal deficits over the last two decades and the rapid growth of the total federal debt. In the early 1970s, federal budget deficits averaged around $14 or $15 billion a year; in the 1990s, they have been running in the vicinity of $100 to $200 billion dollars a year. The total gross federal debt in 1994 was over $4.5 trillion dollars, and expected to grow further in the years ahead. Even accounting for inflation and economic growth, the debt was spiralling upward. In 1974, for example, the gross debt was estimated at less than a quarter of annual GDP; by 1994, it had risen to over two-thirds of annual GDP.[16] Clearly, critics maintained, the United States was living way beyond its means and imposing massive costs on future generations.

What made this even more alarming to many observers was the fact that, despite all the rhetoric about balancing future budgets, there are a number of factors that could easily make federal deficits much larger in the future. A major factor is the aging of the population. Since per capita public expenditures are much greater for the elderly than for other age groups, the increasing proportions of old people, and especially the "old old," in our population is virtually guaranteed to put further upward pressure on federal expenditures. This upward pressure will be felt generally but also specifically in the area of health care costs, whose runaway growth is likely, in itself, to be a major factor in the growth of federal expenditures even apart from the aging of the population. An older America, with exploding health care costs, could easily lead to "unthinkable deficits" by the year 2020. Indeed, according to some accounts, continuation of current policies could be expected to lead to annual federal deficits of as much as 21 percent of GDP, in contrast to the deficits of 3 or 4 percent of GDP we have been experiencing in the early 1990s.[17]

How do these continuing deficits adversely affect the future? The answer most economists would give is that they do so by reducing national saving. Public dissaving, by reducing total national saving, effectively reduces investment and economic growth. As a 1990 report of the Congressional Budget Office put it succinctly: "The purpose of reducing the deficit is to increase national saving, which can spur economic growth and capital formation."[18] On this view of the matter, we can visualize the economy as financing government expenditures and private investment by a combination of taxes and private savings. If government expenditures exceed taxes (producing a deficit), then there will be less saving available to finance investment. Capital formation will fall, fewer assets will be bequeathed to the future, productivity growth will slow down, and in general the next generation will suffer as a result. Foreign investors may, of course, step in and maintain a level of capital formation above that allowed by domestic savings. Indeed, during the last decade, foreign investors did help sustain U.S. investment by buying up our government bonds, private plants, businesses, real estate, and the like. On this scenario, we accumulate foreign indebtedness and it is this burden we bequeath to future generations.[19]

Not all economists agree that the burdens of the debt are as serious as others suggest. For example, Professor Robert Eisner, a former president of the American Economics Association, has argued that we effectively mismeasure federal indebtedness and its impact on the economy in a variety of ways. Inflation reduces the real interest rate that the government must pay on its bonds well below the nominal rate; some government expenditures are themselves capital investments in the future of the economy; we ought also to consider state and local finances as we assess the impact of government on the economy; and so on. The net effect of all these adjustments, he believes, is to make the future burden of the debt far less than commonly calculated.[20]

On the other hand, there are quite different adjustments that suggest that these common calculations vastly understate the true burdens we are placing on the future. In particular, the way in which the federal debt is measured does not take into account unfunded liabilities that past and current legislation is passing along to the future. These include all sorts of programs from Social Security to Federal Deposit Insurance to numerous other insurance and credit commitments including pension guarantees, home mortgages, student loans, agricultural loans, and implicit guarantees of other government-sponsored enterprises. As the 1993 *Economic Report of the President* put it: "Significant long-term commitments are being passed to future generations through a number of government programs. The Federal budget does not report the cost of the commitments entailed until the year payments are actually made."[21]

Taking such federal commitments into account and trying to assess the real burdens that present generations are placing on the generations yet to come leads to some extraordinary numbers. The approach is called "generational accounting." One such accounting concludes that, even on the hopeful assumption that the government gets health care expenditures under control so that these expenditures grow no faster than the rest of the economy, unborn generations of Americans will have net tax payments (lifetime) that are 21 percent higher than those of generations already born. If, by contrast, Medicare expenditures grow faster than the economy as a whole—say, by a not unreasonable 4 percent a year—then future generations may end up paying nearly 50 percent more in taxes than today's youngest generation.[22]

Rather than building for the future, the U.S. government is, by most measurements, creating a number of stumbling blocks that future generations will have to work very hard to get around. Instead of sacrificing now for a better future, it is the sacrifice itself that is being passed on.

SAVING AND THE BABY BOOM GENERATION

All this would not be so worrisome if the personal saving of the working generation, including now the whole of the very large Baby

Boom generation, was taking up the slack. Since this generation has been widely known as the "now generation," one may well suspect that their saving behavior, rather than solving, is actually deepening the overall problem. The suspicion is well-founded.

We can begin by making the universally agreed upon points that U.S. savings rates in recent years have been very low compared to most of our foreign competitors and that they have been declining. In 1970, for example, U.S. personal saving as a percentage of disposable personal income was a rather meager 8.0 percent. By 1990, it had fallen to a quite shocking 4.3 percent. The 1995 *President's Economic Report* considers net saving over the whole economy to be "a meaningful measure of the domestic resources available for increasing the capital stock." "Unfortunately," the report adds, "the trend in net saving has been even more disturbing [than that in gross saving]." Their chart reveals that there was a "decline in net saving—from an average of 8 percent of GDP in the 1960s to an average of 2 percent of GDP between 1990 and 1993." A small uptick in net saving in 1994 was due solely to a downtick in the federal deficit in that year. Basically, net saving in the United States in the 1990s was running at little more than a quarter of the percentage rate of the 1960s.[23]

Since the Baby Boomers will place an enormous strain on the fiscal capacity of the federal government in their retirement years, and since many Boomers have expressed the opinion that Social Security and Medicare won't even be around when they retire, how well, one might ask, are they preparing themselves for this future eventuality? Actually, there are two relevant questions here, the second of which particularly pertains to the current standing of the Idea of Progress: (1) How well are the Boomers preparing specifically for their own retirement years? (2) To what degree are the Boomers working hard to contribute to the well-being of the generations that will follow them? As I have frequently noted, an essential feature of the Idea of Progress as a great motivating force in the late nineteenth and early twentieth centuries was a vision of the better, happier life to be led by future generations.

With respect to the first question, there is, rather surprisingly, some disagreement. Thus, a 1993 study by Richard Easterlin et al. found that the Boomers are preparing quite adequately for their retirement years. The study noted that the data do not support the popular impression that "the savings rates of the boomers are considerably lower than those of their predecessors. . . . Indeed, if allowance is made for saving through employer pension plans," their saving rates may actually be slightly higher.[24]

By contrast, another 1993 study (by Dr. B. Douglas Bernheim, then of Princeton University, for Merrill Lynch) found that the savings rates of the Boomers are shockingly low and, unless increased, may force them "to accept dramatically lower standards of living during retirement, or else to forgo retirement altogether." The Bernheim study concluded that the Boomers are, on average, saving only a third (33.79 percent) of what they should be saving to maintain a retirement standard of living consistent with preretirement years.[25]

The uncertainty factor in all these studies is quite large. For example, with regard to those employer pension plans that Easterlin et al. mention as favoring the Boomers over their predecessors (because of "longer participation and higher vesting"), there is at least some question as to how reliable they will prove to be. Business "shortsightedness has," according to Brookings scholar, James Smalhout, "pushed total payments from defined-benefit plans ahead of contributions by $100 billion each year since 1989 despite the need to prepare for the unprecedented burden of supporting baby boomers in retirement. . . . With the huge baby-boom generation moving into its peak earning years, contributions to private pension plans should greatly exceed benefit payments—not the other way around."[26] Add to this the basic insecurity about the status of Social Security and Medicare down the road, not to mention the great uncertainty about what may be happening to future life expectancies— will there be still more years added to Boomers' lives, and specifically to their retirements?—and one can begin to see why opinions may differ on this matter.

From the point of view of the present study, the minimum conclusion must be that Baby Boomers as a group are taking very serious risks in providing for their own retirements. Their savings rates are low, their private and public pensions shaky, their numbers huge, and their preparation for possible and, in fact, reasonably predictable further extensions of their life expectancies essentially nonexistent. Mind you, the crucial basic point concerning the decline of the Idea of Progress in no way requires that the Boomers prepare inadequately for their own retirements. With lengthened life expectancies, every generation will presumably have some tendency to focus on its own personal future, a future which extends futher forward in time for each successive generation of Americans. Indeed, I will later focus specifically on the contest that develops between considerations of *self* and consideration for *posterity*. (See chapter 12.)

All of which is to say that it is really our second question—the degree to which the Boomers are making provision for their children and heirs after they are gone—that is of special interest to us. This question, too, is a complicated one since provisions for one's children obviously include not only what one leaves them after one's death, but also what one does for them while one is still alive—feed them, clothe them, read stories to them, fix their lunches for school, contribute to their college educations, sometimes help them buy their first homes, and so on. Since we know that there has been a sharp decline in the number of hours parents actually spend with their children over the past quarter century, and also that fathers have been fleeing (or never appearing in) their children's homes in record numbers, we may at least entertain a strong suspicion that many of today's parents are making far less "provision" for their children's needs than in times past.

But what about inheritances in particular? What is the evidence here? Actually, there is some, and it is quite striking. An October, 1992 National Bureau of Economic Research (NBER) Working Paper by A. J. Auerbach, L. J. Kotlikoff, and D. N. Weil suggests that there was a substantial shift between 1962 and 1983 in the direction of U.S. saving, reducing the proportion aimed at providing for one's heirs and increasing the proportion designed for the later consumption of the elderly themselves.[27]

The way the authors try to measure saving designed for bequests and inheritances is by separating increases in "annuitized wealth" from increases in "nonannuitized wealth." The latter is conventional wealth: "assets which can be sold, transferred, or, in the event of an individual's death, bequeathed." The former, by contrast, is "the claim to a stream of future payments that will not continue beyond a person's death." If, at death, all a person's wealth is annuitized, nothing will go to his or her heirs. If it is nonannuitized, all can be bequeathed, subject, of course, to inheritance taxes. And what the study finds is a major shift in emphasis toward annuitized wealth over these two decades. Their conclusions:

> According to our estimates, the 1983 flow of bequests would have been approximately 20% larger had the elderly had the same total

resources, but the 1962 degree of annuitization. Given the conservative nature of the assumptions we made in calculating the change in the degree of annuitization, we guess that bequests in 1983 would have been as much as 30% higher if the degree of annuitization had remained at its 1962 level. . . .

The estimated reduction in bequests in 1983 ($11.1 billion by one estimate, $13.7 billion by another) amounts to a substantial sum when compared to the $106.2 billion of total net national saving in 1983. The implied reduction of national saving in 1983 was not a one time event. Rather the increased annuitization means an ongoing reduction in national saving and national investment that saving finances. While increased annuitization can not explain all of the remarkable recent decline in U.S. saving, it appears to be an important part of the puzzle.[28]

This trend to increased annuitization applies to the pre-Boomer generation, as well as to the Baby Boomers. There is, however, at least some fairly convincing impressionistic evidence that the decline in bequest saving will be even greater among the latter. Thus, Mary Malgoire, a financial planner with Malgoire Drucker, Inc., of Bethesda, Maryland, expects that the Boomers will actually receive significant inheritances from their parents, but doubts that much of anything will be left over for the Boomers' children. "The financial security of our generation," she says, "will be made by inheritance, but nothing will be passed on" to the next.[29]

This apparent falling off in bequest saving suggests just how far the priority given the future—a central feature of the Idea of Progress—has declined in typical Boomer thinking. The "now generation" turns out not to be too bad a description after all.

PROMISCUITY AND SELF-DESTRUCTIVE BEHAVIOR AMONG THE YOUNG

If the Boomer generation is taking certain risks with its own future, and considerable risks with its children's futures, what about those children themselves? Have they been taught about the rewards promised, and the disciplines required, by the Idea of Progress? Are they patiently building their lives towards a better future for themselves and for the children that they might have one day?

As always, the issues are mixed and difficult to sort out. Today's American children spend far more time in formal educational institutions than they did thirty, fifty, or a hundred years ago. A plus for Progress! On the other hand, achievement scores have been declining, and the gap between the educational requirements of our high-tech society and the educational qualifications of large numbers of our young people seems to be growing—not such a plus, maybe even a minus. Similarly, we can say that most young people today do not commit suicide or engage in violent crime. On the other hand, teenage suicide and teenage violence are sharply higher than they were a few decades ago. And so on.

In certain respects, however, the behavior of many of today's American teenagers shows a clearcut and increasing tendency to discount some very obvious and threatening future consequences of their actions. The characteristic tendency of young people to give priority to pressing present above future needs and desires is thus carried to such an extreme as to become potentially self destructive.

Sexual promiscuity is a good case in point. Actually, one might well imagine that there would be at least some trend toward greater sexual restraint among today's teenagers. Certainly there has been a great deal of discussion of the plight of single teenage mothers and their descent into poverty and welfare dependence. Even more to the point, one would think that a growing awareness of the spread of sexually transmitted diseases (STDs), and especially the vast amount of publicity given to the AIDS epidemic, would act as a serious wet blanket on promiscuous sexual behavior. Indeed, in 1987, Cheryl Russell, editor-in-chief of *American Demographics*, proclaimed that "the fear of AIDS will end the sexual revolution. After a 25-year hiatus, once again there is good reason to say no: Fear of death is a cold shower for casual sex, a more effective deterrent than fear of pregnancy."[30]

But it hasn't happened. One thing Russell was right about, and that is that fear of pregnancy has evidently ceased to be an "effective deterrent" to casual sex. A 1993 Census Bureau report showed that between 1982 and 1992, the percentage of American women who had a baby while single went up from 15 to 24 percent, and 63 percent of these women in 1992 were under twenty-five. In fact, two of every three teenagers who had children were unmarried, and this occurred in an era when the termination of pregnancies by abortion was legal in all fifty states.

Even more striking is the evidence on the increase in premarital sexual intercourse among teenagers. Table 10.1, based on a 1991 study in the *Morbidity and Mortality Weekly Report (MMWR)* of the Centers for Disease Control, indicates that, as far as young people are concerned, the sexual revolution not only is not over but actually accelerated in the late 1980s when the word about AIDS and other STDs was already out. Furthermore, not shown in table 10.1 are facts about the numbers of sexual partners of these young women, and the racial breakdown of the incidence of premarital intercourse.

With regard to the numbers of partners, the basic fact is that "adolescents who had had sexual intercourse earlier in life reported greater numbers of sex partners." Thus, for example, among fifteen to twenty-four year-old females who had initiated sexual intercourse before age eighteen, 45 percent reported having had four or more different partners. Early sex, now majority behavior, is also promiscuous sex.

The racial breakdown is interesting not so much because it shows, as expected, that Black teenage women have more active sex lives than White teenage women, but rather because it shows that White teenage sexual intercourse increased much more rapidly over the years 1970–1988 than was the case for Black teenagers. Thus, if table 10.1 numbers are broken down by race for 1970–1988, White women show a 90

Table 10.1   Percentage of Women Aged 15–19 Years Who Reported Having Had Premarital Sexual Intercourse—United States—1970–1988

Age (yrs)	1970	1975	1980	1985	1988
15	4.6	9.8	16.7	20.0	25.6
16	20.3	18.9	26.8	30.4	31.8
17	32.3	36.6	35.5	41.7	51.0
18	39.4	49.1	56.2	53.2	69.5
19	48.2	63.9	66.9	70.7	75.3
Overall	28.6	36.4	42.0	44.1	51.5

Source: "Premarital Sexual Experience Among Adolescent Women—United States, 1970–1988," *Morbidity and Mortality Weekly Report,* Centers for Disease Control, 39, nos. 51 and 52 (4 January 1991).

percent increase (from 26.7 to 50.6%), while Black women show only a 28 percent increase (from 46.0 to 58.8%). Indeed, the difference in behavior is quite small, with White women in 1988 approximating the behavior of Black women in 1975. It is important to stress this point since it is quite common these days to attribute changed social behaviors to minority groups without acknowledging the increasingly strong penetration of such behaviors among the majority of young Americans.

Active premarital sex lives not only contradict previously accepted moral standards, and especially what we think of as "Victorian morality," but they contradict them, I believe, in a quite specific way. They represent a striking emphasis on instant, immediate, and often transitory gratifications at the risk of serious, and very negative, long-run consequences. The vision of the future that dominates the Idea of Progress is discounted almost out of existence.

It might be objected that this analysis fails to take into account one very positive incentive (or at least the removal of a disincentive) to early sexual activity in today's America—namely, a welfare system that offers to eliminate, or greatly reduce, the immediate financial burdens of pregnancy. Some commentators attribute our great increase in single parenthood largely to this one factor. This kind of reasoning undoubtedly played a part in the decision of the president and Congress in 1996 to scale down some aspects of our welfare system.

While undoubtedly that system has aggravated the problems of early sex and illegitimacy, it certainly cannot lay claim to being their entire, or even main, explanation. And this, for the simple reason that such future-risking, ultimately self-destructive youthful behavior is on the rise today in a whole host of other areas of teenage life where the welfare system plays little or no role. The obvious example here is teenage crime and violence. Even more self-destructive than promiscuous sex and early pregnancy, such antisocial juvenile behavior is on the increase today even when adult crime appears, at least superficially, to be on the wane.

And it is not just criminal activity that is on the increase among our young people today. Just in the last five years, the national campaign against teenage smoking and alcohol and drug abuse, which earlier had seemed to produce some favorable results, has floundered very badly. A 1995 survey from the University of Michigan Survey Research Center found that "among both eighth- and 10th-graders, the proportion who reported smoking in the 30 days prior to the survey has increased by one-third since 1991. Some 19 percent of eighth-graders and 28 percent of 10th-graders now report such use." According to principal investigator Lloyd D. Johnston, "these increases in smoking among our children are very broad, occurring among virtually all social classes, all regions of the country, communities of all sizes, those who do and do not plan to attend college, boys as well as girls, and so on. This suggests that there are culture-wide forces leading to these substantial increases."[31] Clearly, our welfare system has very little to do with this particular form of self-destructive behavior.

Nor can it explain the recent, and very sharp, increase in drug use among our young people. Another 1995 report from the Michigan center informs us that "the proportion of eighth-graders taking any illicit drug in the 12 months prior to the survey has almost doubled since 1991 (from 11 percent to 21 percent). Since 1992 the proportion using any illicit drugs in the prior 12 months has risen by nearly two-thirds among 10th-graders (from 20 percent to 33 percent) and by nearly half among 12th-graders (from 27 percent to 39 percent)."[32]

Meanwhile serious alcohol problems continue to plague our youngsters. In the above survey, it was also noted that, "in 1995 the proportions of students having five or more drinks in a row during the two weeks preceding the survey were 15 percent, 24 percent, and 30 percent for eighth-, 10th-, and 12th-graders respectively. Actually, in colleges the problem of alcoholism has become epidemic. Defining "binge drinking" as downing five drinks in a row for men and four in a row for women, a Harvard School of Public Health study covering 17,592 students on 140 college campuses in 1994 found that 44 percent of college students engaged in such binges at least once in the two weeks before the survey.[33]

In short, sexual promiscuity at increasingly early ages is only one example of a whole syndrome of youthful activities in today's America that carries the natural tendency to present-mindedness among the young to new and alarming limits. And what all these activities have in common is that, far from building toward a more promising and better future, they virtually guarantee problems and, in some cases, literally, even early death in the years ahead.

THE GREAT NEW GROWTH INDUSTRY: GAMBLING

From the great grab bag of examples of current behaviors totally at odds with the Idea of Progress, I will pull out one last, and perhaps curious, example: the recent and explosive growth of the U.S. gambling industry. I choose this industry not only because it represents such a sharp change from Victorian morality and, indeed, from fairly recent principles and practices—after all, gambling was illegal throughout most of the nation until a relatively few years ago—but also because the nature of the change represents such a clear reversal of the values embodied in the Idea of Progress.

In a certain sense, of course, all the entrepreneurs who helped fashion and sustain the process of progress during the nineteenth century were "gamblers." What characterized their risk-taking, however, was the exact opposite of what characterizes that of the modern casino or lottery gambler. In particular, these entrepreneurs and capitalists made current sacrifices in the hope and/or expectation of long-term gains. The effort, hard work, saving, and doing without came now, the potential reward much later in time. In the case of today's gambler, the reward that is sought, if it comes at all, comes now. It is a present, not a future, gain that is at stake. William A. Galston and David Wasserman put it this way: "There are . . . important differences of individual motivation and behavior between gambling and business risk-taking: The entrepreneur is focused on the future; the gambler, on the present. The entrepreneur innovates; the gambler at best calculates."[34]

In these calculations, moreover, the gambler has to give exceptional weight to present possibilities over potential long-run risks. However much he may delude himself at the moment, the fact is, as everyone knows, that the gambler loses over the long haul. The percentage of the take varies from casino to casino, from one state lottery to another, from racetrack to racetrack, and so on. But the take is always there, guaranteeing that, on average, and over time, gamblers will lose, and in cumulative terms lose big. This is why, in the traditional morality, gambling is coupled with excessive drinking, promiscuous sex, and, in terms of ultimate consequences, the spread of crime. All such activities overvalue the present and undervalue the future—the most basic reversal possible of the underlying psychology of the Idea of Progress.

Is gambling big enough today to spend any time on? Actually, although Americans have always gambled in one way or another throughout our history, it is only in recent times that gambling could quite accurately be described as *the* leisure-time hobby of the United States. We currently spend more on legal gambling (illegal gambling is, of course, not officially recorded) than on movie theaters, books, amusement park attractions, and recorded music combined. Over the past decade, gambling revenues have been increasing at an annual compound rate of 11.1 percent and forecasts are that total revenues will double over the next decade. Salomon Brothers, in a report on nationwide gambling, estimates that Americans lost $41.9 billion in legal gambling in 1993.[35] To give some sense of the magnitude of this sum, it amounted in 1993 to around eight times the amount spent on movies. It was also, to change field completely, around four times the entire amount the United States spent on funeral and burial expenses during that year. And this sum deals with legal gambling only.

Although there are some indications of a public backlash against the feverish growth of U.S. gambling in recent years, there are other indications suggesting that gambling revenues (and losses) will only increase in the years ahead. There already exist some countries (like Australia) where gambling is even bigger business than in the United States. Also, the number of gambling venues is growing rapidly. Already we have, along with the now traditional lotteries, casinos and bingo parlors, riverboat gambling, gambling cruises "to nowhere," and gambling on airline flights outside U.S. limits. The really big possibilities for the future, however, undoubtedly lie in the realm of electronic gambling. With the development of the internet and the enormous expansion of personal computers, experts are predicting that the great new growth of gaming in the United States may take place right in one's own home, in one's living rooms perhaps, or possibly in the bedroom in our pajamas. For the moment at least, no end is in sight.

How could this be? Until 1930, only two states in the nation (Kentucky and Maryland) even had racetracks. Until 1964 there were no state lotteries anywhere. What could have brought such a dramatic change in American attitudes and behaviors? There are, of course, many elements involved. For example, lotteries have proved to be a fairly painless way of raising state revenues in an era of governmental expansion. Native Americans have discovered a vast new income source. Gambling also is a "sport" well suited to an aging population—it requires very little physical exertion!

Still, the fundamental change goes much deeper than such considerations and it involves a basic shift in morality. This shift, in turn, consists in a turning away from hard work, preparation, discipline, and sacrifice in favor of casual, undisciplined, easygoing risk-taking. And the reason behind this transformation, I strongly suggest, is a different view of the future. When you could count on the future—or, rather, believed that you could count on the future—to be better than the present, then the hard work, sacrifice, and discipline were easily justified as appropriate behavior models. When faith in the future begins to waver, so also does that justification waver, and ultimately fail. In such circumstances, why not take a chance? Why not give it a go?

After all, *somebody* has to win the lottery! Even the Publishers' Clearinghouse Sweepstakes! Certainly it beats struggling all your life and finding that it wasn't worth it, that you've ended up no better than when you started out, and probably a lot worse! In such a futureless world, a few hundred billion dollars doesn't seem all that much to take a chance on. Who knows what might happen?

THE VICIOUS CIRCLE OF POSTMODERNISM

Who knows what might happen? The postmodern question and, in many respects, the postmodern disease. The Idea of Progress increasingly seems a doubtful proposition to Americans, and very probably to all advanced, industrial populations in the world. The question—who knows?—is ultimately that of the agnostic, rather than of the out-and-out pessimist. Although, as most polls indicate, there is in fact a good deal of pessimism about the future in the air, the more basic hurdle for the Idea of Progress seems to be uncertainty. After all, the gambling behavior we have just been talking about probably expresses an optimistic, rather than a pessimistic, view of life. If one really thought, "I'll never, ever win the lottery"—a quite realistic view—one would probably never play in the first place. For the gambler, hope, one presumes, springs eternal.

Still, hope, as Christopher Lasch has noted, is in many crucial dimensions different from optimism. It lacks confidence. It is also, in the gambler's case, focused on the moment and not on the more distant future. What we have in the United States now is a kind of vicious circle in which old moralities—whether having to do with sex, crime, gambling, saving, disciplined hard work, or whatever—are all breaking down and, in their fragmentation, making it almost impossible for anyone to foresee the future path that our society is taking. The circle is vicious because it is the increasing difficulty of foreseeing that future, caused ultimately by the fundamental predicament of progress, that renders these older moralities less appropriate in the first place. Temporal agnosticism breeds a diverse and diffuse morality, which increases uncertainty and hence furthers the underlying basis for agnosticism. In the working out of this vicious circle, the Idea of Progress increasingly finds itself cast aside, regarded as naïve, unjustifiable, and archaic.

And what happens to the institution of the family in a world in which that once-dominant modern Idea slips and falls by the wayside? It is time now to bring the two large themes of this study—declining institution and ideology—into one comprehensive analysis.

POSTSCRIPT: PRESENT-MINDEDNESS ABROAD

Before continuing on, however, I would like to say just a word in passing to place our discussion in something like an international context. The focus of this book is clearly, and centrally, on the United States. Still, since the basic factors that have undermined the Idea of Progress in this country are located in the process of progress in a quite general sense, we would expect to find at least some echoes of the American experience in other industrialized countries. Earlier we did, in fact, note that the traditional family was weakening in virtually all economically advanced nations (chapter three, pp. 60–62). Can the same thing be said about the Idea of Progress abroad? In particular, do we find evidence of the same kind of present-minded, now-centered behavior that we have just noted in the United States and that seems so clearly to deny that special elevation of future claims which we associate with the progressive ideal?

The answer almost certainly is yes, although, as in the case of family structures, with many variations. In one respect—the case of public deficits—Europe mirrors our own situation almost exactly. Mind you, the variations *among* European countries are huge. In 1991, for example, Belgium's gross public debt as a percentage of GDP was an extraordinary 129.4 percent, while at the other extreme, Luxembourg's was only 6.9 percent. Taking the European Community as a whole, however, the ratio of the gross public debt to GDP came out to be 61.8 percent in

1991, while in that same year the ratio of our gross federal debt to GDP was a remarkably similar 62.9 percent.[36]

Actually, in terms of "unthinkable deficits," the rest of the industrialized world seems currently to be having a much harder time than the United States in reducing its spending propensities. Thus the 1996 *Economic Report of the President* proclaimed rather grandly that, in 1994, and taking into account our state and local government surpluses, we had "the lowest general government deficit-to-GDP ratio of any major industrialized country."[37] Countries like Italy were in much deeper trouble in this respect than we were. Even Japan had a larger annual deficit in 1994 than the United States. Since all of these countries have low birthrates and very long life expectancies (in most cases, longer than those in the United States), they are all likely to face very heavy social security, medical, and other, possibly unsustainable, demands in the future.

Of course, in some respects—one thinks particularly of teenage behavior—the United States seems more now-oriented than any of these other societies. Even here, however, the difference is more one of degree than kind. Consider, for example, sexual promiscuity among the young. As Gertrude Himmelfarb has pointed out, "England is second only to the United States in teenage illegitimacy" and, indeed, "the rate of increase in the past three decades has been even more rapid. In both countries, teenagers are far more 'sexually active' . . . than ever before, and at an earlier age."[38] Himmelfarb's discussion of British illegitimacy rates is quite telling for she points out that, in the nineteenth century, from about 1845 to 1900, these rates in England and Wales were not only very low but actually falling. This is clearly future-oriented behavior and is what we would expect in a society increasingly dominated by the Idea of Progress. Similarly, the dramatic rise in British illegitimacy rates (and, of course, our own as well) since the early 1960s is very indicative of the weakening of that Idea in our postmodern era.

Although mentioned only briefly in this chapter, teenage crime is also a very good indicator of shortened time horizons among the young and an area in which the United States rather clearly, and unfortunately, holds the lead. But again, the differences are only of degree. Thus, England has similarly shown sharp increases in youthful crime in recent decades. Even Sweden has not escaped unscathed. David Popenoe writes:

Once a society where following the letter of the law was one of the
supreme commandments. . . . Sweden has witnessed in [1960–1985]
a widespread increase in lawbreaking. . . . The leading criminal age
group in Sweden (as in most advanced societies) is 15 to 19, which
commits more than double the number of reported crimes as the next
leading group—that between ages 20 and 24. While the crime rate
for cleared serious crimes (those resulting in sanctions more severe
than fines) in Sweden increased for all age groups more than four
times in the past 30 years, the increase was fivefold for the 18 to
20–year-old group, and sevenfold for the 17–year-old group.[39]

It is true, as Popenoe notes, that most juvenile crime in Sweden is
not very serious, and certainly not comparable to the near-epidemic of
teenage violence we are now seeing in the United States. However,
there are some respects in which other industrialized nations, including
Sweden, may actually be showing attitudes and behaviors that are even
more present-oriented than those current in this country. One of the
greatest socio-political differences between the United States and most
European countries, for example, is in the extensiveness of their welfare
state programs. Government involvement in these societies is uniformly
greater than in ours, and the range of welfare services—for the poor, the
unemployed, the elderly, families with children, and so on—is far more
wide-ranging and detailed.

Now what can be argued here is that these very extensive welfare
states ultimately reflect, or reflected as they grew, a very present-minded
set of policies. That is to say, they offered very clear and attractive short-
run benefits, which, however, turn out to involve unacceptable long-
run problems and sacrifices. Indeed, at the present time, and throughout
most of Europe, efforts are being made, and with great difficulty, to scale
back the excesses of many of these programs.

Return now to the case of Sweden, the exemplar in many ways of
the very best of what the modern large-scale welfare state has to offer.
Until quite recently, Sweden, with her "Middle Way," was considered
by many to represent almost an ideal way of organizing a modern society's socioeconomic life. The elderly were well taken care of; the unemployed were given training for re-entry into the labor force; mothers
(and fathers) of babies were given wonderful leave arrangements; child
care for infants and preschoolers was amply provided—in short, virtually

all individual and social needs were provided for. Even as late as 1988, a British scholar (Arthur Gould) could claim that "in comparison with other western countries and Japan the Swedish welfare state stands out as a remarkable achievement. . . . Not only has the commitment to the welfare state, high public spending and full employment been maintained in years of growth and prosperity but it has weathered the recent years of recession to emerge relatively unscathed." [40] Apparently, what one might have thought of as the potentially heavy long-run costs of all these wonderful benefits—devastatingly high taxes, a reduced sense of personal initiative and responsibility, and the like—had had no negative effects. The "Middle Way" was a clear winner on all accounts!

Or was it? Ironically, in 1988, the very year when Gould's book was published, Sweden's Social Democratic government, pointing to epidemic tax evasion and tax avoidance, acknowledged the need for a sweeping tax reform program. And the worst was yet to come. By 1990, newspapers were reporting the increasing stagnation of the Swedish economy. In the early 1990s, the problems only intensified. In a May, 1995 issue of the *American Economic Review*, Mancur Olson, Jr. described the growth performance of the Swedish economy thus: "In 1970 Sweden still had one of the two highest per capita incomes in Europe, and its 'Middle Way' was widely admired. But Swedish economic performance was gradually deteriorating. This became increasingly evident as Swedish growth rates fell behind those of most other OECD countries in the 1970's and 1980's, and dramatically apparent with the country's disastrous economic performance in the 1990's." [41]

Olson's article, entitled "The Devolution of the Nordic and Teutonic Economies," was part of a general symposium under the heading, "The End of the Middle Way? The Large Welfare States of Europe." From our point of view, what is interesting about all three articles from this symposium is that each, in one way or another, contrasts the short-term successes of the large welfare state model, and the Swedish case in particular, with its intrinsic longer run problems. In Olson's essay, the early success of Sweden (as in varying degrees of Austria, Norway, and West Germany) is attributed in substantial part to the existence of "encompassing interest organizations," such as society-wide labor unions and employers' federations, which place the interests of the whole economy above those of any narrow special interest groups. In the long run, however, special interest groups do emerge in these societies, and this process of "devolution" can leave the society with a case of "severe institutional sclerosis."

Harvard economist Richard B. Freeman, in his article "The Large Welfare State as a System," also points to certain short-run successes of extensive welfare states, but also serious long-run costs. Basically, the problem he sees is that a tightly integrated system may work very well for a time and under certain given circumstances, but that this very integration may make it resistant to future change. In the particular case of Sweden, "the extensive welfare state worked well for some period because of the tight connections between its parts, but that made it less adaptable to a changing economic environment and made it costly to make the changes that should raise efficiency and create a better long-term economic outcome."[42] In other words, a substantial long-run cost of the large welfare state may be the difficulty of reforming it once it starts breaking down.

The third article in the symposium, "Hazardous Welfare-State Dynamics," by Swedish economist Assar Lindbeck is even more germane from our point of view. While he, like the others, also notes the great difficulties involved in reforming welfare states once they run into trouble, his article focuses mainly on showing how problems, barely evident when welfare policies are first adopted, become increasingly hazardous over time. He writes:

> A strongly humanitarian case can no doubt be made for generous benefits to people in connection with contingencies such as unemployment, sickness, work injury, permanent disability, single-motherhood, and old age. The basic dilemma of the welfare state, however, is that the more generous the benefits, the greater will be not only the tax distortions, but also, because of moral hazard and benefit cheating, the number of beneficiaries. . . . Indeed, moral hazard and cheating are, in my judgment, the weakest spots of the welfare state. My basic hypothesis is that such hazardous adjustments tend to be stronger in the long run than in the short and medium term.[43]

What he suggests is that it takes time to adjust to welfare state arrangements, both informationally—finding out what kinds of benefits are actually available—and morally—it is only over time that social norms change permitting one to take advantage of, and frequently to abuse, these benefits. And when this happens, the welfare state may well "destroy its own economic foundations. That risk is a reality today in several countries."[44] In short, the welfare state works well only until its beneficiaries begin to adjust fully to its many rewards and promises; then, at this later point in time, its equally many disincentive effects and temptations begin to dominate, posing a need for basic reforms which are peculiarly difficult to enact.

Actually, in recent years, Sweden has taken a number of steps to reduce the level of government intervention in her economy. The rate of government spending in Sweden reportedly has fallen from around 75 percent of GDP to about 50 percent of GDP. There has also been an attempt to privatize a number of public companies. Indeed, in many respects, the long-run burdens of the large-scale welfare state are proving harder to alleviate in some of the bigger countries, such as Italy, France, and Germany.

My main conclusion from this admittedly brief look abroad would seem to be that the United States is by no means alone in its tendency to emphasize the short run above the long run. In some respects—in the case of juvenile crime, certainly, and very probably also in the case of our low national saving rate—we may be considerably more present-minded than some other nations. On the other hand, and with particular reference to the more extensive welfare states of many European countries, it can be argued that the American system has more long-run flexibility and adaptability than those other systems and, indeed, that several countries in Europe have purchased short-term benefits only at the expense of very serious long-run problems. It is no accident that the term "Eurosclerosis" is more and more frequently heard these days.

Apparently then, neither here nor abroad have the claims of the distant future above those of the near and immediate term been given the same weight as in days of yore. The era when such future claims were paramount—when the Idea of Progress was a central, and even dominating, creed in the Western world—seems largely to have faded away.

Part III

THE BATTLE:
THE WAR OVER FAMILY VALUES

11

FAMILY VALUES: EVOLUTION OR REVOLUTION?

I return now to the American family, its recent history and future fate. Since we have spent a considerable amount of time on the fortunes of the Idea of Progress, it would be well to begin this discussion with an explicit indication of why I maintain that these ideological fortunes and those of the American family are so much intertwined. I start off by sorting out the general relationships between the Idea of Progress, time horizons, and family values as I perceive them

PROGRESS, TIME HORIZONS, AND FAMILY VALUES

The Idea of Progress, in the sense in which I have been using the term, and in the sense in which I believe it had an enormous practical impact on motivations and behavior in nineteenth- and early twentieth-century America, contains within itself the notion of great concern for and interest in the distant future. Thus, we can say that long time horizons are a necessary condition for the existence of the Idea of Progress as used throughout this book. This is why, in chapter 10, we presented so many examples of temporal myopia, or "present-mindedness," to indicate that, as a matter of empirical fact, the Idea of Progress was losing its hold over Americans (and, indeed, over much of the Western world) in these closing decades of the twentieth century.

Long time horizons are not, however, a sufficient condition for the Idea of Progress since it is also possible to believe that the long-run future is heading for decline and ruin, and to be quite concerned about this matter. Thus, for example, the Doomsday writers of the 1960s and

1970s, discussed in chapter 8, took a very long-run view of things, held that the future was likely to be worse than the present, and argued that, in order to forestall this fate and preserve something like our present living standards, we had immediately to halt the process of progress (industrialization, urbanization, fossil fuel consumption, etc.) and return to a much simpler, nonprogressive pattern of life. In other words, they had long time horizons, showed a great concern about the future, but were definitely not believers in the Idea of Progress. In fact, quite the contrary.

So it is that while it is proper to conclude that short time horizons imply the decline of the Idea of Progress, we cannot claim that long time horizons imply its acceptance. More is needed. In particular, we require a basic optimism, a faith that the future, carried forward on the wings of a continuing process of progress, will more or less inevitably be "better" than the present, just as the present is judged to be "better" than the premodern past.

It is this basic optimism about the distant future that made nineteenth- and early twentieth-century Americans so eager to contemplate, dwell on, and in a certain sense live for the future lives of their children and grandchildren. Or so my analysis claims. The parents and grandparents themselves would not live to see more than a tiny fraction of the wonderful future that science, technology and economic advance would ultimately unveil. But their children would. Their grandchildren would see even more. And so on and on through countless generations to come. This was why there was an intimate historical connection between the triumph of the Idea of Progress and an intense celebration of "traditional" family values in our national past.

Up to this point in our study, we have mainly traced this connection in its positive phase, that is, when both Idea and institution were flourishing, and when Americans were displaying a special and increasing interest in the well-being of their children. I have stressed that this happy state of affairs did not happen automatically but rather was the product of a number of special circumstances in the late nineteenth and early twentieth centuries. In particular, I have pointed out that cultural values and a rather restrictive morality were very important for they enabled a rapidly changing society to maintain a long-run, future-oriented view in the face of growing uncertainty and complexity. In a word, they allowed society to ward off in part, and for a time, the disruptive effects of the fundamental predicament of progress. Children, posterity, family life, the Idea of Progress, Victorian morality, long time horizons—all went together.

For a time. And then this harmonious conjunction of ideas, sentiments and unfolding events started to break apart. The "wake-up call," as I earlier referred to it, was World War I. This shocking event represented a kind of watershed as far as the Idea of Progress is concerned in the Western world, particularly in Europe but also to some degree in the United States. From the point of view of the present analysis, what the war signified was that the behavioral limits that were to keep the new powers of man over nature on a certain path over time had been violated. These limits, if rigid, were also apparently extremely fragile. Barbarism was evidently just around the corner. It had not been truly banished at all. Suddenly, the distant future was called into question. How dependable was that future? And if it was quite undependable, did one really have anything more than the present, the "now"?

The logic of the argument of this book on these points is quite clear, namely, that there is an intimate connection between the Great War, the beginning of the breakdown of Victorian morality, the waning of the Idea of Progress and, ultimately, changing attitudes toward the institution of the family, and especially toward children. In this connection, I found it quite extraordinary to run across some comments from John Galsworthy in the preface he wrote to the second part of the Forsyte Chronicles, *A Modern Comedy*. Having traced the generations of the Forsyte family from the nineteenth century into the twentieth, Galsworthy notes the essential change as follows:

> The generation which came in when Queen Victoria went out, through new ideas about the treatment of children, because of new modes of locomotion, and owing to the Great War, has decided that everything requires revaluation. And, since there is, seemingly, very little future before property, and less before life, is determined to live now or never, without bothering about the fate of such offspring as it may chance to have. Not that the present generation is less fond of its children than were past generations—human nature does not change on points so elementary—but when everything is keyed to such a pitch of uncertainty, to secure the future at the expense of the present no longer seems worthwhile. This is really the fundamental difference between the present and the past generations. People will not provide against what they cannot see ahead.[1]

One could hardly ask for an account of the matter more consonant with the general themes developed in this book. The values that had obtained before the Great War no longer hold (require "revaluation"). The future has become basically unknowable (people "cannot see ahead"). In such a world, although people may care about their children in some elemental sense, they no longer care for them (they no longer bother about their "offspring"). And this, in Galsworthy's view, is not a small and incidental change, but basic ("the fundamental difference between the present and past generations"). Putting this into the terminology we have been using, he anticipates the fundamental predicament of progress, the breakdown of the Idea of Progress as uncertainty about the future replaces faith in the future, the new focus on the present, and the deep connection of all this with the way in which families bring up their children.

THE FAMILY VALUES DEBATE

Galsworthy was writing with reference to Europe and Britain in particular. In the case of the United States, which had suffered much less intensely, the impact of World War I, though apparent in a number of ways, was not quite so direct and emphatic. This was almost certainly also true subsequently of the impact of World War II. Indeed, in the United States, the present debate over "family values" seems almost exclusively confined to the *post*-World War II period. What we appear to have is a simple and straightforward conflict between the 1950s—with *Ozzie and Harriet* and *Leave It to Beaver*—and the 1990s—with Phil Donahue, Geraldo Rivera, and, especially *Murphy Brown*. The Murphy Brown-Dan Quayle debate over unwed motherhood by choice came to symbolize the whole issue of family values as they had altered so dramatically over those few postwar decades. As Barbara Dafoe Whitehead pointed out, "on the night Murphy Brown became an unwed mother, 34 million Americans tuned in, and CBS posted a 35 percent share of the audience. . . . The actress Candice Bergen subsequently appeared on the cover of nearly every women's and news magazine in the country and received an honorary degree at the University of Pennsylvania as well as an Emmy award."[2] Dan Quayle meanwhile was widely ridiculed, a typical comment being that he did not seem to realize that Murphy Brown was not a real but a fictional character.

"Judged by conventional measures of approval," Whitehead added, "Murphy Brown's motherhood was a hit at the box office." But was the view about unwed motherhood expressed in that show really typical of popular feelings generally? James Q. Wilson has argued that there is a sharp difference between views held by the general public—mostly supportive of the "traditional" American family—and those promoted by sociology professors, liberal elites, and the media—supportive of Murphy Brown.[3] And, indeed, Whitehead's own article in *The Atlantic Monthly*, provocatively titled, "Dan Quayle Was Right," has not only been widely quoted ever since but apparently sold more copies of the *Atlantic* than any issue in the entire history of that illustrious periodical.

My own view is that, while sociology professors and the like are undoubtedly complicit in producing changed attitudes to the family, they are not wholly responsible. That is, it seems clear that there also have been very substantial changes in public attitudes as well. The actual and striking transformations of today's American families that were described in chapter 1 indicate, at a minimum, a general willingness to live with institutional changes of unprecedented dimension.

What has to be done now is to try to tie these more recent experiences in with our general theorizing about the effects of both the process of progress and the Idea of Progress on family life. In the remainder of this chapter, I take up the contrast between the 1950s and 1990s in terms of the rather broad question: evolution or revolution? Between the two periods, the changes in attitude to family life clearly appear to be revolutionary. But does that mean that the late 1960s was the revolutionary period, as clearly many young radicals at the time believed? Or was the real revolution in the 1950s? And, above all, how does all this relate to the more general theories about the process and ideology of progress that we have been discussing in parts 1 and 2?

THE TRUE RADICALS: PARENTS OF THE BABY BOOM

I begin by suggesting that the real radicals of the post–World War II period were the parents of the Baby Boomers, not their children. The popularity of *Ozzie and Harriet* and *Leave It to Beaver*, on this view, is not to be taken as a datum from which subsequent changes must be explained, but as a phenomenon that itself badly needs an explanation. The behavior of those Baby Boom parents was not in any way expected or predictable. It was a stunning development that, among other things, falsified virtually every projection of U.S. population made by expert demographers in the immediate prewar period.

If we think of radical or revolutionary change as involving a sharp break in previous trends, then the Baby Boomer parents were revolutionaries in at least three major respects affecting family life. The first and most obvious was in the numbers of babies these families had. In 1940, before our entry into World War II, the U.S. fertility rate was 2.2, this number measuring how many children on average American women would have during their childbearing years. Although just above the "replacement" level (the rate at which population replaces itself and, and in the absence of net immigration, remains constant in the long run), this low rate represented the end product of a general fall in U.S. fertility that had been going on since the beginning of the nineteenth century. In sharp contrast, the rate during the Baby Boom period (1946 to 1964), rose sharply and, at its maximum in 1957 reached 3.8, or nearly twice the prewar level. This was a "revolutionary" change in direction and, as I say, totally unforeseen by the experts.

Subsequently, the U.S. fertility rate fell, and even more sharply than it had risen. By 1976, it had fallen to the extraordinarily low level of 1.7, 55 percent below what it had been nineteen years before and well below the replacement level. Since that time, the rate has hovered at or just below 2.0, where, indeed, one would expect it to be if there had been no Baby Boom at all and past trends had simply maintained themselves.

A second way in which the Baby Boom parents were at odds with previous trends was in the matter of divorce. In general the U.S. divorce rate has been rising ever since the late nineteenth century although until recently it remained at quite a low level. Also there have been temporary downs—as, for example, during the Depression years when many married couples couldn't afford to get divorced—and ups—immediately after World War II when all those unhappy couples made up for lost time. Sociologist Andrew Cherlin has, however, constructed a series which estimates the proportion of marriages that will end in divorce over the period 1867 to 1973, showing both the general trend and departures from the trend (figure 11.1). Here we see that in the period

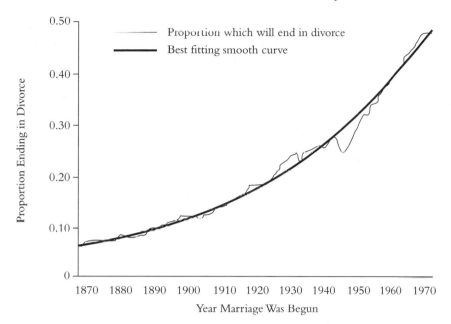

Fig. 11.1   Proportion of marriages begun in each year that will end in divorce, 1867–1973

Source: Taken from Andrew Cherlin, *Marriage, Divorce, Remarriage,* figure 1-5. Copyright © 1981 by the President and Fellows of Harvard College. Reprinted by permission of Harvard University Press.

after World War I—the 1920s—divorces accelerated and rose above the trend line. By contrast, during the Baby Boom period, divorces fell well below the trend line. Cherlin concludes, "Those who married in the decade or so following the war were the only cohorts in the last hundred years to show a substantial, sustained shortfall in their lifetime levels of divorce."[4] Again, after the end of the Baby Boom period (1964) the upward trend is reestablished, and, as in the 1920s, divorces begin to exceed trend rates. Thus, not only did the parents of the Boomers have exceptional numbers of children, but they tended to stay together in intact marriages relative to what went before and what came after.

Finally, there is a third surprising development during this period: the tendency of the mothers of the Boomers to stay at home rather than to take jobs in the labor force. This is surprising both because it again represents a reversal of the long-range trend, and also because one would have thought that the economic factor—the expense of raising all those children—would more or less have forced these mothers into paying jobs in the marketplace. But it didn't happen. Actually, this fact is somewhat disguised because the general upward trend in female labor force participation was so strong and did, indeed, continue during this Baby Boom period. Thus, measuring in terms of national census years, we have female labor force participation rates of 22 percent in 1930, 25.4 percent in 1940, 30.9 percent in 1950, and 34.9 percent in 1960. What is not shown in these aggregate figures is that, between 1940 and 1960, participation rates declined for women under thirty-five—the mothers of the Baby Boom. The increased general participation rate shown above indicates only the very rapid increase in employment of women above thirty-five.[5]

Mind you, the parents of the Boomers were not radical in all respects. For example, their tendency to marry at very young ages was actually a continuation of a long-run trend toward declining marriage ages dating back into the nineteenth century. The sharp increase in marriage age notable in our most recent period is, in fact, totally a post-Boom phenomenon. However, even the lowering of marriages ages during the Baby Boom period is at least consistent with the general mood of the times. And that mood was clearly profamily in what was later to be regarded as extreme by many (and as a kind of paradise lost to others). Big families, mother at home in the kitchen, daddy taking his role of sole provider and family man seriously, it wasn't just a fantasy. Exaggerated perhaps in *Father Knows Best, Leave It to Beaver,* and *Ozzie and Harriet* (though, as James Wilson notes, Harriet actually did have a sometime job)[6], nevertheless the Baby Boom parents did put their money where their mouth was in a crucial way—i.e., statistically. Families did actually count with them!

THE BABY BOOM AND THE IDEA OF PROGRESS

Families counted with them because the future counted with them. Essentially what my overall analysis suggests is that there was an important change in attitudes about the future between the interwar period and the immediate post-World War II period. Faith in the future and in the Idea of Progress generally had been shaken by World War I and, to some degree, by the subsequent Great Depression and also by the ominous buildup in the 1930s toward a still greater and more threatening world war. According to my general hypothesis, this weakened faith in the future should have been reflected in changes in people's attitudes to family life, and especially to the priority they gave their children. In short, the kind of attitudinal changes Galsworthy noted in his description of post–World War I England, though perhaps not quite so strongly in the American case, should have become evident.

As, in fact, they did. We have already discussed the trends of this period. Americans had fewer children. The U.S. total fertility rate not only fell in line with long-term trends, but plummeted sharply to what, up to that point, was an all-time historic low. Divorce rates in the 1920s not only rose in line with historic trends but clearly exceeded them. Women's participation in the labor force continued its long-term increase. Liberation was in the air. Mae West, who has been described as America's first completely liberated woman, became the highest paid star in her movie studio and a huge hit at the box office. Miss West, incidentally, had no children, nor any apparent interest in having children, and her one, youthful marriage was very early terminated in divorce.

In short, all the long standing corrosive effects of the process of progress on the institution of the traditional American family were at play during the interwar period while the protective cover provided by the Idea of Progress was increasingly vague and uncertain. Battered by the Great Depression, one senseless, horrible war, and another even more senseless and horrible war on the way, the Idea of Progress carried little conviction to members of the self-proclaimed "lost generation." Many felt, as Ralph Gabriel noted in the mid–1930s (see p. 191), that they had lost their "moorings" and inhabited "a cosmos in which all appears to be flux."

Then suddenly everything changed. World War II ended. Almost overnight, it seemed, there was this enormous burst of energy in the realm of "family values." Children were everywhere. The child-centered home became a national, almost a patriotic, ideal. Young mothers retreated from the labor force. Divorce rates fell relative to trend. How could these dramatic developments, as described above, have come about?

If the general analysis of this book is correct, the only possible explanation for these phenomenal, and wholly unexpected, changes would
be a sudden, unequivocal reinvigoration of the Idea of Progress in the
two decades following the end of World War II. And this is exactly what
I claim, though the claim will have to be qualified somewhat in a moment. Basically, however, I consider that the end of the war was suc-
ceeded by a strong revival of faith in the future. Did any of those postwar
parents of the Baby Boom have even a moment's flickering doubt that
their children would lead better and happier lives than they had? Not
very likely. Their faith in their children's futures was as strong, and in
some respects even more intense, than that of their Victorian forebears
half a century before.

But why? Let us begin the analysis with one of the most well-
known theories about the Baby Boom, that of Richard Easterlin of the
University of Southern California. His theory centers on what is usually
called the "relative income hypothesis."[7] According to this theory, decisions about family formation depend largely on how young people assess
their future prospects and how they see their chances of achieving the
kind of lifestyles they aspire to. The rosier they feel these prospects are,
the younger they will tend to get married and the greater number of
children they are likely to have. The basis for judging these prospects is
not absolute income, but relative income—that is, income relative to
what they believe they have reason to expect.

Going on, the theory suggests that what young people have reason
to expect in the way of income is largely determined by their past income experience, namely, the past incomes of their parents (during the
pre-Boom period, largely the incomes of their fathers). Relative income,
then, refers to what these young people are earning compared to what
their parents were, or are, earning. The higher this relative income, the
more babies young couples will want to have.

The Baby Boom is then explained by the tremendous jump in
young peoples' relative incomes, in the above sense, after World War II.
Their parents had brought them up during the depression and the war.
Parental earnings during those periods of great national strife were far
below the earning opportunities of young people entering the labor
force in the late 1940s and 1950s. In fact, the country as a whole went
on a growth spree during the immediate postwar period that was almost
unparalleled in our entire national history. Hence, young people were,

and above all *felt*, extremely well off and thus could easily afford marriage and babies. From this feeling of well-being, one could also conclude that mothers would not find any really pressing economic need to enter the labor force. Women, being thus dependent on their husbands, and husbands, having obvious responsibilities to their families, thus created a situation in which the divorce rate might well be expected to fall or at least taper off a bit.

The Easterlin theory, taken as a whole, does have some problems in explaining recent developments, but with respect to the Baby Boom period itself, it is, I would argue, notably consistent with the theory I have presented in this book.[8] My own summary of the matter would go like this: The young people who came of marrying age after the end of World War II were materially and economically probably the most successful generation in American history in terms of the overall trajectory of their life experience. The only serious competitor generations would be those in the latter part of the nineteenth century, after the Civil War, not coincidentally, the generations for whom the Idea of Progress was a dominating social ideology. Born in the 1920s, 1930s, or early 1940s, these young people started out in conditions of extreme economic and/or national insecurity. In 1933, a quarter of the American labor force was out of work. Even by 1939, unemployment was still rampant. Then came World War II with rationing and many fathers in the armed forces and in great personal danger. Following the war, these young people entered a world of extremely rapid growth in personal incomes. By the mid- to late fifties, the "affluent society" was not only born but already certified by John Kenneth Galbraith. Rising almost from ashes to unprecedented wealth, how could these young people not believe that the overwhelming tendency of things was ever onward and upward? How could they fail to take satisfaction in the wonderful, upward-spiralling world they would be handing on to their children and heirs?

Obviously this is all a bit too simple, and, as mentioned, it will have to be qualified in a moment. Still, the fact is that the relative income approach—the notion of doing better over time, of improving on the past—is extremely consistent with the notion that the Idea of Progress was making a strong comeback at this particular period. There were, of course, many general problems, most of which we have discussed earlier in the book—the bomb, the Soviet menace, and so on. But in personal terms, this was a period of extraordinary good fortune, and, above all, good fortune that seemed to be getting better and better all the time. Owning one's own home? Well, why not? Wouldn't that investment simply grow and grow and grow? Was not home ownership, far from being a burden, a more or less automatic way to get rich? And as far as the stock market was concerned, in the 1950s the Dow Jones Industrial Average had its best decade ever, up 239.5 percent over the ten-year span.

Actually, the economic side of it was surely only one feature of the process of progress that suddenly seemed enormously appealing. I think particularly of the discovery of the sulfa drugs, then penicillin, and a host of other antibiotics. The war against infectious diseases, until then rather modest at best, became almost overnight it seemed a positive rout with scientists definitely "mastering" nature to the great benefit of humanity. Even the bomb apparently had its good side. "Atoms for Peace," President Eisenhower proclaimed, creating the tantalizing prospect that the energy problem might possibly be solved for all time. Again, how could one not believe in the benefits of science and the process of progress in general?

This then is my way of generalizing the relative income approach to the Baby Boom period and connecting it up with the overall hypotheses I have been advancing. The process of progress continued to work its slow undermining of the American family. But now against this we had the conquest of a Great Depression, the successful prosecution of a great war, and a cornucopia of abundance—economic, scientific, personal abundance—spilling out all around. The Idea of Progress took on new life. And young people could once again dream of children and the wonderful world they would be passing on to them!

WHY IT ALL COLLAPSED

And then it collapsed: the Baby Boom, the brief respite in the secular trend toward greater and greater marital instability and divorce, the small pause in the mounting trend of young mothers into the labor force, even the one trend during the Baby Boom that had some claim to historic roots—the ever younger ages of first marriages. All gone. Not only gone, but gone so rapidly that, within a few years it was almost impossible to believe that the 1950s had ever really happened. Indeed, people who yearned for a return to the 1950s were accused of the worst kind of nostalgia. Ozzie and Harriet became a kind of joke. The 1950s came to seem to many to have been an anachronistic attempt to return to the values of the late nineteenth and early twentieth centuries. How absurd! The Victorian world was long dead and gone. Good riddance!

In the very first chapter of this book, I spelled out in some detail the factual side of the changes that have taken place during the past twenty-five or thirty years: the soaring divorce rate, the never-married mothers, the headlong flight from responsibility of biological fathers, the farming out of infants to inadequate and even unsafe child care arrangements, the latchkey kids, and so on. We need not go back over that already covered ground except to begin tying it into the overall analysis. In this chapter we have been talking about evolution versus revolution, and certainly the speed of change in the institution of the family since the 1960s deserves a revolutionary designation.

One can go further and say that these changes also deserve a revolutionary designation with respect to the larger prior history of the family in America from colonial times to at least World War I, and indeed with respect to the larger prior history of the family in virtually the whole of human experience. Let there be no doubt about it. Our experiment with broken, fatherless homes and children placed wholesale with extrafamily caretakers is, with respect to the record of the mass of humanity through the ages, a truly revolutionary development. The experiment is obviously not universal yet, in America or elsewhere. Still, it is increasingly the standard pattern for a minority of our children and the occasional (and more and more common) pattern for a majority of our children.

At the same time, viewed from the perspective of the twentieth century only, this development is clearly not particularly revolutionary. On the contrary, it seems the result of a rather natural, evolutionary unfolding. According to my general analysis, the process of progress has been working to undermine the institution of the family at least since the Industrial Revolution. For a long time, this corrosive effect was offset by an ideology—the Idea of Progress—which placed the future, posterity, our children, grandchildren, and heirs in the very forefront of our thoughts. "Family values," so established, more than offset the loss of family functions that had been characteristic since at least the middle of the nineteenth century.

In the course of the twentieth century, however, the Idea of Progress, beset by one predicament after another, and finally, and seemingly rather conclusively, by the fundamental predicament, has faded badly. Faith in the future has been replaced by agnosticism about the future. The ideology protecting the family from the underlying process has been gradually eaten away. In this sense, what has happened since the 1960s is the only-to-be-expected product of an overall evolution dating back at least to World War I. It seems revolutionary only because of the unexpected, and wholly transitory, reversion to the Idea of Progress and turn-of-the-century family values that occurred just after World War II. Thus, as already indicated, what immediately cries out for explanation is not so much what happened since the 1960s as what preceded that development and made it seem so radical. My explanation for the Baby Boom period has already been sketched in above.

Still, there is something of a puzzle here that must be faced directly: If the parents of the Boomers were so committed to the Idea of Progress, if furthermore they gave their children all the love and attention and educational, material and other advantages that "family values" are supposed to produce at their best, if, in fact, by such standards, the Boomers had virtually ideal upbringings—if all this is true, then how do we explain the rebellion of this younger generation against virtually everything their parents apparently held dear? I speak not just of the famous motto of the 1960s—"Never trust anyone over thirty!"—or even the equally famous "generation gap." What I am really referring to is the factual and actual assault on the family unit through divorce, illegitimacy, and general parental neglect that we now see before us. How could children, raised the way *they* were, raise *their* children *this* way?

The answer to this question is, I believe, quite complex but the starting point is what I referred to earlier as a need to qualify the theory that the Baby Boom parents had a restored faith in the Idea of Progress. They did, to a degree, but not completely. There was a major missing ingredient. And this missing ingredient was the morality embodied in the Idea of Progress, or perhaps even more narrowly, the discipline embodied therein.

What, after all, was the general mood in which the children of those early postwar years were raised? Insofar as there is any commonly accepted explanation of their behavior as children (and, indeed, their later behavior as adults), it would be that they received a rather permissive upbringing, in the eyes of many, far too permissive an upbringing. How many grandparents of the period were startled to find their own conversations brought to a halt because "little Jimmy is talking," or "little Susie wants to say something." Credit for such charming scenes was often spread around, but more than anyone else Dr. Spock was charged (actually, somewhat unfairly) for this particular development. "Progressive" schools were sometimes added to the pot, as was Sigmund Freud, and also psychoanalysts, psychologists, and sociologists in general.

My own view of the matter is that, while the parents of the Boomers were clearly infected by the Idea of Progress, it was to an important degree, the Idea of Progress *manqué*. Their children were to enjoy a better life than they themselves had, this was important to them, and they acted on this precept. In that sense, they were effectively back in the world of late-nineteenth- and early twentieth-century America. What was different was that they seemed to see no reason that their children should not sit back and indulge themselves in the better life that was now available. Their children were what counted, but the procession of generations seemed to stop there. Thus, little Jimmy and little Susie somehow got the message that it was perfectly appropriate to enjoy the fruits of the process of progress without mastering its disciplines. A sense of the moral core of the Idea of Progress was missing. The notion that one should not sit back and enjoy, but rather should work hard, save, sacrifice, deny oneself in order to build a still better future in the years ahead—this element was itself sacrificed to a degree that would have been quite shocking to our Victorian forebears.

In truth, the very notion of enjoying the abundance vouchsafed to the young by the process of progress also tore at the moral core of the Idea of Progress more generally. Thus it was that another inheritance of the 1960s and 1970s from the 1940s and 1950s was the slogan "Do your own thing!"—the exact opposite, if you will, of the "straight and narrow." Any clearcut vision of the distant future, morally or otherwise, was effectively shorted out.

A CASCADE OF PROBLEMS FOR THE FAMILY

What I am really saying here is that, although the Idea of Progress was resurrected among the parents of the Baby Boom to an important degree, its resurrection was incomplete and this very incompleteness suggests that the fundamental predicament of progress was at work even with this favored parental generation. For the incompleteness has a special character, namely, the failure of that parental generation to look beyond the fortunes and futures of its children. It is as though its time horizon came to a rather abrupt halt with the lifespans of those children. The latter were given the tools and attitudes to enjoy their own present. They were not instructed as to how to build or even visualize a future beyond their own lives. The parents, effectively agnostic about the distant future, imparted a childhood experience that left their children without any means of visualizing even the fairly near future. The problem, as it were, became compounded.

One exaggerates, of course, to make the point. All these assertions apply only to some families and only to these families some of the time. This caveat must be understood throughout. Still, the general drift of things was almost certainly in the direction described, with three consequences that must be investigated further:

1. *The limited time horizons even of the parents of the Baby Boomers*

Although not as short-sighted, as it were, as their children were to become, even the parents of the Boom have clearly shown the effects of the fundamental predicament of progress in their attitudes to the distant future. Although they "gave their all" to their children, and, in many cases, will be passing on fairly substantial inheritances to those children, they were never able—as were the Progress dreamers of the nineteenth century—to place themselves imaginatively in a still more distant future beyond the lives of their immediate heirs. As this parental generation has grown older, this tendency to focus on the relatively near future and, indeed, increasingly on their own personal futures, has intensified.

2. *The relatively permissive upbringing of the Baby Boomers made the Idea of Progress more or less irrelevant as a guide to their behavior and encouraged a focus on self as opposed to posterity.*

If, in effect, the disciplines implicit in the Idea of Progress were not taught, or at least not heavily emphasized, and great stress was placed on what the Boomers could fairly enjoy during their own lives, then one would expect a tendency to focus on the here-and-now as opposed to the future—on one's self as opposed to one's posterity. This tendency, as I will stress again in the course of this analysis, is already built into the fundamental predicament of progress, particularly when that predicament is combined with longer life expectancies. What is being added here is that if one is also brought up under circumstances where everyone is supposed to stop talking because little Jimmy or little Susie have something to say, then these underlying tendencies to focus on self simply become further magnified. The catchwords of the new era become self-realization, self-fulfillment, development of one's own rich personal potentialities.

3. *The relative absence of instruction in the basic morality of the Idea of Progress also intensifies another natural consequence of the fundamental predicament of progress—an inability to visualize even the general direction of future change.*

As noted at the end of the last chapter, there is already a kind of vicious circle built into the fundamental predicament of progress vis-à-vis morality. Agnosticism about the future, with its consequent shortening of time horizons, tends to undermine morality, or certainly any rigid moral code such as we associate with the Victorians. But that code, we also noted, was vital to making possible long time horizons in an era of wrenching socioeconomic change. As the code is undermined by a foreshortened sense of the future so the ability to foresee the future is itself further undermined—hence, the concept of a vicious circle is involved.

Now we need to add to this already potent mix a still further element: the relatively permissive attitude to morals in general with which the Boomer children were brought up. They were bereft of a defined sense of direction even at the starting gate. And what emerges from this total combination of things is a situation where moral relativism becomes the only moral code—a code that provides no guidance whatever for the future. A code, incidentally, that also denies that there is such a thing as "the family," only "families!"

Thus is the war over "family values" truly and unavoidably launched. Understanding its full scope and dimensions will require us to investigate each of these three points further, the main project for the next two chapters.

12

A MAJOR BATTLEGROUND: SELF VS. POSTERITY

Keynes's example of the "purposive man," who puts off his enjoyment of jam until an unimaginably later future date, points out one of the potential anomalies of the Idea of Progress.[1] If people should put their children's happiness above their own, shouldn't those children also put *their* children's happiness above *their* own, and so on and on and on, in a kind of infinite series, characterized by the fact that everyone, at all times, is always sacrificing him or herself for someone to come who never actually arrives. What kind of sense does that make?

Actually, the Idea of Progress does not create the issue of what I refer to as "self vs. posterity," that is, the balancing of one's own personal interests against those of others to follow, and in the case of the family, especially one's children. The question can arise in the most primitive circumstances where the process of progress isn't even dreamed of. How do we divide up a limited amount of food from the hunt? Natural selection presumably decrees that not everything should go to the hunter. If it did, his issue would not survive. On the other hand, enough must go to the hunter to enable him to hunt again another day. But should the food be so divided that his children will be stronger and more vigorous hunters than he? And how about the hunter's wife and her production? To what degree will she want to favor her children above herself when, among other things, her ability to bear more children may depend on her health and vigor? And so on.

Thus, the Idea of Progress in no way creates the debate over self vs. posterity; what it does do is greatly to strengthen one party to the debate. It lends its force strongly, and in an historically unprecedented way, to the posterity camp. In a shorthand way, we can also say that this happens to be the camp of "family values," or at least of those commonly associated with the "traditional American family." By the same token, the waning of the Idea of Progress can, in itself, be expected to shift the balance in the other direction.

How far in the other direction? No one can be sure, although clearly there would have to be some limits. If we decide collectively that children and grandchildren are really just too much of a nuisance and a bother, getting in the way of our careers and other plans, and, consequently, we decide to have none of them, then, of course, natural selection will come into play again. In the long run, it will be farewell to the human race.

Apart from such unlikely outcomes, there is the important fact that self-interest and interest in the well-being—or at the very least the productivity—of our children are necessarily interrelated. Who is to produce the goods and services with which we hope and intend to furnish our ever-longer retirement years? If we have too few children, or if we neglect their development, education, and general welfare too drastically, we ourselves are likely to pay a price in later years. Thus, determining whether, and to what degree, there has been a shift in our priorities in favor of self and away from posterity in recent decades is a rather complicated matter. Still, the evidence that such a shift has, in fact, taken place seems overwhelming. Three particular developments can be cited.

PARENTAL NEGLECT OF CHILD-RAISING RESPONSIBILITIES

The first and most obvious example is given by all the evidence presented in chapter 1 showing how parents have been sharply reducing their personal commitment to child rearing during the last quarter century. This reduction involves both the partial or total abandonment of their children by many biological fathers and the partial (and sometimes nearly total) abandonment of the child-rearing functions by working mothers. I summarized these developments by noting that, with far fewer children per family today as compared with the Baby Boom period, parental contact hours with the average American child dropped by an estimated 43 percent between 1965 and the late 1980s. It may well have dropped even further since.

This is a dramatic, history-shattering development, and the only question is whether there is any other possible explanation except the blatantly obvious one, namely, that the interests of children today are being given a much lower priority as compared with the interests of their parents. Such alternative explanations are, of course, frequently given, for it is almost certainly true that most parents, regardless of their actual day-to-day behavior, do not like to believe that they are doing anything less than the best for their children. Consider first the case of working mothers and then that of unattentive (and frequently absent) fathers:

Working Mothers

In the case of working mothers, the most common explanation is economic necessity. Since per capita incomes have risen drastically over the past century, and substantially even since the Baby Boom period, it is clear that what is really being talked about here is a psychological necessity. This point is reinforced by the rapid increase in working mothers whose husbands are in the top income quartiles, and this even in cases where we are dealing with infants and toddlers. (See pp. 73–74.)

In recognizing that the pressure that these mothers feel is psychological in nature, one should not in any way minimize the reality of this pressure. It is simply a matter of describing its nature. And what I am suggesting here is that the main reason children tend to come out on the short end of this particular pressure is that the priority given their needs has dropped relative to other priorities available. According to my general analysis, this shift in priorities has two main sources: (1) the process of progress, which opens up so many new and attractive options, including career options, for women, and (2) the waning of the Idea of Progress, meaning that the future world to be occupied by those children has become increasingly vague, uncertain, and of lesser value in terms of present, here-and-now motivations. There are wonderful adult careers to be undertaken and enjoyed today, while any sacrifices these impose on the children will manifest themselves (if at all, of course) only in a rather distant and undependable future.

Needless to say, there is more to be said on this issue. In the great debate over family values, it is commonly pointed out that, although children may appear to suffer somewhat from lack of parental attention when the mother is working, this deficit is more than made up for by the advantage of having that mother serve as a "role model." This aspect of the working mother arrangement is sometimes celebrated not only in popular literature but also by setting aside certain days when mothers bring their daughters to work with them, thus opening the children's eyes to the job and career options that will be available to them later in life.

There are, however, certain difficulties with this line of reasoning. For one thing, this particular advantage, if it is that, is limited to only half the problem—presumably the working mother is a role model for daughters only, since the sons already are aware that men, or at least most men, have always participated in the workforce. More seriously, for those who take a more traditional family approach, this particular argument involves the apparently self-circular notion that a proper role model is a mother who works, even though that working may not in many cases be actually necessary for the family exchequer and may, in some cases at least, involve unfortunate consequences for the children involved. Why, it may be asked, would not a more appropriate role model be a mother (or father, for that matter) who took time off for at least a few years while the children were very small and then resumed her (or his) career at a later stage of life? If, for example, parents working full-time when they have infants or two-year-olds for whom they are responsible is ultimately judged to be harmful for those babies, then in what sense are those parents providing good role models for those same children? Aren't they, in fact, giving them an example of unsatisfactory, rather than "model," behavior?

In any event, the role model defense almost certainly becomes much less tenable as far as children's welfare is concerned if the alternative care arrangements provided for these children are seriously unsatisfactory. Which they clearly are, in actual fact, in America, on average, at this moment in history. Whether and/or how this situation should be repaired is a matter for later discussion. For the moment, the clear and obvious point is that great numbers of very small children in the United States today are being placed in care arrangements that are judged to be woefully unsatisfactory even by those who strongly support the day care route in principle.[2] And it is this real and factual situation that indicates more or less unequivocally that many mothers are willing to take very serious risks with their children's well-being because of other, often more personally attractive, options.

Fatherhood without Responsibility

If mothers are evading at least certain of their traditional responsibilities toward their children, what on earth are we to say about the fathers involved? An absent father is no role model at all, or certainly a very poor one. Furthermore, step-fathers, who could, in theory, serve as paternal substitutes, prove in fact (as always, on average, with many individual exceptions) to be of very little help to the children involved. When it comes to psychological and other difficulties, children in step-father families fare just about as poorly as children in single-mother families.[3]

Some men find it very tempting to assign most of the blame for this paternal irresponsibility to women. After all, it is certainly true that, as women have become more independent, both psychologically and in terms of careers and actual financial resources, the role of the male as sole provider has been seriously diminished. The ironic effect of the liberation of women has, in many cases, been the liberation of men as well—that is to say, their liberation from any sense of responsibility toward wife, children, or the institution of the family in general.

It is, however, not at all clear that all, or perhaps even the greater part, of the initiative here came from the women's side. Barbara Ehrenreich, for example, has suggested that changes in men's attitudes since World War II were generated, at least in the beginning, by a *male* rebellion against the roles traditionally assigned men in modern society. There was the rebellion against the "organization man," and by implication against the burdening of men with all the economic responsibilities involved in the sole-provider role. There was also the sexual revolution and the rebellion against monogamy. *Playboy*, it must be stressed, was an important symbol of the transformation of values occurring in the post-war era. Its first issue was published in 1953, long before women had fled the homemaker role in large numbers and while divorce rates were still quite low. Clearly, the initiative for sexual materials and pornography in general stemmed far more from the male side than from the female side in those early days, and, indeed, still today.

As Ehrenreich put it: "The gray flannel rebel resented his job. The playboy resisted marriage. The short-lived apotheosis of the male rebellion, the Beat, rejected both job and marriage. In the Beat, the two strands of male protest—one directed against the white collar work world and the other against the suburbanized family life that work was supposed to support—come together in the first all-out critique of American consumer culture."[4]

While the Beats, and the hippie culture generally, soon lost popularity, nevertheless it can be argued, at a minimum, that this male rebellion paved the way for what was to happen once women began to assert themselves fully. On this view, what the feminist movement did was to ratify this male role rejection—essentially, by redefining femininity to include a much greater independence of men than in the past—and this gave momentum to a drive that was already on the way. Even women's greater sexual freedom played into this scenario. It turned out that men didn't have to take up the yoke of matrimony at all to enjoy favors hitherto far more restricted and confined. Instead of being chastized for their errant behavior, these new playboys of the Western world were apparently to be rewarded therefor!

Whoever took the primary initiative on all these matters, there simply can be no question that, in terms of actual behavior, very large numbers of American men have given family responsibilities, and especially those involving their children and heirs, a far lower priority than at any time in previous American history. Certainly this is true in comparison to the late nineteenth and early twentieth centuries when the traditional American family was at its peak. At that time, one could not truly have separated off the concepts of "self" and "posterity" in the matter of family men as we are doing in this chapter. For, at that time, to be a "good father" was considered not the opposite of, but an essential component of, a man's *self*-fulfillment. Similarly, of course, with women. Many mothers felt that such success as they had achieved in life was to be measured almost entirely by the happiness, achievements, and general well-being of their children and grandchildren.

How radically all this has now changed! Self-realization, self-fulfillment, development of one's own personality, character, abilities, potentialities—all these universal drives that used to include within them the most profound consideration for posterity, now operate in a world strangely apart. And the risk-takers for this postmodern experiment are unwittingly, and one suspects unwillingly, the children.

SELF-CENTEREDNESS AMONG THE ELDERLY

The parents of the parents of today's children—the parents, that is, of the Baby Boomers we have just been discussing—clearly hold to more traditional family values than do their offspring. However, as suggested in chapter 11, even they have been affected to a degree by the waning of the Idea of Progress. Their time horizons, never really extending quite as far as those of middle-class Americans in the late nineteenth century, have been increasingly shortened over time by the fundamental predicament of progress. The euphoria accompanying the great growth spree of the first postwar decades has abated considerably, and the views of the elderly concerning the distant future are now scarcely less agnostic than those of younger generations.

Furthermore, in terms of the "self vs. posterity" issue, there is, as we know, the further fact that average life expectancies at older ages have been progressively lengthened during the postwar period. This means that the future involving one's own direct and specific self-interest has also been lengthened on average. The combination of a lengthening of personal time horizons and a shortening of more general time horizons has, I suggest, a very strong tendency to tilt the balance among the elderly toward concern for "self" above concern for "posterity."

Actually the extension of life expectancies—while not perhaps an intrinsic, nevertheless a quite characteristic, feature of the process of progress—has potentially enormous consequences for a society's attitude toward children and family institutions generally. These increases are almost certainly not done with yet. What has happened so far is sometimes described as a "squaring" of the survival curve.[5] By this is meant the fact that medical and other advances have brought us nearer and nearer to the point where virtually everyone will live to, or close to, maximum human life span. The latter is variously put in the range of 110 to 120 years or thereabouts.

Note two points: (1) the curve isn't fully squared yet, meaning that we can, in principle, extend average life expectancy still further without altering maximum human life span; and (2) all advances so far have left that maximum human life span unchanged, meaning that there conceivably could be room for truly massive increases in life expectancies if this maximum ultimately proves to be a variable subject to human intervention and control. Is that likely? No one knows for sure, but it would be a rash prophet who argued that this maximum was literally fixed for all time, particularly considering the pell-mell advances in genetic science in recent years.

The reason for mentioning these dazzling and in some ways quite disturbing future possibilities is to suggest an undercurrent here that could, in the long run, massively and perhaps irrevocably affect family life worldwide. The point is that as we come to live really very long lives, we ourselves become our own posterity. If we literally lived forever, there would be no need for children at all, or just a very few perhaps because accidents do happen, and will almost certainly continue to happen, from time to time. Is such thinking wholly far-fetched? Who knows? Already, greatly reduced infant mortality was undoubtedly a factor in the long-run 60 or 70 percent reduction in our fertility rates. If we begin to have massive reductions in mortality at older ages (and these have already begun), might these not also affect our future birthrates?

All this is speculative, but what is not speculative is that Americans of all ages, now very much including elderly Americans, have much longer personal futures to think about than they did, say, at the turn of the century. The future in which one is likely to be specifically and personally engaged has been lengthened. And the question is quite simply this: Has this lengthening of personal and shrinking of general time horizons had the predicted effect on the attitudes of elderly Americans? To put it more bluntly: Have elderly Americans shown a tendency to become more self-centered over time, even when at the rather obvious expense of their children and grandchildren—their posterity?

I strongly believe this to be true, even though I am making the comment (and the clearly implied criticism) about the generation to which I myself belong. The basic evidence is threefold:

1. *Combining longer lives with earlier retirements*

A major change, really a revolution, has taken place in the retirement behavior of the present elderly generation. The great majority of American men above the age of sixty-five used to remain active in the labor force; now only 16 percent do. The same trend is true for males aged fifty-five to sixty-four: in 1948, 89.5 percent were in the labor force; forty years later, only 67 percent were.[6] According to recent research, this trend to earlier retirement is wholly a phenomenon of the past fifty or sixty years, beginning "at the time that falls between the passage of the Social Security Act of 1935 and the granting of tax incentives to corporate employers that established company pension plans with the Revenue Act of 1942."[7] Although many other factors are also involved, there is no doubt that a major factor permitting earlier retirement—and because of extended life expectancies, much longer retirements—has been the extent of public subsidies through Social Security, Medicare, Medicaid, civil service and military pensions, tax-protected private pensions, and numerous other programs. For the most part, these programs represent a direct transfer of resources from the younger, working generation to the older generation, which becomes the beneficiary of an historically unprecedented consumption of goods and services.

2. *Benefits exceeding contributions*

What advocates for the elderly often claim is that the benefits accruing to today's senior citizens are simply repayments of contributions made earlier in life by these same persons when they themselves were members of the working generation. The obvious example offered as a case in point is Social Security. This argument is extremely weak, however, and is so disingenuous as to underline the degree to which defenders of our current arrangements are willing to put the self-interest of today's elderly above that of other generations. The Social Security Trust Fund, to which these prior contributions were supposed to have been made was, in fact, totally exhausted by 1983, and although it is now being reconstituted (by especially heavy contributions from today's working-class generation), those currently in or near retirement are enjoying a level of benefits that it is very doubtful future generations of elderly will be able to maintain.

3. *Elderly versus the present generation of children*

If we, in today's elderly generation, were in fact one of the poorer groups in society, then this special treatment might not seem to reflect any particular degree of generational self-centeredness, though, even then, one might want to know why, if we are so poor, we have abandoned the labor force in such huge numbers. But the opposite is the case. While poverty rates among the elderly have been falling sharply in recent years, those of America's children have, as we know, been rising sharply. At the present time, American children under the age of five have more than double the poverty rate of American adults over sixty-five. Despite this fact, and despite a general trend at the moment to limit all federal expenditures so as to reduce our huge budget deficits, it appears to be politically suicidal to suggest any restraint at all in the growth of federal spending on the elderly.

Consider, for example, the situation with respect to Medicare. Ballooning expenses with this program have brought it to the point where, without changes, it will go bankrupt in four or five years. Further, its long-run financial prospects are even more grim because of the aging of the huge Baby Boom generation. Yet when Republicans proposed a plan to cut, not the absolute level but the rate of growth, of future Medicare benefits, they were savaged in the 1996 elections by Democratic Party and AFL-CIO ads claiming that they were sabotaging the entire program. The effectiveness of this attack with elderly citizens may be observed in Florida and Arizona, two states with large retiree populations that hadn't been won by the Democrats since 1976 (Florida) and 1952 (Arizona). Clinton carried both.

In late 1996, politicians were also facing an issue that can seriously impact future Social Security payments. A distinguished group of economists reported their conviction that the Consumer Price Index (CPI) seriously overstates the rise in the U.S. cost of living. Since Social Security payments are indexed to the CPI, this implied that the elderly have regularly been getting increases in their benefits far in excess of what was intended by the program. To continue with the old CPI would be to project this error into the future. Since a correction to a more accurate index would have the added advantage of reducing the federal debt, it might be imagined that all politicians would immediately rally to the cause—using this technical adjustment as a convenient way to help solve a larger problem. In point of fact, initial reactions from most politicians seemed to be to offer members of the opposite party the chance to take the initiative on this matter. After you, Alphonse! The media presentations of the issue—almost invariably featuring some elderly person or couple saying how they just didn't know how they would manage if this money were taken away from them—hardly helped. It is easy to understand why these elderly entitlement programs have been called the "third rail" of American politics: if your career depends on getting votes, you'd better not touch!

The present generation of children has no vote in these matters and, of course, poses no immediate political threat. Bringing this generation into the picture makes it clear that it is, in fact, our posterity that is being short-changed in this whole area of generational subsidies. Thus, Sylvia Ann Hewlett, a children's advocate, writing of "the increasingly massive transfer of income from the young to the old in American society," discerns a pattern of "Now-now-nowism."[8] The "now" and the immediate future of the elderly—that is to say, the future in which we ourselves are personally and directly involved—appears to be taking clear precedence over the more distant future represented by our children's children, and now, in truth, even over the less distant future of our own children who comprise the majority of the working generation. In this context, self-interest equates to short-term interest. Posterity is left to cope for itself.

DECLINING MEMORIALIZATION OF THE DEAD

The two major developments we have been considering—the relative reduction of direct parental care for children and the tendency of the elderly to absorb social resources with comparatively little thought for future generations—are reasonably well-known. Not everyone will agree with the way in which I have characterized these developments, but the issues themselves are frequently discussed, and will represent nothing particularly novel or newsworthy to most readers.

My third example of a shift of interest from "posterity" to "self" is, however, a rather different matter. With a few exceptions, it has received almost no public attention in the press or other media, and this despite the fact that it involves one of the most significant aspects of any society's family and communal life—the way it treats its dead. Very quietly, a revolution has been taking place in this basic feature of American life, a revolution which has, I believe, a direct bearing on the issue of "self vs. posterity," and, in consequence, on the ultimate meaning and value we attribute to the institution of the family.[9]

In order to follow these interconnections through, one has to describe briefly how funerary practices have changed over the course of

American history. The important points for our purposes are two: (1) The nineteenth century showed a very strong increase in the ceremonies, expenses, and material attentions paid to the dead in the United States. (2) The twentieth century, at least from World War I, and accelerating since the 1960s, has seen a general downplaying of attention to and memorialization of our dead.

In each case we are speaking of this-worldly attentions to the dead: physical preservation of the corpse through embalming; elaborate and expensive caskets and burial paraphernalia; stones, monuments, and other markers; and also restrictive dress codes, complicated funeral rites, and so on. In early Puritan times, although death was obviously a common and significant event, the actual physical memorialization of the dead was most often minimal.

In his study, *Welcome Joy: Death in Puritan New England,* Gordon E. Geddes notes that in the Puritan world, the notion that "the body should be preserved and the grave remain forever inviolate was unthinkable in a world of change and decay." Although graveyards did exist, "yet the majority of New Englanders were buried without gravestones. Uninscribed stone markers might be used, or flat stones, or perhaps wooden markers that no longer survive. But for the majority no permanent marker was used." The burial grounds were owned not by the church but by the towns, but "such upkeep as the town provided was minimal, and the upkeep of grave stones and tombs was the responsibility of relatives. Both town and relatives frequently took their responsibility lightly." Even the funeral, though obviously a spiritual event of great importance, did not involve an extended rite of passage. In Geddes' description: "The community gathered, ate and drank, marched in procession, and met the need of closing its own ranks at the loss of a member. After the funeral, after honoring the dead, life would go on. . . . The dead awaited resurrection; the living returned to the tasks of living."[10]

In a material sense, then, our early forebears left surprisingly little in the way of a lasting memorialization of their dead. Physical death meant impermanence and decay. What was truly important, the immortality of the soul, was not of this world.

In the course of the eighteenth and especially the nineteenth centuries, there was a substantial change in attitude toward death involving, among other things, a desire to leave durable evidence of the deceased in the burial context. The rural cemetery movement, beginning in the first third of the nineteenth century, involved a new attention to a this-worldly memorialization of the dead. "A prime characteristic of the cemeteries," David Charles Sloan notes in his 1991 study, "was their permanence." Their most significant features "were family monuments, which emerged from the landscape and stood outlined against the trees."[11] These monuments were often ornate and by the late ninetecth century included, according to Robert Habenstein and William Lamers, "cornices, fancy caps, arabesques, scrolls, imitation tree trunks, statuary." Although the result was often a "forest of petrified and very indifferent art," still, "the impulse to create beauty even in death was strong."[12]

Along with the rural cemetery movement went increasingly ornate caskets, elaborate displays of mourning in dress and behavior, the beginnings of what were to become extravagant floral displays, and, from the Civil War on, the gradual spread of embalming. Embalming permitted, in the case of war dead, transportation to distant burial sites. In the case of ordinary civilian deaths it permitted a longer period for viewing and other funeral rites. James F. Farrell notes that in Vermillion County, Illinois, the average (mean) number of days between death and burial increased from 1.24 in the 1870s to 2.14 in the 1910s, largely thanks to the introduction of embalming. "At first sight," he writes, "this change of nine-tenths of a day in a period of fifty years may not seem momentous, but in fact it represents a revolution in funeral service. . . . Within a generation, the practice of embalming enabled undertakers to preserve bodies for extended and elaborate funeral services."[13]

With these more elaborate funeral services came a corresponding expansion in the number of undertakers. In the United States as a whole between 1880 and 1920, the number of undertakers rose from eleven thousand to nearly twenty-five thousand, and the number of deaths per undertaker fell from 194.2 to 56.6. In sum, and simultaneously with the growing celebration both of the institution of the family and the Idea of Progress, there occurred, in the words of Charles Jackson, "a domestication and beautification of death . . . between the late eighteenth and late nineteenth centuries. The effect of this movement was to increase significantly the place of death and the dead in the world of the living."[14] All this is in support of the first point above concerning nineteenth-century developments.

And what of the second point with regard to what has been happening in the twentieth century, at least since World War I? Jackson's summary statement here is that there has been a "withdrawal on the part of the living from communion with and commitment to the dying and the dead. Death became alienated from life and the world of the dead and dying was essentially lost." In practical terms, "the elaborate Victorian funeral began to fade in the World War I era."[15]

These statements may strike some readers as rather odd, particularly those who remember reading Jessica Mitford's best-selling 1963 book, *The American Way of Death*.[16] In Mitford's view, the problem with American funerary practices, circa 1960, was that they were tawdry, sentimentalized, overly commercialized, and, above all, excessively expensive. She found it absurd and even obscene to think of "what we spend to bury the dead" compared to "what we spend for the health and welfare of the living." She even implied that we could have a full-scale national health insurance program for far less than what it was costing us to dispose of our dearly departed.

Actually, a careful study of Mitford's numbers suggests that she vastly overstated her case. Even in the year (1960) she chose for study, total funeral and burial expenses in the United States came to less than half a percent of Gross Domestic Product (0.35 percent according to the U.S. Bureau of Economic Analysis). This figure isn't even in the same ball park with any kind of national health insurance program as our experience with Medicare and Medicaid amply demonstrates. Furthermore, this low percentage of GDP was almost certainly already on the decline when she wrote, and, without any question whatever, it has declined massively since. Figure 12.1 shows the Bureau of Economic Analysis estimates from 1960 to 1993, indicating a decline in U.S. funeral and burial expenses as a percentage of GDP from 0.35 percent to 0.15 percent, or well under half the prior number.

Similarly dramatic results are obtained if we compare funeral and burial expenses per individual death to per capita GDP over the same period, roughly measuring the cost of death in relation to annual individual incomes. In 1960, as shown in figure 12.2, this cost percentage was 37.5 percent. By 1993, it had fallen to 17.0 percent, again to less than half in terms of the real hit to the consumer's pocketbook. Equally dramatic has been the rise of a less costly method of disposal, cremation as opposed to earth burial. Table 12.1 shows the extraordinary rise of cremations in the United States since 1960 and their projected further increase into the twenty-first century. We are dealing here with a revo-

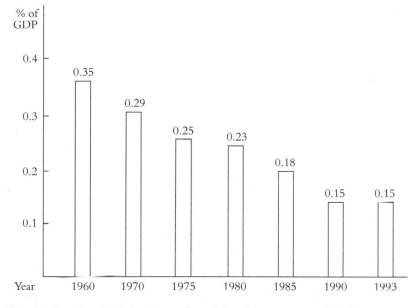

Fig. 12.1   Total U.S. funeral and burial expenses (F&B) as a percentage of GDP (1987$)

Source: Bureau of Economic Analysis.

lution in one of the most basic communal and family rites, a revolution that has been accelerating over the past thirty or forty years.

And what we are in process of discarding here is not really the "American way of death" but the "Victorian way of death." My claim, in fact, is that the discarding of this Victorian way of death is closely interconnected with the decline of the Idea of Progress, with the breakdown of the American family, and, specifically from the point of view of this chapter, with the mounting victory of "self" over "posterity."

How is such a large claim to be justified? The argument I would make is based on the following two points.

1. *A focus on posterity will usually lead to a tendency to increase one's emphasis on memorializing the dead.*

Since the Idea of Progress is basically a secular idea—that is, deals

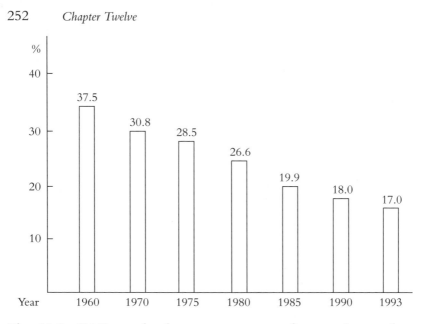

Fig. 12.2   F&B per death as a percentage of per capita product (1987$)

Source: Bureau of Economic Analysis

Table 12.1   U.S. Percent of Cremations to Deaths, 1960–2010

Year	Percent	Year	Percent
1960	3.56	1990	17.0
1965	3.87	1993	19.8
1970	4.58	Projected	
1975	6.55	1994	20.8
1980	9.74	2000	25.6
1985	13.81	2010	32.5

Source: Cremation Association of North America (CANA), 501 North Michigan Avenue, Chicago, Illinois 60611, (312) 644-6610.

essentially with what is happening and will happen on this earth—it is appropriate under its aegis to consider the memorialization of the dead in a material, this-worldly context. The consequence of this secularity is to make a prima facie case for various tangible displays, ceremonies, markers, and monuments observable for all to see in a physical context.

This contrasts with the earlier Puritan idea which minimizes the material world and in which such displays would be out of place. Since the Idea of Progress is also very long term in its outlook, the search for an increased degree of "permanence" in the cemetery-marker-monument context is also very natural and appropriate.

Finally, the interconnections between family values and the Idea of Progress, which I have been stressing throughout this book, make it natural that this physical and long-term honoring of the dead should be fashioned in terms of *family* memorials. The great family monument, standing large and solid behind small individual family-member headstones, is a characteristic feature of Victorian-style cemetery plots.

There is a basic inner consistency in all this. At the deepest level, and in terms of psychological motivation, the Idea of Progress envisioned the future (posterity) as giving meaning, vindication, and judgment to the present. In the same psychological mood in which individuals could take satisfaction—in some cases their greatest satisfaction—in the thought that their children and heirs would live richer, better, and happier lives than they themselves had after they departed this earth, these same individuals would almost certainly imagine their children and heirs as thinking of them, remembering them, perhaps even being a little grateful to them for having helped bring about this very happy outcome. Their stake in the future was real and important to them and essentially took the form of being remembered and memorialized in one way or another.

In this context, neither the rotting graves of the Puritans, nor the later disposable ashes of today's crematoria, would have satisfied those in the late nineteenth and early twentieth centuries who were in important respects living in and for the future. As they passed the torch to their children and heirs, they wanted to be remembered—remembered in this world and, ideally, for generations to come.

2. *How a declining interest in memorialization of the dead reflects an increasing focus on self*

Actually, we no longer pass the torch to our children in quite the way it was done in earlier years. We live too long for that. By the time we get ready to pass the torch, our children are middle-aged or, in some cases, elderly themselves. We not only live long but we also have great difficulty envisioning the more distant future after we are gone. It is hard enough to see what will be happening to the world (and to us personally) a few years down the road; to try to imagine what the world will be like long after we have departed the scene becomes an exercise in total futility. Who can possibly imagine what America will be like in a century, fifty years, even a few years ahead?

To put the contrast in a nutshell: In the nineteenth century and perhaps up to World War I or so, Americans thought they knew the general shape of things to come and they could therefore live imaginatively and in a purely psychological sense in the world that would exist after they themselves were dead. In the twentieth century, or at least during the past sixty or seventy years, Americans have found it more and more difficult to envision the life that will go on in this world after they have departed the scene. This ultimately reflects the combination of longer life expectancies and the fundamental predicament of progress.

The result today is, generally, that each generation tends to think more of itself than of other generations, previous or subsequent, and, specifically, that individuals care increasingly less about what happens to their bodies after they have shuffled off this mortal coil. To put it bluntly: if one is solely interested in self, and if one's basic outlook is secular, then that interest in self dies with the self and what happens after death— the whole paraphernalia of funerals, memorials, cemeteries, and monuments—has no meaning whatsoever.

Indeed, in today's world, funerals are really held primarily not as memorials but as temporary therapy for the still living. In an extremely interesting 1990 survey conducted by the Wirthlin Group, the result was that "about two-thirds of the participants in the study expressed their belief that funerals and other ceremonies are primarily 'for the comfort of those attending' rather than to 'honor and show respect for the deceased.'" [17] What all this really seems to be saying to us is that the only thing that matters is what happens in this world and in this world now. The future after we are gone is a blank. Forget about it. Live your life for your life. All the rest is basically incomprehensible![18]

THE INNER BATTLE

In some respects, the ongoing changes in our funerary practices will seem to many Americans as evidence of good sense and increasingly rational behavior. Why spend all this money on funerals and monuments when the dearly departed can in no way know, or be affected by, our actions? The general reaction in the 1960s to Jessica Mitford's rather exaggerated account of our funeral excesses was that we should be ashamed of ourselves for wasting so much money, and in such tasteless ways, when we could be doing really useful things for the living—more health care, better universities, and so on. So perhaps what we have just described might be thought of as an advance, evidence of an increasingly sensible society.

My own view is that this last example of emphasis on self above posterity is really of a piece with the two earlier examples we discussed—the tendency to neglect our children and an increasing self-centeredness on the part of our elderly. All conspire to weaken the family unit. All suggest that what happens in this physical and material world of ours after we have left the scene really matters very little to us. This is in fact one of the major battlegrounds where the issue of "family values" will ultimately have to be worked out. This battleground is within ourselves, involving finally our judgement as to how to evaluate our own claims as compared to the claims of those who will succeed us. If those successor claims mean very little to us, then, of course, we will certainly care very little what those successors think of us after we are gone. Nor, for that matter, will we adequately attend to their claims while we are still living.

Perhaps, however, at least for some of us, such answers are less than wholly satisfactory. A renewed interest in what happens to this imperfect earthly dwelling of ours after we have departed the scene may still seem worth encouraging. If this renewal might lead to the occasional funeral procession or even monument, perhaps that would not be too great a price to pay for the ancillary benefits that might well accrue.

13

EQUALITY, FAMILY ADVANTAGES, AND MORAL RELATIVISM

I f balancing the claims of self and posterity is one of the central battle-fields in the war over family values, another equally important locus of strife is one mentioned at the very beginning of chapter 1: the issue of "the family" versus "families." Is there one kind of family structure that, with limited variations, has a social and ultimately moral priority above all other such structures? Or are all family structures—rather like Tolstoy's "happy families"—basically the same, that is, socially and morally equivalent? Are POSSLQS (to use the Census Bureau shorthand for "persons of the opposite sex sharing living quarters") to be considered family units when marriage is neither involved nor even contemplated? How about homosexual unions? Never-married single-parent households? Once-divorced single-parent households? Thrice-divorced single-parent households? Marriages that last five years? two years? six weeks? Communal marriages? Communal POSSLQS?

Interestingly, although important commentators like James Q. Wilson correctly argue that the general public is more attached to traditional family values than the media and intelligentsia usually allow, there is at least some evidence to suggest that even that general public has switched over toward the "families" end of the spectrum. A widely reported 1988 poll of 1,200 randomly selected adults, conducted by the Massachusetts Mutual Life Insurance Company, showed that less than one-fourth of respondents defined the family in terms of people related by blood, marriage, or adoption (the Census Bureau definition), while almost three-fourths defined it as "a group of people who love and care for each other."[1] By such a definition, virtually any collection of friendly human beings, whether "sharing living quarters" or not, becomes a family.

What is ultimately at stake here is the moral core of that celebrated (and reviled) phrase, "family values." Also at stake, and very much related to those family values is the moral core of the Idea of Progress. I have repeatedly stressed that during the nineteenth and early twentieth centuries a certain morality was built into the Idea of Progress and that this morality not only placed great emphasis on the future, but constrained choices and options so as to limit acceptable paths of development, while also prescribing future-oriented behaviors like industry, abstinence, and sacrificing for the well-being of one's children and heirs. This morality enabled American society to bear the basically disruptive and complicating effects of the process of progress while maintaining a vivid future orientation. It required strong, cohesive, family units in which divorce was virtually unheard of, mothers worked only in the case of extreme economic need, fathers took their responsibilities as sole providers seriously, and all deviations from these middle-class norms—of which, understandably, there were many—were frowned upon, or in some cases legally prohibited.

The family—not famil*ies*—was the moral agent of the Idea of Progress. And it is precisely with the fading of that Idea under the pressure of the fundamental predicament of progress that the latter has begun seriously to replace the former. In this chapter, I will follow through the logic of this process, placing special emphasis on the concept of "equality." For the judgment that sees a moral equivalence among all conceivable family structures is ultimately based on a moral relativism that is itself founded on the principle of equality writ large. The task of the following pages is to explain how the fundamental predicament of progress tends sharply to elevate the general principle of equality and how this elevation tends to devastate the moral standing of the traditional American family.

PRESENT EQUALITY VERSUS FUTURE GROWTH

Let us begin by acknowledging that the principle of equality, in one form or another, is itself embodied in the morality we usually associate with the Idea of Progress. Although dishonored by slavery, the suppression of women's rights, the shabby treatment of immigrants and the poor generally, the notion that, in principle, there is a certain fundamental equality among all human beings was not only written into the Declaration of Independence but was clearly a part of the American experiment generally. I earlier mentioned Horace Mann's paean to Progress in relation to the need for universal education. Notably, education was to be not just "the creator of wealth undreamed of," but also the "great equalizer" of human conditions. The eventual abolition of slavery, the protection of poor children through child labor laws, the granting of women's suffrage and increasing women's rights in general—all this was not a rejection of the Idea of Progress but an intrinsic feature of its moral program. That is to say, part of the great nineteenth-century American project was to increase the degree of equality among the various individuals and groups in society, or at least to reduce the grosser inequalities that were apparent all around. And these equalities and inequalities involved all phases of human life—economic, political, social, and personal.

Thus, promotion of greater equality, or somewhat reduced inequality, in this very broad sense was part of the morality of capital "P" Progress in nineteenth- and early twentieth century America, not in any way a rejection of that morality. Still it was just that—a part, but not the whole, of that morality. As in the case of "self" vs. "posterity," we have a kind of balancing act to consider here. In particular, equality (always understood in terms of relative not total equality) was considered a generally good thing to achieve, provided that it didn't interfere too much with other good things that were also potentially achievable through the process of progress.

Tocqueville, for example, while acknowledging the appeal of greater equality worried about the effect of its achievement on freedom. In general, he argued that equality's advantages were near term while its costs emerged only much later in time. Writing in 1840, he pointed out: "The advantages of equality are instantaneous. . . . Equality every day confers a number of small enjoyments on every man. The charms of equality are felt every instant, and are within the reach of all; the noblest hearts are not insensible to them, and the most vulgar souls exult in them."

The possible untoward consequences of equality are, however, typically felt much later in time. Thus:

> None but attentive and clear-sighted men perceive the perils with
> which equality threatens us, and they commonly avoid pointing them

out. They know that the calamities they apprehend are remote, and
flatter themselves that they will only fall upon future generations. . . .
The evils which extreme equality may produce are slowly disclosed;
they creep gradually into the social frame; they are seen only at inter-
vals, and at the moment they become most violent habit already causes
them to be no longer felt.[2]

This emphasis on the short-term appeal of equality in contrast to its
potential long-run costs is readily applicable to the economic arena,
where it would appear as a kind of trade-off between equality and economic growth. There is little question that one of the reasons societies
have historically not moved more drastically in the direction of reducing
inequalities of income and wealth is the fear that, in doing so, they
would seriously impair long-run growth. This is probably *the* major constraint on income equalization measures acknowledged in one degree or
another by both liberal and conservative observers. As Kermit Gordon,
then president of the Brookings Institution, wrote some years ago:
"Economic institutions . . . generate substantial disparities among citizens in living standards and material welfare. The differentials in income
are meant to serve as incentives—rewards and penalties—to promote
efficiency in the use of resources and to generate a great, and growing,
national output."[3]

Not only are inequalities often justified in terms of providing potential incentives for productivity and growth, they are also sometimes cited
as necessary to provide the resources needed for saving and capital accumulation. Rich individuals, and rich firms and corporations, do the bulk
of such private saving as is accomplished in most societies. Spread those
surplus incomes and assets over the entire society in a massive equalization campaign, and the result would be—or so it is argued—a possibly
serious reduction in net saving and investment in the society at large.

This inverse relationship between equality and growth is certainly
not the only manner in which these two social goals are related. In the
Affluent Society, for example, John Kenneth Galbraith opined that by
giving more resources to the poor (equality), one might well increase
their productivity (growth).[4] Fred Hirsch, in a frequently discussed
study, *Social Limits to Growth*, argued that as economic growth meets
more and more of our basic economic needs, the struggle over relative
income shares becomes more and more intense. This explains, he sug-

gests, why "economic equality has been a compulsive political idea of the twentieth century."[5]

Just how compulsive this idea has been in the postwar era is shown by the influential book by John Rawls, *A Theory of Justice*.[6] Rawls would permit no inequalities at all unless they could be shown to be to the advantage of the least favored (poorest) members of society. If, by allowing one person to have a higher income than the rest of the society, additional income is generated for the poorest members of society then and only then is the inequality permissible. Actually, this exception to his general rule does in itself suggest a recognition that there is at least some trade-off between equality, on the one hand, and productivity and growth on the other.

Many other possible interconnections between equality and growth could be mentioned, but my special interest relates to those that involve a time dimension, that is, that may be strongly influenced by the shortening of time horizons produced by the fundamental predicament of progress.[7] In this connection, I focus on two aspects of this interrelationship. The first is what we have already suggested above, namely that there is at least some trade-off between the short-term appeal and advantages of equality and the longer-term prospects for economic growth. In terms both of incentives and resources, the danger of moving too strongly in the direction of income redistribution (and this is apart from the costs incurred in the actual redistributional program[8]), is that it may compromise long-term growth to a greater or lesser degree.

The second point is that, contrary to Hirsch's argument, it is almost certainly the case that economic growth over time has at least some tendency to mitigate, not intensify, the struggle over relative shares. This point is frequently suggested by the phrase, once so popular with President Kennedy, that "a rising tide lifts all boats." If your boat is being lifted fast enough, it is suggested, then it matters much less to individuals how fast the boats of others are being lifted. It is only when one's boat appears to be beached and stranded while other boats sail merrily off into the sunset that envy and resentment rise to the fore. So the argument goes; an argument, incidentally, which was often used to explain why the United States with its rapidly rising general living standards never succumbed to the kind of class warfare so confidently predicted by the Marxists.

But if this second point is true, then how does one explain the phenomenon that Hirsch stressed so heavily? In particular, how does one account for the enormously increased interest in promoting greater economic equality—and, indeed, greater equality in all areas of life—that we have seen in the course of this century?

My basic answer is this: The shortening of time-horizons produced by the fundamental predicament of progress tilts the balance between equality and growth in favor of equality with respect to both the major points we have been discussing. Insofar as one has come to discount the future more heavily because of all the uncertainties and complexities of postmodern living, to that degree one is also discounting the costs of any and all income redistribution programs. The *disadvantages* of such programs count for less when the future counts for less. At the same time, the *advantages* of economic growth, being subject to such great uncertainty, are also increasingly discounted. If one is losing faith in the future, then it is a vain comfort to be told to be patient and wait for a future that may never come. One increasingly doubts whether the tide will, in fact, rise, and, if it does rise, whether one's own boat will, in fact, be lifted.

In short, as present and near-term considerations increasingly dominate future and long-term considerations, the balance between equality and growth, like the balance between self and posterity, tends to be shifted toward the nearer term objective—in one case, equality, in the other, self. The negative aspects of income redistribution and other equalization measures are more easily discounted while the promised benefits of future growth become increasingly less persuasive. As Tocqueville put it in his own specific context, the advantages that are "instantaneous" take priority over the consequences which are "remote" and "only fall upon future generations."

EQUALITY AND FAMILY ADVANTAGES

Two questions arise: (1) Has there, in point of actual fact, been this great surge of interest in equality in American society in the course of this century? And (2), if there has, what exactly is its relationship to the fate of the American family?

The first question is a bit complicated to answer for the simple reason that, by most indicators, income inequality has been increasing in the United States since the late 1960s or early 1970s. Newspaper articles are filled with accounts of the extraordinarily high compensations (salaries, bonuses, and stock options) received by many U.S. corporate CEOs and how the gap between these payments and the wages of the average worker has been growing by leaps and bounds. Also, many politicians have made much of the fact that the immigration to the United States of large numbers of unskilled (including illegal) foreign workers and the rapid growth of imports of low-skill-intensive goods from the less developed world have hit our own unskilled, low-income workers with particular ferocity.

It would take us much too far afield to discuss these and other reasons for recent changes in the U.S. income distribution, including, one might add, the question of how properly to measure the extent of income and wealth inequalities. Suffice it to say that the main explanation given by most commentators—an explanation very consistent with the general themes of this book—is that inequality has risen because of the increasing technological complexity of our high-tech society, with the consequent relative and rapid rise of returns to skills and education. The relatively unskilled and uneducated are the ones to suffer, while the more fortunately endowed and trained benefit handsomely. This is a basically reasonable explanation and poses no problems whatever for my general argument—if anything, quite the contrary.[9]

However, the main point to be made here is that whatever drift to greater inequality there may be at the moment, and however temporary or permanent it may turn out to be, such facts really say nothing at all about the intensity of the national drive to reduce inequality in American society. Taking any kind of historical perspective at all, the increasing intensity of this effort over the past century, and certainly over the past thirty or forty years simply cannot be doubted.

Consider, for example, the efforts made by way of income redistribution in U.S. society since the 1960s. This period, incidentally, includes all the Reagan years, when, it is sometimes said, the federal government massively favored the well-to-do over the poor. In point of fact, total federal spending on means-tested and social insurance programs rose from 4.3 percent of U.S. GDP in 1967 to 9.2 percent in 1990. Although there was some drop between 1978 and 1982, the overall level of federal and state spending per poor person was up more than 300 percent between 1967 and 1990. Even eliminating the large increase in Medicaid spending on the poor, real spending per poor person through other means-tested programs increased by 230 percent between 1967 and 1990.

Furthermore, during much of this period, the tax system was taking not less but far more money from the well-to-do. During the largely Reagan years of 1980 through 1989, for example, the share of the federal income tax paid by the top 20 percent of the population by income group rose from 67.2 percent to 72.3 percent and that of the top 5 percent from 37.1 percent to 44.2 percent. Taking taxes and transfer payments together, the President's Council of Economic Advisers estimated that in 1991, households in the lowest income quintile received an average annual net subsidy of $8,808, while households in the highest quintile paid out an annual negative subsidy of $22,022.[10]

To keep these developments in proper historical perspective, it must be recalled that it was only a century ago (1895) that the U.S. Supreme Court declared income taxes unconstitutional, and only in 1913 that the Sixteenth Amendment providing for such a tax was ratified.

This historical point is not of antiquarian interest only, for this book is precisely concerned with these long-run developments, and in particular the shift in priorities from the Idea of Progress to what we might well now call the Idea of Equality. It is this major historical shift in priorities that our analysis would predict, not the actual achievement of greater income equality over time. The latter, as already suggested, may be increasingly difficult to achieve as our postmodern society becomes ever more complex, although there is fairly clear evidence that, notwithstanding current trends, the degree of income equality has in fact increased notably since the turn of the century.[11]

When we turn to our second question—the effect of this shift in priorities on the status of the American family—the answer fairly leaps out at us. Whereas from a Progress perspective, the traditional American family is not only a useful but an indispensable institution, from an Equality perspective it becomes highly suspect, no longer a real friend, and in many ways the enemy.

The argument here is clear and simple: The intact, biological-parent home where primary child care is provided by a biological parent is arguably the greatest single advantage a young person can have in life. Such an advantage virtually guarantees that the child will never suffer the manifold effects of poverty. Equally or even more significantly, it strongly suggests that the child will do better in school, be much less likely to require psychological or psychiatric treatment, be quite unlikely to engage in criminal activities, be physically more healthy, and, indeed, be less likely to wander around the house lighting matches, testing electrical outlets, or orally experimenting with rat-poison or ammonia. (See chapter 2, pp. 38–45.) This child will not only have a much preferred childhood but will have a very strong chance of ultimately entering that elite of well-trained, well-educated adults who have always done well economically in the course of American history and who are especially successful in the present era of increasing technological and cognitive demands.

But what these seemingly positive features also mean is that the institution of the intact, parent-nurturing, biological family is the main source of personal, educational, and socioeconomic inequalities in present-day America. To grow up in such a family affords inestimable advantages for certain individuals, which they themselves have done nothing in particular to deserve, as compared to the disadvantages of all other children, which they themselves have equally done nothing to deserve. Given such an obvious injustice, and given our new and dramatic emphasis on equality, how can such an institution be tolerated? How, indeed, can the institution of the traditional American family be tolerated?

This dissonance between the equality ideal and an institution that is the source of great de facto inequality in the society leads to numerous media attempts to denigrate traditional family life (e.g., the Murphy Brown-Dan Quayle flap), and also various pieces of legislation and/or court decisions, which either undermine traditional family values or actually penalize the institution itself. No-fault divorce, where the deeper interests of the children involved are basically ignored, is a good example of the state effectively scorning the significance and solemnity of the marriage vow, not to mention parental responsibilities for children. Aid to Families with Dependent Children (AFDC), with its well-known bias in favor of father-absent households, is another good example. Similarly, moves already instituted or underway to increase subsidies to extra-family day care illustrate the way in which parental care for infants and toddlers is not only treated as expendable, but is actually penalized. In a large-scale day-care regime, mothers (or fathers) who choose to stay at home to raise their babies not only lose income but are actually taxed to help pay subsidies to those who use day care instead of providing parental care.

This last example is rather similar to the school choice issue, an issue that can also be interpreted in family-friendly or family-unfriendly terms. Should families (parents) have the right to use whatever schools they feel are best for their children (public, private, or parochial) or is the state effectively to penalize any family which attempts to go outside the public school system? Any family that chooses the alternative route will not only have to pay private tuition, but will, of course, also continue to pay taxes for the support of the public schools. In this case, the state is effectively determining what the appropriate education for the child should be rather than the family, or at least it is very heavily penalizing the family for making any other than the state-approved choice. In general, the equality principle is very hard on families, or any other institution, which seeks to secure advantages for its members, when those advantages are not available for all, or at least the great generality of, children and citizens.

MORAL RELATIVISM AND THE ISSUE OF FAMILY VERSUS FAMILIES

The actions just described have a tendency to penalize, or at least limit, the intrinsic advantages that intact, well-functioning families have above other institutional forms. In a way, however, the deeper attack on the family is somewhat different, and it consists primarily in denying that such advantages actually exist in the first place. The claim is not that the traditional family has too many things going for it, but rather that it is neither better nor worse than any other family form. This claim is expressed in many different ways. Bad marriages, it is said, are quite common and actually worse than divorces. Single mothers are heroically doing a wonderful job in the vast majority of cases. Homosexual lovers should have every right that married couples have, including pension privileges and the inheritance of rent-controlled apartments. Extended families are often far more loving and in general superior to nuclear families. The supposed advantages of the traditional American family are a result of a mythologizing of history by family apologists. Actually, that institution was more commonly a prison than a source of personal fulfillment.

The denial of the advantages of traditional family life above any other forms of cohabitation and child rearing is to be interpreted, I believe, as a type of moral relativism under which the equality principle has been extended to virtually all aspects of human behavior. Actually, the leap from: (1) a heavy discounting of the future and the new priority given equality, to (2) a thoroughgoing moral relativism, is an amazingly short one. Indeed, moral relativism is in many ways the natural and consistent morality—for it *is* a moral system, and at times a rather fierce one—for a myopic, equality-oriented, and essentially nonprogressive world.

The leap is made—or the small step taken—via the concepts of *multiculturalism* and *diversity*. At first glance, the connection seems obscure. For when we think of a seriously egalitarian society, our tendency is to envision great uniformities—people having the same incomes, the same kinds of houses, the same degrees of power and prestige, and so on. In contrast, both "multiculturalism" and "diversity" appear to call attention to the differences among groups rather than to their similarities. In common usage among both intellectuals and public officials, these terms represent a rejection of the kind of uniformity suggested by older concepts such as the "melting pot," in which, over time, individual and group identities are recast into something peculiarly "American."

In fact, however, it is just the opposite. For one thing, as a matter of practical observation, it is clear that most individuals who espouse the virtues of "diversity" are also in the forefront of those who argue for quotas or their equivalents. In a university setting, as one example, this would involve trying to make faculty appointments, administrative positions, student admissions, and the like more closely approximate various demographic percentages. In public life, officials often try to staff boards and agencies in such a way that they will "look like the nation." Such approaches are sometimes described as replacing the old-fashioned equality-of-opportunity principle with that of equality-of-result.

What is most interesting about quotas and similar equalization measures, however, is the underlying logic that justifies them within a diversity framework. For the essential justification is not that, over time, differences among these groups will disappear—that those who function poorly today will, given these new opportunities, soon enough come to function exactly as do other more advantaged groups. On the contrary, within this framework, the differences among groups are, in principle, a cause for celebration. These differences are not expected to disappear but to remain. Thus, what is being equalized here is not the behavior of different groups, but the moral value of different behaviors. In brief, groups behave differently, and they must be allowed to do so, but this must not affect their positions in the economy or their standing in society because all behaviors are morally equivalent.

Notice that the foregoing statement actually involves a certain inconsistency for it says both (1) that all behaviors are morally equivalent, and (2) that we must tolerate all these different behaviors. The clear implication is that there is one kind of behavior that is *not* morally equivalent and that we must *not* tolerate: intolerant behavior. The ultimate expression of the principle of moral relativism is that there are no fixed standards of value other than one, and that one fixed standard is the equivalence of all standards of value. *The one thing we will not tolerate is intolerance!*

The paradox embodied in that last statement readily gives rise to paradoxical behavior, and specifically to the phenomenon of what critics have come to call "political correctness." What starts out as a pluralistic, everything-is-acceptable philosophy is fairly easily transformed into a requirement of basic conformity of thought. Many examples could be cited here, but we need not linger over them.[12] Instead, I would emphasize three quite general points relevant to the over-all purposes of this study:

1. *Moral relativism, as a serious morality, is really inconceivable except in a society in which future consequences are almost wholly ignored.*

The claim here is that different behaviors are, in general, not equivalent, morally or otherwise, but that their lack of equivalence is mainly manifested in terms of their future consequences. The only way in which one can even entertain the relativistic hypothesis is by largely ignoring, or heavily discounting, these future consequences of present behaviors. Thus the basic agnosticism about the future which, according to our analysis, derives ultimately from the fundamental predicament of progress, is almost certainly a necessary condition for the emergence of moral relativism as a widespread (though, of course, never universal) popular philosophy.

2. Moral relativism, by sanctioning wide varieties of different behaviors, makes the future ever more difficult to predict or envision, further undercuts the anticipatable consequences of those different behaviors, and thus effectively creates a self-reinforcing environment.

If moral relativism succeeds in creating such chaos in society that no one really has any idea whatever as to what may or may not happen tomorrow, then it becomes increasingly difficult to form judgments as to what "good" or "bad" behavior really is. Or, rather, one's judgments will almost wholly be formed by the immediate consequences and characteristics of the behavior in question. In such terms, tolerance of different behaviors is very likely to become the most reasonable attitude and intolerance the only real vice. For tolerance obviously has certain immediate advantages. It allows people to do what they want to do at the moment without interference. Similarly, intolerance has certain equally obvious immediate disadvantages. In one way or another, the intolerant person is chastizing, bullying, ignoring or in other ways discomfitting other individuals and thus restricting their lives and generally rendering them less pleasant and fruitful. The admitted fly in the ointment is the strict lack of tolerance for the intolerant, à la the problem of political correctness. However, if moral relativism is increasingly and ultimately universally accepted, then the problem of "correcting" the "incorrect" will vanish and this particular paradox will have little or no bearing on the practical application of the relativistic principle.

3. Just as moral relativism renders the Idea of Progress totally archaic, it also asserts the fundamental equivalence of all family structures, thus rendering the traditional American family simply one option out of the universe of "families" generally.

I return here to the question with which we began this chapter, the issue of "the family" versus "families." What is the bearing of this discussion of moral relativism on this particular issue? The rather obvious point is that the moral relativist insists that we must be tolerant of, and equally respectful of, all family structures. What I have added by the foregoing analysis is the notion that such moral relativism with respect to familial institutions is maintainable only if we largely ignore future consequences and that such a present or near-term orientation is one of the likely products of the fundamental predicament of progress.

I can perhaps make this general point clearer by a particular example: attitudes toward what has been happening to the American Black family in recent decades. Of all family structures in the United States, the Black family has on average probably departed most clearly from the model of the traditional American family. Well over two-thirds of Black children are born out of wedlock, divorce and separation are rampant, single-mother families are the rule more than the exception, and the whole institution is deeply mired in a welfare system that, despite recent reforms, has largely taken over the economic role once assigned to husbands and fathers. Since we know that fatherless households can be a positive breeding ground for crime and other antisocial behaviors, what does American society make of this particular deviation from traditional norms?

The answer some years ago was fairly clear. It was simply that one was not allowed to call attention to the weaknesses of Black families and the profound consequences of such weaknesses for the future of American society. The person who learned this lesson most sharply was Daniel Patrick Moynihan who, in 1965, wrote a report, "The Negro Family in America: The Case for National Action," in which he called attention to the changing structures of Black families and spoke explicitly of the growing "pathology" of Negro family life. The response, especially from some Black scholars, was immediate and harsh. It was said that Moynihan had failed to consult the existing literature on Black families, that numerous research studies had been misinterpreted, and that impermissible generalizations about the Black population had been based on a limited number of cases. In short, the messenger was condemned and the message—which actually turned out to be prophetic—was basically suppressed.

Implicit in this condemnation and suppression was not only the notion that the moral values of all behaviors are equivalent, but also a sense that group behavior, if it is to be judged at all, should be judged not by a common standard but by standards internal to the group itself. In a 1978 study, sociologist W. R. Allen classified views as to the history and culture of Black Americans under three perspectives: "cultural deviant," "cultural equivalent," and "cultural variant." The "cultural deviant" position (attributed to Moynihan and others) reflected the view that Black families with their never-married mothers, absent fathers, and increasing state of disorganization represented a kind of social "pathology." The "cultural equivalent" perspective suggested that there is nothing special about the situation of Blacks that better incomes, living standards, and the like would not change—that is, Blacks would under better socioeconomic conditions live with much the same attitudes and behaviors as Whites. And, finally, the "cultural variant" perspective claimed that there are fundamental cultural differences between Blacks and Whites and ultimately that Blacks must be judged by their own cultural standards, and not by those of an essentially alien White culture.[13]

What moral relativism does, in essence, is to elevate the "cultural variant" perspective to a dominant position. It says that only Blacks can understand Blacks. Only Blacks can be allowed to judge or criticize Blacks. Indeed, in the long run, it goes even further than this and suggests that only those Blacks with proper attitudes towards Black culture—politically correct attitudes—should be heeded. The worst offenders of all are Blacks with "White"—in essence, critical—attitudes. These suffer a particularly cruel kind of ostracism within the Black community.

The Black family is only one example of many. The same morally relativistic attitudes can be applied to Hispanics, Native Americans, women, homosexuals, and any other demographic or cultural subgroup one can imagine. And it is by such logic and argument that "the family" is replaced by "families" and the fate of our future generations placed at fundamental risk.

WHERE THE BATTLE STANDS NOW

It was back in the late 1960s when Moynihan was sent to the cultural woodshed for his presumptuous analysis. Much has happened since then. For one thing, the Black family has proceeded much, much further down the very road that Moynihan warned about in 1965. For another, the American White family has started moving down that very same road and, in many respects, stands in 1995 where the Black family stood thirty years earlier. For still another thing, the messenger has not only been forgiven but is increasingly praised for his prescience. Moynihan, it is now frequently suggested by Blacks as well as Whites, had it right after all!

Does this suggest that we are entering a period of, as it were, revising the revisionists, that is, returning to a more traditional view in which different family structures are once again differentiated from each other, and at least some attention is given to intact, two-biological-parent families as especially favorable to the raising of children? From this author's point of view, this possibility is a very hopeful one, and one that will be explored at some length in the next two chapters. Before embarking on this somewhat optimistic voyage, however, we should heed a few warnings.

One such warning concerns the fate of the "cultural deviant" point of view which allegedly characterized Moynihan's initial analysis of the Black family. Moynihan himself has raised some red flags on this issue, not so much specifically with regard to family structures, as with regard to the concept of "deviancy" in general. In a brilliant 1993 paper in *The American Scholar,* and following the earlier analysis of Durkheim, he suggested that societies can only tolerate a certain amount of deviancy, neither too little nor too much.[14] When behavior changes so as to become much more deviant by an earlier standard, society adjusts by altering the standard of deviancy. Whereas bad table manners were once considered very regrettable if all too common, now spraying innocent bystanders with gunfire from a passing car is considered very regrettable, but also all too common. What was once considered unthinkable has now ceased to be the least bit surprising.

What this lowering of the standard of deviancy does in the family context is, of course, to permit wider and wider ranges of family structures and behaviors to be considered perfectly normal and appropriate. Even the vocabulary changes. Having children out of wedlock is now seldom spoken of in terms of "illegitimacy" (and certainly never in terms of the earlier and more explicitly derogatory word), but more commonly in terms of as the value-free "single-mother parenting." Insofar as we are, in fact, increasingly "defining deviancy down," (Moynihan's phrase), then the trend of things would appear to be toward an even more pervasive moral relativism than in the past.

Another warning (though possibly also hopeful?) sign relates to the Black family itself. In October, 1995, there was the dramatic "Million Man March" on Washington, D.C., arranged, orchestrated, and attended almost exclusively by Black men. The hopeful aspect of this demonstration was that virtually all the speakers referred to the present structure of Black families not as a "cultural variant" possessing its own inner vitality and integrity, but specifically and explicitly as a serious social "problem," and one that needs serious correction. The Black men present were uniformly urged to take much greater responsibility for their women and their children.

But there was a great warning in this demonstration as well. It was not just the rather disturbing presence and leadership of Louis Farrakhan, but the fact that the whole episode was conceived as an exercise exclusively within the Black community (and, in fact, within the Black male community only). Martin Luther King's march on Washington in 1963 was explicitly multiracial and its message was clearly premised on the dream of a society in which character, not race, would be determinant. By contrast, the 1995 march carried a sometimes subliminal, often actually open and explicit, message that only Blacks can resolve Black problems. This message suggests a potentially separatist future for the Blacks within American society, and also clearly underlines the fundamentally relativist position that each group in our society is the only certifiable judge of its own standards and behavior.

This overriding message is, in fact, anathema for anyone who hopes to see a serious resurrection of the institution of "the family" in America. For internal standards, internally certified, are what give advocates of "famil*ies*" their most (seemingly) plausible argument in the great family values debate. Despite the fine talk of strengthening Black families, this argument must give great pause to anyone seriously concerned about the future of our nation's children.

14

RECLAIMING THE FAMILY: PRINCIPLES AND PROGRAMS

M any studies of the current breakdown of the American family, having reached by whatever route conclusions similar to those we have been discussing—that is, that family breakdown is real and that its consequences are potentially tragic for our children and heirs—then go on to suggest that only a massive change in our cultural attitudes will enable us to avert this future disaster. However, since this suggestion is sometimes accompanied by detailed proposals that often seem weak, vague, rather unrealistic or even irrelevant, one is frequently left with the feeling that the required cultural change will never come, that our course into the future is already plotted, and that it is a very grim course indeed.

In this chapter and the next, I will investigate the possibility and likelihood of reclaiming something like the traditional American family, if that is to be our national purpose. It may not be. Even for those who might agree that our present arrangements are harmful to later generations, the claims of the present above the future, of self above posterity, of equality above growth, and of moral relativism above family values might still seem worth honoring. There is little doubt that what the changed cultural climate that is being urged upon us would entail would be a greater sense of personal limits, self-restraint, even occasionally self-sacrifice. Do we really want to undergo this kind of culture shock? Do we really want to give up the many attractive features of the now for the uncertain promises of the later? It is perhaps because of this underlying ambivalence that so many of us can proclaim the need for a cultural revolution to restore family values, while our concrete proposals for change seem so pathetically inadequate to the task.

In this chapter, I will investigate a few concrete proposals that might seriously alter the American family landscape. In chapter 15, I will question whether or not such proposals actually have any chance of adoption especially given the underlying problems posed by the fundamental predicament of progress.

THREE BASIC PRINCIPLES

However concrete or specific proposals for family reform might be, they must embody certain more general principles that explain what it is one is trying to achieve. If, as I believe, there is no way of ever returning to the Victorian family with its sole-provider husband and full-time homemaker wife, then what exactly is the institution that we might reasonably wish to restore? I limit the basic principles that I believe should underlie future family reform to three:

1. *Any governmental programs that, under the guise of helping individual family members, actually displace or otherwise undermine basic family functions should be avoided.*

What we have here is a generic difficulty common to virtually all government-sponsored programs designed to help the family. For what most of these programs help are family members, not the institution of the family. Indeed, by helping family members outside the institutional framework of the family, they cannot help but weaken that framework. How serious this problem is is a matter of dispute. In my own particular analysis, I do not attribute the primary reason for family breakdown—as some do—to the massive growth of the welfare state and especially to programs like AFDC, which, in recent decades, have greatly reduced the penalties for illegitimacy among young mothers. However, that such programs have had some effect on the rapid rise of single-parent families, and that this effect is certainly negative from a societal point of view, seems impossible to deny.

Moreover, as we suggest above, such negative effects seem endemic to the great majority of government-sponsored "family" programs. Steps to improve the quality of day care in recent federal legislation, while they may be beneficial to children in day care, also give further encouragement and support to parents to hand off their responsibility for rearing their young children to nonfamilies agencies.[1] The family leave legislation passed by the Congress in 1992 was fine for encouraging parental care for children in the first weeks of life, but also almost certainly encourages an earlier return to work by parents, thus discouraging parental care after those first weeks.[2] Even the Earned Income Tax Credit (EITC), which is intended to give economic support to the working poor turns out to have a serious "marriage penalty" involved. Since the credit applies only to one child per family, a couple with two children can, by divorcing, actually gain a net subsidy estimated at $5,000.[3]

Often these negative effects are unintended and they are almost always difficult to avoid. What our principle suggests, however, is that the cumulative result of all these unintended consequences can, over time, have very serious repercussions on U.S. family life. The first test of any new program in this area (or, indeed, of any programs already in existence) should be: What is its actual effect not just on individuals but on the institution of the family itself? If, as a nation, we truly wish to save that institution, then this principle has to be given a very high priority.

2. It should be considered a responsibility of parents to provide primary care for their children until they are of school age except in the most unusual circumstances.

The escape clause ("except in the most unusual circumstances") is obviously necessary in that it is very easy to imagine situations either where the parent has no choice but to use day care or, conversely, where society believes it is overwhelmingly in the child's interest not to be raised at home. Demonstrable, physical evidence that a child is being abused at home sexually or otherwise can and should cancel out both parental responsibilities and parental rights. Similarly, there may be cases where sheer economic necessity makes it unavoidable or at least very clearly desirable to substitute day care for parental care for preschoolers, toddlers, and even infants.

Still, what this second principle claims is that such a clause should be invoked only very sparingly. It bases this claim on the view that parental care for very young children is in the great generality of cases far superior to extrafamily care, and also that some at least temporary sacrifice of self in favor of posterity is required once parents have assumed the role of parenthood. It says, more or less unequivocally, that if parents want the rights, privileges, and joys of having children, they must also be prepared to accept this major responsibility therefrom.

This principle does not, however, take us all the way back to the Victorian "cult of domesticity," with its homemaker-in-the-home and its sole provider off somewhere in the commercial and industrial marketplace. For one thing, it is neutral about the question of which parent will provide the early nurturing for the children. If, as is most likely, that nurturing takes place primarily with the mothers, that is fine, but not required. One's guess is that paternal exceptions will be rare but will exist in a few cases.

More significantly, however, this second principle does not apply for the whole time children are living at home but only roughly until they reach the age of five. This differentiates it sharply from the Victorian household where the mother who raised the young children also remained confined, whether by personal choice or social pressure, largely to the domestic sphere for the rest of her life. Because of the reduction in the average number of children women have and because of extensions in women's life expectancies, the percentage of a woman's life during which she will have a child of five or under in the house has declined precipitously since the last century, probably now to 10 percent or even less.[4] Thus, what is being asked of parents here, and especially of women, is some small sacrifice of the benefits of jobs and careers, but a sacrifice that does not even compare to that of the Victorian world where virtually 100 percent of a woman's life was centered in the home, first that of her parents and later that of her husband and children.

3. *Men who achieve the fact of fatherhood must, again except in the most unusual circumstances, accept the full responsibilities of fatherhood.*

As before, we have an escape clause, and the weight of this third principle depends both on the frequency with which such a clause is invoked, and also what is actually meant by "the full responsibilities of fatherhood." The looser interpretation of this phrase would limit it essentially to financial responsibilities. Under this interpretation, the central thrust of the principle would be that fathers, whether married, divorced, separated, or never married at all, would have essentially the same financial responsibilities toward their children, and thus effectively to the mothers of their children, as if they were living with them in the most securely intact, two-biological parent household. One would not be allowed to get off the hook by failing in one way or another to honor the equivalent of a marriage commitment.

A stronger interpretation would imply that, except in unusual circumstances, fathers should also be expected to assume the nurturing, disciplining, role-modeling, generally caring role that fathers have always been expected to assume (though, of course, have not always achieved) through most of human history. This stronger interpretation thus also implies at least some degree of actual physical presence of the father in the lives of his children, not simply sending a check, or visiting once every few months or years.

My own view is that the stronger interpretation, perhaps limited, as in the case of parental child care, to the years when the children are quite young, is desirable. The two-parent household is thus set up as the ideal to be supported and striven for at least during those early years when so much vital child development takes place. Like the case of principle two, we are dealing here with a step, but really only a small step, back in the direction of the Victorian family where never married parents were virtually unknown and divorce, even when there were no children involved, was quite uncommon.

Even this small step, however, would involve something of a revolution in the laws and mores of late-twentieth-century America. Would we really be willing to represent our children's interests in a serious way in our divorce proceedings? Would we really be willing to entertain any sanctions at all on fatherless households and unmarried child bearing? Thus, this third principle, perhaps even more than the first two, would involve a real test of our interest in the kind of cultural revolution many American voices are now calling for.

A PARENTAL BILL OF RIGHTS

Let us first consider the question of encouraging parental care for preschool-age children. Professor T. Grandon Gill and I have, in a number of papers, sketched out the financial and other implications of a program we call a "Parental Bill of Rights."[5] We believe that such a program, properly formulated, would impose very few if any costs on society at large and would very likely produce enormous social benefits.

As its title suggests, the Parental Bill of Rights is to a large degree modeled on the World War II GI Bill of Rights. It is based on the premise that parents who raise their own children perform an extremely important social service and that, in so doing, they may seriously imperil their long-run career prospects. In this respect, there is at least some analogy between their situations and that of soldiers who went off to war in World War II and whose careers were interrupted for periods ranging from several months to several years. The analogy is not complete since serving in battle obviously involves dangers and risks that have no counterpart in the rearing of young children. Still, mothers who forgo labor force participation during their child-rearing years do have to pay a substantial price for having done so. Recent estimates are that the returning wage for such women is 33 percent lower than it otherwise would have been and that most of them never fully make up this difference later in life.[6]

Under the proposed Parental Bill of Rights, those mothers, or fathers as the case may be, will receive a subsidy in return for the career sacrifice they are making for a socially desirable end. As in the case of the GI Bill, this subsidy will take the form of educational benefits, these to apply after their children have started school so that these parents can more effectively reenter the labor force or initiate a long-run career path. Again, as under the original GI Bill, this educational subsidy could be applied at the high school, vocational school, college, graduate school, or even post-graduate school levels. It also could include subsidized apprenticeship or other on-the-job training programs in industry.

Clearly, there are many different ways in which this program could be set up. Rather than go into these details here, I will summarize what I believe to be the central and essential features of the Parental Bill approach, and how these are specifically related to the three general principles described above:

1. It seems quite clear that the Parental Bill would meet the first general principle for family-oriented programs, namely, that it tends to reinforce not displace basic family functions. The alternative to parental

care for young children is care of one kind or another outside the structure of the nuclear family. The Parental Bill clearly subsidizes child care
within that family structure.

2. The program also quite definitely promotes the second general
principle, that is, that primary child care for young children should be
considered a fundamental parental responsibility. The program an-
nounces a significant societal commitment to, and respect for, parental
care for infants and preschoolers, thereby raising the cultural status and
prestige of stay-at-home parenting. It would hopefully both increase the
number of young adults who provide parental care for their young children and also enable these former "homemakers" eventually to become
among the better educated and more highly trained members of the
labor force.

3. It would directly address the question of the employment and
career prospects of the spouse (either wife or husband) who stays home
to take care of the children. Essentially, what is being suggested here is
that rather than combining career and family all the way ("doing it all"),
or following a scaled-down career all the way (the "Mommy track"7),
there might characteristically be a sequencing pattern in which a relatively short "parenting track" was followed by a relatively uninterrupted
subsequent "career track." Dealing with two children to the age of five
(and our own model program limits the benefits to two children per
family), we are envisioning a parenting track of perhaps seven or eight
years on average. It is quite possible that the subsequent career track,
being relatively uninterrupted by major parenting responsibilities, would
have considerable advantages for both employees and employers. The
latter, in particular, could have more confidence that the employees involved would now be able to give 100 percent or at least near–100
percent attention to their work and future careers.

4. The proposal clearly involves an investment approach, with the
payoff to parental education being higher productivity, higher incomes,
and very possibly higher tax revenues for the government. One recent
study finds as much as a 16 percent increase in wage rates for each additional year of schooling completed.[8] This study is confirmed by a 1992
Census Bureau report which estimates the following:[9]

Educational Level	*Monthly Average Earnings in 1990*
No high school diploma	$ 492
High school diploma	1,077
College diploma	2,116
Professional degree	4,961

There are really two important investment gains here: (1) the increased human capital invested in the parent, and (2) the beneficial effect on the child's development of closer parental care and attention. Both investment gains would help combat our relative shortage of highly trained workers relative to job demand and our predicted surplus of unskilled workers relative to the availability of low skill jobs. These problems, as suggested earlier, have contributed substantially to the present inequalities in our national income distribution.

5. The real costs of this program in terms of the reduced labor force participation by the parents providing increased child care at home are likely to be minimal. The reasons are twofold. First, and most significantly, if the parents do not provide primary care for these children, someone else has to. Calculations of what it would actually cost society to provide "quality" day care to these very young children suggest that there would be very little net economic gain to society from having these parents in the labor force instead of raising their own children at home. Second, when the additional costs of labor force participation (commuting, clothes, etc.) are added in, even this little net economic gain is likely to disappear.[10]

6. Last, but not least, insofar as this program involves any net long-run cost in terms of expenditures above revenues for the government, we believe the burden should be experienced at the other, retirement, end of life, and not during the young, parenting stage of life. In labor force terms, if the Parental Bill should succeed in reducing participation rates of young parents to some degree, our notion is that this could, and should, be compensated by slightly higher labor force participation by workers in their later years. It seems incredible that, with the generally better health and longer life expectancies of older Americans, retirement ages should actually be dropping as they have in recent decades. Just as

our Social Security and pension systems have been major factors enabling this earlier retirement to take place, so these systems can be modified to encourage later labor force participation than at present.

In effect, what is being suggested is a change in life patterns whereby the stress and heavy burdens of the young parenting years are eased under the auspices of the Parental Bill while some (as it works out, quite small) burdens are added to one's senior years. A few months, or a year or two at most, longer in the labor force, encouraged by reduced public subsidies, would be more than enough to finance a program that, because of its investment features, is likely to be virtually self-sustaining to begin with.

Thus, in brief presentation, we have the concept of a Parental Bill of Rights. Its main drawback would seem to be that it would delay the flowering of certain careers for a few years. Its main career advantage would be that, like the original GI Bill, it might in the long run mean a far better educated labor force than would emerge without it. It is interesting that Peter Drucker has dated the beginning of the entire "information age" from the passage of the GI Bill in 1944.[11] On a somewhat smaller scale, could comparable educational advantages emerge from a Parental Bill?

And what of this alleged drawback—the possible delay in one's full participation in what we have called the "career track?" How serious is that? Actually, except for pure mathematicians and potential Mozarts, there would seem to be relatively few professionals who must accomplish their life works at especially young ages. Is it so important to start practicing law at age twenty-five as opposed, say, to age thirty-two or thirty-three? In how many service sector jobs can it be said that the twenty-year old does better work than the thirty-year old, the forty-year old than the fifty-year old, the fifty-year old than the sixty-year old, and so on? And will there really be any great loss to society in most jobs if a few years are forgone in one's twenties and retirement is delayed from, say, sixty-one or sixty-two to (what it always used to be) sixty-five? Actually, one of the great advantages of our move from a heavy-industrial to an office-service style economy is that the physical demands of work are continually lessened and age becomes less and less consequential as far as our productivity is concerned.

In short, if a Parental Bill approach is rejected, it will almost have to be for quite different reasons—reasons, indeed, that reflect that basic conflict between self and posterity that we have already discussed at some length. That is to say, it will be rejected because we so value the immediate options and advantages for our own self-realization and personal development that we will not let anything interfere even temporarily—including the ultimate well-being of our children.

A PROGRAM FOR TEENAGE SINGLE MOTHERS

Although the Parental Bill can, in principle, do much to promote family values in American society—including, possibly, even some reduction in some of the stresses that lead to divorce—it obviously cannot accomplish everything that is needed. One particular area where it is quite weak, and in many ways irrelevant, is the case of single mothers on welfare and especially teenage single mothers. Is there anything that can be done in the case where, literally, "children are having children"? In particular, is there anything that can be done that does not further destroy the role of the family in the upbringing of the children of these children?

Clearly, one thing that should be done is to try to engage the fathers—who in some cases may also be children—in this particular enterprise, a possibility to be discussed in a moment. Assuming, however, that this effort is being made (and very likely only partially successful at best), then how do we overcome, or at least mitigate, the disadvantages of the two obvious alternative arrangements: (1) having these young girls bring up their children on their own while being supported primarily through the state welfare system, or (2) placing these children in day care while the mothers go on either to finish school or take entry-level jobs?

The disadvantages of the first method include the likely beginning of prolonged stays on welfare, the isolation of these child-mothers with the strong risks of further pregnancies occurring, and, perhaps above all, the total lack of knowledge of how to rear infants and toddlers on the part of many, and probably most, of these teenage mothers. These are almost universally children who have received extremely poor parenting themselves. How could they conceivably be expected to become successful parents themselves? The odds surely are very much against them.

The second approach, which has received some reinforcement in the welfare reforms of 1996 with their emphasis on workfare, also has massive disadvantages. This approach necessarily involves providing primary care for the teenagers' children through extrafamily agencies. This day-care route clearly violates both our first and second basic principles of family reform, that is, it displaces a clearly important family function, and it specifically reduces the role of parental care for very small children. It can be argued further that this second approach, by relieving the teenage parent of the primary responsibility for raising her own infant or toddler, is also likely to encourage further childbearing. Apparently, or so it may well seem to such a teenager, there are very few burdens involved in having children. Why bother to protect too carefully against future pregnancies?

Obviously, what we need here is a new, inventive approach to the problem, and one such approach has been developed by Elizabeth Bjornson Gill, the author's wife, who has worked for a number of years as a *Guardian ad litem* representing abused and neglected children in the Florida Court system.[12] Her proposal involves the development of what she calls a Parent-Child Center (PCC), which may roughly be described as a center providing day care for *both* the teenager's children *and* the teenagers themselves. The teenage mothers will have primary responsibility for caring for their babies, but they will do so in a setting in which a group of other teenage mothers and children will be present along with a small supervisory staff.

The following excerpts from Elizabeth Gill's recent pilot program proposal suggest both the novelty of the program and the way in which it attempts to navigate between the hazards of the two standard approaches discussed above:

Proposal for a Parent-Child Center Pilot Program

The following proposed pilot program targets teenage mothers, expectant mothers, and infants and toddlers from birth up to age four.

Summary: The following is a brief summary of the proposed pilot program:

A. Groups of eight teenage mothers and their babies would be formed with a Program Coordinator (Super-Mom) and an Assistant Coordinator (Big Sister).

B. This is a twelve-month a year program. Each weekday (and, ideally, on Saturday mornings as well), instead of dropping her infant or toddler off at a day care center, the mother will remain at the center and take primary responsibility for the care of her child.

C. Twice a month, a home visit will be made by the Coordinator or her Assistant.

D. In addition, formal and informal instruction will be offered each day. A certified teacher will come to each PCC unit one day a week. Use will be made of self-programmed workbooks and computer software so that each girl can proceed at her own pace. The teacher will monitor the young mother's progress and create a study plan with achievable objectives.

E. The curriculum will include: 1. Literacy training; the ability to read a newspaper; 2. Competence in arithmetic at the level necessary for shopping and managing personal finances; 3. American social history with illustrations of core values and behavior which are part of our heritage, the goal being self-motivated behavior modification; 4. A basic knowledge of child development.

F. Informal instruction will include those skills most often taught by a parent in a functional family: 1. Housekeeping: how to clean most efficiently, laundry, care of appliances, etc. 2. First Aid; 3. Cooking and Nutrition; 4. Games, Sports, Art, and Music: exposure and participation in a variety of interesting activities.

G. The infants' and toddlers' schedule and activities will be the same as those in any well-ordered home.

H. In addition to the services of the Program Coordinator and the Assistant Coordinator, the program calls for a part-time teacher (1 day per week at each unit), a nurse (1/2 day per week), and a part-time worker who will help locate fathers and attempt to encourage them to participate in some of the program activities.

Distinctive Features: This program is unique in a number of ways, including the following:

A. It is a twelve-month, full-time day-care program in which the teenage mother cares for her own child under supervision.

B. Teenage mothers participate in the program over a period long enough to permit them to practice their parenting skills, and also to develop general skills necessary as preparation for functioning in the labor force.

C. Academic credentials are not required of the Program Coordinator or the Assistant Coordinator. This proposal recognizes the need for personnel who have already in their own lives successfully completed the family-building and child-nurturing tasks we are setting out to communicate. Excellent character references, as well as references proving that the candidate has successfully raised a family, provide the background necessary to accomplish our aims.

This then, in brief, is the Parent-Child Center concept as recently proposed to the Florida Department of Health and Rehabilitative Services. The last "distinctive feature," discussed above is a significant and symbolic one. The people who run these small PCC units are thought of, not as social workers with academic qualifications, but as successful parents, proved, say, by the fact that they have successfully raised their own children all of whom have graduated from high school. These women are meant to exemplify by their own lifestyles and behavior the kind of "family values" the program wishes to instill in these young mothers.

Notice also the concept of a group of such mothers, creating in effect a little neighborhood for them. This provision of companionship in a mutually purposive and nurturing atmosphere may well reduce the sense of isolation and loneliness that many teenage mothers experience and this, in turn, may make them less prone to the casual affairs and relationships leading to still more pregnancies and babies.

Finally, the program is also novel in suggesting the possible and extensive use of computer technology to further the education of these young girls. There will be many hours each day when the infants and toddlers will not need the direct attention of their mothers. What the program hopes to do is to use these hours for self-instructional computer work under the weekly supervision of a professionally licensed teacher.[13]

Ultimately, the PCC program, like the Parental Bill of Rights program discussed earlier, are attempts to formulate novel approaches which avoid the very obvious defects of state-supported programs which almost invariably displace, rather than support, the institution of the family, and ultimately undermine the very family values they are trying to sustain. In the case of the PCC program, an attempt is made to render what are usually very dysfunctional family units (teenage mothers raising babies) more functional by bringing them together in a group context and placing them under the supervision of women who, by their own life experiences, have shown themselves to be deeply committed to those family values we wish to affirm.

PROGRAMS AIMED AT FATHERS

In both proposals discussed so far, there has been a notable lacuna, that is, any real attempt to face the problem of wayward, and often totally disappearing, fathers. In the case of the PCC program, it is intended that an effort be made to engage fathers in the program to the extent that they can be found and persuaded to do so. One can imagine a great variety of activities, both social (dances, arts and crafts, movies, etc.) and educational (especially parenting classes) through which a young father's interest in his children, and the mother of his children, might well be kindled. These young men would, in effect, be invited to become a part of the small neighborhood that each PCC unit creates. Some, at least, might find this participation attractive, and their willingness to sustain a longer-run role of active fatherhood might even be affected.

In the case of the Parental Bill of Rights, the hope would be that the program might have some favorable effect on keeping currently intact marriages from fragmenting. Numerous specific provisions—as, for example, concerning the transferability of the educational benefits from one spouse to another—can be written in to increase the advantages of maintaining marital unions. Further, one would hope that, in the case of the wife and mother (if, as would probably happen in most cases, she was the one to provide primary child care for the preschoolers), the program would ease at least some of the psychological stresses that so many young women are under today. Essentially, the mother is offered a middle choice between having favorable long-run career prospects while neglecting her children, or damaging her long-run career prospects while fulfilling her maternal responsibilities. The Parental Bill option provides the middle ground in which career-deferring activities do not mean career-ending activities, where one can focus primarily on one important activity during one period of life and another in another, where one really can "do it all," but in sequence. In this way, the Parental Bill should help reduce somewhat the wife's inner tensions and thus contribute to the overall mood of harmony in the marriage.

More specifically from the husband's point of view, it seems almost certain that one of the bonds that is likely to tie a man more securely to his marriage is the feeling that his wife is devoting herself in a serious way to the beneficial rearing of their children. Or, to put it the other way around, if the wife is not showing such devotion, one of the greatest benefits of married life from the man's point of view is likely to disappear. One may object that, if the wife is working, her income would be part of the cement potentially holding a marriage together. Actually, in the case of high-income wives, the evidence is that marriages are likely to be very shaky indeed, possibly because of the deflation of male ego involved, possibly simply because the husband loses any real sense of being needed in the marriage. In the case of low-income wives, the costs of day care, working expenses, taxes, and so on, are likely to eat up the greater part of the additional income the wife is bringing in. Also, the Parental Bill holds out the promise of future economic benefits resulting from the subsidy to further education—a subsidy which, indeed, the wife could, if she wished, transfer in whole or in part to the husband. Under any circumstance, it seems very doubtful that any of these economic considerations would have the emotional impact on the husband that would come from seeing his wife lovingly, carefully, and even (dare one say it?) self-sacrificially providing for the needs of his little daughters and sons.

The direction of the effects of both these programs, then, is likely to be favorable as far as engaging more fathers in the great project of family life. What is much less clear is that these effects would be anything more than marginal as far as the problem of missing fathers is concerned. Indeed, that problem becomes more and more massive with each passing day. In 1995, a Census Bureau report indicated that the percentage of families with children headed by a single parent—mostly women—had risen to 31 percent, up from 13 percent in 1970. When other family forms, such as step-father families, are considered, we are rapidly approaching a situation where, at a given moment in time, nearly half of all children are being raised in the absence of their biological fathers, and where, during the course of their whole childhoods, the majority of children will actually go through a period in a biological-father-less household. It is no wonder that David Blankenhorn has described "Fatherless America" as "our most urgent social problem."

What then can be done about this matter? Blankenhorn himself offers "twelve proposals" that might help reset the nation's compass in the direction of the fatherhood idea. If one has a serious interest in restoring family values, one would find it difficult to disagree with any of these proposals. They are direct, simple, occasionally almost embarrassingly simple, but it is, in a way, a need to restore a sense of embarrassment, if not shame, over our rearing of today's fatherless children that is at stake here. He begins with a pledge that "every man in the United States should be requested to take": "Many people today believe that fathers are unnecessary. I believe the opposite. I pledge to live my life according to the principle that every child deserves a father; that marriage is the pathway to effective fatherhood; that part of being a good man means being a good father; and that America needs more good men."[14]

He then goes on through the other proposals, similar in basic intention, and ends with proposal twelve, urging family scholars to rewrite our high school textbooks about marriage and parenthood: "Other than viewing masculinity as a problem to be overcome, most current textbooks have almost nothing to say on the subject. But rather than cursing the darkness, a few scholars could light candles. Instead of more stories featuring the Unnecessary Father, perhaps a new guy could appear in some of these textbooks: the Good Family Man. Perhaps we are ready to attend to his story."[15]

Blankenhorn concludes by admitting that his proposals do not constitute a blueprint, that they are an attempt rather to point away "from a culture of fatherlessness, toward fatherhood." In chapter 15, I will specifically take up the problem of initiating such a cultural change, including the role of scholars, textbook writers, and intellectuals generally in perpetuating our present difficulties.

First, however, we have to look to see if there are any specific programs one might want to introduce, presuming that the cultural climate had in fact changed in the required way. Two basic areas command our attention: (1) trying to limit divorces in cases where children are involved; and (2) trying to encourage fathers and mothers to become husbands and wives in the first place—that is, the general problem of the never-married mother.

1. *Programs to discourage divorce where children are involved*

There are a whole range of programs and policies that could be instituted if we, as nation, decide that we seriously wish to lower the divorce rate for families with dependent children. Essentially, what must be conveyed to all married couples is that when they reach the point of having children, the interests at stake in the perpetuation or break-up of that marriage become threefold: wife, husband, *and* children. The wife and husband can generally be presumed to represent their own interests in the divorce proceedings, while the state must assume that the interests of the children require third-party (state) support and that these interests almost always run in the direction of maintaining the marriage. There are exceptions, of course some marriages should be severed explicitly *for* the children's sake—but the governing presumption in marriages with dependent children should be that a resolution within the context of an intact, two-biological parent family must be diligently searched for and applied. The strong implication is that in almost all marriages in which one of the parties wishes to maintain the union, the addition of the children's interest will create a majority interest in favor of keeping the marriage intact. Even where both husband and wife wish the divorce, the children's interest may be weighed so heavily that the dissolution of the marriage may be denied, or at least substantially delayed, and the potential penalties applied to the noncustodial parent may be sufficient to switch that parent's interest in the direction of maintaining the marriage after all. In short, any marriage involving dependent children should become not easy but extremely difficult to wangle one's way out of.

Specific programs to promote this result are not difficult to imagine and, in fact, have been suggested in a number of public documents: for example, *Families First*, the 1993 Report of the National Commission on America's Urban Families; or *Marriage in America*, a 1995 Report to the Nation from the Council on Families in America.[16] *Families First*, to take one example, suggests the following actions (somewhat abbreviated here) to "reform state laws on marriage and divorce":

a) Marriage laws should state explictly the social importance of marriage, and enumerate the obligations of marriage, especially the obligation of parents to their children.

b) For all divorces involving minor children, legislatures should enact "children-first" divorce laws in order to guarantee that the primary state objective in divorces involving children is to protect the needs of children and the custodial parent.

c) In determining custody, courts should evaluate plans to make sure that the emotional, intellectual, social, and moral development of children is ensured.

d) If one spouse petitions for a no-fault divorce and the no-fault claim is contested, courts should enter the legal process with a presumption favoring the preservation of the marriage. Procedures courts may institute include: (1) Sending the couple, without lawyers, to a mediator to resolve the dispute, or (2) Directing the couple to marital counseling and requiring a waiting period.

e) Especially in cases involving minor children, legislatures should consider adopting or extending meaningful waiting periods for divorce, perhaps coupled with mandatory participation in counseling or marital education.

f) States should consider requiring that parents in divorce proceedings attend a parenting class in which the parents learn the impact of divorce on children and how to minimize the negative consequences of divorce on children.

The clear general drift of all these recommendations is to give greater weight to children's interests than in the past, and to question seriously the present situation where forty of fifty states now maintain a pattern of quite easy "no-fault" divorces. The Council on Families comes basically to the same conclusions, suggesting that legislators "reconsider state marriage laws that lean toward 'nofault' divorces" and "shift the support of the law toward the marital partner trying to save the marriage."

Added on to these recommendations in the two reports, and other similar reports, are more or less stringent measures to ensure that, if the marriage does break up, the noncustodial parent—usually the father—will be charged with substantial financial responsibilities to his ex-wife and children and these will be diligently enforced. In other words, marriages with dependent children will be very hard to get out of, and if one does get out of them, the financial burden of so doing will be great. Incentives for remaining, disincentives for leaving: together, one assumes, these should have a fairly substantial effect in lowering our current divorce rate.

2. *Programs to encourage fathers to marry the mothers of their children*

One of the great disadvantages of the programs just discussed is that they may have a tendency to increase the number of never-married mothers, already a problem as, or more, serious than the divorce problem. That is to say, if you make marriages more difficult to get out of when once entered into, this could, certainly in marginal cases, discourage men (and women as well) from taking on the commitment in the first place. What this means, in turn, is that any strengthening of the marriage commitment must be accompanied by strong incentives *to* get married and strong disincentives to have or sire babies while *not* being married.

It is here, probably more than anywhere else in this whole reform process, that the shoe really begins to pinch. For it is almost impossible to create the relevant incentives and disincentives without in one way or another punishing the children themselves, specifically the children who are born out of wedlock and remain in single-parent households. In the old days, of course, that was exactly what was done. Through ostracism, condemnation, and more or less forced putting-out-for-adoption practices in the case of "illegitimacy," the never-married mother knew perfectly well she had crossed a crucial societal boundary. Effectively, both child and mother were punished for the parental indiscretion.

Although this difficulty is fundamental and is unlikely to be completely avoided, there is at least one point on which almost all supporters of family values tend to agree: the fathers involved should secure no advantages, financial or otherwise, from abandoning their pregnant girl friends. This is likely to involve:

a) Mandatory identification of a father for every child born in the

United States, if necessary through DNA testing. This identification should then become part of the father's official record, probably through the Social Security system, and should follow him for the rest of his life.

b) Whatever financial responsibilities this father would assume by the act of marriage shall at a minimum be attached to his earnings in the event that he does not in fact marry the mother in question. If he marries some other person, his obligation to the earlier mother of his child shall be the same as if he actually had married her and was now divorcing her.

Fathers are thus told that the gains from not marrying are, at least in financial terms, nonexistent. Indeed, since it is invariably more expensive to maintain the same number of people in two (or more) households than in a single household, it can be expected that the fathers will actually suffer economically from not marrying if the above provisions are faithfully and diligently enforced.

One would, however, ideally like to stress the pluses of marrying rather than the negatives of not marrying. And this is where our fundamental problem arises. For if we start talking seriously about offering positive subsidies to married couples, then we are really suggesting reducing or curtailing the subsidies we might give to unmarried mothers. The classic case, of course, is AFDC. For decades now, social commentators have been complaining about the fact that AFDC, by subsidizing single mothers, effectively encourages mothers to remain single—that is, increases the number of never-married mothers. If we were to focus AFDC exclusively, or even mainly, on married couples, then we would necessarily be decreasing the payments to those never-married mothers and their children, a group already disastrously mired in poverty. We have the same question with respect to taxes and housing subsidies. Should we, for example, give preference to married couples in the allocation of subsidized housing loans and public housing, and, if we do, what happens to the probably more needy unmarried mother who is effectively displaced?

It is probably at this point, more than any other in the debate, that our society has to decide which way it really wants to go. In the old days, girls having babies and boys deserting those girls were considered immoral. In countless ways, both publicly and privately, this behavior was punished, and, in consequence, remained limited, at least limited compared to the social tragedy we are dealing with today. While it is inconceivable that we would return exactly to that earlier approach, the question is whether or not we will now begin to experiment with a range of programs which in one way or another actually do give positive rewards to married parenthood and definite penalties to unmarried parenthood. This leads to two further suggestions:

c) On the positive side, that we experiment with programs: that increase AFDC, and any and all other subsidy, payments to married families with children above those received by unmarried families with children; that increase tax exemptions for the former above those for the latter; that eliminate any and all other "marriage taxes" wherever found in the system and transform that system so that these become effectively "marriage subsidies" or "marriage exemptions."

d) On the negative side, that we experiment with programs: that strictly limit the time never-married parents can remain on welfare (already a possibility under the 1996 welfare reform legislation); that limit the number of out-of-wedlock children who can be covered; that encourage placing those children out for adoption; that require young never-married mothers to live in their own parents' home rather than in separate single-family households; and that require both the never-married mothers and the officially identified fathers of these children to take parenting and personal responsibility classes rather akin to the defensive driving classes now required for those who have been in traffic accidents.

If we, as a nation, are serious about the matter, it seems quite likely that some combination of these various approaches and programs could in fact reduce the rate of never-married parenting and, as in the case of more stringent divorce procedures, bring our wayward and wandering fathers back into the charmed circle of active family life. Despite the complications and difficulties, there is ultimately no lack of things that could be done . . . *if* we are serious!

15

WE *CAN* ACT, BUT *WILL* WE?

T he previous chapter ended on the incomplete phrase: . . . *if* we are serious! The good news from that chapter was that there are certain principles and even certain specific programs that could, if adopted with diligence and sincerity, help restore the American family to viability, or at least prevent its further decline. But one has to go into such an effort with one's eyes open, recognizing that it would involve very considerable changes in our current attitudes, with potentially very substantial consequences for different groups in society. It is a serious matter and everyone who thinks seriously about it recognizes that only a major cultural reformation will permit any practically useful programs to be undertaken. One can, indeed, go further than that and suggest that if such a cultural reformation did occur, these practical steps and programs might not even have to be acted on. If "family values" truly sweep the nation again as they have in the past, then the various restrictions, incentives, disincentives, subsidies, and the like that we have been talking about would be almost irrelevant. They wouldn't hurt, but they would hardly be critical.

All of which goes to say that David Blankenhorn and others who focus on the need for cultural change are ultimately correct, and are pointing at the right and underlying problem. My objective in this chapter, however, is to try to take the next step, asking how likely it is that this cultural change will, in fact, take place, and what specific conditions will be necessary for such change to occur. In order to do this, one needs a theory as to how and why our national culture has in recent decades turned away from the values embodied in the traditional American family, and, indeed, so sharply and rapidly.

It is, of course, exactly such a theory that this entire book has been

297

written to offer. In particular, I have tried to connect the breakdown of the American family with the decline of the Idea of Progress. More precisely, I have attributed the undermining of the institution of the family to the process of progress, a development that is counteracted, and for a long time fended off, by the Idea of Progress. Then we come upon our great paradox through which the process of progress goes on to undermine the Idea: the fundamental predicament of progress. When this happens, I have argued, the ideology protective of the family falters and fails and the institution is subjected, without defenses, to the corrosive impact of the process of progress. The result: the triumph of the present over the future, of self over posterity, of equality over growth, of moral relativism over family values, and of "families" over "the family."

These analytic claims are totally familiar to us by now and my present question is: What bearing does all this have on the likelihood of a cultural revolution in which family values are once again placed on a national pedestal, or, at least, given much higher priority than at present? In turn, the simple and obvious answer to this question—simple and obvious, that is, in terms, of our prior analysis—would appear to be: In order to restore family values in the sense required, we would have to achieve a renewed interest and faith in the future, and this through a restoration of a belief in the Idea of Progress or, more likely, some rough moral equivalent thereof.

To put it even more specifically in the terms used in the foregoing analysis: we would have to find some way of defeating, at least partially, the fundamental predicament of progress. If we really are totally agnostic about the future, it is, I believe, inconceivable that we would ever be willing to sacrifice our present interests in any serious way for those who are to follow after us. Why on earth should we?

Thus, the very first question that must be addressed is whether there is any conceivable possibility that the Idea of Progress might one day in the reasonably near future experience some kind of rebirth?

MORALITY AND PREDICTABILITY

Such a rebirth is certainly not unthinkable. Actually, as we well know, Americans have already experimented once with a restoration of the Idea of Progress, or, more accurately, a partial restoration. The cynicism and despair that followed World War I (the "lost generation"), and that persisted in some degree during the Depression and the early years of World War II, were sharply interrupted in the immediate postwar decades by an enormous enthusiasm for science, technology, growth, and development, both nationally and worldwide. The basic reason for the renewal of this faith in Progress was the actual, empirical experience of the generations that came to maturity just after the war. Their lives, starting from depression- and world war-stricken beginnings, followed an amazingly sharp upward trajectory as postwar prosperity, medical advances, comforting social programs, and even a relatively peaceful world in which serious threats existed but actual wars were limited, brought personal and societal benefits literally never before experienced in the history of mankind. Who could sensibly refuse to be a true believer?

But the belief, as I stressed earlier, was essentially flawed. The basic flaw was that it was shortsighted. The parents of the Boomers looked to their children's welfare in many ways, restraining the already evident tendencies to divorce and separation, sacrificing some career advancement possibilities to attend to their children's needs, but they gave relatively little attention to the future world that those children would, in their turn, create. The core morality of the Idea of Progress was shunted aside. The need for hard work, discipline, saving, abstinence, and, in general, for maintaining a strong future orientation was never properly emphasized nor instilled in the minds and hearts of those Boomer children. Thus, it may be said that, for all their talk of both Progress and family values, the parents of the Boomers were already to some degree afflicted by the myopia implicit in the fundamental predicament of progress.

Understandably then, great numbers of their children—the Boomers themselves—were doubly afflicted by this myopia, actually triply afflicted. First, they have not had the exceptional experience of rapidly increasing personal welfare common to members of their parents' generation. Second, and even more forcefully than when their parents joined the labor force, the increasing complexity of today's technological society has meant that the fundamental predicament—the difficulty of seriously envisioning the long-run future—was bound to pose especially deep problems for any future-oriented code of ethics. Third, and finally, compared to their parents, they were morally unprepared to chart anything like a definite and predictable course into that future. With almost nothing whatever remaining of the "straight and narrow," their pre-scription for the future was the wholly indeterminate, "Do your own thing!"

In raising the question of the possibility of a recrudescence of the Idea of Progress in America as we enter the twenty-first century, one is basically asking whether there is any real chance that these three factors that have so fatally afflicted the Boomer generation might somehow be counteracted or sidestepped in the years ahead. No one can possibly know for sure—all of us, after all, are subject to the fundamental predica-ment of progress to some degree. All crystal balls lack clarity these days. It could hardly be otherwise.

Subject to this general caveat, one can nevertheless hazard certain guesses on these matters, and what these guesses tend to produce is something of a mixed bag. With respect to the first issue—the actual physical, material, economic, and medical trajectory of the lives of com-ing generations—can we say anything at all about what science and tech-nology have in store for us? Here, at least, a modicum of optimism seems possible. When we were discussing the various specific predicaments of progress in part 2, we seemed to find in most cases that science and technology might very well disclose solutions to these current predica-ments, as, in general, they did with respect to past predicaments. Is it likely that Americans will live longer, healthier, more economically abundant lives in the future than in the past? No one knows, but techni-cally at least, there seems no necessary reason that it should not happen.

Unfortunately, technical conditions are at best necessary and hardly sufficient conditions for a restoration of our faith in the Idea of Progress. Technical conditions, indeed, are part of the problem implicit in the second issue—the possible intensification of the fundamental predica-ment of progress in the years ahead. As we gain more and more choices, more and more power to affect our environment through new technol-ogies, who can possibly guess what future path our society will be tak-ing? Change, choice, and complexity breed an increasingly near-term, present-orientation in our thinking. Indeed, carried far enough, such an orientation might actually undermine the possibility of further scientific and technological advance. Then even the technical conditions for sus-taining the Idea of Progress might fail us.

Which brings us to what is really the heart of our present exercise: the third problem facing the Boomers—the lack of a sufficiently future-oriented code of morality governing their attitudes and general behavior. It is not that this generation has no moral code. The overriding principle of equality can be a stern moral taskmaster. Moral relativism itself, as already noted, can be fiercely moralistic as its extreme manifestation in "political correctness" clearly demonstrates. Thus, what is lacking isn't morality in general, but the specifically future-oriented morality embedded in the Idea of Progress. This morality contains prescriptions concerning work, self-discipline, saving for the future, and so on—the virtues associated with promoting the process of progress over time—and it also contains prescriptions concerning personal behavior and particularly as this behavior affects the rearing and nurturing of future generations. That is to say, what we usually refer to as "family values" are not apart from, but implicit in, the Idea of Progress.

Thus, we might rephrase our original question as follows: If, by whatever means, such a morality could in large part be reinstated, would this help to lessen or in any way contain the damaging impact of the fundamental predicament of progress? And my answer is, quite simply, yes. It would help. How much it would help no one can be sure. But that it would work in the general direction of counteracting the fundamental predicament seems a certainty. The logic behind this claim derives from the fact that a major reason why the shape of the distant future has become increasingly difficult to discern is that, at the very time when science and technology have vastly increased man's power to affect the future, man's use of this new power has become increasingly variable and unpredictable. Instead of prescribed behaviors that chart a clear and definite direction into the future, we have the putative moral equivalence of virtually any and all behaviors (always excepting intolerance) Everyday we are freshly astonished by what is going on in our world. Deviance, à la Moynihan and Durkheim, is being defined down to the point where virtually everything passes muster. In a word, the present-oriented morality, with which so many of us now indulge ourselves, simply, and really by definition, leaves the future up for grabs.

By contrast, if Americans in general were to restore a more future-oriented moral code, the present vicious circle, by which our short-term morality renders the future increasingly uncertain and this uncertainty promotes an increasingly short-term morality, could very well become a virtuous circle. That is to say, by limiting, guiding, and generally focusing our attitudes, thoughts, behavior and projects on the future, we would very likely have a much clearer image of what that future might turn out to be. Having this clearer image, we might then place even more of our interest and attention on the task of shaping that future in a beneficial way. In essence, this is what happened in the late nineteenth and early twentieth centuries. Living through a period of incredibly wrenching scientific, technological, and socioeconomic changes, the United States, Britain, and to some degree all the industrializing nations, created as it were an approved "tunnel" through which, and only through which, the future was to be approached.

In due course, this tunnel began to crack. Today, it is almost totally broken down. Yet without such a tunnel, or its rough equivalent, any possibility of resurrecting the Idea of Progress seems clearly out of the question.

A FIXED MORALITY IN A CHANGING WORLD?

Let us then move on to the next stage of the analysis. If a particular kind of future-oriented, rather restrictive moral code is necessary to attaining some degree of protection from the fundamental predicament of progress, what possible chance is there that such a limiting—some would even say archaic—morality could possibly be sustained in our rapidly changing world? Insofar as we are a basically secular society—and the Idea of Progress ultimately is concerned with things of this world—then traditional religion is unlikely to sustain us in the morality required of Progress. (Which is, of course, not to say that many people, faced with the dilemmas I have been discussing, will not choose to abandon secularity in general and focus in a basically premodern way on a religious conception of the universe.) Further, evolution is likely to be a poor guide for the Progress moralist, partly because of the basically nasty ring associated with Social Darwinism, the "survival of the fittest," and the like, but also because the process of progress tends slowly but surely to increase humanity's power to alter the evolutionary process. In an age poised on the edge of possibly truly revolutionary genetic feats, this point hardly needs any further underlining.

So without religious commandment or evolutionary guidance, how is postmodern man to imagine that he could possibly establish anything like a durable, long-lasting code of morality in a world of continuing, and often revolutionary, change? Actually, the deeper question may be the exact opposite of the one just posed, namely: Is it really possible to live in such an endlessly changing world *without* a relatively fixed, and firmly based, morality? Speaking always with reference to things of this world, we might put this quite different contention as follows: Change, it can be argued, is humanly endurable over the long pull only when it takes place within a relatively fixed moral framework. Otherwise it is mere flux. Flux deprives human existence of all significance and deeper meaning. What turns mere "change" into capital "P" Progress is precisely the moral framework within which the change takes place and is seen to offer fulfillment.

What is suggested here is that, without something like the Idea of Progress, or its rough equivalent, the massive and accelerating changes introduced by the Scientific and Industrial Revolutions really become unsupportable. There is no stability left, nothing to hang onto, nothing to certify the purpose and meaning of one's existence.

But surely, the counterargument might go, you don't seriously believe that any traditional, "old-fashioned" values can maintain themselves while each day brings not only some new gadget, invention, and technological advance, but also such vast changes in living arrangements as urbanization, suburbanization, and exurbanization, not to mention new and more efficient methods of birth control, abortion, plastic surgery, organ transplants, biogenetic engineering, and the like? Doesn't every new development in science, demography, and socioeconomic living conditions pose unbearable challenges to any relatively fixed morality?

In my own view, the answer—rather surprising in a way—is no. To put it a bit more carefully, I would argue that there is nothing in the fundamental predicament of progress that requires us to abandon any given set of moral principles. Indeed, I would include in this the morality embodied in the Idea of Progress. For although the fundamental predicament implies that it is increasingly difficult to imagine what the distant future will turn out to be, it in no way mandates that we must change our views as to what a beneficial and desirable future is. In fact, it mandates nothing with respect to our current or future morality.

One has to be a bit careful here, since it might appear that this is simply parroting the comforting rationalization that scientists have been offering for years and years, namely, that science and morality do not conflict, that there is nothing wrong with the products of science (the bomb, genetic engineering, or whatever), but only the uses to which these products are put (wiping out cities, creating monsters in the lab, and so on). Although true enough, it is not very helpful to say that it is not science that is the problem but man, since it is for man, and not the birds and the bees, that science does its work.

My claim runs far deeper than this, however, and, in fact, derives precisely from the underlying circumstances that produce the fundamental predicament of progress. The central problem posed by the process of progress is that it undermines the sense of inevitability of any particular path into the future. The reason our time horizons keep getting shorter and shorter is that we cannot foresee which of the many complicated paths available to us will in fact prevail. Nothing is required, nothing predetermined, and this, alas for the true believers, includes the particular onward and upward path prescribed by the Idea of Progress.

But notice the basic drift of all this. It is away from inevitability to possibility, from the single and inexorable to the multiple and variable. Charles Beard, we recall, defined Progress precisely as a move from "necessity to freedom." The problem posed by the fundamental predicament for the Idea of Progress is not that we are increasingly bound to act in a fixed and certain way, but that we are increasingly free to act in vastly different and often quite unpredictable ways. But to say that we are "free" is to say that we *are* "free"! A rose is a rose is a rose. Increased freedom is increased freedom is increased freedom.

And what this increased freedom allows us is the privilege, if we wish to exercise it, of making our own a great variety of different moral and ethical codes and, in particular, if we so chose, the most restricted, old-fashioned, simple-minded Victorian morality we could possibly imagine. No one may want to do this. But no one can claim that we are prohibited from doing this, that there is something inexorably predetermined in the process of progress that requires us to abstain from such an archaic code. To repeat: To speak of inexorability, predetermination, prohibitions, and requirements is to violate, not fulfill, the terms of the fundamental predicament. Our problem is ultimately not our new restraints, but our new freedoms.

In short, to anyone who says, you can't go back, you can't reinstate those long discarded codes, you can't even reestablish the rather limited set of family values discussed in the last chapter—to such a person, one simply replies, "Why not?" Are you in fact trying to tell me that the future really *is* predetermined, that the morality of that future is already set by you and your colleagues, that despite appearances we are not really free at all but bound to follow one particular, "correct" path into the future? And if that is what you are saying then I say that it is you, not I, who is violating the conditions imposed upon us by the fundamental predicament of progress. It is you, not I, who is denying the kind of freedom that is in many ways the source of the entire problem in the first place.

We are free. We are free to bring back "the family" if we choose to. And insofar as "the family," and its related values contribute to a clearer image of the future, we are also free to bring back at least a modified version of the Idea of Progress—modified in the direction of humility, hope, conjecture rather than assertion, yet still rooting itself in the same basic view of the world.

We could. We can.

Will we?

THE PSYCHOLOGICAL PROSPECT

"We can act, but will we?" is the title of this chapter, and what is implied is that while we are not in any way logically, or by great, inevitable forces of history, required to abandon either Progress or "the family," nevertheless it is quite a different matter to believe that we will, in fact, choose these particular options. The real question is, as always, not logical but psychological. Could we psychologically sustain any kind of traditional values in a scientifically revolutionizing, technologically advancing, materially expanding, fast-paced, competitive, rat-race kind of world? Is this really possible?

Empirical evidence on this point would actually seem to be mixed. Certainly the broad tendencies toward moral relativism, multiculturalism, diversity, and the like that we have so often noted are evidence of a strong move away from traditional values. So, too, obviously, is our increasing abandonment of traditional family structures and the sharply lowered priority we give our children. The path along which the future, in the most general sense, is given pride of place—along which, as it were, we keep looking ahead, rather than from side to side—has certainly been forsaken by many and perhaps ultimately will be forsaken by all.

On the other hand, there has also grown up in our own time—and, in a way, this is the very most recent development—a general feeling that while all this choice is very nice, the way we exercise this wide range of choice is even more important. What we need now, many claim, is limitation, constraint, a restoration of a sense of proportion, of morality, and, indeed, of more traditional values generally. We need to give children more parental care and attention; we need to respect the institution of the family far more deeply and consent to its dissolution with far more restraint and caution than we have shown in recent decades; we need to develop precepts and programs such as those suggested by the Council on Families, the National Commission on America's Urban Families, or the various plans and proposals presented in chapter 14. These views, in turn, are often combined with other more or less traditional attitudes: respect for the work ethic, calls for a greater sense of responsibility with respect to drugs, sexual promiscuity, violence, crime, and even the current craze for gambling.

There is a whole constellation of views here that is quite familiar to anyone who looks and listens in upon the contemporary American scene. What is most interesting to me in the present connection is that this quite traditional, "old-fashioned" point of view is most frequently associated with a faith in scientific progress, new technologies, economic growth, and, in general, the benefits of change and novelty in the actual circumstances of life. Not always, of course. For many of these same views are held by religion fundamentalists who, as we have already noted, are essentially rejecting the whole theater within which the process of progress takes place. Their heaven *is* heaven.

But there is also a constellation of views of this sort held by those who still rely primarily on a heaven on this planet, a heaven that is to some degree being enjoyed by themselves, but hopefully will be enjoyed increasingly by their children. Within this secular-minded group, there are those who continue to look to the future for a kind of personal redemption, purpose, and meaning in life beyond the temporary and transient. In general, indeed, it can be claimed as a matter of empirical fact that, in today's America, the celebration of traditional, relatively fixed values and the celebration of economic growth, scientific advance, and other forms of material change tend to go together. By contrast, it is in the camp of the moral relativists that the process of progress, and rapid future change of any kind, tend to be treated with suspicion and concern.

Thus, for some Americans at least, the psychological balancing act of combining constraining values with the active celebration of change seems viable. To this constituency, the contrary balancing act—doing one's own thing at the moment while largely ignoring future consequences—is the really difficult act to bring off. In short, one can fairly claim that charting our future path along more or less traditional lines is not only a logical possibility—nothing prevents our making this choice—but is an option which, for some at least, is psychologically acceptable and even deeply satisfying. For those who believe in family values, all the above is basically good news.

THE POLITICS OF DENIAL

Unfortunately for those believers, however, this good news represents only part of the story. For although the foregoing analysis suggests that we are free to act in a certain way and that many contemporary Americans would be psychologically comfortable with such a choice, we also know that very large numbers of Americans are making quite different choices. Furthermore, this same analysis prohibits us from concluding that the choice we favor—if, indeed, that happens to be where we stand—is in any way a required or mandated choice. There is nothing inevitable about it. The fundamental predicament precludes anyone from making the claim that "necessity" is on his or her team, not someone else's.

Still, there is something that can be said on the matter. My own view is that the path we do ultimately choose will reflect, more than anything else, our feelings about our children. If, for whatever inherited biological or cultural reason, we are truly and deeply concerned with the lives of others than ourselves, of others who will live after we have departed the scene, of our children, our grandchildren, possibly even our great grandchildren—if this concern is, as we always used to assume, deeply embedded in the human psyche and an unalterable feature of the human condition—if such conditions are fulfilled, then it is hard to believe that Americans will be content to continue risking the fate of those who will succeed us as cavalierly as we have been in recent years. Under such assumptions, the restoration of the family and even, probably in a somewhat modified form, the Idea of Progress itself seems quite likely.

This conclusion assumes, of course, that Americans do, in fact, realize and recognize the harm done to their children and heirs by the current arrangement of things. If, on the contrary, they have come to believe that they have no real choice but to continue acting as they are, or that these actions, after all, impose no real burden of hardship on their children, then, of course, there is no warrant whatever for believing that the changes we have been discussing will occur.

All of which is to say that the first requirement for those who wish to restore the family and related values must be to try to make their fellow citizens conscious of the real harm actually being inflicted upon today's American children. Facing this fundamental fact is crucial. By the same token, denial of this fact represents the worst thing that can happen from a pro-family point of view—actually, a betrayal of our children, indeed a betrayal of overwhelmingly objective evidence.

So far, at least, one has to say that, not all but many, American intellectuals have an extremely poor track record on this particular subject. The push in schools and universities in the direction of multiculturalism, diversity, universal tolerance, and, of course, families above the family is both well known and disturbing. I mentioned in the last chapter David Blankenhorn's twelfth and final proposal which was that textbook writers ought to pull up their socks and give intact, father-present, families at least equal time in the minds of our young. The disparagement of the traditional American family is, in fact, a staple of modern American intellectual life.

There is, of course, one possible (and not very attractive) explanation of why so many intellectuals support the culture of divorce, separation, day care, latchkey kids, and general child neglect rampant in today's society. Could it be because they themselves are frequently complicit, parties at interest? It is certainly clear that, in many cases, they themselves are, or have been, divorced, separated, professionally occupied parents of day-care children, absent from home when the kids return from school, reduced to spending a few hours a week of so-called "quality" time with emotionally and spiritually undernourished children. Since one can assume that none of these professionals wishes to believe that his or her actions have done harm to their own children, what alternative do they have except to deny that such harm has in fact occurred? And how can they exempt themselves without also exempting the great generality of American parents who are doing similar, or (being much poorer on average) far worse things to their own children?

One almost has to resort to this kind of distasteful *ad hominem* explanation, or something rather similar to it, for how otherwise can one understand the torrent of psychological and sociological literature that purports to show that, after all (and despite their poverty, school failures, psychological problems, suicides, homicides, teenage violence, increased smoking, drug abuse, sexual promiscuity, illegitimacy rates, obesity, and widespread mental depression), our children are really doing just fine these days? Admittedly there are a few problems in the underclass, the ghetto . . . but for the rest . . .

Three different claims to support these seemingly transparent rationalizations are common:

1. *There is really no alternative to continuing, or expanding, our present arrangements for bringing up our children.*

This is the standard argument as to why mothers of infants and toddlers have no alternative but to join the labor force and farm their children out to extrafamily care arrangements which are deemed, even by their strongest supporters, to be wholly inadequate and even unsafe. The "sheer necessity" argument is put forward with an absolutely straight face even though average real incomes per capita are five times what they were a century ago, and even though many of the mothers who are farming out those infants and toddlers have husbands in the very highest income quartile.

A favorite stratagem in this we-have-no-alternative connection is to project certain trends into the future, take the projections as firmly fixed, and then show that we have no real future option except to follow certain favored policies. In the 1990 National Research Council report on U.S. child care policies, for example, there is a section labeled "Future Trends," featuring two graphs which project large increases in (1) the percentage of children with mothers in the labor force, and (2) the percentage of children living in single-parent families for the year 2000.[1] Based on these trends, the report concludes that one can predict "with some certainty" that "the demand for out-of-home child-care services will continue to increase well into the 1990s." Since quality services are clearly desirable, and current services are often not of high quality, is it not obvious, implies the report, that the government must throw its full weight behind an effort to improve day-care quality and accessibility? Given the trends in labor force participation and family structure, there is, of course, no real alternative to the proposed policy. But this is a totally bogus argument when one believes—as family supporters clearly do—that policy ought to be specifically directed at discouraging single-parent families and encouraging parental care for small children. If, as in this report, one rules out all other alternatives by fiat, then naturally there is only one left. What else would one expect from such an exercise?[2]

2. *Find some way of "proving," ideally statistically, that children today, despite overwhelming contrary evidence, are not really harmed by the break-up of intact, two-biological-parent families.*

This is not an easy task. It requires enormous ingenuity. For the fact is that there is seemingly indisputable evidence from countless studies that children in single-parent and step-parent families fare worse on almost every single dimension—psychological, educational, or economic—than children in intact biological-parent families.[3] Still, if we are to justify our very high rates of divorce, separation, and never-married parenting, we have to find some way around this mountain of evidence. Surely, we would not willingly do such harm to our children as these studies imply.

There does, in fact, appear to be one sure way out of this dilemma. For one can claim that the real problem isn't with the broken family but with the intact family before it broke up. It is the bad marriages that precede the divorces that harm the children, not the divorces themselves. By the same logic, never-married parents also do well to prefer not being married to entering into one of those bad marriages that would only break up very quickly anyway. The beauty of this line of argument is that the fault—the ultimate source of the harm being done our children—is placed squarely at the feet of the traditional family. The implication is that it is actually a good thing in many, very probably most, cases that these terrible traditional marriages are breaking up. For the harm done the children by continuing these bad marriages (hints of sexual and other abuses are often found lurking in the shadows) would obviously be greater than by allowing such unions to be dissolved.

One of the most egregious articles—egregious because it was authored by a slew of very distinguished social scientists and was published in one of our most reputable journals, *Science*—that took this line of attack came out in 1991 and purported to show that a great deal of the harm experienced by the children of divorce was due to conditions that existed well before the separation occurred, especially "family dysfunction and marital conflict."[4] It can be seen that, if accurate, this study would be very reassuring to many divorced parents of young children by supporting their hopeful view that, in dissolving their marriages, they have not harmed, and may even have improved, the health, happiness, and life prospects of their children.

If accurate. Yet, in point of fact, the article was full of holes. The study treated both British and American children and reached inconsistent results for the two groups. It reached inconsistent results for American boys versus American girls. In the case of U.S. girls, it showed that these children experienced *fewer* behavioral problems after divorce than did girls from intact families. This was such a startling result considering all other known studies on this subject that the lead author, when queried on the matter, was forced to reply that girls showed the effects of divorce in very different ways from boys. Later, it was revealed that another of the authors of the *Science* study had earlier published an article showing that such gender differences did not exist. And this was only the beginning of the problems evinced by this particular article. Indeed, the ensuing controversy prompted at least one observor, Senator Moynihan, to wonder what could possibly have happened to *Science*. In the old days, he remarked sadly, it used to publish serious, verifiable articles![5]

The point is not to revisit this particular controversy but to show the willingness, indeed one might almost say eagerness, even of a distinguished group of scholars to publish material that could serve to exonerate divorcing parents of any real responsibility for the harm that their children might suffer in consequence. This is exactly the kind of rationalization that makes the resurrection of the institution of the family so very difficult for its supporters to promote.

3. *If any studies appear showing that present societal arrangements are, in fact, harming our children, attack the author or authors with all guns blazing!*

This approach is probably particularly common when the issue involves mothers of young children entering the labor force. The claim that any mother anywhere is harming her child by virtue of her full-time job or career is probably the claim most violently rejected by supporters of the present status quo. Many of these supporters, needless to say, are mothers who have full-time careers or fathers whose wives have full-time careers. A case in point has to do with psychologist Jay Belsky of Pennsylvania State University whose researches we discussed at some length earlier (see chapter 2, pp. 49–51). His early studies had suggested the possibility that day care in a child's first year of life might be harmful for later development. This immediately produced a flood of protest. Sociologist Sandra Scarr claimed that Belsky's views represented a backlash against the women's movement: "The advice for women has always been to get out of the work force. This is just another way of saying the same thing." Tiffany Field, a professor of pediatrics and psychology at the University of Miami was even more direct: "I think it's bunkum," she was quoted as saying.[6]

Belsky and his colleagues, undeterred, carried on, and in 1991, he and D. Eggebeen reported their study suggesting that day care might possibly be harmful not only for infants but over the first three years of a child's life. This conclusion has also been reached by other qualified observers, though it has been questioned too, most recently by the NICHD study dealing with infant attachment-security. But what was interesting about this 1991 episode was that the editor of the journal involved (*The Journal of Marriage and the Family*) found it necessary to publish immediately, indeed, in the very same issue, a series of rebuttals, mostly very hostile, to the Belsky-Eggebeen article. The title of one critique may give the flavor of the debate: "On Comparing Apples and Oranges and Making Inferences about Bananas." At the end of this barrage of contrary articles, Belsky and Eggebeen could only wonder if, had their results been different, their methods would have been subject to quite such a massive attack.[7]

The above three strategies constitute, in my judgment, what psychologists, using one of their favorite current words, might term a species of "denial." For those personally complicit in the present pattern of infant and child care neglect, the reasons for denial are obvious. For others, the notably short-term, present orientation of much postmodern thought may form a more generalized, depersonalized framework in which this denial can be understood. Under any circumstances, it can well be argued that the harm such patterns of thought do to our youngest generations is incalculable.

A CRUCIAL FIRST STEP

What this finally boils down to is a concept that is as simple to state as it will be difficult to apply. If we truly wish to save the family, we must, individually, and as a nation, face the fact that we are not giving adequate attention to our children and our children's futures. The one trend that we must *not* project into the future is the continuing reduction of parental hours spent with our children and, perhaps especially, the virtual or total absence of any paternal care or even fatherly presence in the home in many instances.

If we can agree that our current practices are, in fact, harming our children, that we have given priority to other self-oriented, now-focused objectives even at our children's expense, then we will have an opportunity to test the hypothesis I mentioned a few pages ago, namely, that the great majority of parents would not willingly do harm to their children and that there is some deep biological or cultural tie between parents and children such that, being forced to face such harmful behavior squarely, most of us would want to change that behavior.

This hypothesis may not in fact be valid. Under the time-shrinking influence of the fundamental predicament of progress, we may simply and deeply care more about the now than the later, more about ourselves than our issue. Certainly, many of us seem to be behaving that way in contemporary America.

All that can be said ultimately is that if we truly care about our children and if, after all the rationalizations are stripped away, we really do want to do better by them, then there is nothing to stop us from doing so. The process of progress ultimately endows us with choices, and this particular choice is clearly ours to make.

NOTES

PREFACE

1. Robert H. Nelson, *Reaching for Heaven on Earth: The Theological Meaning of Economics* (Savage, Md.: Rowman & Littlefield Publishers, 1991), xxi–xxii.

INTRODUCTION

1. The use of the term "pathology" to refer to certain conditions in American Black families was, of course, a feature of Daniel Patrick Moynihan's well known 1965 government report, "The Negro Family in America: The Case for National Action." Moynihan was often faulted for his analysis at the time; later, frequently praised for his foresight. What is significant for us is that, on many dimensions, the American White family of 1996 approximates conditions in the Black family of 1965.

2. Henry George, *Progress and Poverty*, 50th Anniversary Edition (New York: Robert Schalkenback Foundation, 1946), 538.

3. J. B. Bury, *The Idea of Progress: An Inquiry into Its Growth and Origin* (London: Macmillan, 1932; Dover Edition, 1955), 347. Bury's classic was originally published in 1920.

4. For discussion of the "cult of domesticity," see Carl Degler, *At Odds: Women and Family in America from the Revolution to the Present* (New York: Oxford University Press, 1980)

CHAPTER 1

1. This account of the institution of the family follows closely that presented in Richard Gill, Nathan Glazer, and Stephan Thernstrom, *Our Changing Population* (Englewood Cliffs, N.J.: Prentice-Hall, 1992), esp. 144–48.

2. Phon Hudkins, quoted in William Raspberry, "Bring Back the Family," *Washington Post*, 17 July 1989.

315

3. Degler, *At Odds*, 3–4.

4. Kathleen Gough, "The Origin of the Family," in Arlene S. Skolnick and Jerome H. Skolnick, eds., *Family in Transition*, 5th ed. (Boston: Little, Brown, 1985), 32.

5. Degler, *At Odds*, 367.

6. John Demos, *A Little Commonwealth: Family Life in Plymouth Colony* (New York: Oxford University Press, 1970), 183–4.

7. Ralph Waldo Emerson, "Woman," (1855), from *Emerson's Complete Works*, vol. 11 (Boston: Houghton Mifflin and Company, 1893).

8. Catharine E. Beecher and Harriet Beecher Stowe, *American Woman's Home, or Principles of Domestic Science* (New York: J. B. Ford & Co., 1869), 214.

9. U.S.Congress, 1914: Citation for legislation establishing Mother's Day.

10. Thomas J. Espenshade, "Illegitimacy and Public Policy," *Population and Development Review* 11, no. 2 (June 1985). For the most recent available numbers on American family structures, see Ken Bryson, "Household and Family Characteristics, March 1995," U.S. Bureau of the Census, *Current Population Reports,* P20–488, 1996.

11. Teresa C. Martin and Larry L. Bumpass, "Recent Trends in Marital Disruption," *Demography* 26, no. 1 (February, 1989): 44.

12. Sociologist Andrew Cherlin notes in an article, "Nostalgia as Family Policy," in *The Public Interest* (110, winter 1993) that the U.S. "divorce rate has declined about 10 percent from its 1981 peak." However, Larry Bumpass questions the significance of this decline:

> Although annual rates of divorce have fluctuated around the trend line, the underlying rate of increase in the level of lifetime divorce has been virtually constant for more than 100 years, generating the accelerating curve from 7% of marriages in 1860 to current expectations of well over half. It is too soon to conclude that the plateau in the divorce rate of the last decade represents the end of the trend—we must remember that there was a similar 15–year plateau before the takeoff of the late 1960s. In any event, the current level of marital disruption is very high. Martin and Bumpass (1989) recently estimated that almost two-thirds of recent first marriages would be likely to disrupt if current levels persist. Further work leads us to suspect that 60% may be closer to the mark.

(Larry L. Bumpass, "What's Happening to the Family? Interactions between Demographic and Institutional Change," *Demography,* 25, no. 4 (November 1990.)

13. U.S. Bureau of the Census, *Current Population Reports*, P23–181, "Households, Families, and Children: A 30–Year Perspective," 1992, 38.

14. Steve W. Rawlings and Arlene F. Saluter, "Household and Family

Characteristics, March 1994," U.S. Bureau of the Census, *Current Population Reports,* P20–483, 1995.

15. David Blankenhorn, *Fatherless America: Confronting Our Most Urgent Social Problem* (New York: Basic Books, 1995), 18–19.

16. See Kathryn A. London, "Children of Divorce," *Vital and Health Statistics,* Series 21, no. 46, NCHS, 1989. London noted that, whereas in 1956 the average number of children per divorce (0.95) was less than that of the average number of children per married-couple household (1.30), by 1984 the numbers were identical (0.92). She suggested that one reason was that "parents who were unhappy with their marriages became less likely to stay together for the sake of the children." (2).

17. The latest available edition is Lynne M. Casper, "Who's Minding Our Preschoolers?" U.S. Bureau of the Census, *Current Population Reports,* P70–53, April 1996.

18. These arrangements with out-of-home and nonrelative infant care are, as the text indicates, basically new in our American experience, though other societies, in other historical periods, have sometimes used nannies, wetnurses, and all sorts of curious child-care arrangements, most of which would be judged unsatisfactory by modern standards, and certainly by American standards during the nineteenth and early twentieth centuries.

19. Lynne M. Casper, Mary Hawkins, and Martin O'Connell, "Who's Minding the Kids? Child Care Arrangements, Fall 1991," U.S. Bureau of the Census, *Current Population Reports,* P70–36, June 1994, 10.

20. Gill et al., *Our Changing Population,* 276.

21. Robert Haveman and Barbara Wolfe, "Children's Prospects and Children's Policy," *Journal of Economic Perspectives* 7, no. 4 (fall 1993): 155.

CHAPTER 2

1. The surprising increase in sex at very early ages among American teenagers is discussed at greater length in chapter 10.

2. William Damon, *Greater Expectations* (New York: The Free Press, 1995), 7.

3. Fordham Institute for Innovation in Social Policy, *1996 Index of Social Health: Monitoring the Social Well-Being of the Nation* (Tarrytown, N.Y.: Fordham Graduate Center, 1996): 1–19.

4. Elizabeth Kolbert, "Americans Despair of Popular Culture," *New York Times,* Sunday, 20 August 1995.

5. Gill et al., *Our Changing Population,* 290.

6. Haveman and Wolfe, "Children's Prospects," 159–61.

7. John H. Bishop, "Is the Test Score Decline Responsible for the Productivity Growth Decline?" *American Economic Review* 79, no. 1 (March 1989).

8. Damon, *Greater Expectations*, xiii.

9. *AARP Bulletin* 37, no. 10 (November 1996), 3.

10. Suzanne Bianchi and Edith McArthur, "Family Disruption and Economic Hardship: The Short-Run Picture for Children," *Current Population Reports*, Series P–70, no. 23, 1991, 10.

11. National Commission on America's Urban Families, *Families First*, Washington, D.C., January 1993, 25.

12. *Families First*, 25.

13. It is actually difficult to interpret the frequently repeated statement that adult crime in the United States has been declining in recent years, (a) because different studies give different results, and (b) because the measured decline in crime may reflect more than anything else the major increase in the number of criminals actually in jail over the last few years.

14. Elaine C. Kamarck and William A. Galston, "Putting Children First: A Progressive Family Policy for the 1990s" (Washington, D.C.: Progressive Policy Institute, September, 1990), 14.

15. Richard Neely, "Too Many Divorces and Not Enough Guns," *Wall Street Journal*, 24 March 1995. See also John R. Lott, Jr., "More Guns, Less Violent Crime," *Wall Street Journal*, 28 August 1996.

16. In addition to the National Longitudinal Survey of Youth (NLSY), McLanahan and Sandefur report basically similar results from the Panel Study of Income Dynamics (PSID), High School and Beyond Study (HSB), and National Survey of Families and Households (NSFH 1 = Cohort 1, and NSFH 2 = Cohort 2). See Sara McLanahan and Gary Sandefur, *Growing Up with a Single Parent* (Cambridge, Mass.: Harvard University Press, 1994), esp. chapter 3.

17. Nicholas Zill and Charlotte A. Schoenbron, "Developmental, Learning, and Emotional Problems: Health of Our Nation's Children, United States, 1988," *Advance Data from Vital and Health Statistics*, No. 190, NCHS, 1990.

18. Deborah A. Dawson, "Family Structure and Children's Health: United States, 1988," NCHS, *Vital Health Statistics* 10 (no.178), 1991.

19. Nicholas Zill, Donna Morrison, Mary Joe Coiro, "Long-Term Effects of Parental Divorce on Parent-Child Relationships, Adjustment, and Achievement in Young Adulthood," *Journal of Family Psychology* 7, no. 1(1993): 93–103.

20. McLanahan and Sandefur, *Single Parent*, 1.

21. The problematic status of stepfamilies, as far as children are concerned, is also brought out in Zill et al., "Long-Term Effects," and Dawson, "Family Structure," studies as well as numerous other studies, including, James H. Bray et al., "Longitudinal Changes in Stepfamilies: Impact on Children" (Washington, D.C.: American Psychological Association, 15 August 1992). Among other

things, the evidence is that child sexual abuse in stepfamilies is much higher than in biological parent families.

22. Daniel Patrick Moynihan, "Defining Deviancy Down," *American Scholar* 62, no. 1 (winter, 1993): 17–30.

23. Cheryl D. Hayes, John L. Palmer, and Martha J. Zaslow, eds., *Who Cares for America's Children? Child Care Policies for the 1990s* (Washington, D.C.: National Academy Press, 1990). For a general critique of this report, see Richard Gill, "Day Care or Parental Care?" *The Public Interest* no. 105 (fall 1991): 3–16.

24. See, for example, John Bowlby, *Attachment and Loss*, vols. 1–3 (New York: Basic Books, 1969, 1973, 1980); Robert N. Emde, ed., *Rene A. Spitz: Dialogues from Infancy: Selected Papers* (New York: International Universities Press, Inc., 1983); Mary D. Salter Ainsworth et al., *Patterns of Attachment: A Psychological Study of the Strange Situation* (Hillsdale, N.J.: Lawrence Erlbaum Associates, 1978); Selma Fraiberg, *Every Child's Birthright: In Defense of Mothering* (New York: Basic Books, 1977); Marshall Klaus, John Kennell, and Phyllis Klaus, *Bonding: Building the Foundations of Secure Attachment and Independence* (Reading, Mass.: Addison-Wesley, 1995); T. Berry Brazelton and Bertrand G. Cramer, *The Earliest Relationship* (Reading, Mass.: Addison-Wesley, 1990).

25. Jay Belsky, Richard M. Lerner, and Graham B. Spanier, *The Child in the Family* (Reading, Mass.: Addison-Wesley, 1984): 48.

26. J. Belsky and D. Eggebeen, "Early and Extensive Maternal Employment and Young Children's Socioemotional Development: Children of the National Longitudinal Survey of Youth," *Journal of Marriage and the Family* 53, no. 4 (November 1991): 1083–1098.

27. NICDH Early Child Care Research Network, "Infant Child Care and Attachment Security: Results of the NICDH Study of Early Child Care," 20 April 1996, 15.

28. NICHD, 15.

29. Jay Belsky, letter to the author, 20 May 1996.

30. Burton L. White, *The First Three Years of Life*, new and revised edition (New York: Simon & Schuster, 1990), 267.

31. Fredelle Maynard, *The Child Care Crisis* (New York: Viking Penguin, 1985), 119.

32. Marion Blum, *The Day-Care Dilemma: Women and Children First* (Lexington, Mass.: D.C. Heath, 1983), 24.

33. Suzanne W. Helburn, ed., *Cost, Quality, and Child Outcomes in Child Care Centers, Technical Report,* Center for Research in Economic and Social Policy, University of Colorado at Denver, 1995.

34. Ibid, 319–20.

35. Ibid, 320.

CHAPTER 3

1. Thus, AFDC plus food stamps benefits were decreasing in real terms between the 1980s and the 1990s while single-parenthood was increasing sharply. Also, the facts that well-to-do mothers are also increasingly single parents and that Europe, with higher welfare benefits, has lower rates of single-motherhood than the United States suggest that deeper explanations are required. This is not to say that our welfare system has had no effect on promoting single motherhood. It almost certainly has provided a necessary, though not sufficient, condition for this development to occur.

2. One of the sharpest downward departures from this trend took place in the Baby Boom period. See figure 11.1 on page 225.

3. Herman E. Krooss, *American Economic Development*, 2d ed., (Englewood Cliffs, N.J.: Prentice-Hall, 1966), 451–52.

4. Sara McLanahan and Lynne Casper, "Growing Diversity and Inequality in the American Family," in Reynolds Farley, ed., *State of the Union: America in the 1990s*, vol. 2 (New York: Russell Sage Foundation, 1995), 15.

5. David Popenoe, *Disturbing the Nest: Family Change and Decline in Modern Societies* (New York: Aldine de Gruyter, 1988), 173.

6. For a discussion of these growth estimates, see Richard T. Gill, *Economics: A Concise Micro/Macro Text* (Mountain View, Calif.: Mayfield Publishing, 1993), chapter 26.

7. Adam Smith, *The Wealth of Nations* (New York: Modern Library, Random House, 1937), 3.

8. Paul Mantoux, *The Industrial Revolution in the Eighteenth Century: An Outline of the Beginnings of the Modern Factory System in England*, rev. ed. (New York: Harper & Row, 1962).

9. Peter F. Drucker, *The New Realities* (New York: Harper & Row, 1989), 173.

10. For a discussion of this issue, see a number of papers in the *American Economic Review* 83, no. 2 (May 1993), esp. 104–26. A common conclusion is that there was a "strong increase in the demand for skill over the 1940–1990 period" in the United States. (K. M. Murphy and Finis Welch, "Occupational Change and the Demand for Skill, 1940–1990," 126.)

11. Charles A. Beard. "Introduction" to Bury, *The Idea of Progress*, xl.

12. At the end of the nineteenth century, Herbert Spencer defined evolution as "a change from a relatively indefinite, incoherent, homogeneity to a state of relatively definite, coherent, heterogeneity." (Herbert Spencer, "What is Social Evolution?" *Nineteenth Century* 44 [1898]: 353.)

13. John Scanzoni, *Shaping Tomorrow's Families: Theory and Policy for the 21st Century* (Beverly Hills, Calif.: Sage Publications, 1983), 33.

14. For a general discussion of the changing nature of women's work, see Judith A. Matthaei, *An Economic History of Women in America: Women's Work, the Sexual Division of Labor, and the Development of Capitalism* (New York: Schocken Books, 1982).

15. Gary S. Becker, *A Treatise on the Family* (Cambridge, Mass.: Harvard University Press, 1981), 242.

16. Talcott Parsons and Robert F. Bales, *Family, Socialization and Interaction Process* (New York: The Free Press, 1955), 16–17.

17. Barrington Moore, Jr., *Political Power and Social Theory* (Cambridge, Mass.: Harvard University Press, 1958), 172–73, 178.

18. W. W. Rostow, *The Stages of Economic Growth: A Non-Communist Manifesto* (Cambridge: Cambridge University Press, 1960), 80. 91.

19. John Kenneth Galbraith, *The Affluent Society*, 2d ed. rev. (Boston: Houghton Mifflin, 1969), 2.

20. Paul Ryscavage, "More Working Wives Have Husbands with 'Above-Average' Incomes," *Monthly Labor Review* 102, no. 6 (June 1989): 41.

21. For example, Italy, in the early 1990s was reported to have a fertility rate of 1.4 whereas replacement fertility is slightly above 2. For trends in the U.S. fertility rate, see Gill et al., *Our Changing Population*, chapter 3.

22. Simon Kuznets, "Notes on Demographic Change," in Martin Feldstein, ed., *The American Economy in Transition* (Chicago: University of Chicago Press, 1980), 335.

23. Kingsley Davis, "Wives and Work: Consequences of the Sex Role Revolution," *Population and Development Review* 10, no. 3 (September 1984): 405.

24. Bureau of the Census, Household and Family, *Current Population Reports*, Series P–20, No. 447, 6.

25. Joseph A. Schumpeter, *Capitalism, Socialism, and Democracy*, 3d ed. (New York: Harper & Brothers, 1950), 246.

26. These quotations are in order from: (1) Elin McCoy, "Childhood Through the Ages," in James M. Henslin, ed., *Marriage and the Family in a Changing Society*, 2d ed. (New York: Free Press, 1985), 393; (2) Degler, *At Odds*, 9; (3) Brigitte Berger and Peter L. Berger, *The War over the Family: Capturing the Middle Ground* (Garden City, N.Y.: Anchor Press/Doubleday, 1983), 7; (4) Viviana Zelizer, *Pricing the Priceless Child* (New York: Basic Books, 1985), 8–9; (5) James Lincoln Collier, *The Rise of Selfishness in America* (New York: Oxford University Press, 1991), 14; (6) Popenoe, *Disturbing the Nest*, 302; (7) John Sommerville, *The Rise and Fall of Childhood* (Beverly Hills, Calif.: Sage Publications, 1982), 228; and (8) Jack Larkin, *The Reshaping of Everyday Life, 1790–1840* (New York: Harper & Row, 1988), 53.

27. Degler, *At Odds*, 74.

28. However, even Lawrence Stone admits that, while the upper-and middle-class children were suffering from their Victorian fathers during the nineteenth century, "contraception, humanitarian legislation, slowly improving economic conditions, welfare services, and schools probably improved the lot of the children of the poor." (Lawrence Stone, *The Past and the Present* [Boston: Routledge & Kegan Paul, 1981], 227.)

29. Thus, Steven Mintz and Susan Kellogg write about the nineteenth century: "Within marriage the old ideals of patriarchal authority and strict wifely obedience were replaced by new ideals of mutual esteem, mutual friendship, mutual confidence." (Mintz and Kellogg, *Domestic Revolutions: A Social History of Family Life* [New York: The Free Press, 1988], 46.) This softening of attitudes from the early nineteenth century on also seemingly applied to the treatment of American children.

30. Edward Shorter, *The Making of the Modern Family* (New York: Basic Books, 1975), 168.

31. Lloyd deMause, "The Evolution of Childhood," in Lloyd deMause, ed., *The History of Childhood* (New York: The Psychohistory Press, 1974), 1.

32. These rather extreme views are, moreover, not commonly shared among historians. In our own pre-industrial period, for example, most evidence is that colonial parents did indeed have a warm and positive interest in their children. In explaining the custom of many Puritan parents of placing their children with other families, Edmund Morgan, for example, suggests "that Puritan parents did not trust themselves with their own children, that they were afraid of spoiling them by too great affection." As to Puritan discipline, he writes: "Granted its purposes and assumptions, Puritan education was intelligently planned, and the relationship between parent and child it envisaged was not one of harshness and severity but of tenderness and sympathy." (Edmund S. Morgan, *The Puritan Family: Religion and Domestic Relations in Seventeenth Century New England* [New York: Harper & Row, 1966], 77, 108.)

33. Becker, *Treatise,* esp. chapter 5, "The Demand for Children."

CHAPTER 4

1. For general surveys of the literature on the Idea of Progress, see the classic Bury, *The Idea of Progress*; Charles Van Doren, *The Idea of Progress* (New York: Frederick A. Praeger, 1967); Robert Nisbet, *History of the Idea of Progress* (New York: Basic Books, 1980), and a number of essays in Leo Marx and Bruce Mazlish, eds., *Progress: Fact or Illusion?* (Ann Arbor: University of Michigan Press, 1996). Literally, hundreds of thinkers are classified by various indices in these books.

2. These quotes are, in order, from George Bancroft, James Harvey Rob-

inson, Charles A. Beard, and Henry George. George is the one described as a "critic" of Progress, since he argued that it could happen that "progress may pass into retrogression" if right policies (notably his famous single tax) were not adopted. With good policies in effect, however, he joined the throng of others who believed that future ahead could be marvellous indeed. See his classic work, Henry George, *Progress and Poverty*, 50th Anniversary Edition (New York: Robert Schalkenback Foundation, 1946).

3. Oscar Handlin, *Chance or Destiny: Turning Points in American History* (Boston: Little, Brown, 1955), 194–95.

4. The Index Number Problem in economics involves the possibility that the rate of growth of, say, national income between any two dates will be different depending on whether one measures it from the past looking forward or from the present looking back. Commonly, the rate of growth is greater looking forward than looking back. Without stretching the analogy too far, one can easily imagine that the moral progress over a given period might be very differently assessed depending on whether one was using the initial set of values or the later set of values as one's measuring rod.

5. This issue is discussed in Van Doren, *Idea of Progress*, esp. 238–39.

6. From Adam Smith's *Wealth of Nations* (1776) to the 8th edition of Alfred Marshall's *Principles of Economics* (1920), "abstinence"—variously called "parsimony," "frugality," or, in Marshall's term, "Waiting"—played a major role in British classical economics. Abstinence produced saving which produced capital which produced wealth. Interestingly, it was only in the mid-twentieth century, with the writings of John Maynard Keynes that saving, abstinence, frugality, etc. took on the guise of villains—because they reduced demand and could lead to unemployment. For Keynes's very "short-run" outlook in general, see below, page 332n4.

7. Thorstein Veblen was the writer who most emphasized the "invidious" impulse to impress our neighbors through conspicuous consumption, vicarious leisure, and the like. While Veblen's analysis makes clear that upper- and middle-class American families in the late nineteenth century were very much involved in displays of wealth—that is, were hardly in "retreat" from the larger society—he does not in fact spend any time at all discussing what we might think of as "conspicuous bequests" to one's heirs. The only comment about inheritance in his classic work is that "wealth acquired passively by transmission from ancestors or other antecedents presently becomes even more honorific than wealth acquired by the possessor's own efforts." (Thorstein Veblen, *The Theory of the Leisure Class* [1899, New York: Augustus M. Kelley, 1975] 29.)

8. Alexis de Tocqueville, *Democracy in America*, trans. Henry Reeve (New York: Oxford University Press, 1947), 337.

9. Christopher Lasch, *Haven in a Heartless World: The Family Besieged* (New

York: Basic Books, 1977), 168. Lasch's reference to "some historians" is specifically pointed at Edward Shorter (see page 80).

10. Demos, *Past, Present, and Personal*, chapter 2.

11. Kirk Jeffrey, "The Family as Utopian Retreat from the City: The Nineteenth Century Contribution," *Soundings: An Interdisciplinary Journal* 55, no. 1 (spring, 1972), 21–42.

12. Thus, Demos points out that the nineteenth-century family did continue to relate to the larger society in a number of ways, mentioning family units in mills and some manufacturing establishments, the "chain migration" of immigrants, family bookkeepers for businesses, and the like. Jeffrey speaks of some of our nineteenth-century ancestors who viewed the family as a "nursery and school," preparing individuals to "go forth and remake American society." Even Lasch, in a later book, conjectured that "the doctrine of maternal influence commended itself, to an enterprising and forward-looking people, because it served to assure them that moral and material progress went hand in hand." (Christopher Lasch, *The True and Only Heaven: Progress and its Critics* [New York: W.W. Norton, 1991], 62–63). This notion of moral and material progress going hand in hand is exactly what the present book proposes as the main thread running through late-nineteenth-century family life.

13. This is the title of James Laver's book, *The Age of Optimism: Manners and Morals, 1848–1914* (London: Weidenfeld and Nicolson, 1966). Although much of the book is concerned with European countries, especially Britain, its comments are clearly meant also to apply to the prevailing American mood.

14. The James quote, like that from Emerson, are cited in Kenneth Lynn, *The Dream of Success* (Westport, Conn: Greenwood Press, 1955), 122.

15. John L. Rury, "Who Became Teachers?" in Donald Warren, ed., *American Teachers: Histories of a Profession at Work* (New York: Macmillan, 1989), 17, 25.

16. Benjamin Franklin, *Poor Richard's Almanack* (Mount Vernon, N.Y.: A Peter Pauper Press Book), 10, 21, 41.

17. Lawrence A. Cremin, *The Transformation of the School: Progressivism in American Education, 1876–1957* (New York: Vintage Books, 1964), 8.

18. Ruth Miller Elson, *Guardians of Tradition: American Schoolbooks in the Nineteenth Century* (Lincoln: University of Nebraska Press, 1964), 258.

CHAPTER 5

1. Carl Becker, *Progress and Power* (New York: Alfred A. Knopf, 1949), 6.

2. Thus, Lewis Mumford refers to the clock as a "key invention" which "became the source of a whole line of inventions which completed in the realm of time and motion what the magnifying glass had done in space." (Lewis Mum-

ford, *The Myth of the Machine* [New York: Harcourt, Brace, & World, Inc., 1967], 285–86. And again: "The clock, not the steam-engine, is the key machine of the modern industrial age." (Lewis Mumford, *Interpretations and Forecasts, 1922–1972* [New York: Harcourt Brace Jovanovich, 1973], 271–72.)

3. See Anthony F. Aveni, *Empires of Time: Calendars, Clocks, and Cultures* (New York: Basic Books, 1989), 129, 134.

4. Richard Morris, *Time's Arrows: Scientific Attitudes toward Time* (New York: Simon and Schuster, 1985), 84.

5. Stephen Toulmin and June Goodfield, *The Discovery of Time* (New York: Octagon Books, 1983), 161.

6. Charles Lyell, *Principles of Geology*, vol. 1 (Chicago: University of Chicago Press, 1990), 24.

7. The standard reference here is Arthur O. Lovejoy, *The Great Chain of Being* (New York: Harper & Row, 1960). The conception—which, according to Lovejoy, "through the Middle Ages and down to the late eighteenth century . . . most educated men were to accept without question"—involved the notion that all possible creatures from the lowest to the highest had been created, that is, that every possible niche was filled. This conception made no room for evolution or development and was "inconsistent with any belief in progress, or indeed, any sort of significant change in the universe as a whole." (59, 242).

8. After the fact, Spencer did actually invent the phrase "survival of the fittest" and, according to one critic, "wallowed for decades in evolutionary speculation of the boldest sort." His deductive approach was, however, not deeply trusted by Darwin. See William Irvine, *Apes, Angels, and Victorians* (Alexandria, Va.: Time-Life Books, 1963).

9. Charles Darwin, *The Origin of Species* (New York: P. F. Collier & Son, 1909), 528.

10. Charles Van Doren suggests that "the theory that sees progress occurring because mankind has a social or collective memory, such that the knowledge of past ages is handed down to later generations, which in turn add to it, is probably the most familiar, and is, in one sense, the most basic of all theories of progress." He then cites twenty-two major thinkers who can be classified as subscribing to this view. (Van Doren, *Idea of Progress*, 33–34). The reason I do not give more emphasis to this notion of the cumulative character of knowledge is that I am most concerned with the Idea of Progress as it affected the general public in the nineteeth and early twentieth centuries. In this connection, I believe that the *fruits* of this accumulating knowledge in the form of inventions, innovations, and rising living standards were probably most important.

11. Bury, *Idea of Progress*, 324–25.

12. Galbraith, *Affluent Society*, 1.

13. For an interesting discussion of medieval society's reliance on "For-

tune" to explain the inexplicable, see J. G. A. Pocock, *Politics, Language, and Time: Essays in Political Thought and History* (New York: Atheneum, 1971).

14. Stone, *Past and Present*, 155.

15. Pre-Industrial Revolution life expectancies must have been very low, especially because of high infant mortality. In America in colonial times, life expectancy at birth may have averaged around 35 years. Among Native Americans, before Columbus, burial sites suggest that as many as 40 percent of deaths were of children aged five or under.

16. J. Huizinga, *The Waning of the Middle Ages* (Garden City, N.Y.: Doubleday & Company, 1954), 30.

17. Mantoux, *The Industrial Revolution*, 405 *et seq.*

18. For example, an 1828 geography textbook is typical in claiming that "no nation, either in ancient or modern times, has increased so steadily and rapidly, in everything which indicates national wealth and prosperity as the people of the United States." This theme is repeated endlessly in readers, spellers, and geographies well into the twentieth century. See Elson, *Guardians of Tradition*, 258.

19. James Q. Wilson, "On Gender," *The Public Interest* no. 112 (summer 1993): 10.

20. Collier, *Rise of Selfishness*, 14.

21. David S. Landes, *The Unbound Prometheus: Technological Change and Industrial Development in Western Europe from 1750 to the Present* (Cambridge: Cambridge University Press, 1969), 21.

CHAPTER 6

1. Thomas Robert Malthus, *Population: The First Essay* (Ann Arbor: University of Michigan Press, 1959).

2. Charles Van Doren also notes that Malthus, in later versions of his essay, "holds that some progress must occur. But it is rather a distant progress, far removed from the present day." (Van Doren, *The Idea of Progress*, 242.)

3. Keynes was referring specifically to the Malthus-Ricardo debate over unemployment and "general gluts." Overall, however, Ricardo clearly had a more direct impact on subsequent economic theory than did Malthus. J. M. Keynes, *The General Theory of Employment, Interest, and Money* (New York: Harcourt, Brace and Co., 1936), 32.

4. William Godwin, *An Enquiry Concerning Political Justice and its Influence on General Virtue and Happiness*, vol. 1 (Toronto: University of Toronto Press, 1946), 93.

5. Malthus, *Population: The First Essay*, 95.

6. David Ricardo, *On the Principles of Political Economy and Taxation*, vol. 1

of Piero Sraffa, ed., *The Works and Correspondence of David Ricardo* (Cambridge: Cambridge University Press, 1951).

7. Ricardo, *Principles*, 120–21.

8. The evolution of Malthus's thought between first and second editions of the essay is discussed in George J. Stigler, *Essays in the History of Economics* (Chicago: University of Chicago Press, 1965), 160–66.

9. Landes, *The Unbound Prometheus*, 21–22.

10. Stigler, *Essays*, 172.

11. Paul R. Ehrlich, *The Population Bomb*, rev. ed. (New York: Ballantine Books, 1978), xi, 24–25, 224.

12. Gerald M. Meier, *Emerging from Poverty* (New York: Oxford University Press, 1984), 55–56. Other similarly positive assessments are cited in Gill et al., *Our Changing Population*, 448–49.

13. Stigler, *Essays*, 172.

14. Thus, even at a somewhat slower rate of population increase than at present, Pranay Gupte has calculated that, by a thousand years from now, world population could reach the totally implausible number of 60 million billion people. Pranay Gupte, *The Crowded Earth· People and the Politics of Population* (New York: W. W. Norton, 1984), 20.

15. Lloyd G. Reynolds, *Economic Growth in the Third World, 1850–1980* (New Haven: Yale University Press, 1985), 405. Examples of rapid declines in birthrates over a twenty-year period are: South Korea,–44%; Taiwan,–48%; Thailand,–32%; Malaysia,–31%; Brazil,–30%; Turkey,–26%; and Indonesia,–24%.

16. Richard Easterlin and Eileen Crimmins, *The Fertility Revolution: A Supply and Demand Analysis* (Chicago: University of Chicago Press, 1985), 191.

CHAPTER 7

1. We might even say, man's "animal nature" was at fault. At least, Darwin considered that his own work was, in some ways, a simple extension of the Malthusian thesis to other forms of life. Thus, "the Struggle for Existence amongst all organic beings throughout the world, which inevitably follows from the high geometrical ratio of their increase, will be considered. This is the doctrine of Malthus, applied to the whole animal and vegetable kingdom." (Darwin, Introduction, *Origin,* 23.)

2. Thus, World War I could be looked upon, in Woodrow Wilson's phrase, as an opportunity "to make the world safe for democracy." The League of Nations could also be viewed, in theory, as a notable advance in the cause of world peace occasioned by the horrors of war. This same kind of logic has been applied to the atomic bomb as an agency of world peace (see pp. 142–44).

3. C. P. Snow, the scientist/novelist, has been quoted as making such comments. Since "statistical certainty" is something of an oxymoron, it is to be hoped that Lord Snow was speaking in his capacity as novelist rather than as scientist.

4. Even in the tense decades preceding World Wars I and II, it is difficult to find any period as filled with potentially explosive incidents and deep-seated ideological rivalries as the post-World War II decades. From the Berlin blockade of the 1940s to the shooting down of an unarmed Korean airliner in the 1980s, the number of likely *casus belli* was legion, including, one might add, two serious actual wars in which the U.S. and Soviet-supported (and/or Chinese) troops were involved. Clearly, the problem to be explained here is why, under these circumstances, World War III did *not* come.

5. Rostow, *Stages of Growth*, 14.

6. Alfred Russel Wallace actually urged Darwin to substitute Spencer's phrase, "survival of the fittest," for his own term, "natural selection." Darwin replied that he agreed about "the advantages of H. Spencer's excellent expression" but would keep his own phrase since it was already in wide use. Whether the phrase "natural selection" would in due course, "be rejected," Darwin wrote, "must now depend on the 'survival of the fittest.'" Quoted in Robert L. Carneiro, "Introduction" to *The Evolution of Society, Selections from Herbert Spencer's Principles of Sociology* (Chicago: University of Chicago Press, 1967), xx.

7. Ibid, xxxvii.

8. Herbert Spencer, *Social Statics: Or Conditions Essential to Human Happiness*, (1851; New York: Augustus M. Kelley Publishers, 1969), 65, 64.

9. John U. Nef, *War and Human Progress: An Essay on the Rise of Industrial Civilization* (Cambridge, Mass: Harvard University Press, 1950), 381, 377.

10. This point was made by former President Nixon in an excellent article some years ago (Richard Nixon, "Superpower Summitry," *Foreign Affairs* [fall 1985]: 1–11). While acknowledging the difficulties of achieving an effective defense against an all-out Soviet attack, he stressed the practicality of a "thin population defense" which "*would* be effective against an accidental launch or an attack by a minor nuclear power." It is at least arguable that, in the 1990s, when a version of SDI might actually be useful, the United States has completely, and foolishly, lost interest in the project.

11. A defense of SDI on the grounds that almost nothing in science is "impossible," was once offered by Zbigniew Brzezinski, formerly President Carter's National Security Adviser, among others. "The 'impossible' is a concept we should use with great hesitation. It is foolhardy to predict the timing of innovations. We are persuaded that the laws of physics do not in any way prevent the technical requirements of a defensive shield that would protect populations as well as weapons." (Z. Brzezinski, R. Jastrow, and M. Kampelman, "Defense in

Space is not 'Star Wars,'" *New York Times Magazine*, 27 January 1985.) Unfortunately, as we suggest in the text, the nothing is "impossible" argument can also
be used against the long-run efficacy of SDI or any other defensive system.

12. Nobel is quoted in Herta E. Pauli, *Alfred Nobel: Dynamite King—
Architect of Peace* (New York: L. B. Fischer, 1942), 232. Pauli added that toward
the end of his life Nobel realized that this theory was "one of the most colossal
fallacies in the history of human thought." Pauli's book was published in 1942
in the midst of World War II and before the "bomb." As indicated in our text,
there has effectively been a small rebirth of this "colossal fallacy" in more recent
years.

13. Numerous scenarios were developed during the MAD era by Freeman
Dyson and many others, whereby escalation to World War III could easily occur.
At that time, for example, the great superiority of Russian conventional forces
in Europe suggested that an adventurous Russian regime could pick off pieces
virtually at will unless the United States resorted to a "first use" (tactical nuclear)
response. Should we have so responded—and this was what we were set up to
do—then the Russians would be highly tempted to reply with a "first strike"
(massive strategic attack) on the United States. Since there is always at least some
advantage to a "first strike," and since, by hypothesis, we would already have
shown our willingness to introduce nuclear weapons into combat, what else
would there be for the Russians to do? But if our limited response might produce this result, then we would likely conclude that it was a totally inadequate
way of handling the situation. Thus, we would be faced with two unacceptable
alternatives: (1) let the Russians chew up increasing chunks of Europe, or (2)
initiate a "first strike" on our own, thus launching World War III. The point is
that one didn't really need insane dictators to see big trouble brewing under the
MAD approach. Moderately ambitious regimes might be quite enough to get the
nuclear-war ball rolling.

14. The chart, referred to in the text, showing higher rates of growth for
industrial democracies as opposed to centrally planned economies, was based on
material in R. Summers and A. Heston, "Improved International Comparisons
of Real Product and its Composition, 1950–1980," *Review of Income and Wealth*
30 (June 1984): 207–262.

15. Adam Przeworski and Fernando Limongi, "Political Regimes and Economic Growth," *Journal of Economic Perspectives* 7, no. 3 (summer 1993): 60.

16. For a summary of Robert Barro's arguments and those of the Heritage
Foundation, see the following articles in the *Wall Street Journal*: Barro, "Pushing
Democracy is No Key to Prosperity"(12/14/93); Barro, "Democracy: A Recipe
for Growth?" (12/1/94); and Kim R. Holmes, "In Search of Free Markets,"
(12/12/94).

17. Henry S. Rowen, "Cheer Up, Troubled World," *Wall Street Journal*,

31 August 1993. Rowen cites political scientists R. J. Rummel of the University of Hawaii and Michael Doyle of Johns Hopkins University as arguing that "no democracy has ever waged war against another democracy." Rowen is sympathetic to the point, but notes that the "claim obviously rests on the definition of democracy."

18. Actually, Kennedy may have exaggerated this likelihood since the USSR never even went on a military alert during the Cuban missile crisis. He also clearly overestimated the dangers of nuclear proliferation, having foreseen fifteen to twenty nuclear powers by the 1970s.

19. Jacobs, *Short-Term America*, 1, note 1.

20. Matthew L. Wald, "Today's Drama: Twilight of the Nukes," *New York Times* (Sunday, 16 July 1995).

21. One measure of the degree of anxiety in America about the possibility of nuclear war is the setting of the Doomsday Clock by the Board of Directors of *The Bulletin of the Atomic Scientists*. The setting began at seven minutes to midnight in 1947 and reached its closest point (two minutes to midnight) in 1953 after the United States developed the hydrogen bomb. By 1991, it was moved steadily backward until it reached seventeen minutes to midnight. In September, 1995, the Board of Directors believed "a move may be warranted. but there is no consensus on which direction." (*Bulletin* 51, no. 5 [September/October, 1995]). However, later in the year, in view of the threats to peace in the post–Cold War era, the Board did finally move the hands from seventeen to fourteen minutes to midnight (*Bulletin* 51, no. 6 [November/December, 1995]), still much further back than in the 1950s and early 1960s.

CHAPTER 8

1. "A Blueprint for Survival," copyright 1972 by *The Ecologist*, published by Tom Stacey Ltd. and Penguin Books.

2. Jay Forrester, *World Dynamics* (Cambridge, Mass.: Wright-Allen Press, 1971), 11–13. For a general discussion of limits-to-growth theories, see Richard T. Gill, ed., *Great Debates in Economics* (Pacific Palisades, Calif.: Goodyear Publishing Company, Inc., 1976), 131–86.

3. Robert M. Solow, "Is the End of the World at Hand?" in Gill, *Great Debates*, 180.

4. "Good News on U.S. Oil and Gas Reserves," *Science News* 147 (18 March 1995): 171. Actually, the good news is not confined to the United States. The American Petroleum Institute estimates that the world's proven oil reserves have nearly doubled since OPEC I to a trillion barrels. Also, it should be noted that the price performance of oil is fascinating in that shortages, real or manufactured by OPEC, led to much higher prices which, in turn, led to greatly increased

exploration which, in turn, led to greater supplies and a sharp fall in prices. At the present time, oil prices in real, inflation-adjusted, terms are approximately where they were before OPEC was ever heard from and only a fraction of their average levels during the 1970s and 1980s.

5. Hansen is quoted in R. Monastersky, "Scientist Says Greenhouse Warming is Here," *Science News* 134, no. 1 (2 July 1988).

6. S. Fred Singer, "No Scientific Consensus on Greenhouse Warming," *Wall Street Journal*, 23 September 1991.

7. Jonathan D. Kahl et al., "Absence of evidence for Greenhouse Warming over the Arctic Ocean in the Past 40 Years," *Nature*, 361 (28 January 1991): 335–40.

8. William K. Stevens, "Global Warming Experts Call Human Role Likely," *New York Times*, 10 September 1995.

9. R. Monastersky, "World Climate Panel Charts Path for Action," *Science News* 148, 4 November 1995.

10. Baliunas is quoted in George Melloan, "Waterworld, Bootleg Freon and a Berlin Plot," *Wall Street Journal*, 3 April 1995.

11. If, for no other reason, the Heidelberg Appeal is notable for indicating that the Idea of Progress is not altogether dead, certainly not among world-renowned scientists. Thus the Appeal states. "Humanity has always progressed by harnessing Nature to its needs and not the reverse. . . We stress that progress and development have always involved increasing control over hostile forces, to the benefit of mankind. We therefore consider that scientific ecology is no more than an extension of this continual progress toward the improved life of future generations."

12. Gene M. Grossman and Alan B. Krueger, "Economic Growth and the Environment," *Quarterly Journal of Economics* 110, no. 1 (May 1995): 353–377.

13. See Ron Bailey, ed., *The True State of the Planet* (New York: The Free Press, 1995); Bill McKibben, "Not So Fast," *New York Times Magazine*, 23 July 1995; and Greg Easterbrook, *A Moment on the Earth: The Coming Age of Environmental Optimism* (New York: Viking, 1995).

14. "Blueprint for Survival," 155–56.

15. Ben Wattenberg, *The Birth Dearth: What Happens When People in Free Countries Don't Have Enough Babies* (New York: Pharos Books, 1987).

16. Michael D. Lemonick, "The Ice Age Cometh?" *Time Magazine*, 31 January 1994.

CHAPTER 9

1. Schumpeter, *Capitalism, Socialism, and Democracy*, 61.

2. Schumpeter was quite out of step with the prevailing views of the

immediate postwar years as exemplified by his Harvard colleague, and probably the leading American Keynesian of the time, Alvin Hansen. Interestingly, the stagnationists, of whom Hansen was the main proponent, argued that past American progress had been due to very special circumstances—the existence of a frontier, rapid population growth, capital-intensive investments, and the like—and that, if it were to continue in the absence of these past stimuli, the government would have to be much more active in the future. Thus, continued progress was seen as increasingly dependent not only on human choices, but very specifically on collective choices via the State.

3. Lasch, *The True and Only Heaven*, 80.

4. John Maynard Keynes, "Economic Possibilities for our Grandchildren," *Essays on Persuasion* in *Collected Writings of John Maynard Keynes*, vol. 9 (London: Macmillan, St. Martin's Press), 358–73. This celebration of the present moment above the future is actually quite consistent with Keynes's economic theorizing, which was, in essence, very short-term in emphasis. Thus, it was that in his formal theoretical structure in the *General Theory*, we had investment but no actual capital accumulation, and saving—the hero of classical economics because of its effect on long-run growth—became the villain of Keynesian economics because of its putative effect on short-term unemployment.

5. The view that "change is accelerating" these days is frequently heard. Sometimes the position seems to be that we just happen to be in one of those periods when change is especially rapid. See, for example, Ronald Brownstein in the *Los Angeles Times Magazine*, 8 May 1994: "Change is constant in American life. But now, as at other times in our history, it has become a more pressing, tangible, accelerated social phenomenon." At other times, the view is expressed that present-day change is uniquely rapid; for example, Robert M. White, president of the National Academy of Engineering: "The pace and intensity of technological advance are without historical precedent" (*Wall Street Journal*, 8 June 1995). Our own position is that, whether change in present-day America is or is not accelerating, it certainly continues to be very rapid and shows no particular signs of deceleration.

6. Two of the classic works in this field are, of course, Max Weber, *The Protestant Ethic and the Spirit of Capitalism* (New York: Charles Scribner, 1952), first published in 1905; and R. H. Tawney, *Religion and the Rise of Capitalism: A Historical Study* (New York: Harcourt, Brace, 1926). For later critics of the Weberian thesis, see Nelson, *Reaching for Heaven*, especially pp. 74–80.

7. Elson, *Guardians of Tradition*, 27–29.

8. John Wesley was acutely conscious of this problem. He wrote: "I fear, wherever riches have increased, the essence of religion has decreased in the same proportion. Therefore I do not see how it is possible, in the nature of things, for any revival of true religion to continue long. For religion must necessarily pro-

duce both industry and frugality, and these cannot but produce riches. But as riches increase, so will pride, anger, and love of the world in all its branches." Quoted in Weber, *The Protestant Ethic*, 175.

9. See Edward C. Banfield, *The Unheavenly City Revisited* (Boston: Little, Brown, 1974).

10. Schumpeter, *Capitalism, Socialism, and Democracy*, 160–61.

11. An interesting question, which we may touch on from time to time, but which is essentially beyond the range of this book, is whether the fundamental predicament of progress is likely to undermine not only the Idea of Progress but the process of progress itself. Certainly, there are many ways in which the Idea has, in the past, facilitated the process—for example, by its emphasis on saving, investment, hard work, innovations that pay off only in the long run, and so on. On the other hand, the workings of modern science have a tendency to keep the process of progress going through a kind of internal momentum of their own. Possibly the result will be that the process will have a tendency, other things equal, to outlast the Idea, at least for some reasonable period of time. Other things, of course, are seldom equal!

CHAPTER 10

1. Becker, *Progress and Power*, 6–7.

2. Ralph Gabriel, Review of vols. 11–13 of the *Encyclopedia of the Social Sciences*, in *American Historical Review* 40 (January 1935): 307.

3. For discussion of the evolution of Beard's views on progress, see Robert A. Skotheim, *American Intellectual Histories and Historians* (Westport, Conn.: Greenwood Press, 1978; originally Princeton University Press, 1966), esp, 95–108.

4. Harry Levin, "English Literature of the Renaissance," in Tinsley Helton, ed., *The Renaissance: A Reconsideration of the Theories and Interpretations of the Age* (Westport, Conn.: Greenwood Press, 1961), 147.

5. Nisbet, *History of the Idea of Progress*, 177.

6. Lasch, *The True and Only Heaven*, 80–81.

7. Bruce Mazlish, "Progress: A Historical and Critical Perspective," in Marx and Mazlish, eds., *Progress*, 28. In this volume also see Gerald Holton, "Science and Progress Revisited," esp. 9.

8. Robert Heilbroner, *Visions of the Future* (New York: Oxord University Press, 1995), 69.

9. Irving Kristol, "America Dreaming," *Wall Street Journal*, 31 August 31 1995. Kristol could have been referring to any number of articles that have appeared right in the *Wall Street Journal* itself. A typical example: Clare Ansberry and Thomas F. O'Boyle, "Voices of a Generation Fear for the Status of the

American Dream" *Wall Street Journal*, 11 August 1992. The first sentence of the article is also characteristic: "For many Americans, the future seems about as secure as a dandelion puff."

10. Northwestern National Life Insurance Company, "Children's Health at Risk: Attitudes of American Children and Parents," 1993.

11. The Roper poll results are summarized in Alan L. Otten, "People Patterns," *Wall Street Journal*, 27 September 1993. Not all polls show these results, of course. For example, the *Boston Globe*, 4 September 1994, reported a poll conducted by Arthur Levine of Columbia Teachers College showing college students optimistic (92 percent) about their personal futures and optimistic (67 percent) about the future of the United States. However, these particular results seem a bit strange, to say the least, not only because they are inconsistent with most other polls, but because other answers in this very same poll seem to refute this general optimism. Thus, 82 percent agree that most people look out only for themselves, 83 percent agree that family values are breaking down in America, 68 percent believe that most people will take advantage of you if they can, and only 21 percent feel that Congress has the interests of the people at heart. One has to wonder where the students' alleged optimism is coming from!

12. An amusing (and puzzling) example of confusion about the nature of the demand for labor in the United States is given in a book edited by Gary Burtless, *A Future of Lousy Jobs?* (Washington, D.C.: The Brookings Institution, 1990). The title would seem clearly to imply that the hamburger-flipper hypothesis is valid whereas the book itself demonstrates exactly the opposite point, namely, that "the demand for skilled workers has been growing faster than the supply and the demand for unskilled workers has fallen faster than the supply." (30) One has to wonder why the editor permitted the title to stay as it is.

13. George J. Church, "Are We Better Off?" *Time*, 19 January 1996, 39.

14. Michael E. Porter, "Capital Choices: National Systems of Investment," in Neva R. Goodwin, ed., *As If the Future Mattered: Translating Social and Economic Theory into Human Behavior* (Ann Arbor: University of Michigan Press, 1996), 20. For further discussion of short-term business horizons in America, see Michael T. Jacobs, *Short Term America: The Causes and Cures of Our Business Myopia* (Boston: Harvard Business School Press, 1991); or J. M. Lauderman, "Opening Our Eyes to Market Myopia," *Business Week: Reinventing America*, 1992, 134–48.

15. The term, heading this section, "unthinkable deficits," is taken from Peter G. Peterson, *Facing Up* (New York: Simon & Schuster, 1993), 250.

16. These data are from the *Economic Report of the President*, February 1995.

17. Peterson, *Facing Up*, 250.

18. Congressional Budget Office, *Reducing the Deficit, Spending and Revenue Options: Report to the Senate and the House Committees on the Budget*, Part 2, February, 1990, 5.

19. Formally, the relation of government spending (G), taxes (T), investment (I), saving (S), and capital inflows from abroad is:

$$G + I = T + S + \text{capital inflows}$$

Capital inflows, in turn, are measured by the excess of our imports (IM) over our exports (X). Thus, the budget deficit (G − T) will be equal to:

$$G - T = (S - I) - (X - IM).$$

20. Making all these adjustments, Professor Eisner calculated that an officially measured 1988 federal deficit of $155 billion was transformed into an actual total government *surplus* of $42 billion. (Robert Eisner, "Divergences of Measurement and Theory and Some Implications for Policy," *American Economic Review* 79, no. 1 [March 1989]). Other economists, however, remain unconvinced by his arguments.

21. *Economic Report of the President*, 1993, 264.

22. Laurence J. Kotlikoff, *Generational Accounting* (New York: The Free Press, 1992), 213. For a further discussion by the participants in this new approach, see the symposium on generational accounting in the *Journal of Economic Perspectives* 8, no. 1 (winter, 1994): 73–94.

23. See *Economic Report of the President*, 1995, 118–19.

24. R. Easterlin, C. Schaeffer, and D. Macunovich, "Will the Baby Boomers be Less Well Off Than Their Parents? Income, Wealth, and Family Circumstances over the Life Cycle," Mimeo, 13 May 1993, 11.

25. B. Douglas Bernheim, "Is the Baby Boom Generation Preparing Adequately for Retirement?" (Sponsored by Merrill Lynch, 15 January 1993), 2.

26. Jim Smalhout, "Retirement Woes: Pension Saving is Short of the Mark," *Wall Street Journal*, 4 February 1993.

27. A. J. Auerbach, L. J. Kotlikoff, and D. N. Weil, "The Increasing Annuitization of the Elderly—Estimates and Implications for Intergenerational Transfers, Inequality, and National Saving," NBER Working Paper No. 4182, October 1992.

28. Auerbach et al., "Increasing Annuitization," pp. 25–26.

29. Malgoire is quoted in A. B. Crenshaw, "The Boomers and the Bequests," *Washington Post*, 11 October 1992.

30. Cheryl Russell is quoted in the *Wall Street Journal*, 3 March 1987.

31. Lloyd D. Johnston, quoted in news conference release, 15 December 1995, announcing results of the survey of American teenage smoking as part of the *Monitoring the Future Study* of the University of Michigan Survey Research Center, pp. 1, 3.

32. Survey of teenage drug use, *Monitoring the Future Study*, news conference release, 15 December 1995, 1.

33. The authors of this survey conclude that "these findings support the view of college presidents who believe that alcohol abuse is the No. 1 problem on campus." H. Wechsler, A. Davenport, G. Dowdall, B. Moeykens, and S. Castillo, "Health and Behavioral Consequences of Binge Drinking in College," *Journal of the American Medical Association* 272, no. 21 (7 December 1994): 1672.

34. William A. Galston and David Wasserman, "Gambling Away Our Moral Capital," *The Public Interest,* no. 123 (spring, 1996): 62.

35. Estimates are that total legal betting in the United States in 1993 came to $330 billion; meanwhile "illegal gambling still pulls in billions." (Gerri Hirshey, "Gambling: America's Real National Pastime," *New York Times Magazine,* 17 July 1994, section 6.)

36. Charles R. Bean, "Economic and Monetary Union in Europe," *Journal of Economic Perspectives* 6, no. 4 (fall 1992): 45. Actually, if we limit the U.S. debt to that held in the hands of the public, and also include not just federal but state and local governments, our total debt-to-GDP ratio would be well below the figure cited in the text.

37. *Economic Report of the President,* 1996, 21.

38. Gertrude Himmelfarb, "A De-moralized Society," *The Public Interest* no. 117 (fall 1994): 60.

39. Popenoe, *Disturbing the Nest,* 158.

40. Arthur Gold, *Conflict and Control in Welfare Policy: The Swedish Experience* (London: Longman, 1988), 32.

41. Mancur Olson, Jr. "The Devolution of the Nordic and Teutonic Economies," *American Economic Review* 85, no. 2 (May 1995): 22.

42. Richard B. Freeman, "The Large Welfare State as a System," *American Economic Review* 85, no. 2 (May 1995): 20.

43. Assar Lindbeck, "Hazardous Welfare-State Dynamics," *American Economic Review* 85, no. 2 (May 1995): 9–10.

44. Lindbeck, "Hazardous Dynamics," 9.

CHAPTER 11

1. John Galsworthy, *The Modern Comedy* (New York: Penguin Books, 1979), preface, 15.

2. Barbara Dafoe Whitehead, "Dan Quayle was Right," *The Atlantic Monthly,* April 1993, 55.

3. James Q. Wilson, "The Family-Values Debate," *Commentary,* April 1993. The opening sentence of the article is: "There are two views about the contemporary American family, one held by the public and the other by policy elites." For my own view of the role of intellectuals in the family-values debate, see chapter 15, pp. 307–13.

4. Andrew Cherlin, *Marriage, Divorce, Remarriage* (Cambridge, Mass.: Harvard University Press, 1981).

5. James P. Smith and Michael P. Ward, "Women's Wages and Work in the Twentieth Century," prepared for the National Institute of Child Health and Human Development, R–3119–NICHD, October 1984, xvi.

6. Wilson, "Family-Values Debate," 25. Harriet was, in fact, a singer!

7. For a comprehensive statement of the relative income theory, see Richard A. Easterlin, *Birth and Fortune: The Impact of Numbers on Personal Welfare* (New York: Basic Books, 1980). This account of Easterlin's theory rests heavily on Gill et al., *Our Changing Population*, 47–49

8. Easterlin hypothesized that a kind of cycle might emerge over time: low birthrates lead to economic good fortune, which leads to high birthrates, which lead to lower wages and then low birthrates, and so on. This cycle has not, however, developed quite as predicted.

CHAPTER 12

1. See above chapter 9, pp. 172–73, and note 4. Keynes's comment about cats, their kittens, and their kittens' kittens, when translated into parents, children, and grandchildren, suggests a very strong priority given to self (parents) as compared to posterity (children and grandchildren).

2. Recall the 1995 report on child care centers in the United States, which recommends much more funding for such centers but also concludes that, in actual fact, "child care at most centers in the United States is poor to mediocre, with almost half of the infant and toddler rooms providing poor quality." Helburn, *Cost, Quality,* 1.

3. As noted earlier (page 42), McLanahan and Sandefur, in their analysis of children's outcomes, link single-parent and stepfamilies together (*Single Parent,* chapter 3). David Blankenhorn's survey of the literature on stepfamilies finds that "the social science data regarding outcomes for children in stepfamilies are remarkably consistent and almost uniformly bleak." (*Fatherless America,* 190).

4. Barbara Ehrenreich, *The Hearts of Men: American Dreams and the Flight from Commitment* (Garden City, N.Y.: Anchor Press/Doubleday, 1983), 52.

5. For a discussion of survival curves, their "squaring," and the possibility of extending maximum human life span, see Gill et al., *Our Changing Population,* 390–97.

6. We refer to *male* labor force participation at older ages here because that is where the great change has been. In the case of older women, there has been little change in labor force participation, the trend toward earlier retirement in general and the trend toward increasing female labor force participation in general roughly cancelling out.

7. Roger L. Ransom and Richard Sutch, "The Decline of Retirement Years Before Social Security: U.S. Retirement Patterns, 1870–1940," in Rita Ricardo-Campbell and Edward P. Lazear, eds., *Issues in Contemporary Retirement* (Stanford, Cal.: Hoover Institution Press, 1988), 4. This statement is interesting because it suggests that before public benefits—Social Security, tax-protected pension plans—American workers were not retiring earlier.

8. Sylvia Ann Hewlett, *When the Bough Breaks* (New York: Basic Books, 1991), 163.

9. The following account relies heavily on Richard T. Gill, "Whatever Happened to the American Way of Death?" *The Public Interest*, no. 123 (spring, 1996).

10. Gordon E. Geddes, *Welcome Joy: Death in Puritan New England* (Ann Arbor: UMI Research Press, 1981), 150, 153.

11. David Charles Sloan, *The Last Great Necessity: Cemeteries in American History* (Baltimore: The Johns Hopkins University Press, 1991), 80, 77.

12. R. W. Habenstein and W. M. Lamers, "The Pattern of Late Nineteenth-Century Funerals," in Charles O. Jackson, ed., *Passing: The Vision of Death in America* (Westport, Conn.: Greenwood Press, 1977), 97.

13. James J. Farrell, *Inventing the American Way of Death, 1830–1920* (Philadelphia: Temple University Press, 1980), 204.

14. Charles O. Jackson, "Introduction," in Jackson, *Passing*, 5–6.

15. Ibid, 236.

16. Jessica Mitford, *The American Way of Death* (New York: Simon and Schuster, 1963).

17. The survey was conducted by the Wirthlin Group, McLean, Va., for the Funeral and Memorial Information Council, May and August 1990.

18. This entire discussion refers only to relatively secular-minded Americans. Insofar as religion is making a comeback these days, especially fundamentalist religion, then, of course, the attitude to this-worldly memorialization of the dead may change for much different reasons.

CHAPTER 13

1. A variety of new and different definitions of the family is given in a Special Edition of *Newsweek* (winter-spring 1990) devoted entirely to the "twenty-first century family."

2. Tocqueville, *Democracy in America*, 309.

3. Kermit Gordon, "Foreword," in Arthur M. Okun, *Equality and Efficiency: The Big Tradeoff* (Washington, D.C.: The Brookings Institution, 1975), vii.

4. Galbraith, *Affluent Society*, 330–33, where he points out that increased

human investment in the poor, including educational investment, will produce "increased output . . . as a by-product of the effort to eliminate poverty."

5. Fred Hirsch, *Social Limits to Growth*, A Twentieth Century Fund Study (Cambridge, Mass.: Harvard University Press, 1976), 173.

6. John Rawls, *A Theory of Justice* (Cambridge, Mass.: The Belknap Press of the Harvard University Press, 1971).

7. Thus, in a number of studies in the 1950s and 1960s, Nobel Prize-winning economist Simon Kuznets suggested that the growth process, over time, tended to increase the relative inequality in income distribution at the beginning of the industrialization process and to increase relative equality in its later stages. In writings in 1979 and 1980, however, Kuznets began to worry that continued development in the United States might be accompanied by greater relative inequality owing to the demographic tendency of lower economic groups to outreproduce higher income groups. (See, for example, Simon Kuznets, "Economic Growth and Income Inequality," *American Economic Review* 45, no. 1 (March 1955), and for his later views, *Growth, Population and Income Distribution* (New York: W. W. Norton, 1979). Another very important contribution to the growth-equality issue was made by Schumpeter—a contribution which is almost uniformly ignored in discussions of today's growing income "inequality." Schumpeter put the heart of the issue is a single phrase: "mass production . . . unavoidably also means production for the masses." What he was suggesting was that the usual numerical measures of equality and inequality are flawed because of their failure to take into account the enormous real gains of lower income groups as a result of economic growth. The goods that become increasingly cheap and available in large quantities are those bought by ordinary citizens, while luxury goods (handicrafts, personal services, and the like) bought by the rich become increasingly expensive in a relative sense. Schumpeter's example is worth quoting: "Electric lighting is no great boon to anyone who has money enough to buy a sufficient number of candles and to pay servants to attend to them. It is the cheap cloth, the cheap cotton and rayon fabric, boots, motorcars, and so on that are the typical achievements of capitalist production, and not as a rule improvements that mean much to a rich man. Queen Elizabeth [I] owned silk stockings. The capitalist achievement does not typically consist in providing more silk stockings for queens but in bringing them within the reach of factory girls in return for steadily decreasing amounts of effort." (Schumpeter, *Capitalism, Socialism, and Democracy*, 67.)

8. Arthur Okun (Okun, *Equality and Efficiency*) referred to these redistributional costs in terms of a "leaky bucket," suggesting that, as we carried water (money) from rich to poor, inevitably some would leak out (for administrative costs, etc.) along the way. Some unkind wags later referred to this as the "old Okun bucket!"

9. Although there is nearly universal agreement that the growing spread between the incomes of the highly educated and those of the unskilled is a major factor in the increasing degree of measured U.S. inequality of income, there is fairly substantial evidence that, as suggested in the text, international factors also play a part. (See the symposium, "Income Inequality and Trade," *The Journal of Economic Perspectives* 9, no. 3 (summer 1995):15–80.

10. *Economic Report of the President*, 1992, 137.

11. A study based on Census Bureau numbers and analyzed by Eugene Smolensky of the University of California at Berkeley and Robert Plotnick of the University of Washington suggests a massive movement in the direction of greater equality since World War I, and a small, though definite, movement toward greater inequality since the early 1970s. See "Across the Great Divide," *Wall Street Journal*, 2 October 1995, A12.

12. From the increasingly large library of "political correctness" incidents, we might mention two at the University of Pennsylvania in 1993 that attracted nationwide attention. According to numerous newspaper accounts, a student, kept from studying by the late-night noise of a group of Black sorority sisters, shouted that they were behaving like "water buffalo." This term, as it turned out, was of somewhat ambivalent meaning because of the student's Israeli background. The second incident involved a group of Black activists who seized and destroyed an entire issue of the student newspaper, *The Daily Pennsylvanian*, because of views they considered unfriendly to Blacks. The apparently intolerant behavior of the student in the water buffalo incident brought forth the wrath of the University, whereas the seemingly much more serious matter of the well-orchestrated seizure of an entire press run was basically understood as a legitimate "form of student protest." Astonishingly, an evaluational report of University of Pennsylvania administrators, far from criticizing the students who seized the newspaper, was actually highly critical of the university's security guards for daring to interfere with this activity. Indeed, a museum administrator who pursued the students was charged with "inappropriate" behavior and it was recommended that "his actions should be reviewed by his supervisor for possible disciplinary action." Why this huge difference in treatment? Quite simply, the water buffalo incident expressed, or was alleged to express, intolerant behavior, while the press seizure expressed, or was alleged to express, a legitimate protest against intolerant behavior!

13. Walter R. Allen, "The Search for Applicable Theories of Black Family Life," *Journal of Marriage and the Family* (February 1978): 117–29.

14. Moynihan, "Defining Deviancy Down," 17–30.

CHAPTER 14

1. Admittedly, the 1990 federal day care legislation was rather modest in scope. For example, under section 2 (Child Care and Development Block

Grants), Congress authorized the expenditure of $750 million in 1991, $825 million in 1992, and $925 million in 1993—not very large sums. Still, the general thrust of the legislation—to improve the quality and accessibility of extra-family child care—was unmistakable, and proponents were obviously hoping for much more in the future. Thus, Representative Pat Schroeder (D-CO) was quoted as saying, "We'll take whatever it is and build on it next year."

2. Actually, as in the case of the 1990 day care legislation, the 1992 Family and Medical Leave Act appears to have had a very modest impact at best (see Barbara Sullivan, "Few Workers Make Use of Family Leave Policy," Fort Lauderdale *Sun-Sentinel*, 27 October 1995). This is certainly in part because, in the case of childbirth or family illness, employees are offered up to twelve weeks of unpaid leave only. Offering leave benefits would almost certainly have two contrary effects: (a) increase the number of employees who would make use of the leave option, and (b) decrease the amount of time these employees would devote to early child care. For a study of the issues involved here, as shown by past U.S. experience, see Martin O'Connell, U.S. Bureau of the Census, "Maternity Leave Arrangements, 1961–1985," Paper presented at the annual meetings of the American Statistical Association, 7 August 1989.

3. This estimate is from Marvin Kosters of the American Enterprise Institute, see *Wall Street Journal*, 27 October 1995.

4. For a calculation comparing nineteenth- and twentieth-century mothers in terms of years with young children in the house, see Mary Jo Bane, *Here to Stay: American Families in the Twentieth Century* (New York: Basic Books, 1976), esp. table 2.1, 25.

5. The concept of a Parental Bill of Rights was first developed by Richard T. Gill and T. Grandon Gill in a paper for presentation at a symposium on marriage in America, "Of Families, Children, and a Parental Bill of Rights," A Council on Families in America Working Paper, No. 33, May 1993, 1–77. It was then published in somewhat shorter form as "A New Plan for the Family," *The Public Interest* no. 11 (spring 1993): 86–94, and then again simply as "A Parental Bill of Rights," *Family Affairs*, Institute of America Values, 6, no. 1–2 (winter 1994), with commentary by Janet Zollinger Giele and Allan C. Carlson.

6. This estimate is from Joyce P. Jacobsen and Laurence M. Levin, "The Effects of Intermittent Labor Force Attachment on Female Earnings," paper presented to the American Economic Association conference, 1992. The authors discuss the situation of a woman leaving work at twenty-five and returning seven years later to work full time, and find that the "present value of the difference between her earnings twenty years after she re-enters and what they would have been had she remained constantly employed is $52,000 [1984 dollars] . . . This amount is equal to 15 percent of her prospective earnings had she worked constantly, or approximately three years' worth of wages—a considerable difference. Thus, the cost of taking a seven-year gap is ten years of earning."

7. The well-known and highly controversial concept of the "mommy track," with its basic division of working women into two groups, "career-primary" and "career-and-family" women was advanced by Felice N. Schwartz in "Management Women and the New Facts of Life," *Harvard Business Review* (January–February, 1989): 65–76. Although not totally incompatible with our own approach, we prefer the idea of fairly clearcut "sequences" as implied by the Parental Bill program.

8. This large estimate is from Orley Ashenfelter and Alan Krueger, "Estimates of the Economic Return to Schooling from a New Sample of Twins," Working Paper No. 4143, National Bureau of Economic Research, August 1992. Their conclusion is that "our best estimate is that increased schooling increases average weekly wage rates by about 16% per year completed. This is a far larger estimate than any we have seen in the prior literature. Even if our procedures of adjustment for measurement error are not accepted, within-pair estimates of the returns to schooling are never less than 9% per year completed."

9. U.S. Bureau of the Census, *Current Population Reports*, Series P70–32. "What's It Worth? Educational Background and Economic Status: Spring, 1990." Washington, D.C.: U.S. Government Printing Office, 1992.

10. See, for example, estimates of the costs of labor force participation, in Sandra L. Hanson and Theodora Ooms, "The Economic Costs and Rewards of Two-Earner, Two-Parent Families," *Journal of Marriage and the Family* 53 (August 1991): 622–34.

11. Peter F. Drucker, "The Post-Capitalist World," *The Public Interest* no. 109 (fall 1992): 26.

12. Elizabeth B. Gill, in addition to her work as a *Guardian ad litem*, has at various times taught in elementary, junior high, and senior high schools. She has an Ed. M. from the Harvard Graduate School of Education.

13. Because the main alternative to the PCC program for these teenage mothers would almost certainly involve sending the mothers to school and their children to full-time day care, rough calculations by the author suggest that the PCC program might well be substantially *less* expensive than this main alternative.

14. Blankenhorn, *Fatherless America*, 226

15. Blankenhorn, *Fatherless America*, 233.

16. Commission on Urban Familes, *Families First*, chapter 4, "Recommendations for Change," esp. sec. 6, "Reform State Laws on Marriage and Divorce." Council on Families in America, *Marriage in America: A Report to the Nation*, March 1995: recommendations are presented on pages 13–17.

CHAPTER 15

1. For a full reference to this NRC report, see above, pp. 47–48.

2. My own critique of the NRC report and especially of the notion of

"inexorable" trends in the direction of further reductions in parental care for children, is offered in Richard T. Gill, "Day Care or Parental Care?" *The Public Interest* no. 105 (fall 1991): 3–16.

3. Rather than repeat this material here, the reader is referred back to chapter 2, and such experts as Zill, Dawson, Popenoe, Galston, Blankenhorn, Whitehead, Elshtain, and, even though she almost seems to deny with one hand what she proclaims with the other, Sara McLanahan.

4. A. J. Cherlin, F. F. Furstenberg, P. L. Chase-Lansdale, K. E. Kiernan, P. K. Robbins, D. R. Morrison, and J. O. Teitler, "Longitudinal Studies of Effects of Divorce on Children in Great Britain and the United States," *Science* 252 (June, 1991): 1386–89. What makes this very flawed article so upsetting is that its authors form a virtual honor role of sociologists, psychologists, and economists interested in the fate of the American (and British) family. Probably the main problem with the article, even more serious than those I have mentioned in the text, is that it wholly ignores the possible interaction between free and easy divorces and conditions within intact marriages. Knowing one can escape so easily, why bother trying to hold things reasonably together? These and other criticisms I presented in Richard T. Gill, "For the Sake of the Children," *The Public Interest* no. 108 (summer, 1992): 81–96. This article, in due course, produced a response from Andrew Cherlin, "Nostalgia as Family Policy" and a rebuttal by myself, "Family Breakdown as Family Policy," in *The Public Interest* no. 110 (winter 1993). The reader can decide for him or herself whether my claims about this particular article are or are not justified.

5. One witness to this controversy clearly felt that *Science* had let him down. Senator Moynihan's exact words (to a Congressional Committee) were: "And then [Gill] says, simultaneously, there is an increasing number of papers, one of which was published in "Science" which is the journal of the American Association for the Advancement of Science. (I was once a vice president of the AAAS. You're not supposed to put things in "Science" that won't hold up.) And he [Gill] just takes it apart completely." (Hearings before the House Select Committee on Children, Youth and Families, 7/23/92.)

6. The quotes from Scarr and Field are taken from Thomas E. Ricks, "Day Care for Infants is Challenged by Research on Psychological Risks," *Wall Street Journal*, 3 March 1987.

7. J. Belsky and D. Eggebeen, "Early and Extensive Maternal Employment and Young Children's Socioemotional Development: Children of the National Longitudinal Survey of Youth," *Journal of Marriage and the Family* 53 no. 4 (November 1991): 1083–98. The critiques of this article were as follows: Sandra Scarr, "On Comparing Apples and Oranges and Making Inferences About Bananas"; Deborah Lowe Vandell, "Belsky and Eggebeen's Analysis: Meaningful

Results or Statistical Illusions?" and Kathleen McCartney and Saul Rosenthal, "Maternal Employment Should be Studied Within Social Ecologies." Belsky and Eggebeen's reply to all this was entitled "Scientific Criticism and the Study of Early and Extensive Maternal Employment."

INDEX

Okun, Arthur, 339n8
Olson, Mancur, Jr., 213–14
OPEC, 154
opportunity costs, 74–76
options. *See* choices
Ozzie and Harriet, 18, 222–23, 226

paradox of progress, 7, 57, 98–99, 298
Parental Bill of Rights, 279–84,
    288–89
Parent-Child Center (PCC), 284–88,
    342n13
parent child interaction. *See* children
"parenting track," 281
Parsons, Talcott, 72
pathology of family life, 1, 45, 315n1
permissive child-rearing, 232–35
persons of opposite sex sharing living
    quarters, 257
Pierce, John, 98
Playboy, 241
political correctness, 268, 301, 340n12
pollution, 7, 163–65. *See also* green-
    house effect; environment
polyandry, 15
polygyny, 15
Popenoe, David, xvii, 62, 211–12
population growth, 64, 124–26, 129–
    33, 160, 327n14
population principle (Malthus),
    122–24
Porter, Michael, 195
POSSLQS. *See* persons of opposite sex
    sharing living quarters
posterity: increased interest in (nine-
    teenth century), 4, 8, 93, 103, 180,
    220; two senses of, xvi-xvi; waning
    interest in (postmodern era), xvi,
    180. *See also* self vs. posterity
postmodern era, basic characteristics,
    1, 3

poverty. *See* children
predicaments of progress: defined, 7,
    121–22; Doomsday analyses, 135–
    36, 151, 166, 168, 191, 219–20;
    first great predicament, 122–29;
    fundamental predicament, 8, 171–
    88, 220, 234, 243, 254, 258, 298–
    99, 303, 333n11; limits-to-growth
    predicaments, 7, 151–69; war as
    predicament, 136–49
present-mindedness, 186, 206, 210,
    219, 301. *See also* myopia; time ho-
    rizons
price mechanism, 156, 159, 165
process of progress: basic characteris-
    tics, 63–69, 176; changing relation
    to Idea of Progress, 8, 104–5,
    176–88; defined, 6, 63
progress. *See* Idea of Progress; paradox
    of progress; predicaments of prog-
    ress; and process of progress
Progressive Era, 115, 137
Protestantism, 106, 182

Quayle, Dan, 222–23, 265

rapidity of change. *See* change
Rawls, John, 261
Reagan, President Ronald, 141;
    Reagan administration, 190,
    263–64
relative income hypothesis, 228–29
religion: and morality, 91, 182–84,
    332–33n8; revival of, 3, 191, 302,
    306, 338n18
replacement fertility, 75, 224
resource depletion, 152–58
retirement, 244–45, 282, 338n7
revolution vs. evolution, in family life,
    219–36
Reynolds, Lloyd, 132

ABOUT THE AUTHOR

A former assistant dean, senior tutor, master of Leverett House, and lecturer on economics at Harvard University, Richard T. Gill is the author or editor of nine books in economics and coauthor of *Our Changing Population*. He has published in periodicals ranging from the *Atlantic Monthly* and the *New Yorker* to *The Public Interest* and *Family Matters*. He has also been involved in two major public television series, most recently in "Economics U\$A," a 28–program Annenberg/Corporation for Public Broadcasting project, which continues to be shown both nationally and abroad.

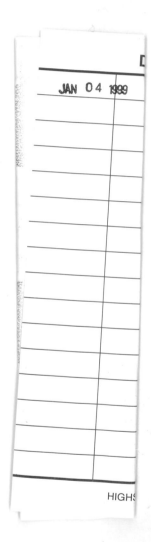

D

JAN 04 1999

HIGHS